SURFACE TENSION

SURFACE TENSION

To all the men, women
and children lost at sea,
in body or soul.

Dedicated to Rosa.

ISBN: 9781782763314

MARCH 2016. FIRST PRINTING.

Published by Titan Comics, a division of Titan
Publishing Group, Ltd. 144 Southwark Street,
London SE1 0UP. Originally published in single
comic form as *Surface Tension* #1-5. *Surface
Tension* is trademark™ and copyright © 2015 Jay
Gunn. All rights reserved.

Printed in China. TC0176.

A CIP catalogue record for this title is available
from the British Library.

 WWW.TITAN-COMICS.COM

 @COMICSTITAN

 FACEBOOK.COM/COMICSTITAN

Lettered by
Comicraft's Jimmy Betancourt
& Albert Deschesne

Editor
Andrew James

Assistant Editor Emeritus
Kirsten Murray

Collection Designer
Rob Farmer

TITAN COMICS

SENIOR EDITOR
Steve White

EDITORIAL
Lizzie Kaye, Tom Williams

PRODUCTION MANAGER
Jackie Flook, Maria Pearson

PRODUCTION ASSISTANT
Peter James

STUDIO MANAGER
Selina Juneja

SENIOR SALES MANAGER
Steve Tothill

SENIOR MARKETING & PRESS OFFICER
Owen Johnson

**DIRECT SALES AND
MARKETING MANAGER**
Ricky Claydon

COMMERCIAL MANAGER
Michelle Fairlamb

PUBLISHING MANAGER
Darryl Tothill

PUBLISHING DIRECTOR
Chris Teather

OPERATIONS DIRECTOR
Leigh Baulch

EXECUTIVE DIRECTOR
Vivian Cheung

PUBLISHER
Nick Landau

SURFACE TENSION

WRITTEN AND
ILLUSTRATED BY
JAY GUNN

LETTERS COMICRAFT'S JIMMY BETANCOURT
& ALBERT DESCHESNE

TITAN
COMICS

www.titan-comics.com

CHAPTER ONE
GHOSTS

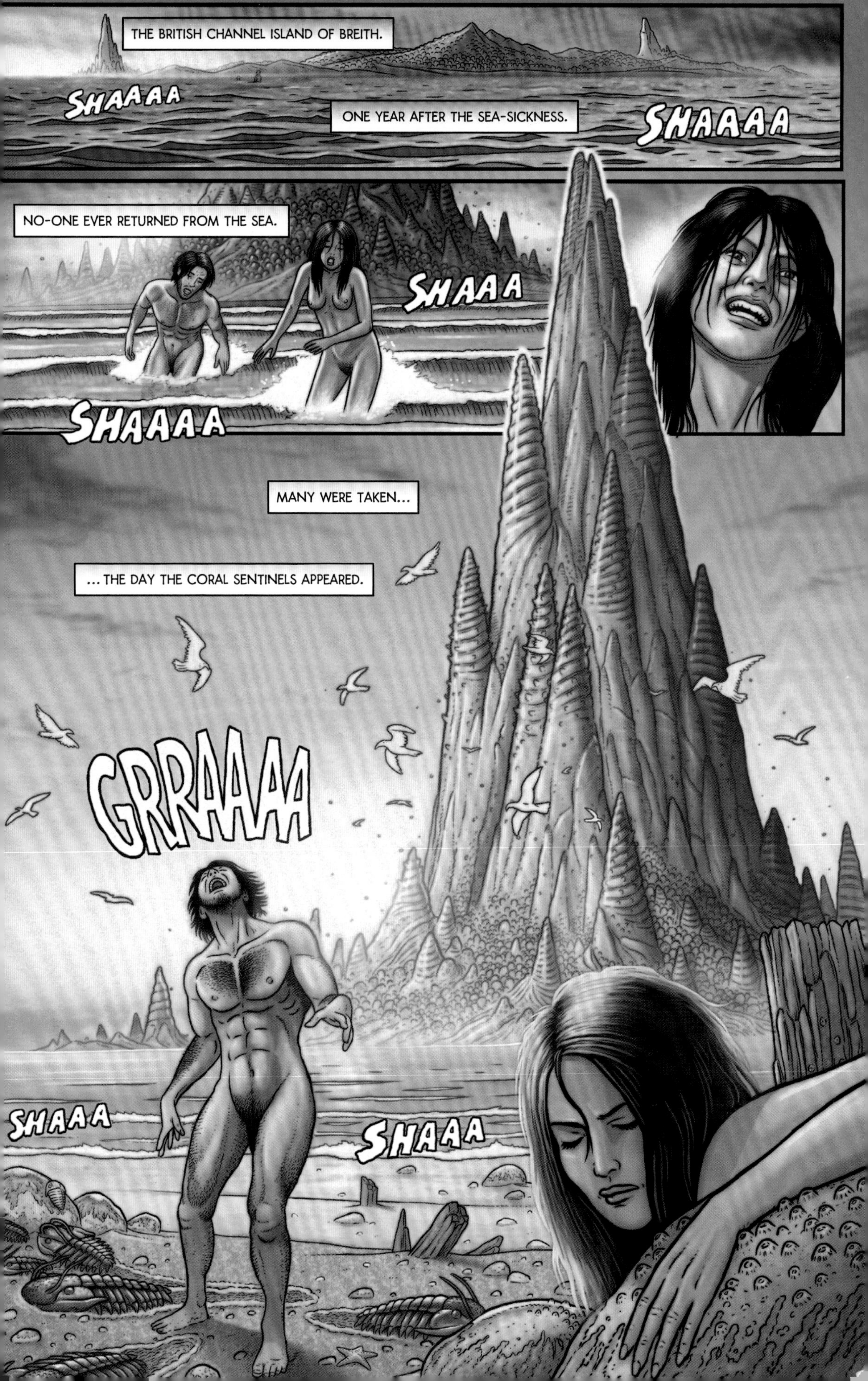
THE BRITISH CHANNEL ISLAND OF BREITH.
SHAAAA
ONE YEAR AFTER THE SEA-SICKNESS.
SHAAAAA
NO-ONE EVER RETURNED FROM THE SEA.
SHAAA
SHAAAAA
MANY WERE TAKEN...
... THE DAY THE CORAL SENTINELS APPEARED.
GRRAAAA
SHAAA
SHAAA

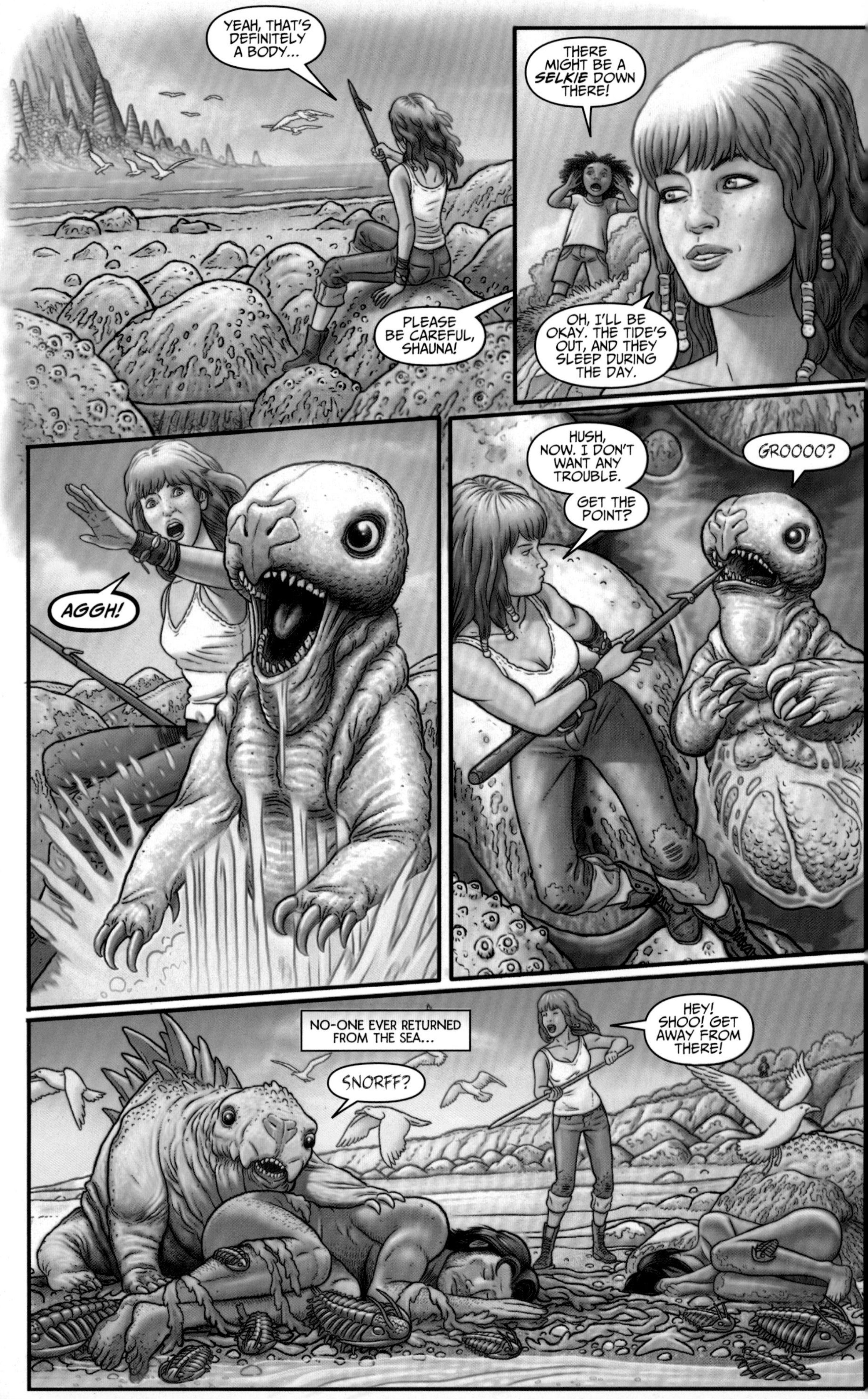
YEAH, THAT'S DEFINITELY A BODY...
PLEASE BE CAREFUL, SHAUNA!
THERE MIGHT BE A SELKIE DOWN THERE!
OH, I'LL BE OKAY. THE TIDE'S OUT, AND THEY SLEEP DURING THE DAY.
AGGH!
HUSH, NOW. I DON'T WANT ANY TROUBLE.
GET THE POINT?
GROOOO?
NO-ONE EVER RETURNED FROM THE SEA...
HEY! SHOO! GET AWAY FROM THERE!
SNORFF?

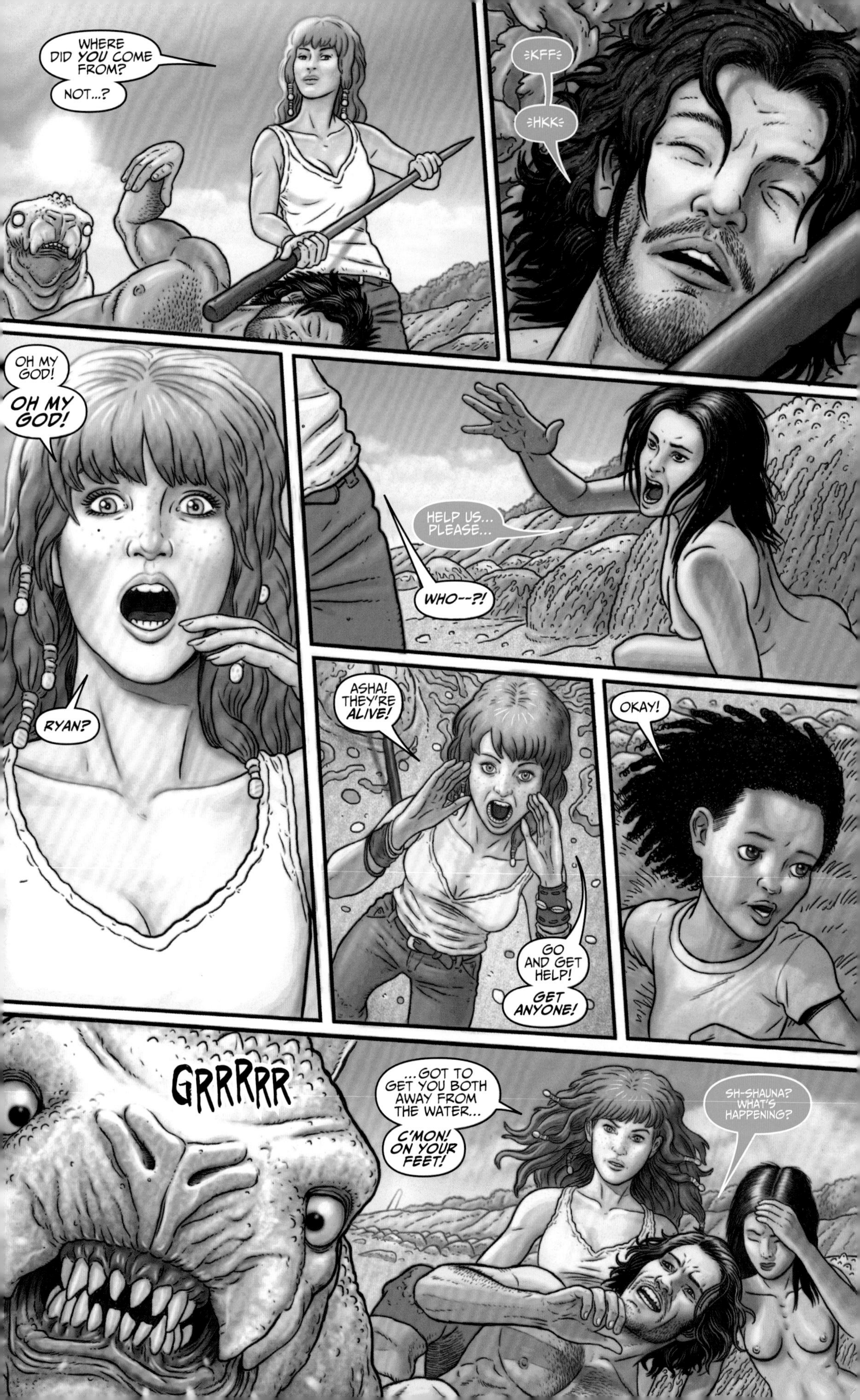

WHERE DID YOU COME FROM?
NOT...?
KFF
HKK
OH MY GOD!
OH MY GOD!
RYAN?
HELP US... PLEASE...
WHO--?!
ASHA! THEY'RE ALIVE!
GO AND GET HELP!
GET ANYONE!
OKAY!
GRRRRR
...GOT TO GET YOU BOTH AWAY FROM THE WATER...
C'MON! ON YOUR FEET!
SH-SHAUNA? WHAT'S HAPPENING?

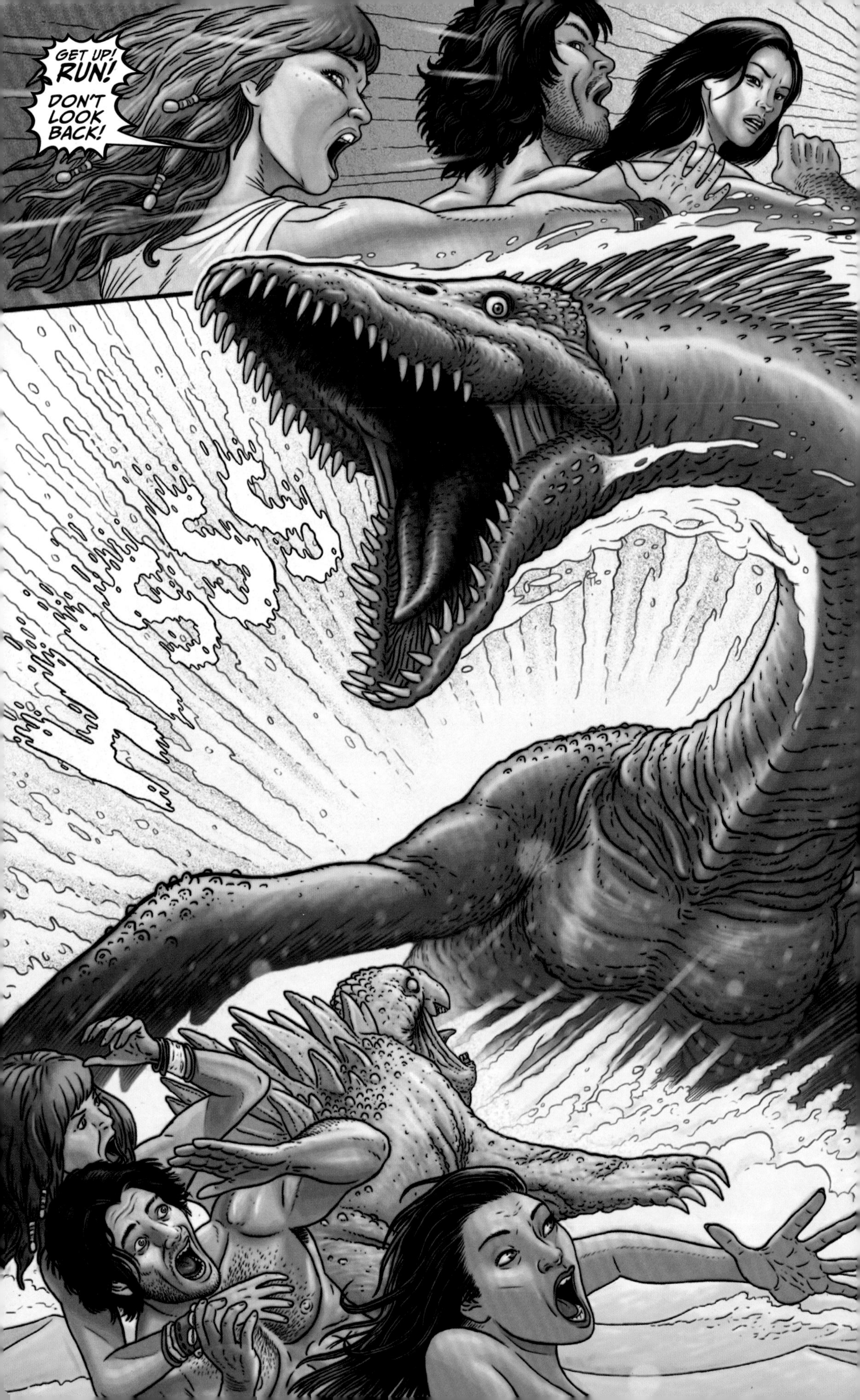
GET UP! RUN!
DON'T LOOK BACK!

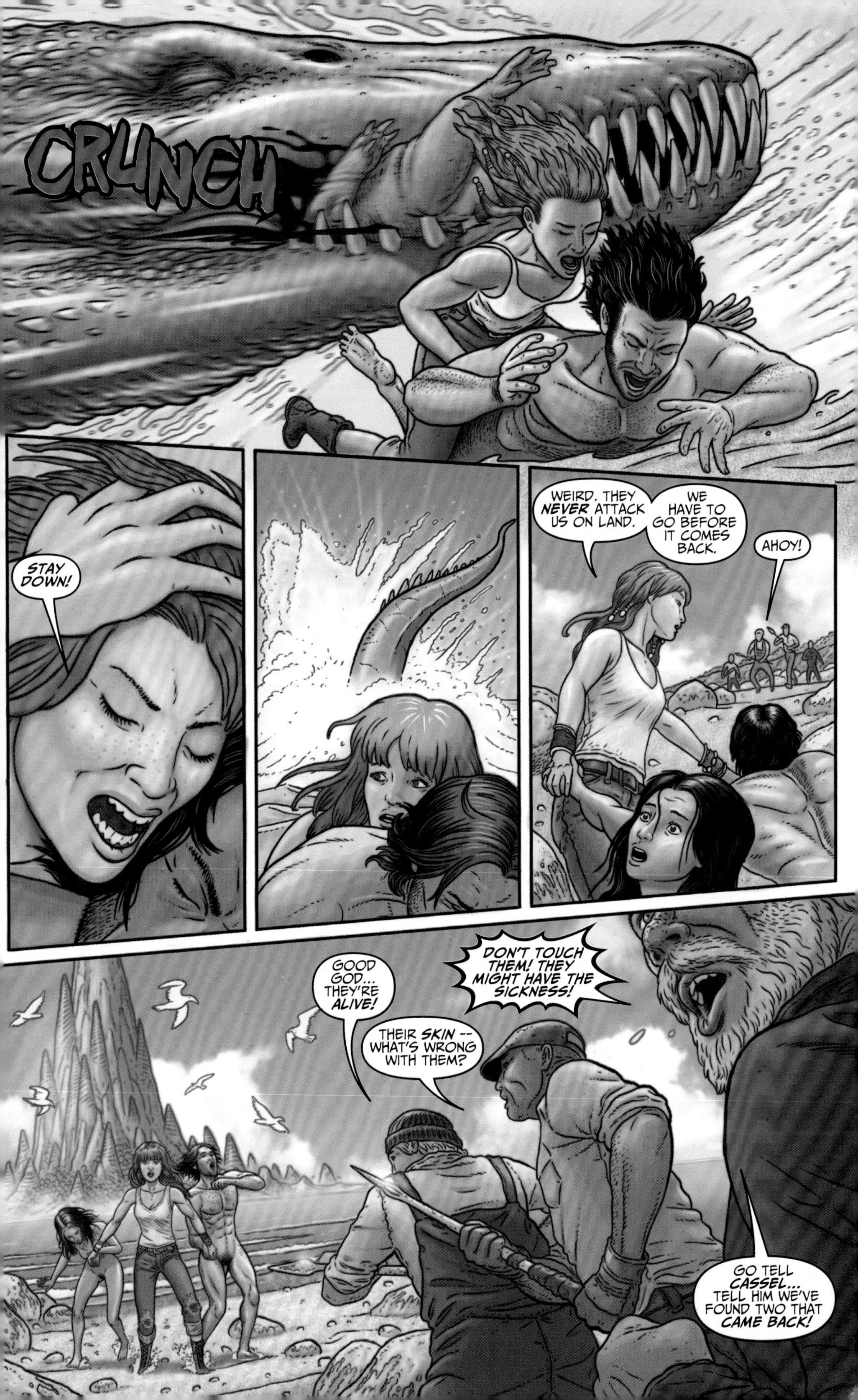
CRUNCH
STAY DOWN!
WEIRD. THEY NEVER ATTACK US ON LAND.
WE HAVE TO GO BEFORE IT COMES BACK.
AHOY!
GOOD GOD... THEY'RE ALIVE!
DON'T TOUCH THEM! THEY MIGHT HAVE THE SICKNESS!
THEIR SKIN -- WHAT'S WRONG WITH THEM?
GO TELL CASSEL... TELL HIM WE'VE FOUND TWO THAT CAME BACK!

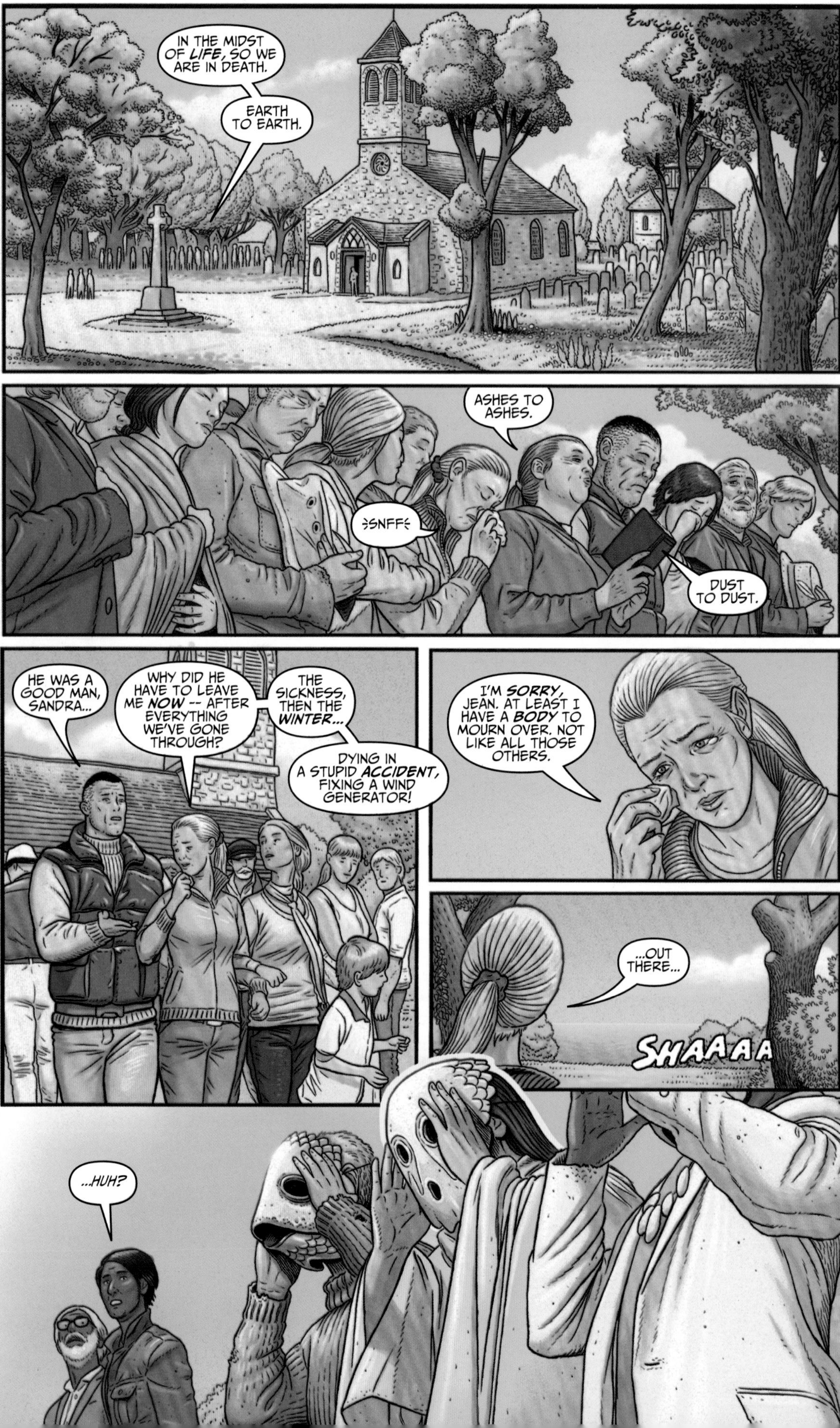
IN THE MIDST OF LIFE, SO WE ARE IN DEATH.
EARTH TO EARTH.
ASHES TO ASHES.
SNFF
DUST TO DUST.
HE WAS A GOOD MAN, SANDRA...
WHY DID HE HAVE TO LEAVE ME NOW -- AFTER EVERYTHING WE'VE GONE THROUGH?
THE SICKNESS, THEN THE WINTER...
DYING IN A STUPID ACCIDENT, FIXING A WIND GENERATOR!
I'M SORRY, JEAN. AT LEAST I HAVE A BODY TO MOURN OVER. NOT LIKE ALL THOSE OTHERS.
...OUT THERE...
SHAAAA
...HUH?

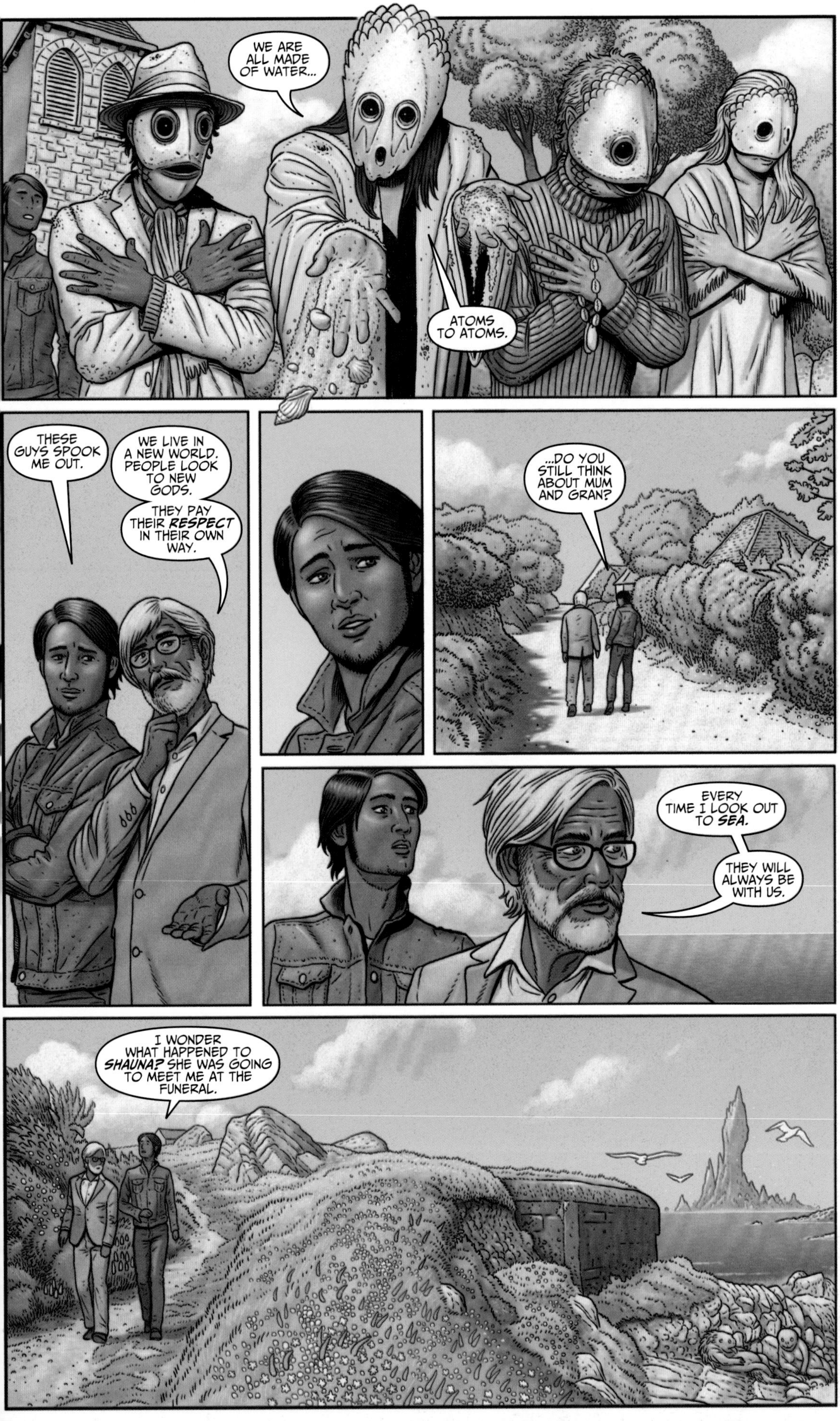
WE ARE ALL MADE OF WATER...
ATOMS TO ATOMS.
THESE GUYS SPOOK ME OUT.
WE LIVE IN A NEW WORLD. PEOPLE LOOK TO NEW GODS.
THEY PAY THEIR RESPECT IN THEIR OWN WAY.
...DO YOU STILL THINK ABOUT MUM AND GRAN?
EVERY TIME I LOOK OUT TO SEA.
THEY WILL ALWAYS BE WITH US.
I WONDER WHAT HAPPENED TO SHAUNA? SHE WAS GOING TO MEET ME AT THE FUNERAL.

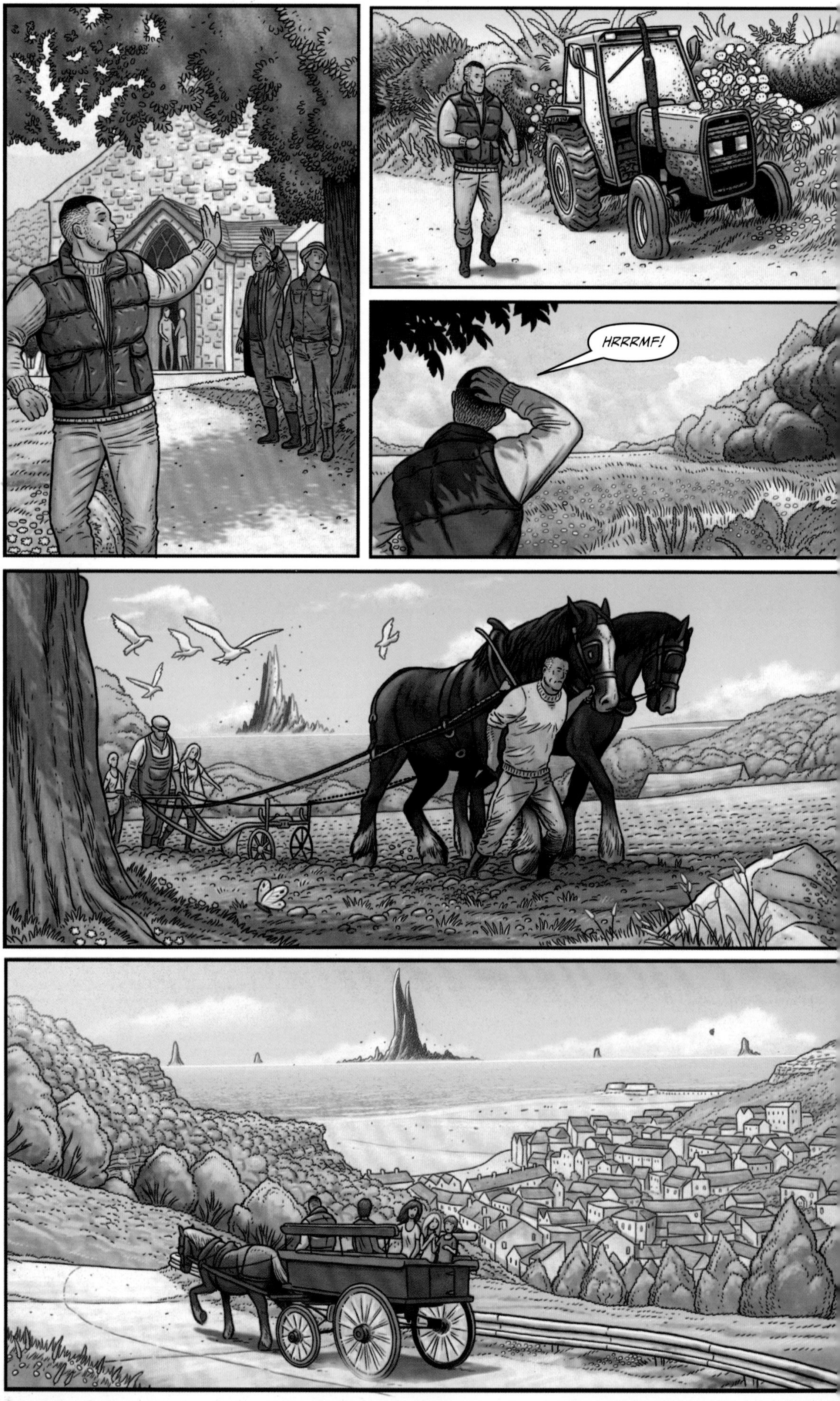
HRRRMF!

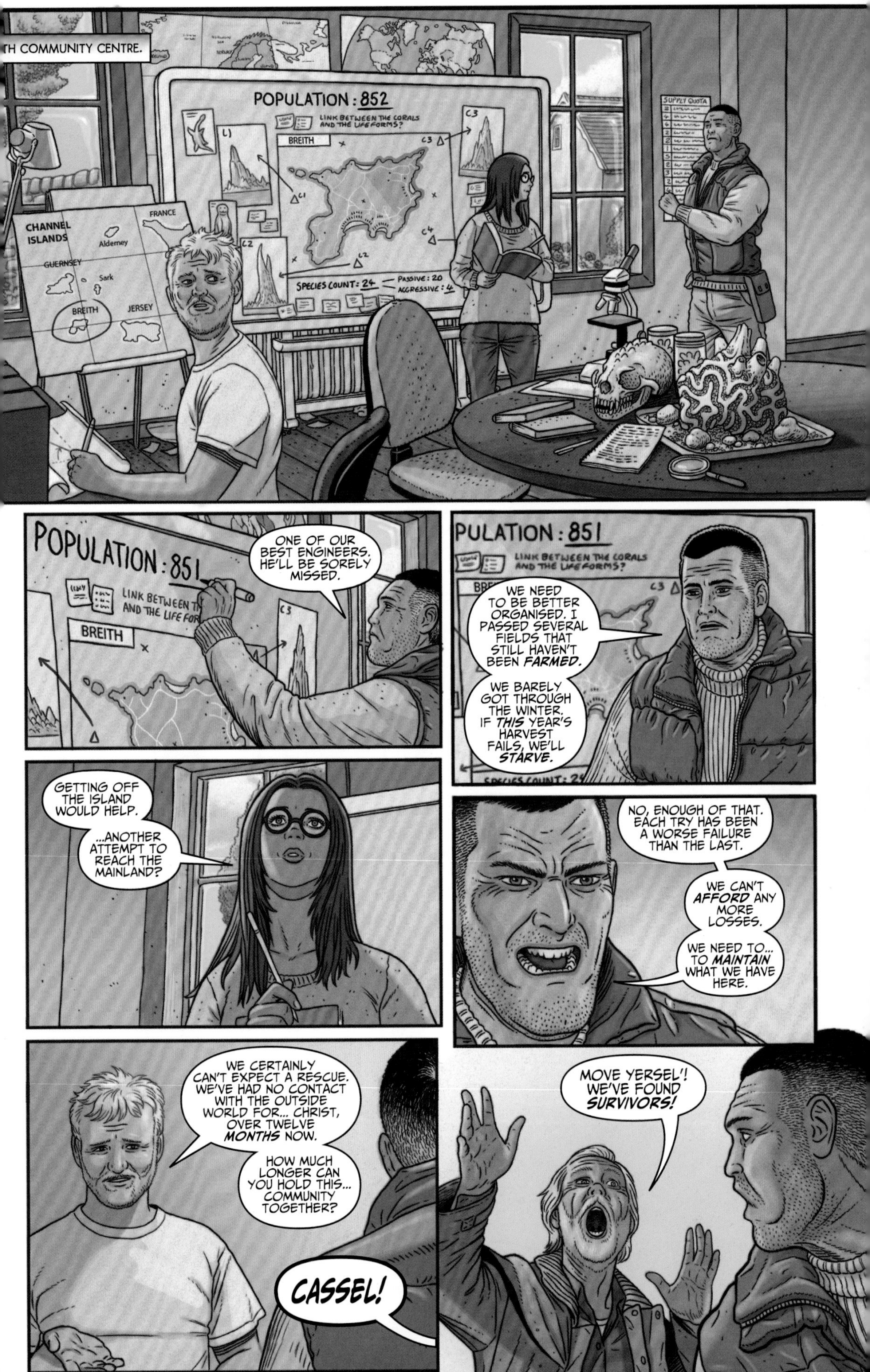

TH COMMUNITY CENTRE.
POPULATION : 852
LINK BETWEEN THE CORALS AND THE LIFEFORMS?
BREITH
SPECIES COUNT : 24 — PASSIVE : 20 AGGRESSIVE : 4
SUPPLY QUOTA
CHANNEL ISLANDS
FRANCE
Alderney
GUERNSEY
Sark
BREITH
JERSEY
POPULATION : 851
LINK BETWEEN TH AND THE LIFE FOR
BREITH
ONE OF OUR BEST ENGINEERS. HE'LL BE SORELY MISSED.
PULATION : 851
WE NEED TO BE BETTER ORGANISED. I PASSED SEVERAL FIELDS THAT STILL HAVEN'T BEEN FARMED.
WE BARELY GOT THROUGH THE WINTER. IF THIS YEAR'S HARVEST FAILS, WE'LL STARVE.
GETTING OFF THE ISLAND WOULD HELP.
...ANOTHER ATTEMPT TO REACH THE MAINLAND?
NO, ENOUGH OF THAT. EACH TRY HAS BEEN A WORSE FAILURE THAN THE LAST.
WE CAN'T AFFORD ANY MORE LOSSES.
WE NEED TO... TO MAINTAIN WHAT WE HAVE HERE.
WE CERTAINLY CAN'T EXPECT A RESCUE. WE'VE HAD NO CONTACT WITH THE OUTSIDE WORLD FOR... CHRIST, OVER TWELVE MONTHS NOW.
HOW MUCH LONGER CAN YOU HOLD THIS... COMMUNITY TOGETHER?
CASSEL!
MOVE YERSEL'! WE'VE FOUND SURVIVORS!

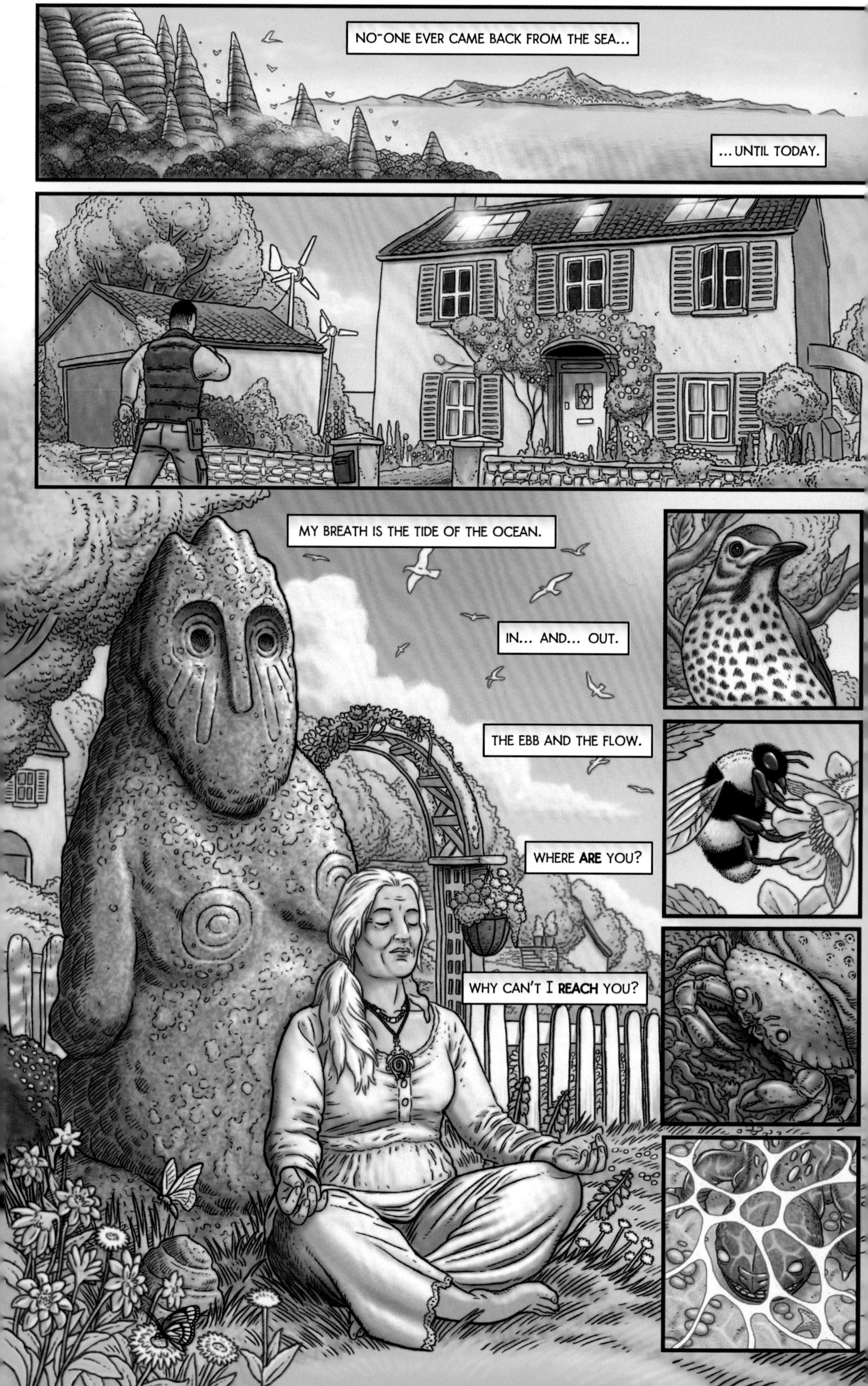
NO-ONE EVER CAME BACK FROM THE SEA...
...UNTIL TODAY.
MY BREATH IS THE TIDE OF THE OCEAN.
IN... AND... OUT.
THE EBB AND THE FLOW.
WHERE **ARE** YOU?
WHY CAN'T I **REACH** YOU?

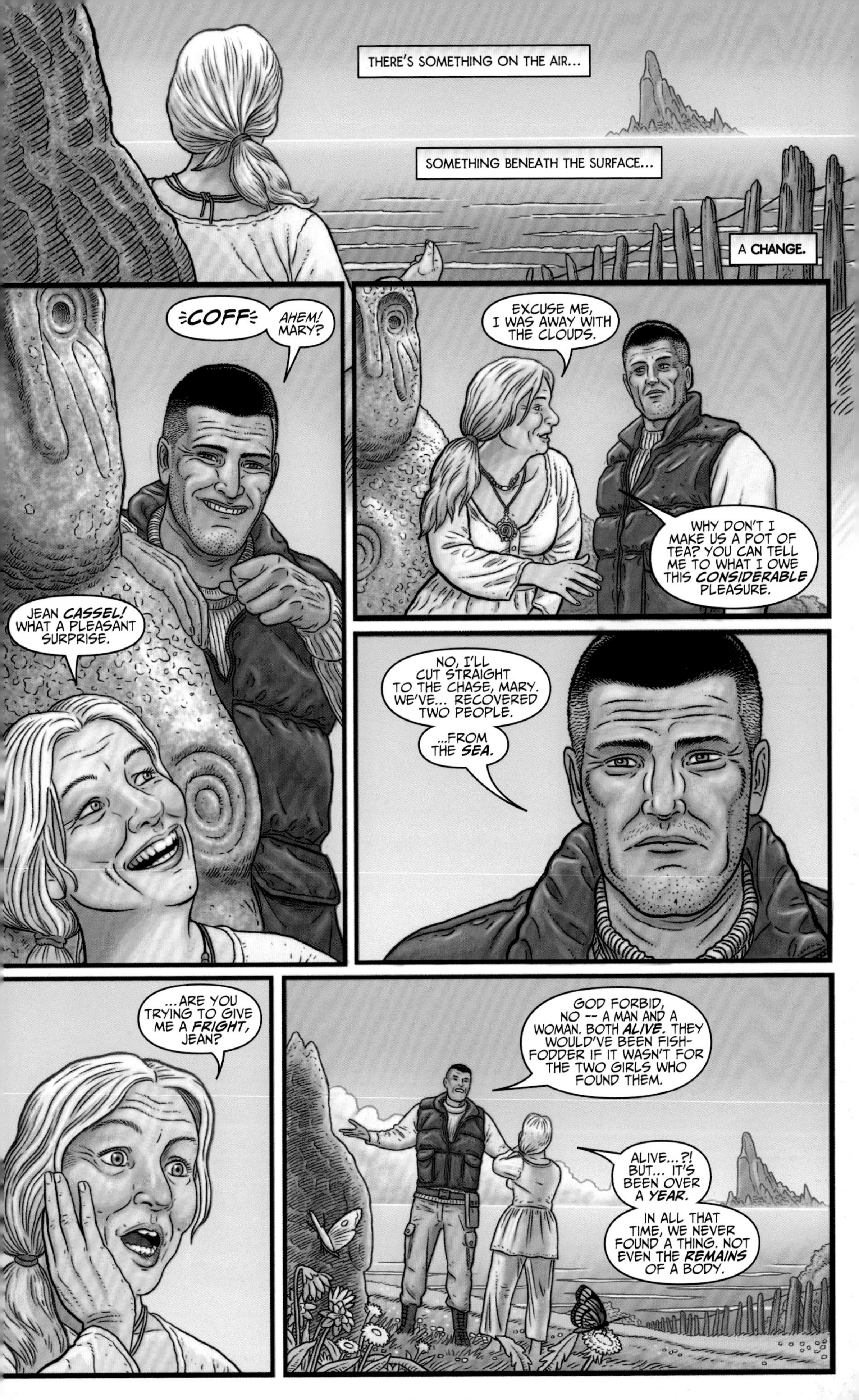

THERE'S SOMETHING ON THE AIR...
SOMETHING BENEATH THE SURFACE...
A CHANGE.
COFF
AHEM! MARY?
JEAN CASSEL! WHAT A PLEASANT SURPRISE.
EXCUSE ME, I WAS AWAY WITH THE CLOUDS.
WHY DON'T I MAKE US A POT OF TEA? YOU CAN TELL ME TO WHAT I OWE THIS CONSIDERABLE PLEASURE.
NO, I'LL CUT STRAIGHT TO THE CHASE, MARY. WE'VE... RECOVERED TWO PEOPLE.
...FROM THE SEA.
...ARE YOU TRYING TO GIVE ME A FRIGHT, JEAN?
GOD FORBID, NO -- A MAN AND A WOMAN. BOTH ALIVE. THEY WOULD'VE BEEN FISH-FODDER IF IT WASN'T FOR THE TWO GIRLS WHO FOUND THEM.
ALIVE...?! BUT... IT'S BEEN OVER A YEAR.
IN ALL THAT TIME, WE NEVER FOUND A THING. NOT EVEN THE REMAINS OF A BODY.

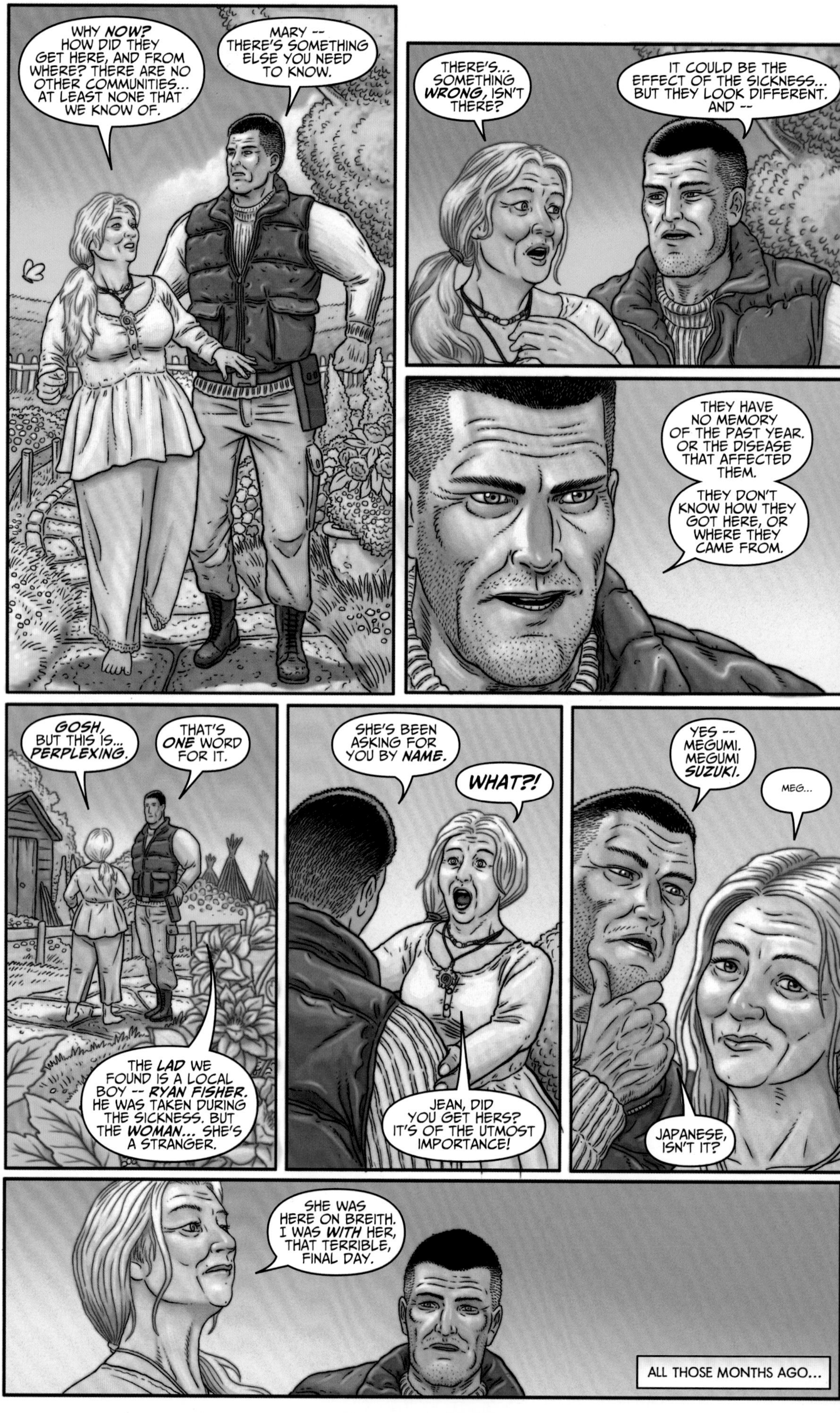
WHY NOW? HOW DID THEY GET HERE, AND FROM WHERE? THERE ARE NO OTHER COMMUNITIES... AT LEAST NONE THAT WE KNOW OF.
MARY -- THERE'S SOMETHING ELSE YOU NEED TO KNOW.
THERE'S... SOMETHING WRONG, ISN'T THERE?
IT COULD BE THE EFFECT OF THE SICKNESS... BUT THEY LOOK DIFFERENT. AND --
THEY HAVE NO MEMORY OF THE PAST YEAR. OR THE DISEASE THAT AFFECTED THEM.
THEY DON'T KNOW HOW THEY GOT HERE, OR WHERE THEY CAME FROM.
GOSH, BUT THIS IS... PERPLEXING.
THAT'S ONE WORD FOR IT.
THE LAD WE FOUND IS A LOCAL BOY -- RYAN FISHER. HE WAS TAKEN DURING THE SICKNESS. BUT THE WOMAN... SHE'S A STRANGER.
SHE'S BEEN ASKING FOR YOU BY NAME.
WHAT?!
JEAN, DID YOU GET HERS? IT'S OF THE UTMOST IMPORTANCE!
YES -- MEGUMI. MEGUMI SUZUKI.
MEG...
JAPANESE, ISN'T IT?
SHE WAS HERE ON BREITH. I WAS WITH HER, THAT TERRIBLE, FINAL DAY.
ALL THOSE MONTHS AGO...

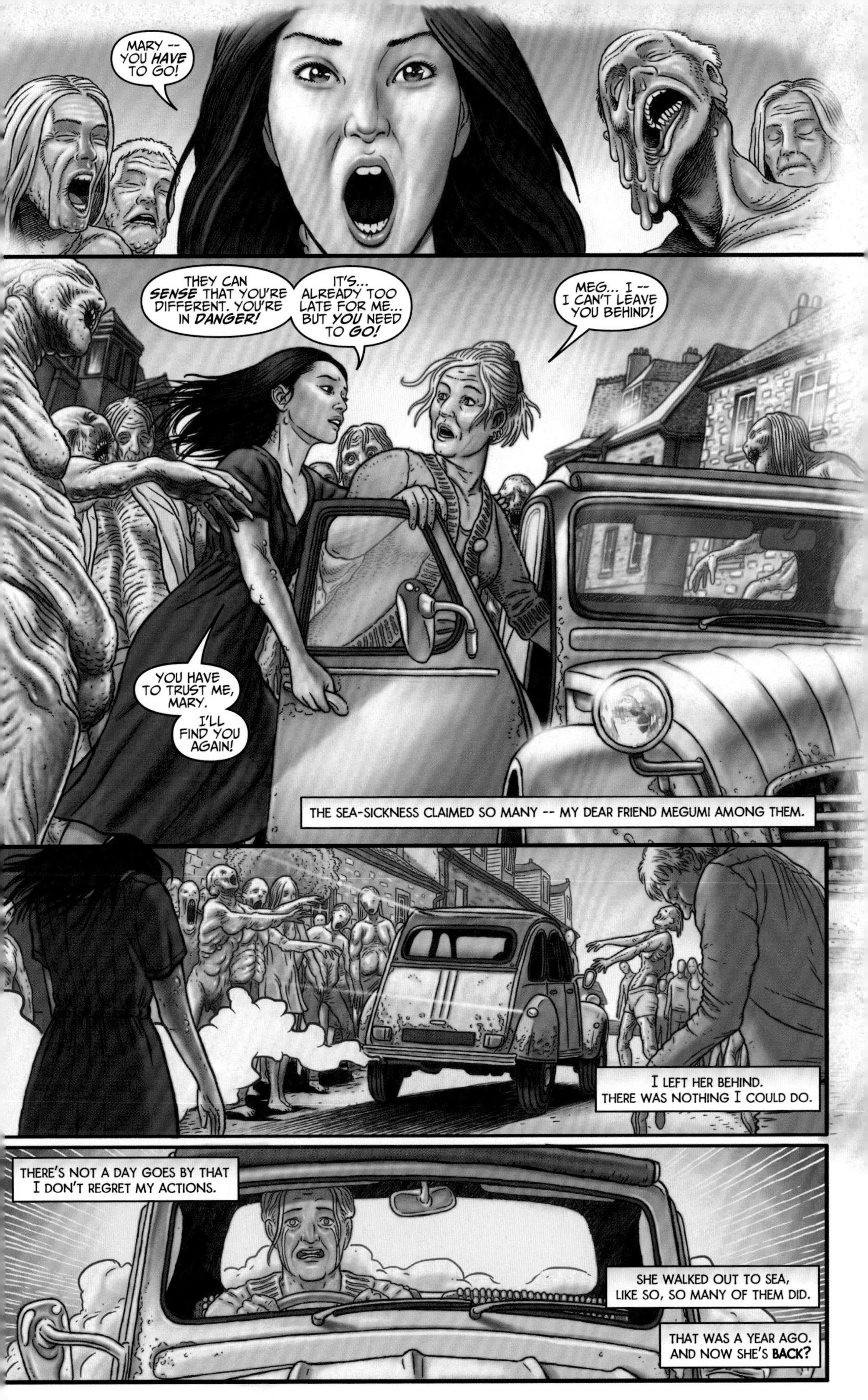
MARY -- YOU **HAVE** TO GO!
THEY CAN **SENSE** THAT YOU'RE DIFFERENT. YOU'RE IN **DANGER!**
IT'S... ALREADY TOO LATE FOR ME... BUT **YOU** NEED TO **GO!**
MEG... I -- I CAN'T LEAVE YOU BEHIND!
YOU HAVE TO TRUST ME, MARY.
I'LL FIND YOU AGAIN!
THE SEA-SICKNESS CLAIMED SO MANY -- MY DEAR FRIEND MEGUMI AMONG THEM.
I LEFT HER BEHIND. THERE WAS NOTHING I COULD DO.
THERE'S NOT A DAY GOES BY THAT I DON'T REGRET MY ACTIONS.
SHE WALKED OUT TO SEA, LIKE SO, SO MANY OF THEM DID.
THAT WAS A YEAR AGO. AND NOW SHE'S **BACK?**

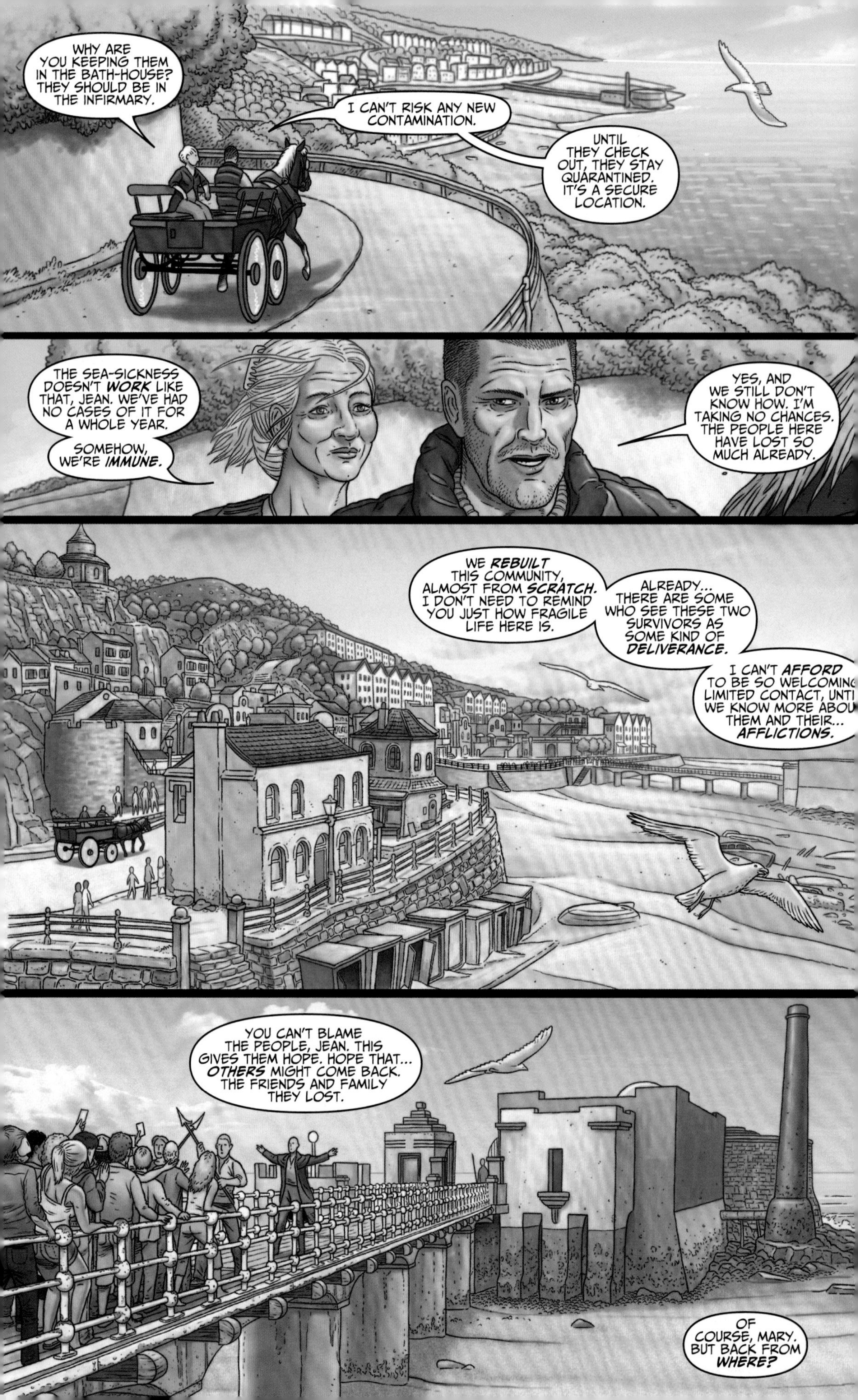
WHY ARE YOU KEEPING THEM IN THE BATH-HOUSE? THEY SHOULD BE IN THE INFIRMARY.
I CAN'T RISK ANY NEW CONTAMINATION.
UNTIL THEY CHECK OUT, THEY STAY QUARANTINED. IT'S A SECURE LOCATION.
THE SEA-SICKNESS DOESN'T WORK LIKE THAT, JEAN. WE'VE HAD NO CASES OF IT FOR A WHOLE YEAR.
SOMEHOW, WE'RE IMMUNE.
YES, AND WE STILL DON'T KNOW HOW. I'M TAKING NO CHANCES. THE PEOPLE HERE HAVE LOST SO MUCH ALREADY.
WE REBUILT THIS COMMUNITY, ALMOST FROM SCRATCH. I DON'T NEED TO REMIND YOU JUST HOW FRAGILE LIFE HERE IS.
ALREADY... THERE ARE SOME WHO SEE THESE TWO SURVIVORS AS SOME KIND OF DELIVERANCE.
I CAN'T AFFORD TO BE SO WELCOMING LIMITED CONTACT, UNTI WE KNOW MORE ABOU THEM AND THEIR... AFFLICTIONS.
YOU CAN'T BLAME THE PEOPLE, JEAN. THIS GIVES THEM HOPE. HOPE THAT... OTHERS MIGHT COME BACK. THE FRIENDS AND FAMILY THEY LOST.
OF COURSE, MARY. BUT BACK FROM WHERE?

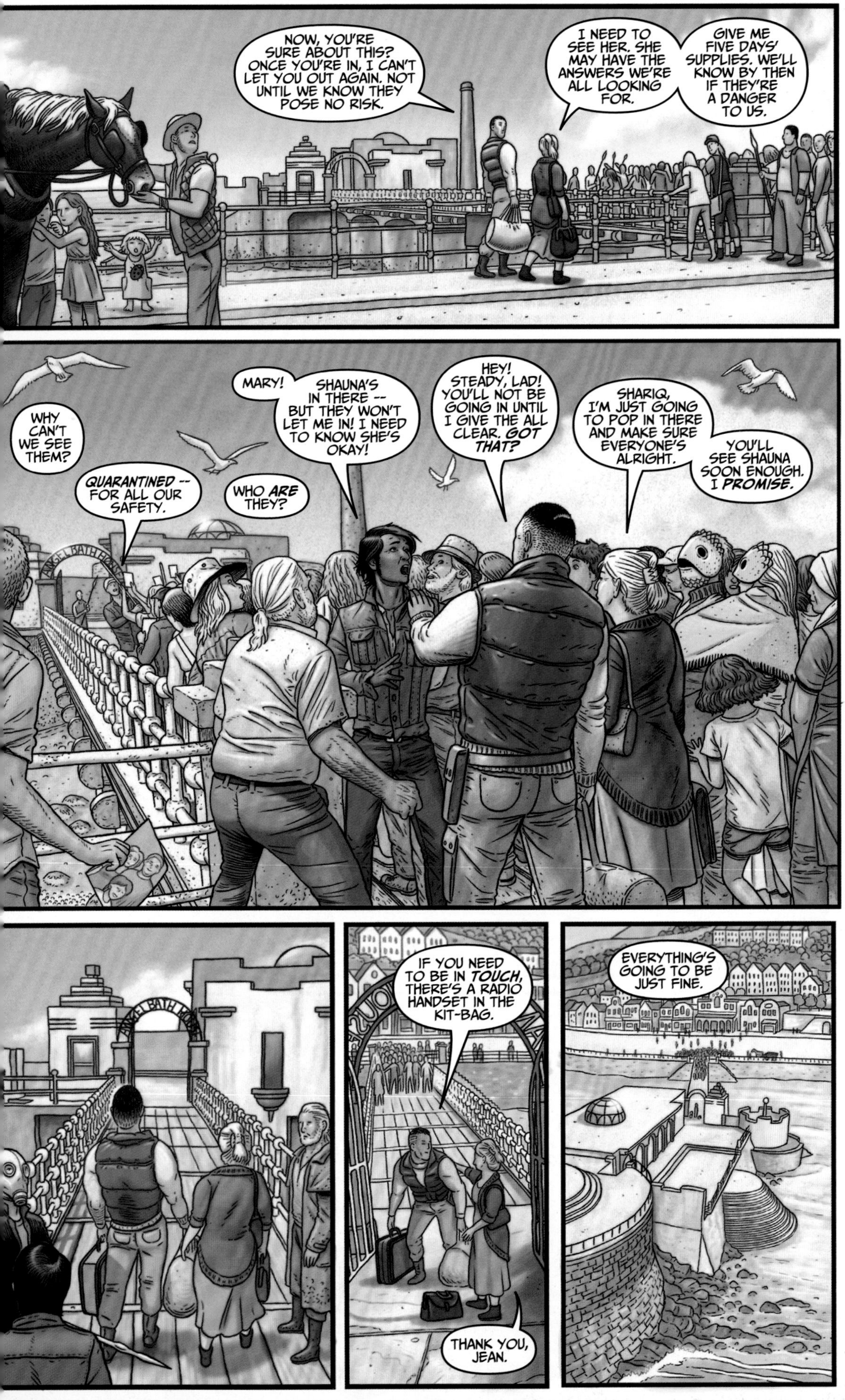
NOW, YOU'RE SURE ABOUT THIS? ONCE YOU'RE IN, I CAN'T LET YOU OUT AGAIN. NOT UNTIL WE KNOW THEY POSE NO RISK.
I NEED TO SEE HER. SHE MAY HAVE THE ANSWERS WE'RE ALL LOOKING FOR.
GIVE ME FIVE DAYS' SUPPLIES. WE'LL KNOW BY THEN IF THEY'RE A DANGER TO US.
WHY CAN'T WE SEE THEM?
QUARANTINED -- FOR ALL OUR SAFETY.
WHO *ARE* THEY?
MARY!
SHAUNA'S IN THERE -- BUT THEY WON'T LET ME IN! I NEED TO KNOW SHE'S OKAY!
HEY! STEADY, LAD! YOU'LL NOT BE GOING IN UNTIL I GIVE THE ALL CLEAR. *GOT THAT?*
SHARIQ, I'M JUST GOING TO POP IN THERE AND MAKE SURE EVERYONE'S ALRIGHT.
YOU'LL SEE SHAUNA SOON ENOUGH. I *PROMISE.*
IF YOU NEED TO BE IN *TOUCH,* THERE'S A RADIO HANDSET IN THE KIT-BAG.
THANK YOU, JEAN.
EVERYTHING'S GOING TO BE JUST FINE.

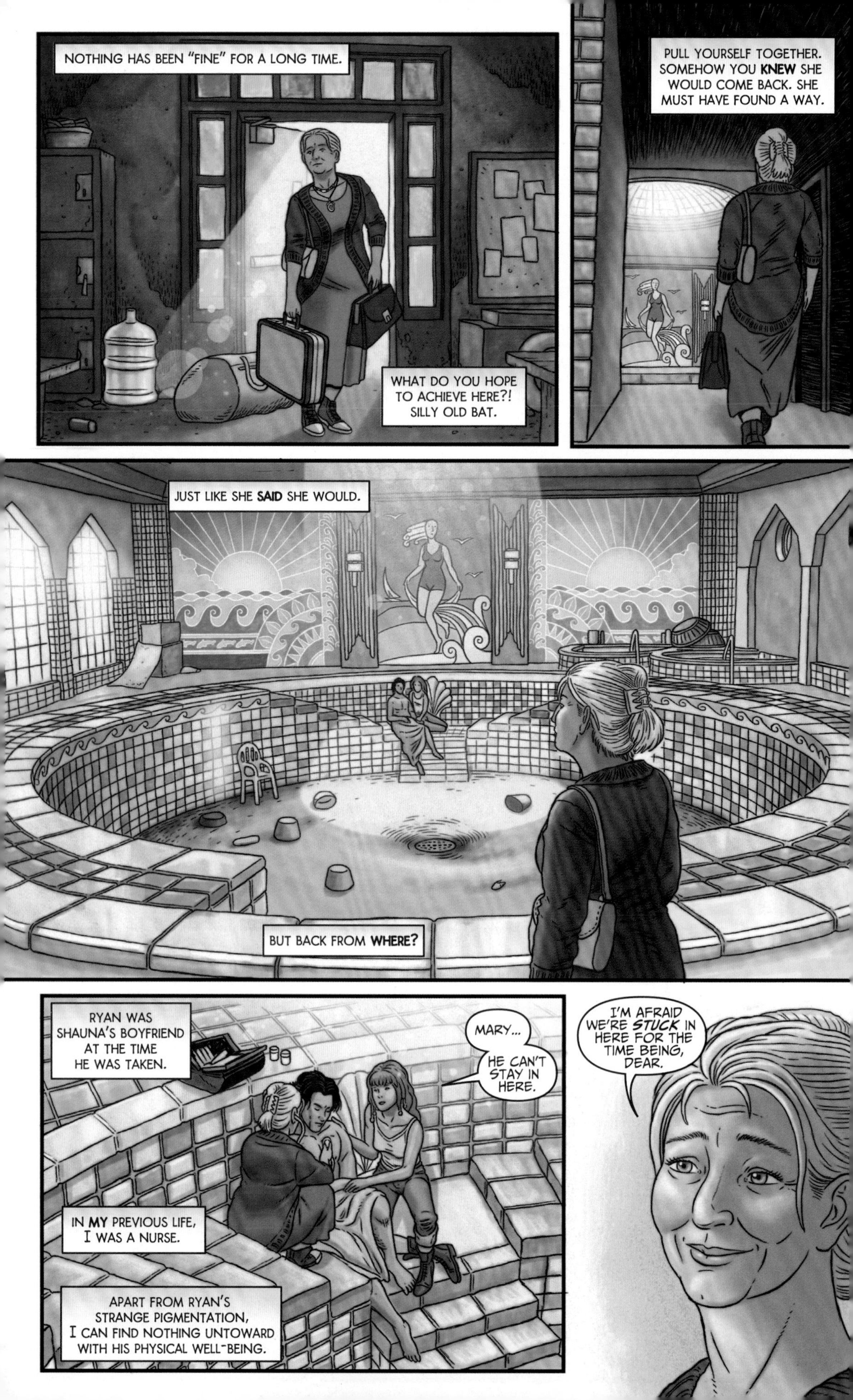
NOTHING HAS BEEN "FINE" FOR A LONG TIME.
WHAT DO YOU HOPE TO ACHIEVE HERE?! SILLY OLD BAT.
PULL YOURSELF TOGETHER. SOMEHOW YOU **KNEW** SHE WOULD COME BACK. SHE MUST HAVE FOUND A WAY.
JUST LIKE SHE **SAID** SHE WOULD.
BUT BACK FROM **WHERE?**
RYAN WAS SHAUNA'S BOYFRIEND AT THE TIME HE WAS TAKEN.
MARY...
HE CAN'T STAY IN HERE.
IN **MY** PREVIOUS LIFE, I WAS A NURSE.
APART FROM RYAN'S STRANGE PIGMENTATION, I CAN FIND NOTHING UNTOWARD WITH HIS PHYSICAL WELL-BEING.
I'M AFRAID WE'RE ***STUCK*** IN HERE FOR THE TIME BEING, DEAR.

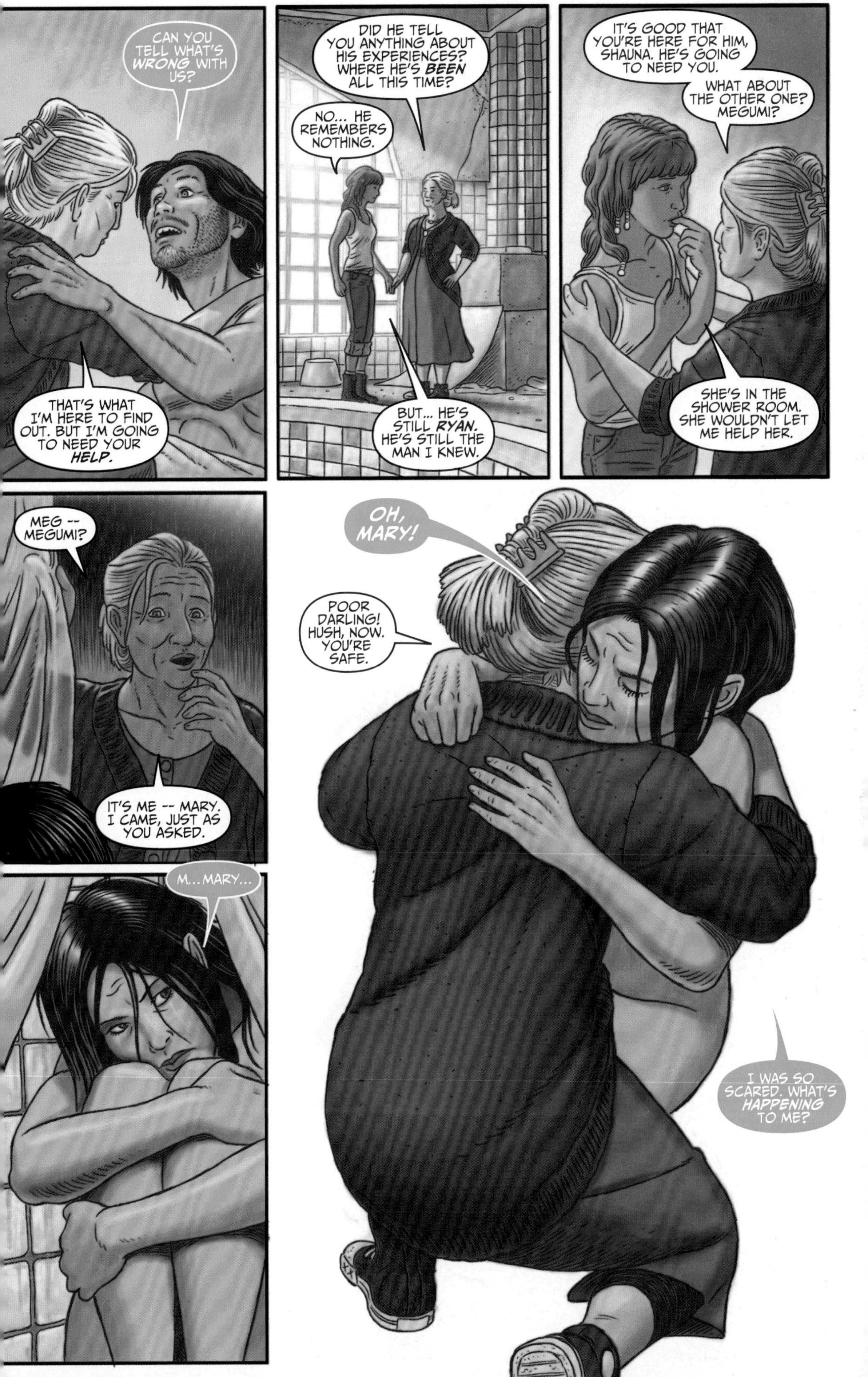
CAN YOU TELL WHAT'S *WRONG* WITH US?
THAT'S WHAT I'M HERE TO FIND OUT. BUT I'M GOING TO NEED YOUR *HELP.*
DID HE TELL YOU ANYTHING ABOUT HIS EXPERIENCES? WHERE HE'S *BEEN* ALL THIS TIME?
NO... HE REMEMBERS NOTHING.
BUT... HE'S STILL *RYAN.* HE'S STILL THE MAN I KNEW.
IT'S GOOD THAT YOU'RE HERE FOR HIM, SHAUNA. HE'S GOING TO NEED YOU.
WHAT ABOUT THE OTHER ONE? MEGUMI?
SHE'S IN THE SHOWER ROOM. SHE WOULDN'T LET ME HELP HER.
MEG -- MEGUMI?
IT'S ME -- MARY. I CAME, JUST AS YOU ASKED.
M...MARY...
OH, MARY!
POOR DARLING! HUSH, NOW. YOU'RE SAFE.
I WAS SO SCARED. WHAT'S *HAPPENING* TO ME?

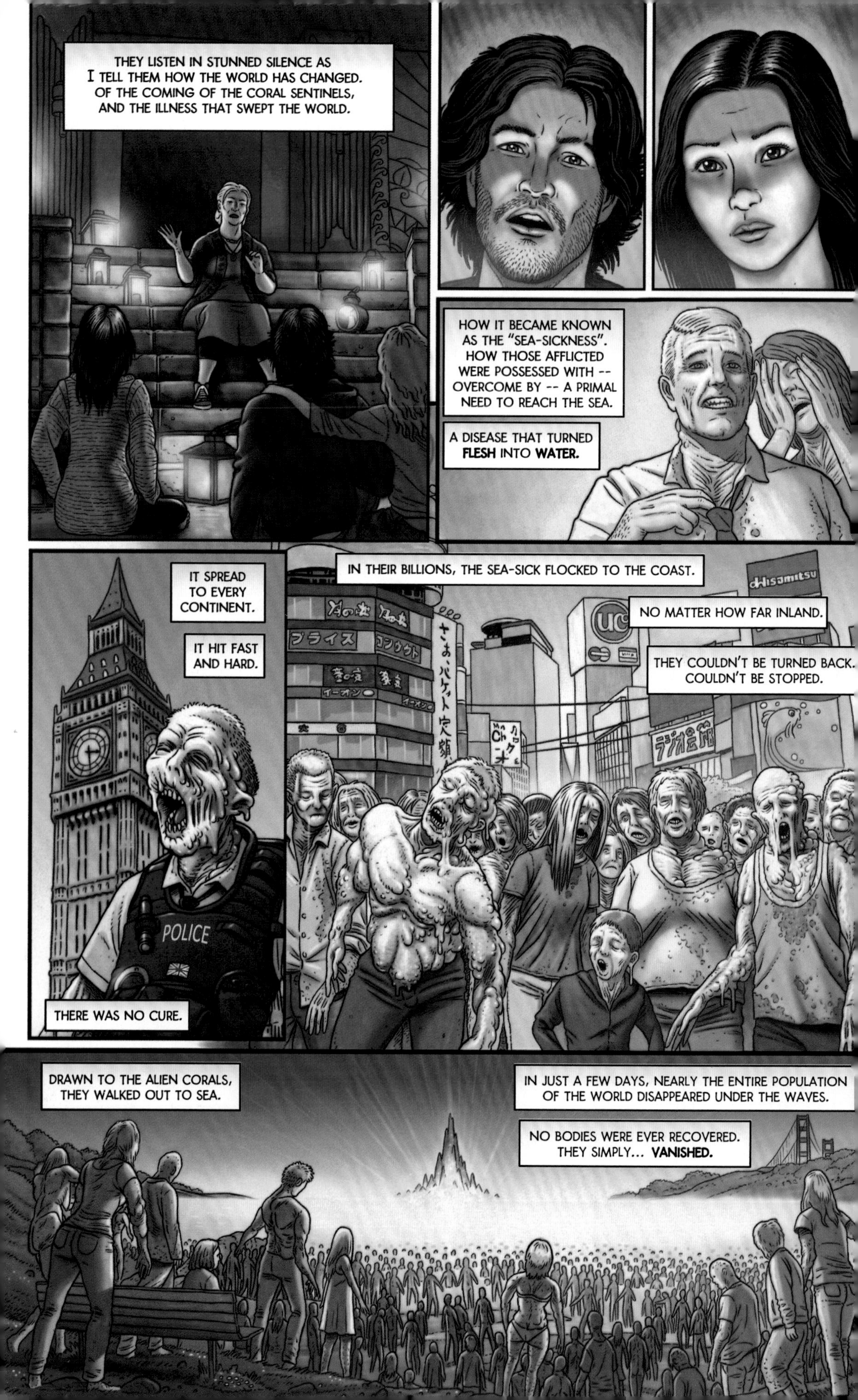
THEY LISTEN IN STUNNED SILENCE AS I TELL THEM HOW THE WORLD HAS CHANGED. OF THE COMING OF THE CORAL SENTINELS, AND THE ILLNESS THAT SWEPT THE WORLD.
HOW IT BECAME KNOWN AS THE "SEA-SICKNESS". HOW THOSE AFFLICTED WERE POSSESSED WITH -- OVERCOME BY -- A PRIMAL NEED TO REACH THE SEA.
A DISEASE THAT TURNED **FLESH** INTO **WATER.**
IT SPREAD TO EVERY CONTINENT.
IT HIT FAST AND HARD.
POLICE
THERE WAS NO CURE.
IN THEIR BILLIONS, THE SEA-SICK FLOCKED TO THE COAST.
Hisamitsu
NO MATTER HOW FAR INLAND.
THEY COULDN'T BE TURNED BACK. COULDN'T BE STOPPED.
ラジオ会館
DRAWN TO THE ALIEN CORALS, THEY WALKED OUT TO SEA.
IN JUST A FEW DAYS, NEARLY THE ENTIRE POPULATION OF THE WORLD DISAPPEARED UNDER THE WAVES.
NO BODIES WERE EVER RECOVERED. THEY SIMPLY... **VANISHED.**

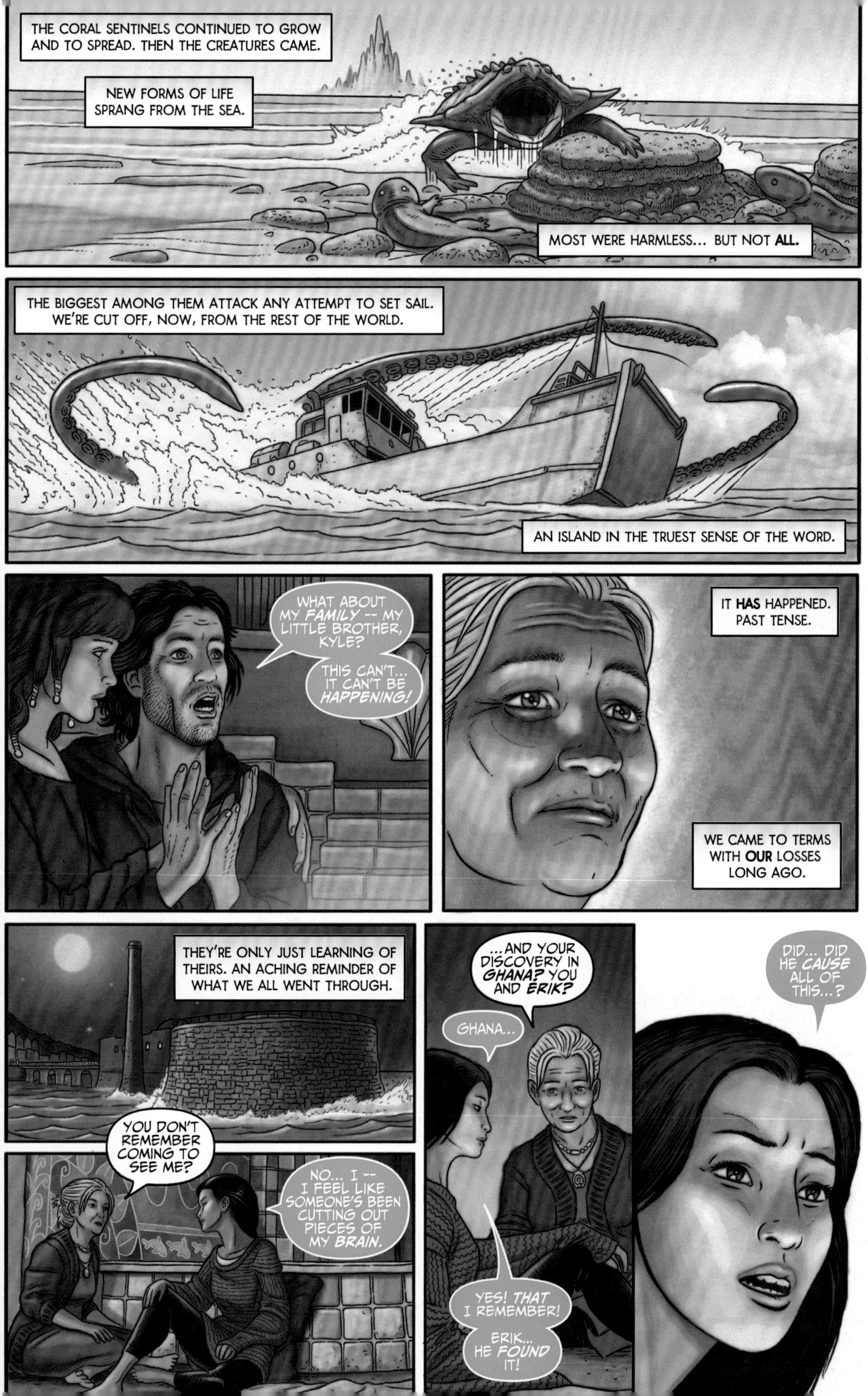
THE CORAL SENTINELS CONTINUED TO GROW AND TO SPREAD. THEN THE CREATURES CAME.
NEW FORMS OF LIFE SPRANG FROM THE SEA.
MOST WERE HARMLESS... BUT NOT ALL.
THE BIGGEST AMONG THEM ATTACK ANY ATTEMPT TO SET SAIL. WE'RE CUT OFF, NOW, FROM THE REST OF THE WORLD.
AN ISLAND IN THE TRUEST SENSE OF THE WORD.
WHAT ABOUT MY FAMILY -- MY LITTLE BROTHER, KYLE?
THIS CAN'T... IT CAN'T BE HAPPENING!
IT HAS HAPPENED. PAST TENSE.
WE CAME TO TERMS WITH OUR LOSSES LONG AGO.
THEY'RE ONLY JUST LEARNING OF THEIRS. AN ACHING REMINDER OF WHAT WE ALL WENT THROUGH.
YOU DON'T REMEMBER COMING TO SEE ME?
NO... I -- I FEEL LIKE SOMEONE'S BEEN CUTTING OUT PIECES OF MY BRAIN.
...AND YOUR DISCOVERY IN GHANA? YOU AND ERIK?
GHANA...
YES! THAT I REMEMBER!
ERIK... HE FOUND IT!
DID... DID HE CAUSE ALL OF THIS...?

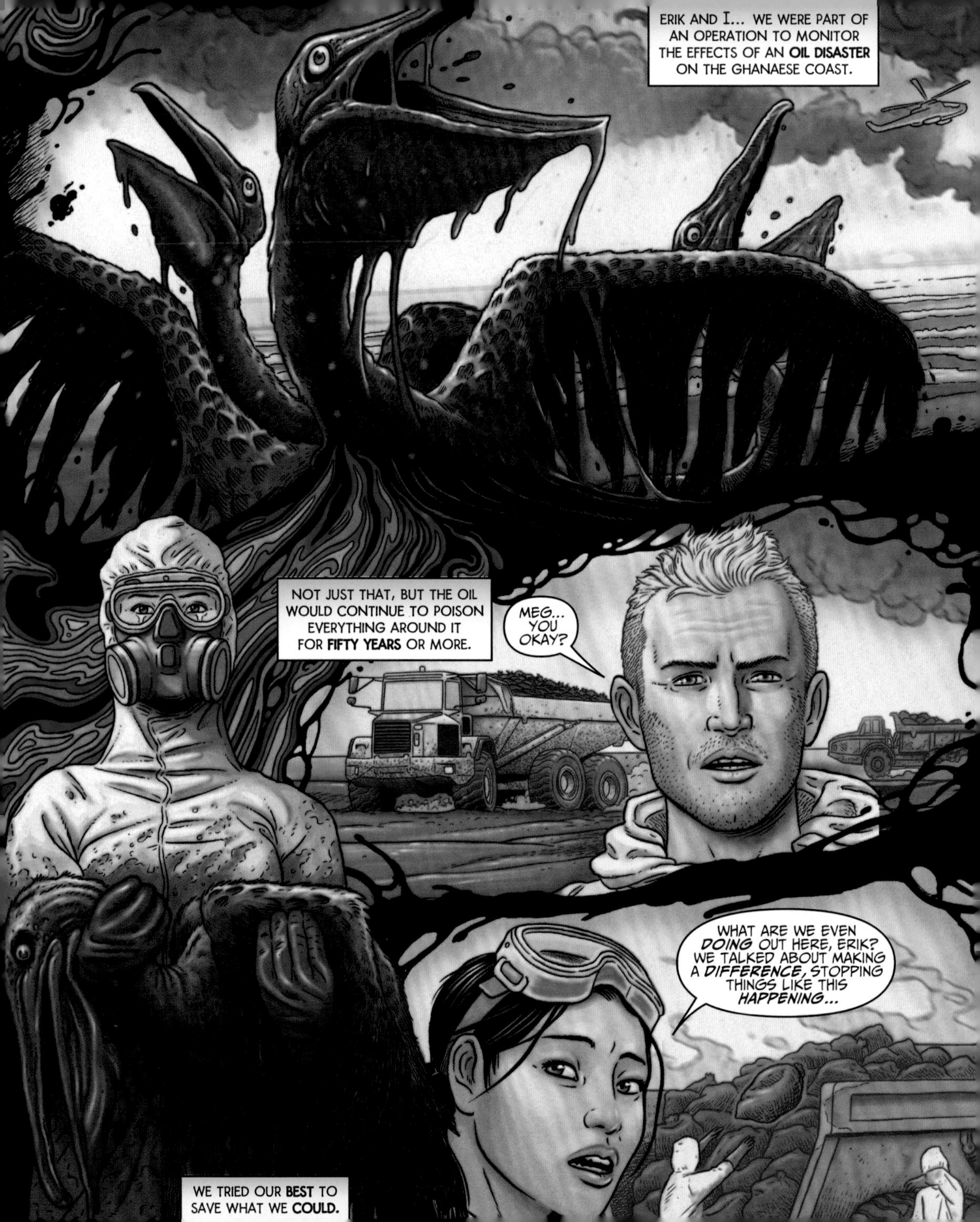
ERIK AND I... WE WERE PART OF AN OPERATION TO MONITOR THE EFFECTS OF AN OIL DISASTER ON THE GHANAESE COAST.
NOT JUST THAT, BUT THE OIL WOULD CONTINUE TO POISON EVERYTHING AROUND IT FOR FIFTY YEARS OR MORE.
MEG... YOU OKAY?
WHAT ARE WE EVEN DOING OUT HERE, ERIK? WE TALKED ABOUT MAKING A DIFFERENCE, STOPPING THINGS LIKE THIS HAPPENING...
WE TRIED OUR BEST TO SAVE WHAT WE COULD.

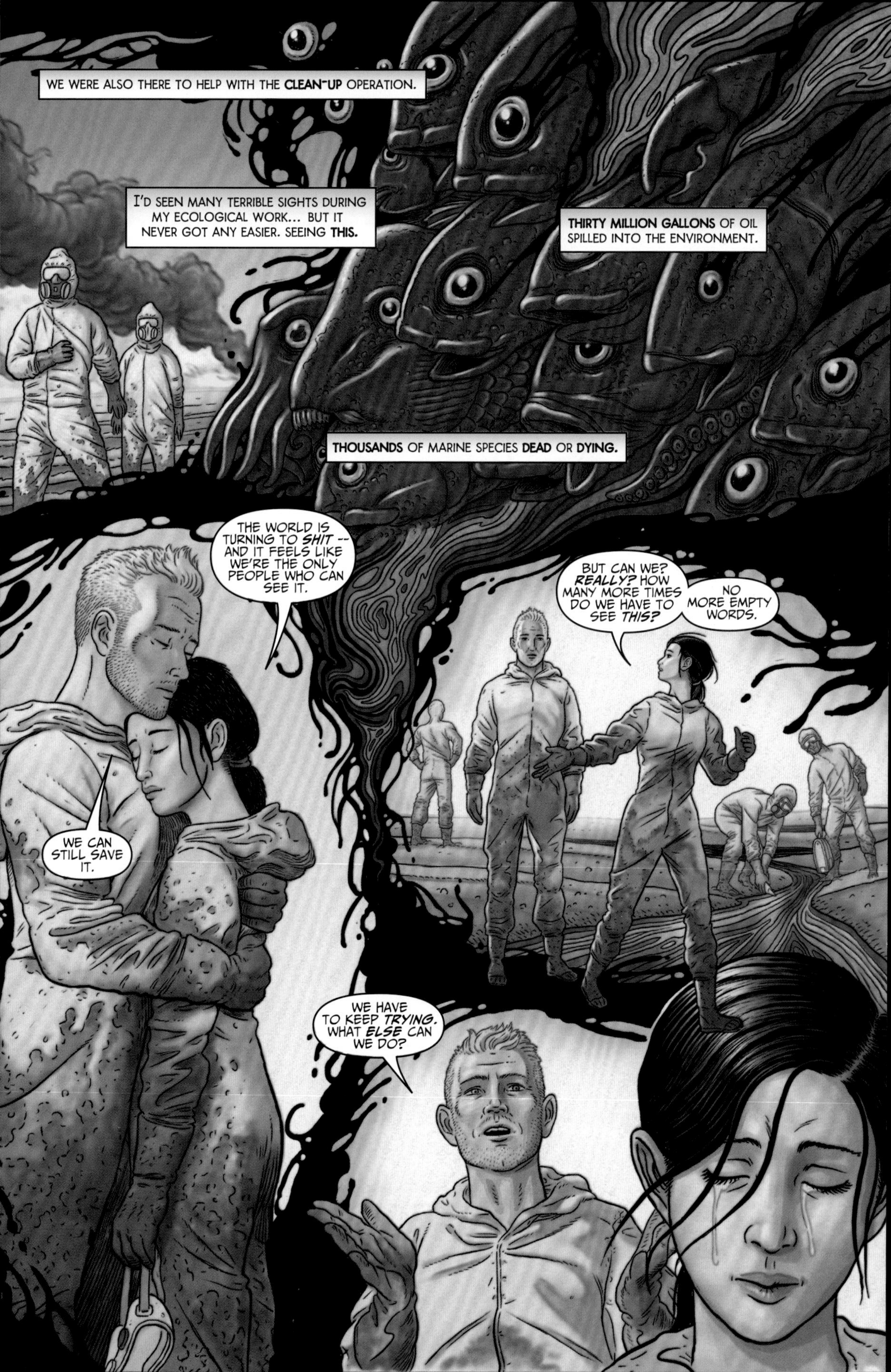
WE WERE ALSO THERE TO HELP WITH THE **CLEAN-UP** OPERATION.
I'D SEEN MANY TERRIBLE SIGHTS DURING MY ECOLOGICAL WORK... BUT IT NEVER GOT ANY EASIER. SEEING **THIS.**
THIRTY MILLION GALLONS OF OIL SPILLED INTO THE ENVIRONMENT.
THOUSANDS OF MARINE SPECIES **DEAD** OR **DYING.**
THE WORLD IS TURNING TO *SHIT* -- AND IT FEELS LIKE WE'RE THE ONLY PEOPLE WHO CAN SEE IT.
WE CAN STILL SAVE IT.
BUT CAN WE? *REALLY?* HOW MANY MORE TIMES DO WE HAVE TO SEE *THIS?*
NO MORE EMPTY WORDS.
WE HAVE TO KEEP *TRYING*. WHAT *ELSE* CAN WE DO?

FOUR MONTHS LATER, WE RETURNED TO GHANA TO CONTINUE OUR RESEARCH.

THE BEACH WAS SCRAPED CLEAN, THE SEA STERILIZED WITH CHEMICALS.

WE CARRIED OUT OUR TESTS, WROTE OUR REPORTS.

ON THE SURFACE, EVERYTHING LOOKED NORMAL... BUT UNDERNEATH, WE KNEW IT WAS **DYING.**

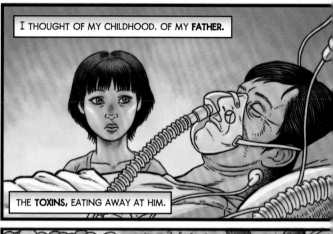

I THOUGHT OF MY CHILDHOOD. OF MY **FATHER.**

THE **TOXINS,** EATING AWAY AT HIM.

THEY DID **THEIR** BEST, TOO -- BUT NO-ONE COULD SAVE **HIM.**

I WAS DOING THIS FOR HIM.

TO BRING REST TO RESTLESS SPIRITS.

THE DAMAGE WAS TOO MUCH. NOT JUST HERE, BUT ACROSS THE **WORLD.**

IT HAD GONE TOO FAR, PAST THE POINT OF NO RETURN. WE COULDN'T SAVE A THING.

WE WERE ONLY KILLING TIME.

...IT WAS IN THE SECOND WEEK THERE THAT ERIK FOUND IT.

GUYS! DROP EVERYTHING, YOU'VE GOT TO **SEE** THIS!

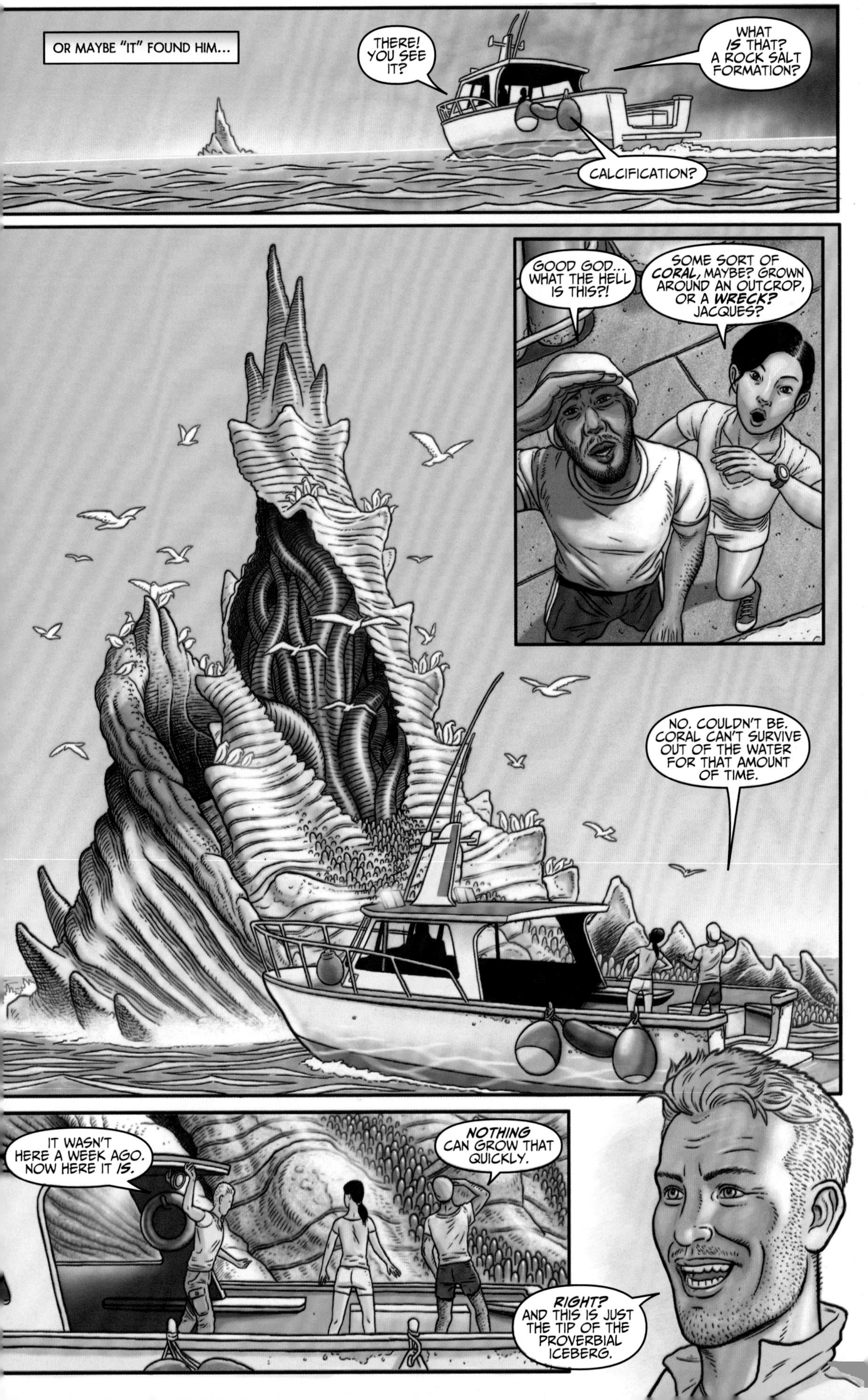
OR MAYBE "IT" FOUND HIM...
THERE! YOU SEE IT?
WHAT IS THAT? A ROCK SALT FORMATION?
CALCIFICATION?
GOOD GOD... WHAT THE HELL IS THIS?!
SOME SORT OF CORAL, MAYBE? GROWN AROUND AN OUTCROP, OR A WRECK? JACQUES?
NO. COULDN'T BE. CORAL CAN'T SURVIVE OUT OF THE WATER FOR THAT AMOUNT OF TIME.
IT WASN'T HERE A WEEK AGO. NOW HERE IT IS.
NOTHING CAN GROW THAT QUICKLY.
RIGHT? AND THIS IS JUST THE TIP OF THE PROVERBIAL ICEBERG.

THE POLLUTANTS IN THE WATER... THEY'VE *KILLED* ALL THE CORAL COLONIES IN THIS AREA.

THIS IS JUST... *IMPOSSIBLE!*

YEAH. BUT IT'S VERY MUCH *ALIVE.* EVEN ON THE SURFACE, IT SEEMS TO BE THRIVING.

HAVE YOU TESTED THE *WATER?*

SEE THE CIRCLE AROUND THE STRUCTURE?

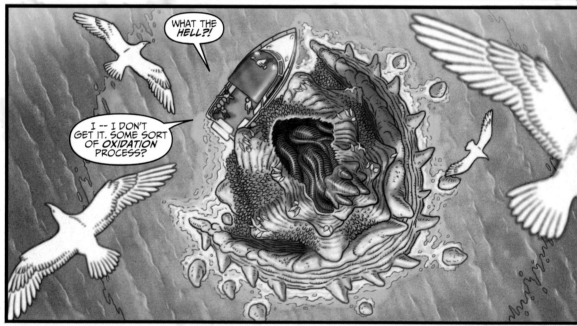

WHAT THE *HELL?!*

I -- I DON'T GET IT. SOME SORT OF *OXIDATION* PROCESS?

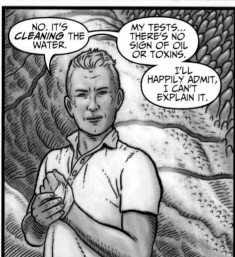

NO. IT'S *CLEANING* THE WATER.

MY TESTS... THERE'S NO SIGN OF OIL OR TOXINS.

I'LL HAPPILY ADMIT, I CAN'T EXPLAIN IT.

MEG. COME HERE. *FEEL* IT.

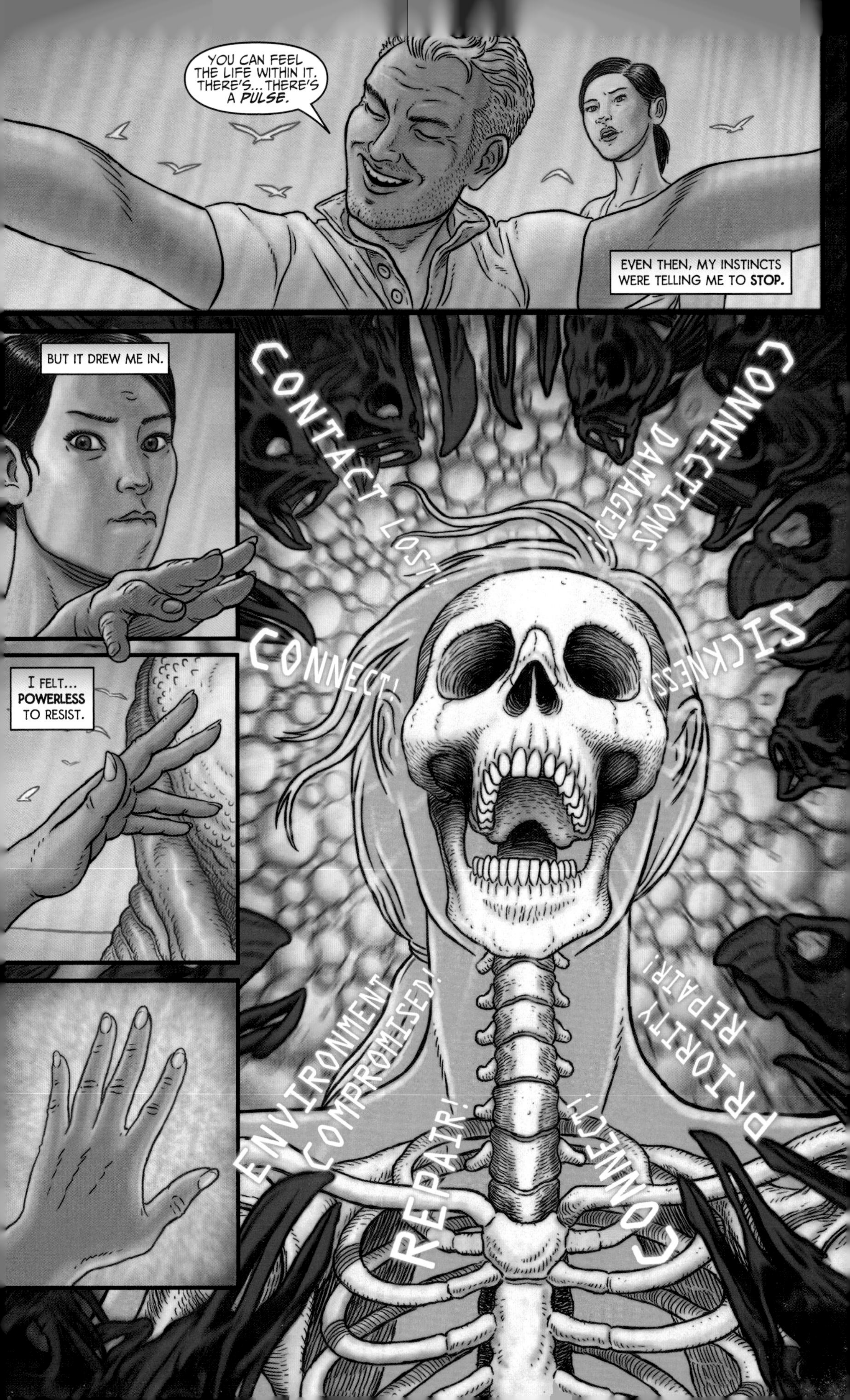
YOU CAN FEEL THE LIFE WITHIN IT. THERE'S... THERE'S A *PULSE.*
EVEN THEN, MY INSTINCTS WERE TELLING ME TO **STOP.**
BUT IT DREW ME IN.
I FELT... **POWERLESS** TO RESIST.
CONTACT LOST!
CONNECTIONS DAMAGED!
CONNECT!
SICKNESS!
ENVIRONMENT COMPROMISED!
PRIORITY REPAIR!
REPAIR!
CONNECT!

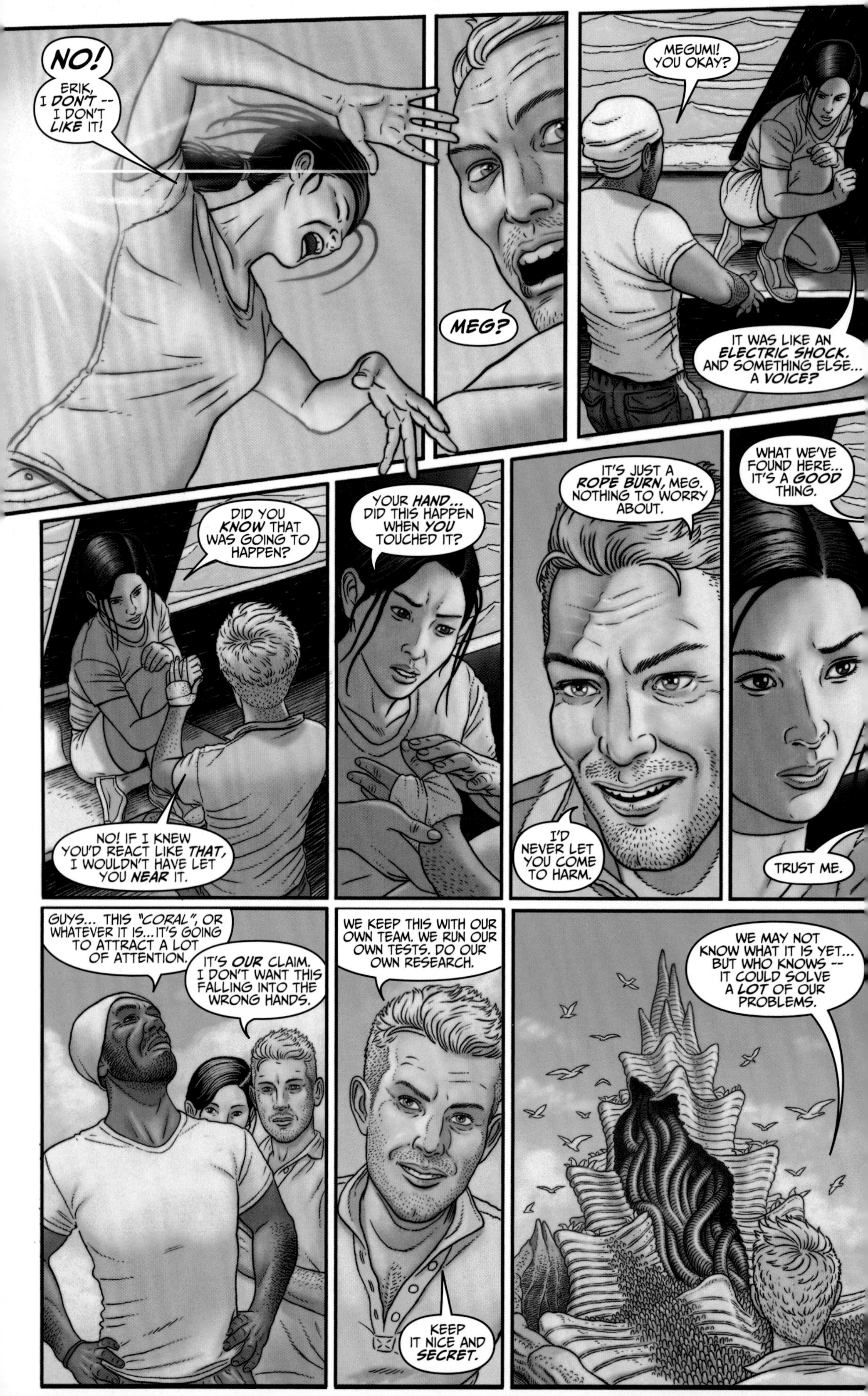
NO!
ERIK, I DON'T -- I DON'T LIKE IT!
MEG?
MEGUMI! YOU OKAY?
IT WAS LIKE AN ELECTRIC SHOCK. AND SOMETHING ELSE... A VOICE?
DID YOU KNOW THAT WAS GOING TO HAPPEN?
NO! IF I KNEW YOU'D REACT LIKE THAT, I WOULDN'T HAVE LET YOU NEAR IT.
YOUR HAND... DID THIS HAPPEN WHEN YOU TOUCHED IT?
IT'S JUST A ROPE BURN, MEG. NOTHING TO WORRY ABOUT.
I'D NEVER LET YOU COME TO HARM.
WHAT WE'VE FOUND HERE... IT'S A GOOD THING.
TRUST ME.
GUYS... THIS "CORAL", OR WHATEVER IT IS...IT'S GOING TO ATTRACT A LOT OF ATTENTION.
IT'S OUR CLAIM. I DON'T WANT THIS FALLING INTO THE WRONG HANDS.
WE KEEP THIS WITH OUR OWN TEAM. WE RUN OUR OWN TESTS. DO OUR OWN RESEARCH.
KEEP IT NICE AND SECRET.
WE MAY NOT KNOW WHAT IT IS YET... BUT WHO KNOWS -- IT COULD SOLVE A LOT OF OUR PROBLEMS.

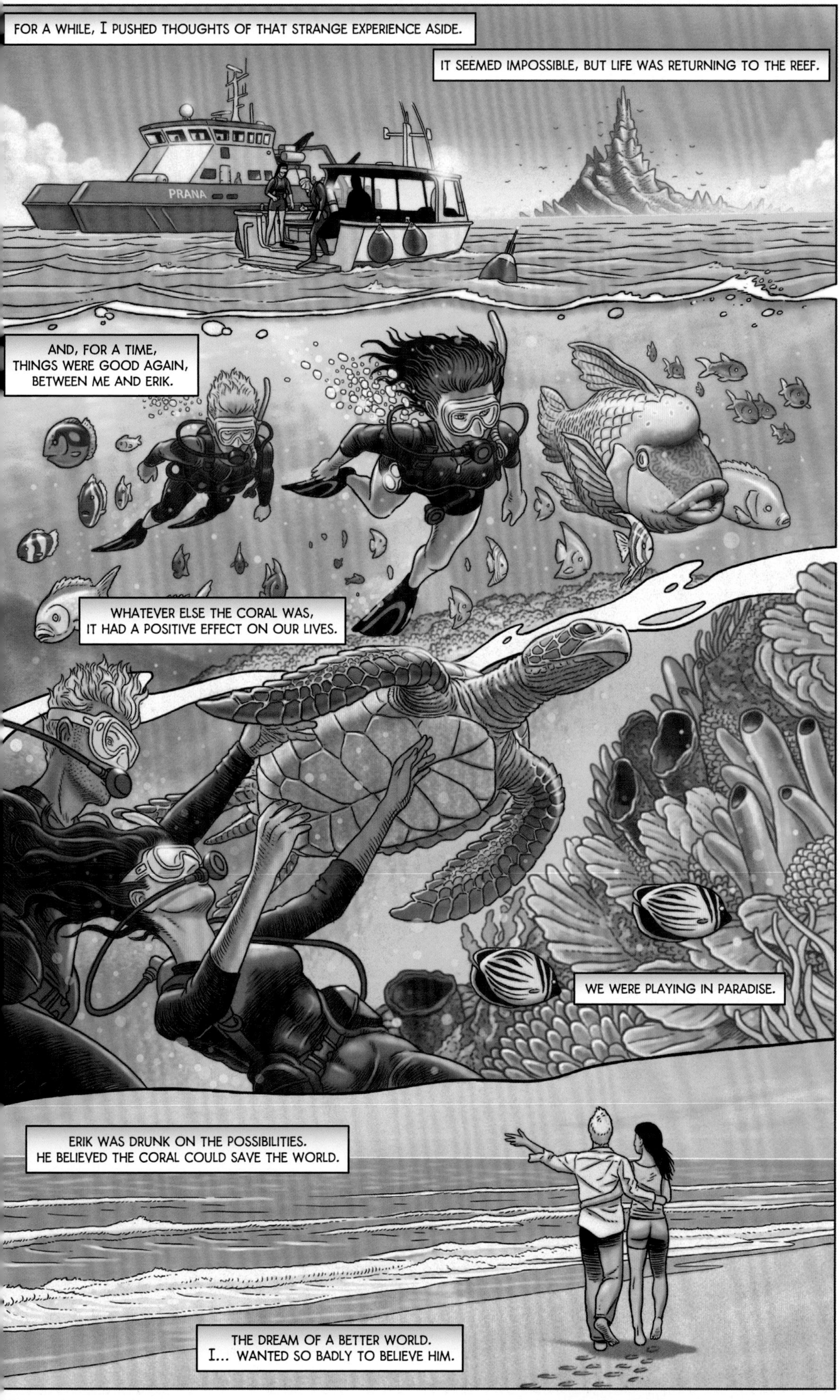

FOR A WHILE, I PUSHED THOUGHTS OF THAT STRANGE EXPERIENCE ASIDE.
IT SEEMED IMPOSSIBLE, BUT LIFE WAS RETURNING TO THE REEF.
PRANA
AND, FOR A TIME, THINGS WERE GOOD AGAIN, BETWEEN ME AND ERIK.
WHATEVER ELSE THE CORAL WAS, IT HAD A POSITIVE EFFECT ON OUR LIVES.
WE WERE PLAYING IN PARADISE.
ERIK WAS DRUNK ON THE POSSIBILITIES. HE BELIEVED THE CORAL COULD SAVE THE WORLD.
THE DREAM OF A BETTER WORLD. I... WANTED SO BADLY TO BELIEVE HIM.

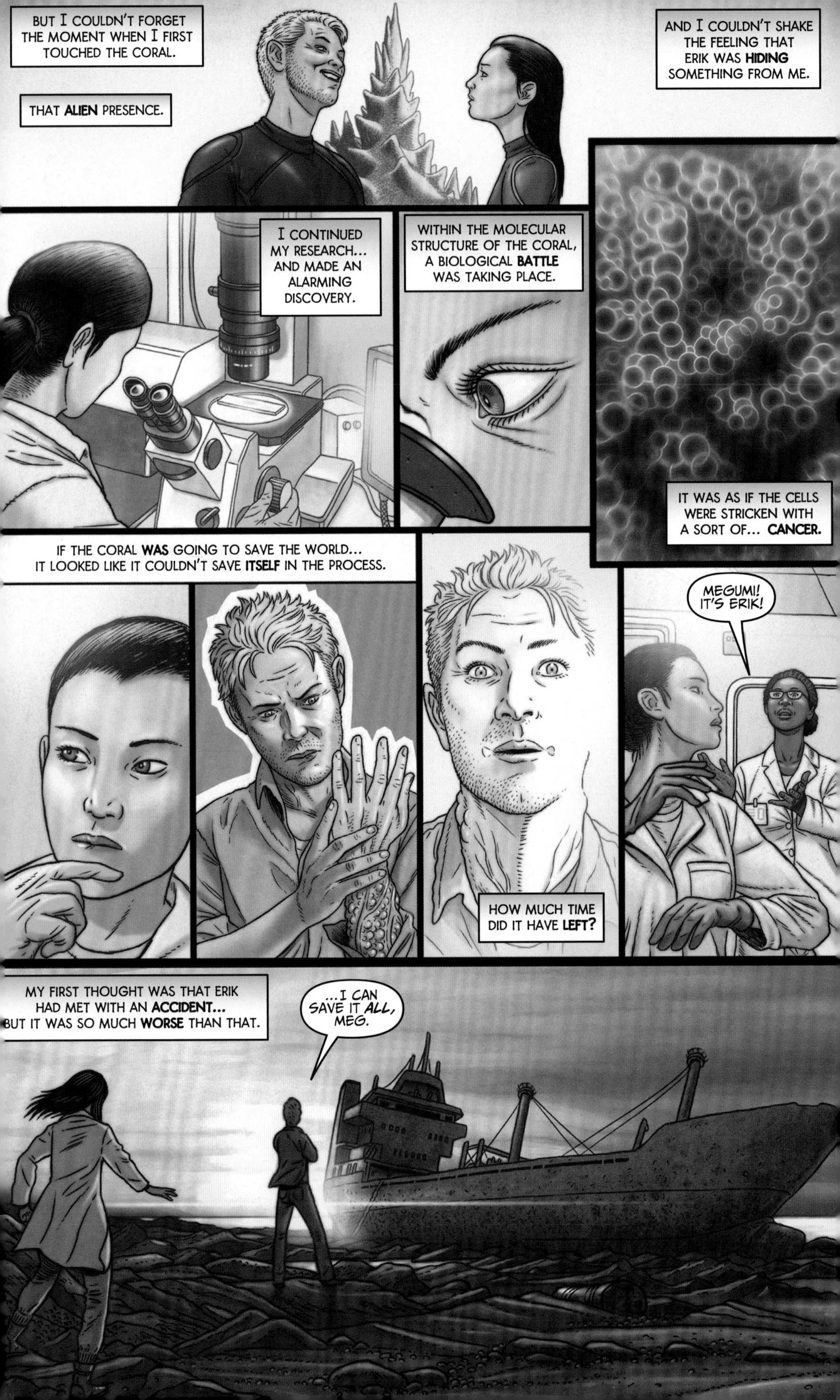
BUT I COULDN'T FORGET THE MOMENT WHEN I FIRST TOUCHED THE CORAL.
THAT ALIEN PRESENCE.
AND I COULDN'T SHAKE THE FEELING THAT ERIK WAS HIDING SOMETHING FROM ME.
I CONTINUED MY RESEARCH... AND MADE AN ALARMING DISCOVERY.
WITHIN THE MOLECULAR STRUCTURE OF THE CORAL, A BIOLOGICAL BATTLE WAS TAKING PLACE.
IT WAS AS IF THE CELLS WERE STRICKEN WITH A SORT OF... CANCER.
IF THE CORAL WAS GOING TO SAVE THE WORLD... IT LOOKED LIKE IT COULDN'T SAVE ITSELF IN THE PROCESS.
HOW MUCH TIME DID IT HAVE LEFT?
MEGUMI! IT'S ERIK!
MY FIRST THOUGHT WAS THAT ERIK HAD MET WITH AN ACCIDENT... BUT IT WAS SO MUCH WORSE THAN THAT.
...I CAN SAVE IT ALL, MEG.

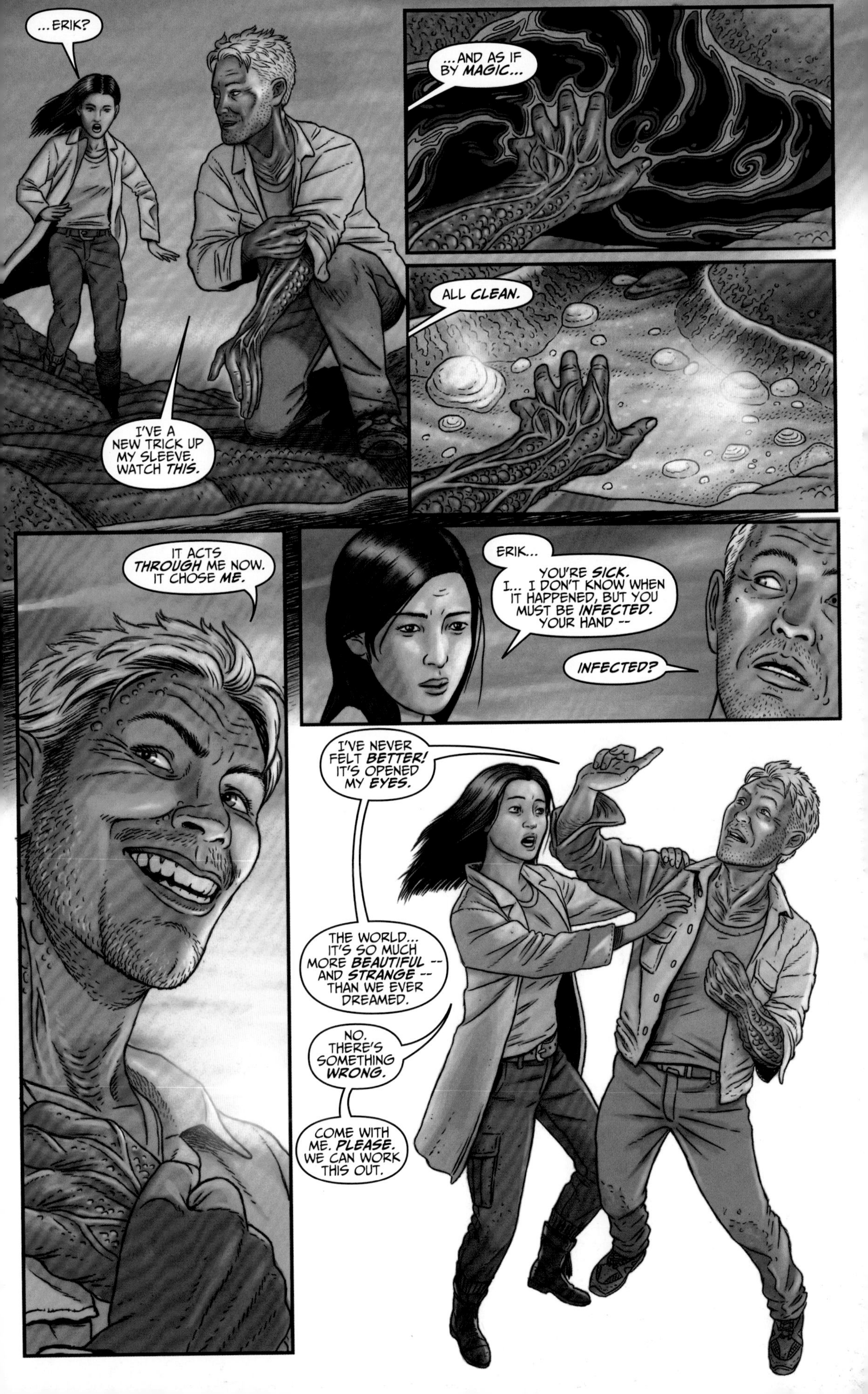
...ERIK?
I'VE A NEW TRICK UP MY SLEEVE. WATCH THIS.
...AND AS IF BY MAGIC...
ALL CLEAN.
IT ACTS THROUGH ME NOW. IT CHOSE ME.
ERIK...
YOU'RE SICK. I... I DON'T KNOW WHEN IT HAPPENED, BUT YOU MUST BE INFECTED. YOUR HAND --
INFECTED?
I'VE NEVER FELT BETTER! IT'S OPENED MY EYES.
THE WORLD... IT'S SO MUCH MORE BEAUTIFUL -- AND STRANGE -- THAN WE EVER DREAMED.
NO. THERE'S SOMETHING WRONG.
COME WITH ME. PLEASE. WE CAN WORK THIS OUT.

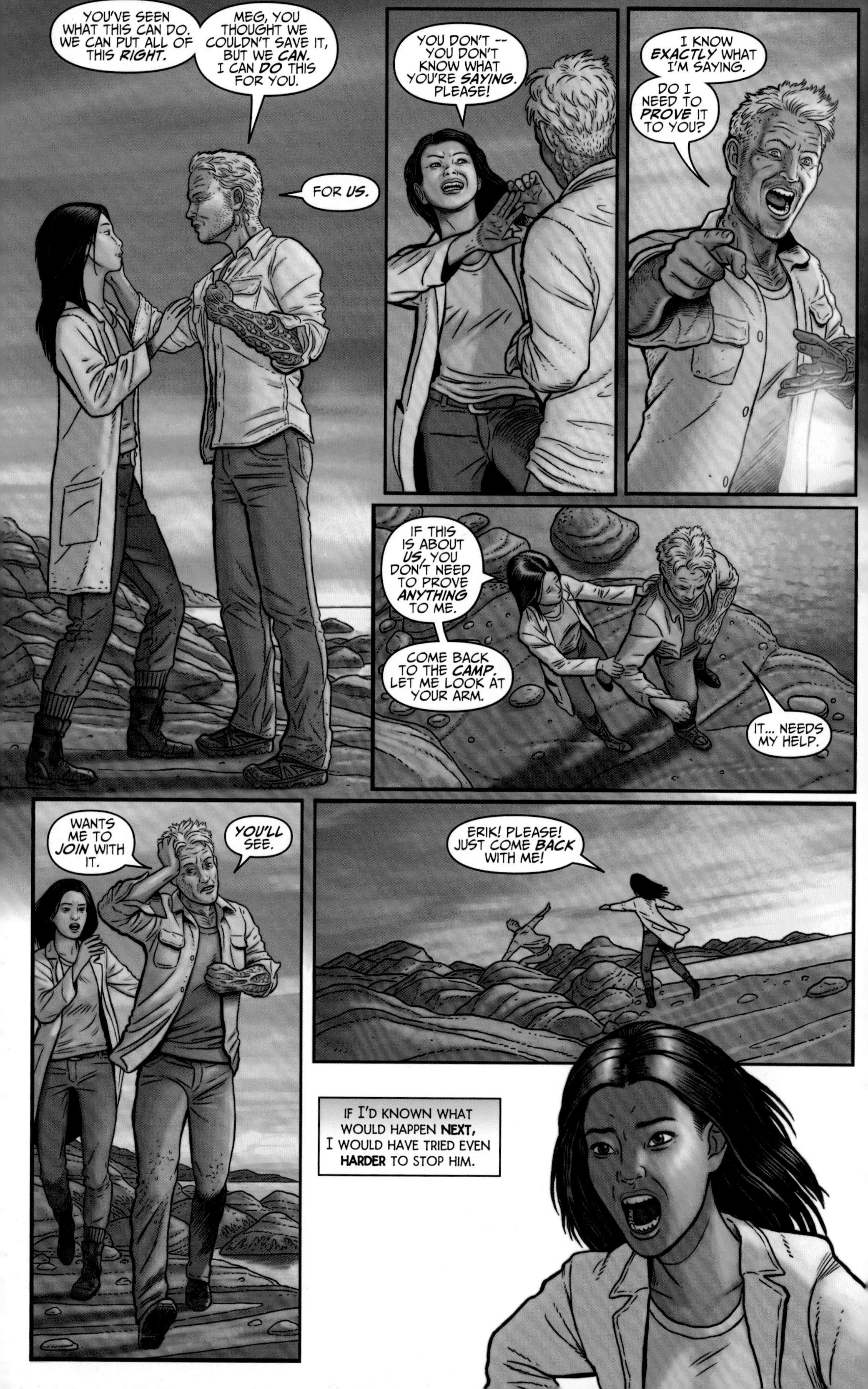
YOU'VE SEEN WHAT THIS CAN DO. WE CAN PUT ALL OF THIS RIGHT.
MEG, YOU THOUGHT WE COULDN'T SAVE IT, BUT WE CAN. I CAN DO THIS FOR YOU.
FOR US.
YOU DON'T -- YOU DON'T KNOW WHAT YOU'RE SAYING. PLEASE!
I KNOW EXACTLY WHAT I'M SAYING.
DO I NEED TO PROVE IT TO YOU?
IF THIS IS ABOUT US, YOU DON'T NEED TO PROVE ANYTHING TO ME.
COME BACK TO THE CAMP. LET ME LOOK AT YOUR ARM.
IT... NEEDS MY HELP.
WANTS ME TO JOIN WITH IT.
YOU'LL SEE.
ERIK! PLEASE! JUST COME BACK WITH ME!
IF I'D KNOWN WHAT WOULD HAPPEN NEXT, I WOULD HAVE TRIED EVEN HARDER TO STOP HIM.

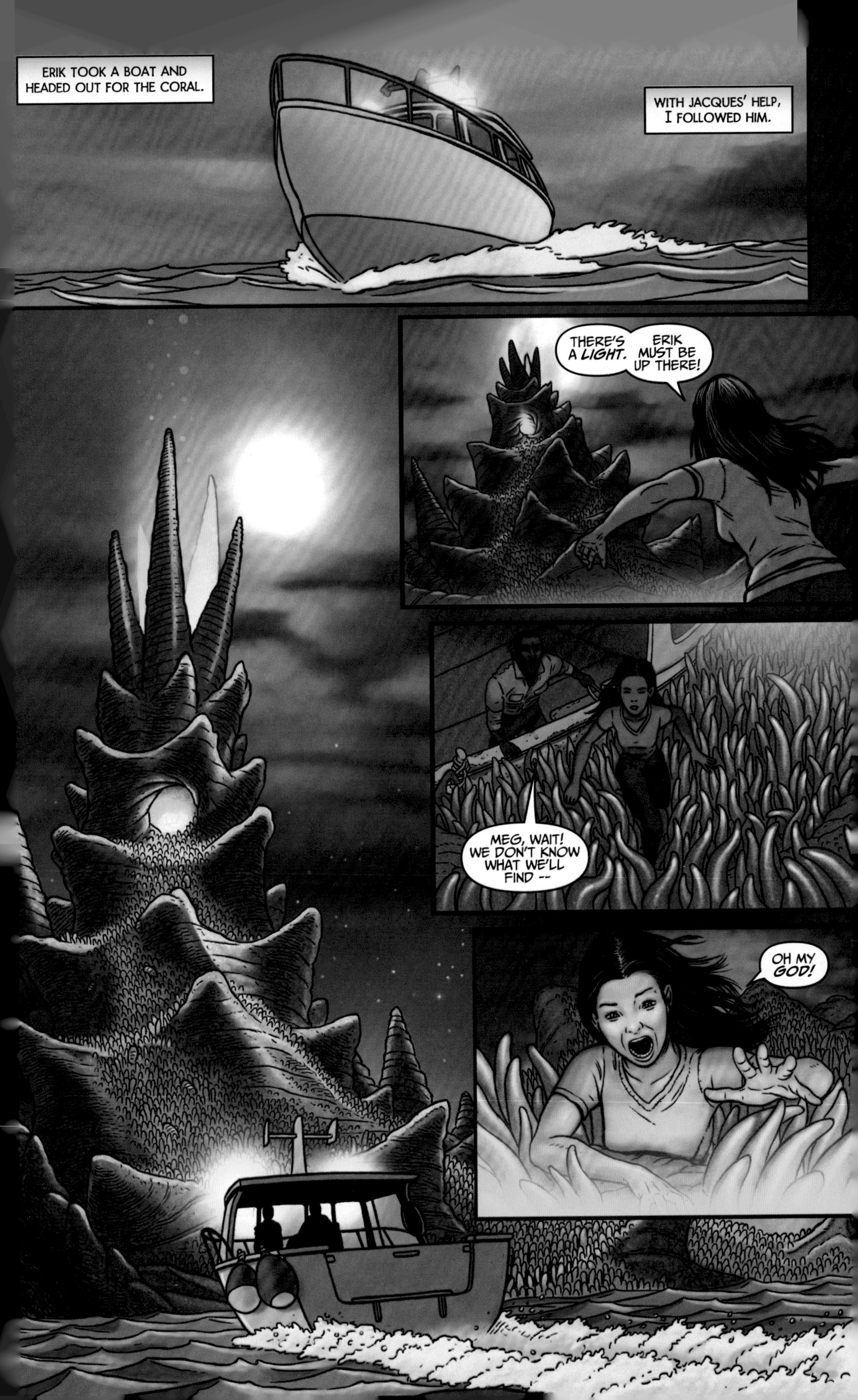
ERIK TOOK A BOAT AND HEADED OUT FOR THE CORAL.
WITH JACQUES' HELP, I FOLLOWED HIM.
THERE'S A *LIGHT.*
ERIK MUST BE UP THERE!
MEG, WAIT! WE DON'T KNOW WHAT WE'LL FIND --
OH MY *GOD!*

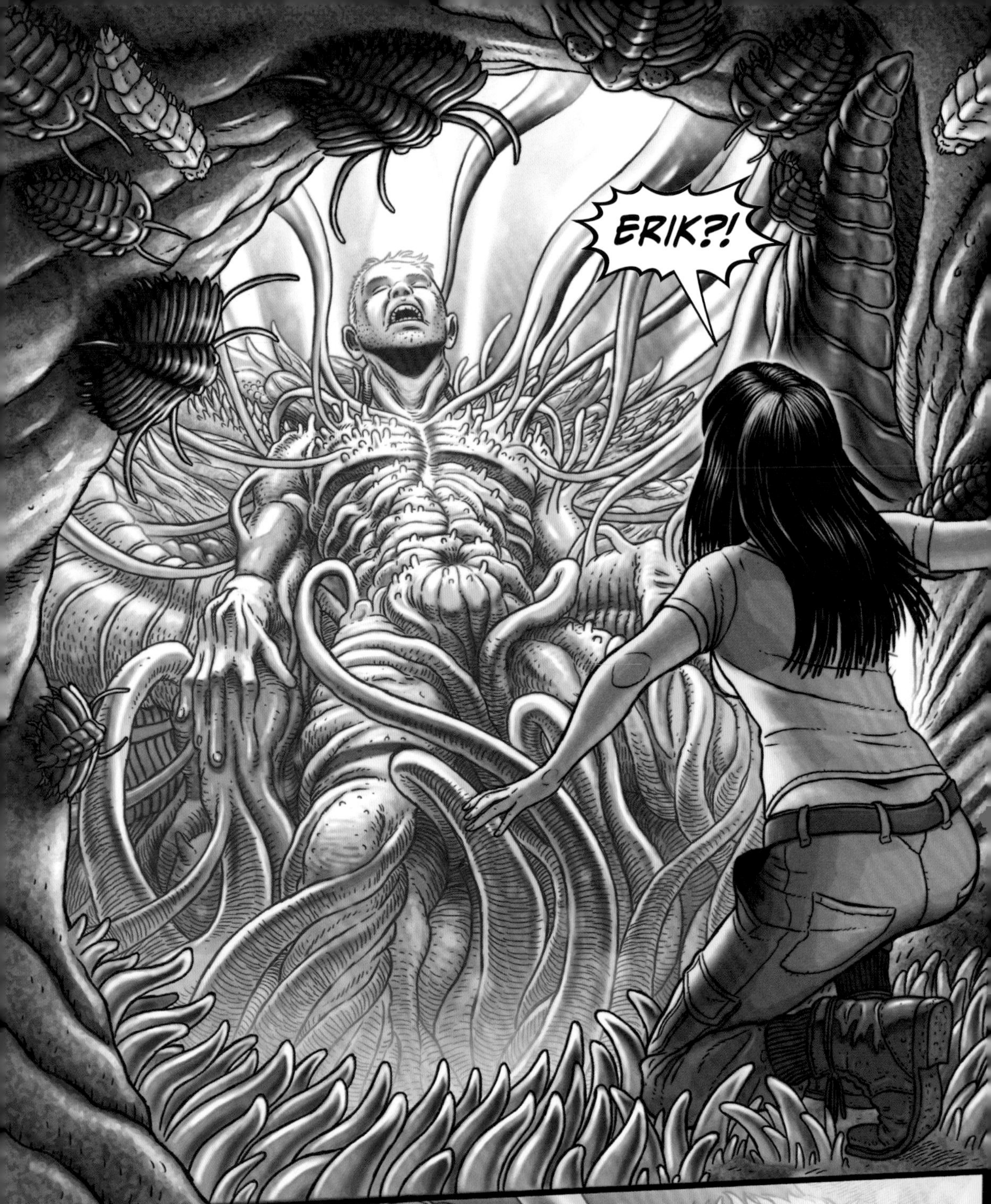
ERIK?!

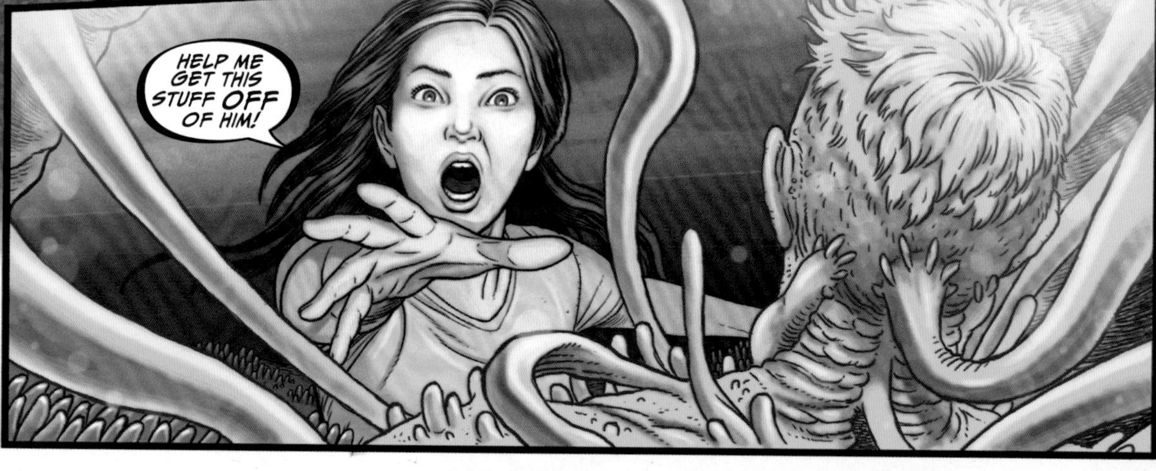
HELP ME GET THIS STUFF OFF OF HIM!

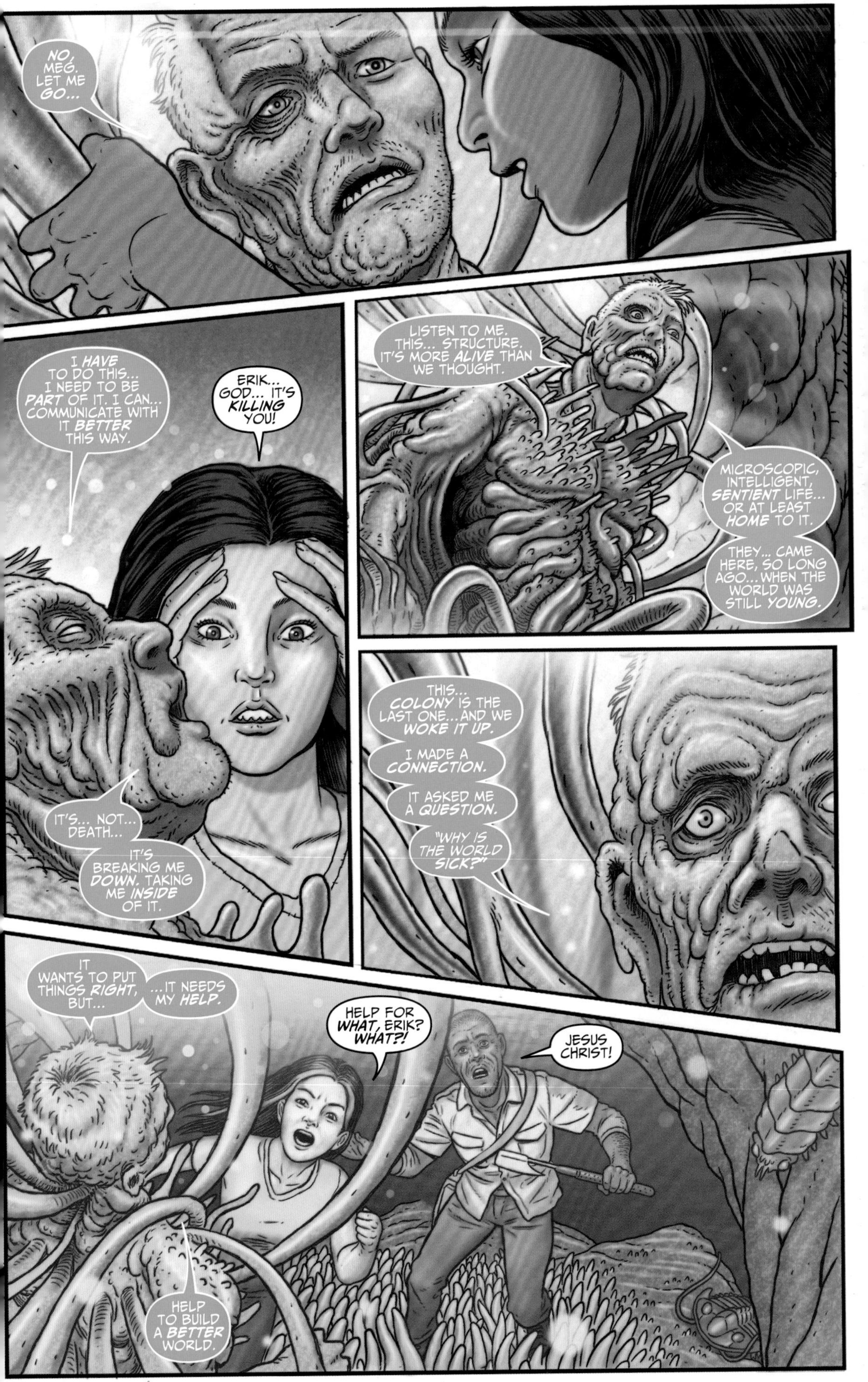
NO, MEG. LET ME GO...
I HAVE TO DO THIS... I NEED TO BE PART OF IT. I CAN... COMMUNICATE WITH IT BETTER THIS WAY.
ERIK... GOD... IT'S KILLING YOU!
IT'S... NOT... DEATH...
IT'S BREAKING ME DOWN. TAKING ME INSIDE OF IT.
LISTEN TO ME. THIS... STRUCTURE. IT'S MORE ALIVE THAN WE THOUGHT.
MICROSCOPIC, INTELLIGENT, SENTIENT LIFE... OR AT LEAST HOME TO IT.
THEY... CAME HERE, SO LONG AGO... WHEN THE WORLD WAS STILL YOUNG.
THIS... COLONY IS THE LAST ONE... AND WE WOKE IT UP.
I MADE A CONNECTION.
IT ASKED ME A QUESTION.
"WHY IS THE WORLD SICK?"
IT WANTS TO PUT THINGS RIGHT, BUT...
...IT NEEDS MY HELP.
HELP FOR WHAT, ERIK? WHAT?!
JESUS CHRIST!
HELP TO BUILD A BETTER WORLD.

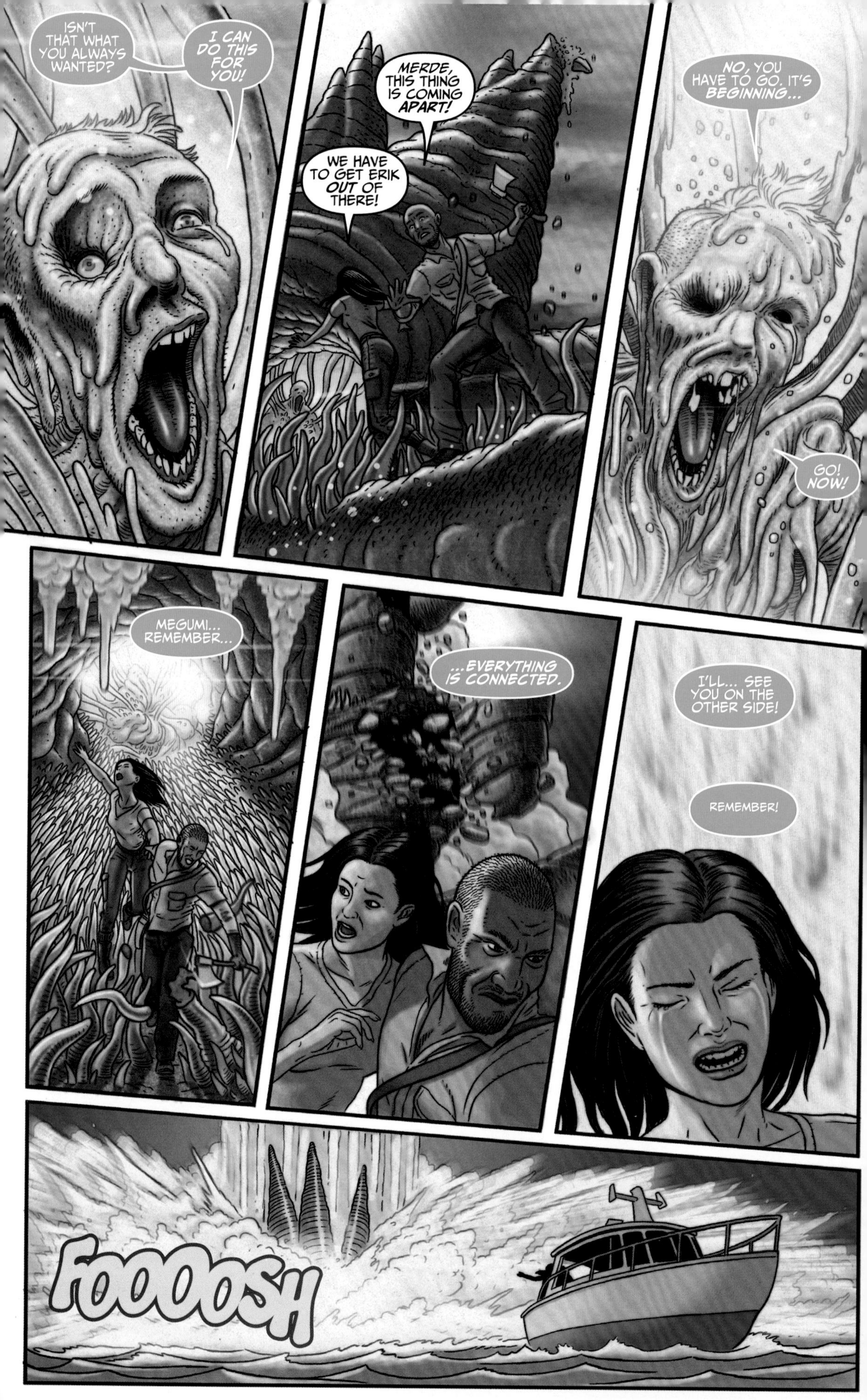
ISN'T THAT WHAT YOU ALWAYS WANTED?
I CAN DO THIS FOR YOU!
MERDE, THIS THING IS COMING APART!
WE HAVE TO GET ERIK OUT OF THERE!
NO, YOU HAVE TO GO. IT'S BEGINNING...
GO! NOW!
MEGUMI... REMEMBER...
...EVERYTHING IS CONNECTED.
I'LL... SEE YOU ON THE OTHER SIDE!
REMEMBER!
FOOOOSH

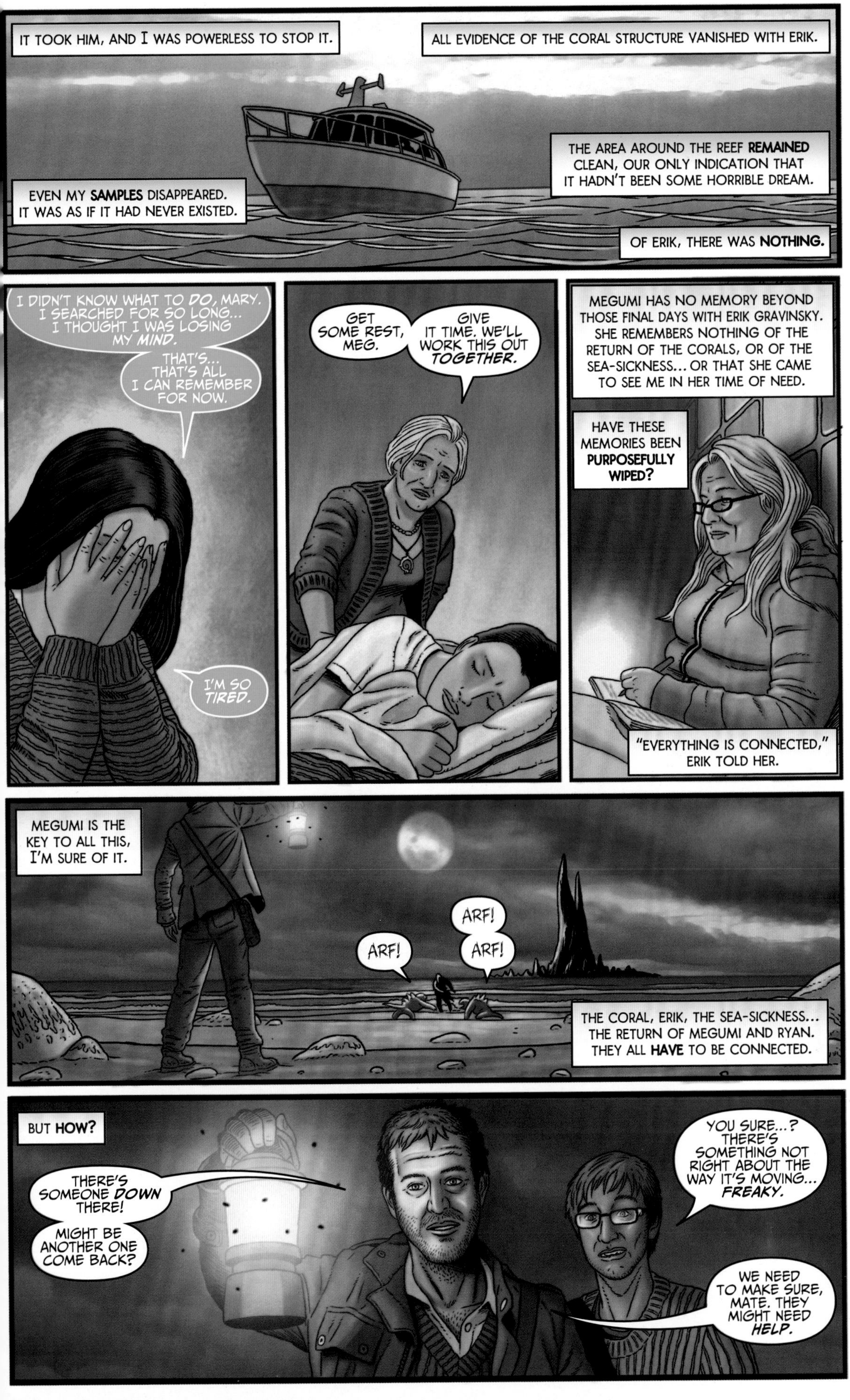
IT TOOK HIM, AND I WAS POWERLESS TO STOP IT.
ALL EVIDENCE OF THE CORAL STRUCTURE VANISHED WITH ERIK.
EVEN MY SAMPLES DISAPPEARED. IT WAS AS IF IT HAD NEVER EXISTED.
THE AREA AROUND THE REEF REMAINED CLEAN, OUR ONLY INDICATION THAT IT HADN'T BEEN SOME HORRIBLE DREAM.
OF ERIK, THERE WAS NOTHING.
I DIDN'T KNOW WHAT TO DO, MARY. I SEARCHED FOR SO LONG... I THOUGHT I WAS LOSING MY MIND.
THAT'S... THAT'S ALL I CAN REMEMBER FOR NOW.
I'M SO TIRED.
GET SOME REST, MEG.
GIVE IT TIME. WE'LL WORK THIS OUT TOGETHER.
MEGUMI HAS NO MEMORY BEYOND THOSE FINAL DAYS WITH ERIK GRAVINSKY. SHE REMEMBERS NOTHING OF THE RETURN OF THE CORALS, OR OF THE SEA-SICKNESS... OR THAT SHE CAME TO SEE ME IN HER TIME OF NEED.
HAVE THESE MEMORIES BEEN PURPOSEFULLY WIPED?
"EVERYTHING IS CONNECTED," ERIK TOLD HER.
MEGUMI IS THE KEY TO ALL THIS, I'M SURE OF IT.
ARF!
ARF!
ARF!
THE CORAL, ERIK, THE SEA-SICKNESS... THE RETURN OF MEGUMI AND RYAN. THEY ALL HAVE TO BE CONNECTED.
BUT HOW?
THERE'S SOMEONE DOWN THERE!
MIGHT BE ANOTHER ONE COME BACK?
YOU SURE...? THERE'S SOMETHING NOT RIGHT ABOUT THE WAY IT'S MOVING... FREAKY.
WE NEED TO MAKE SURE, MATE. THEY MIGHT NEED HELP.

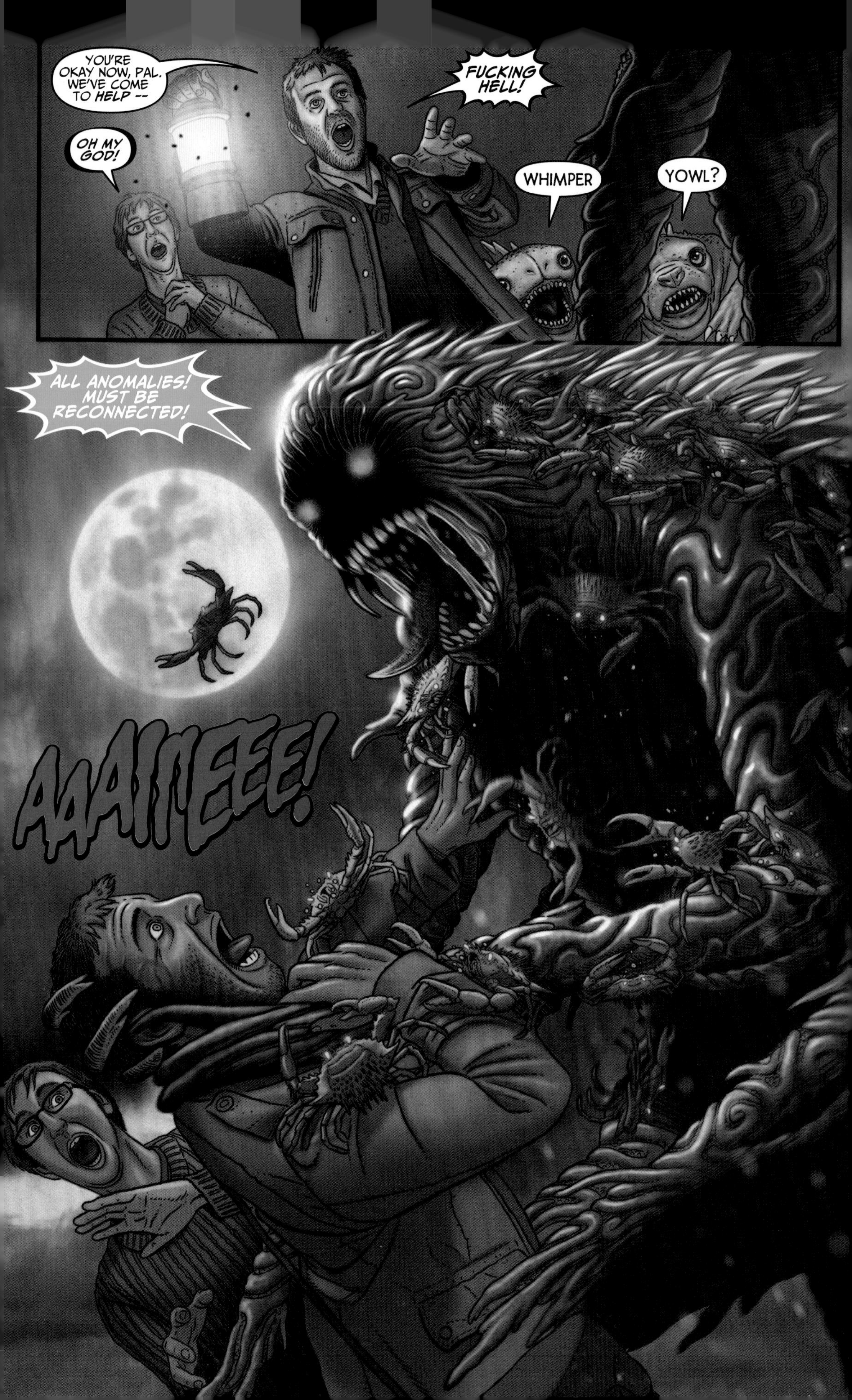
YOU'RE OKAY NOW, PAL. WE'VE COME TO HELP --
OH MY GOD!
FUCKING HELL!
WHIMPER
YOWL?
ALL ANOMALIES! MUST BE RECONNECTED!
AAAIIEEE!

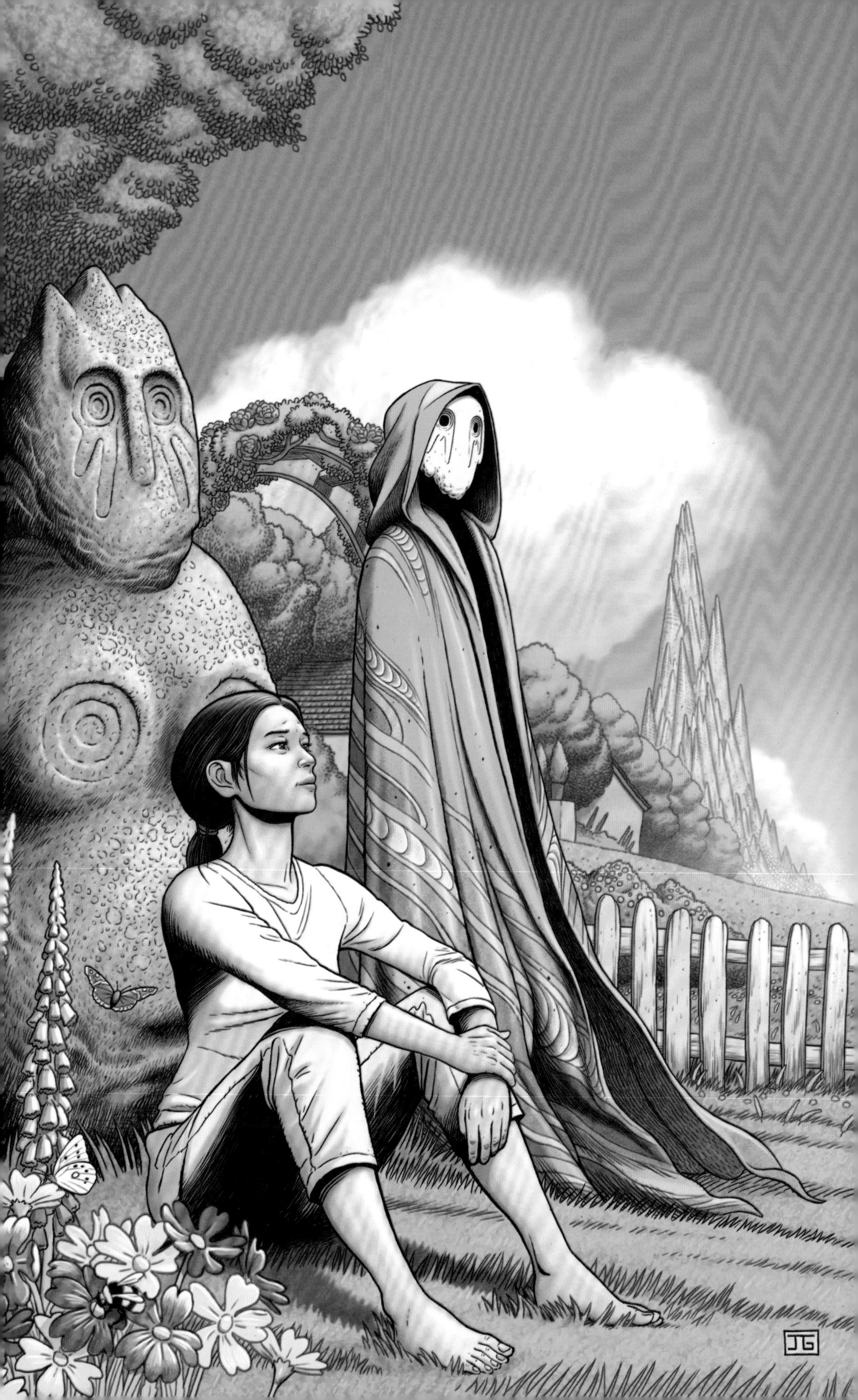
JG

CHAPTER TWO
FAMILY

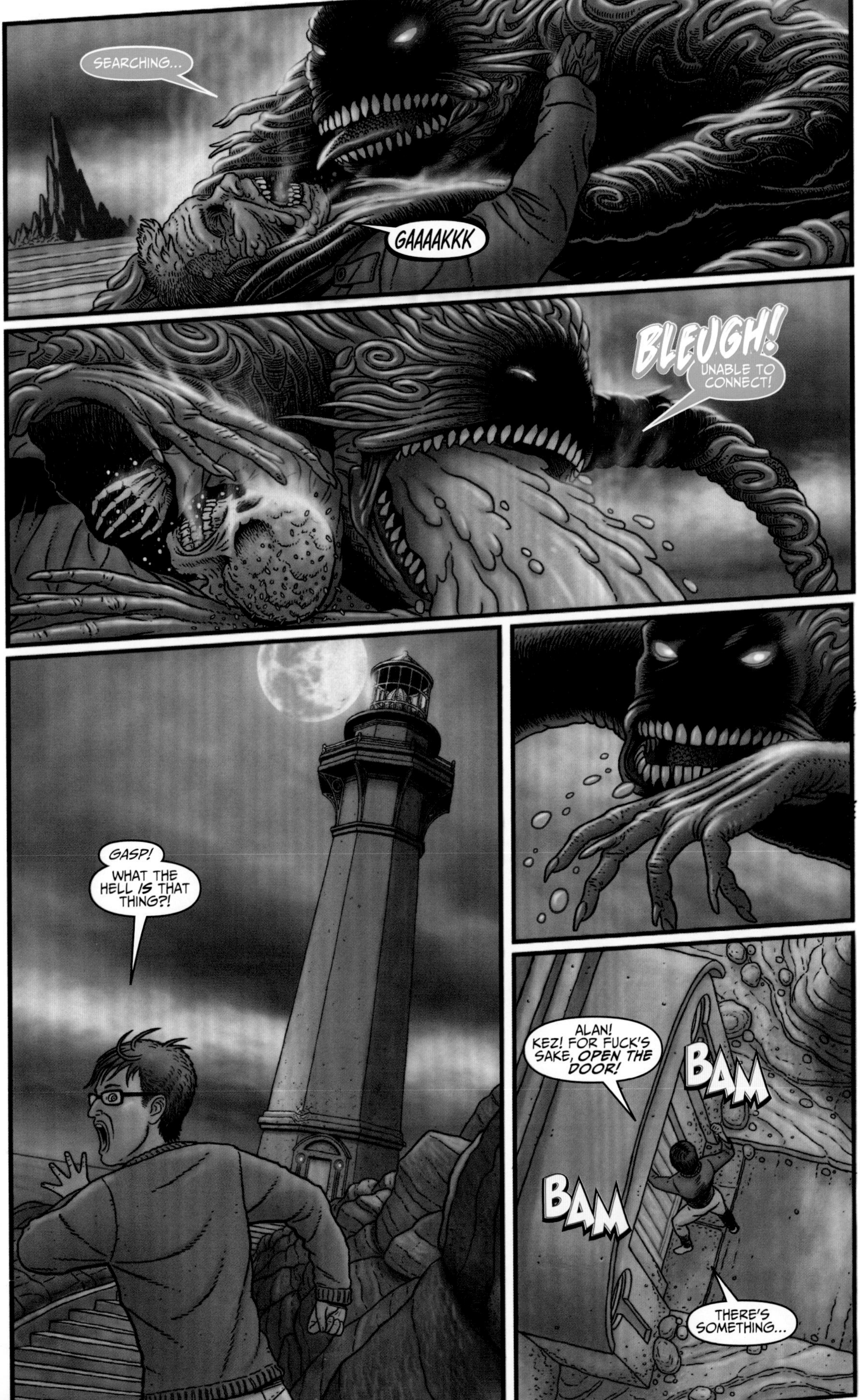
SEARCHING...
GAAAAKKK
BLEUGH!
UNABLE TO CONNECT!
GASP! WHAT THE HELL IS THAT THING?!
ALAN! KEZ! FOR FUCK'S SAKE, OPEN THE DOOR!
BAM
BAM
THERE'S SOMETHING...

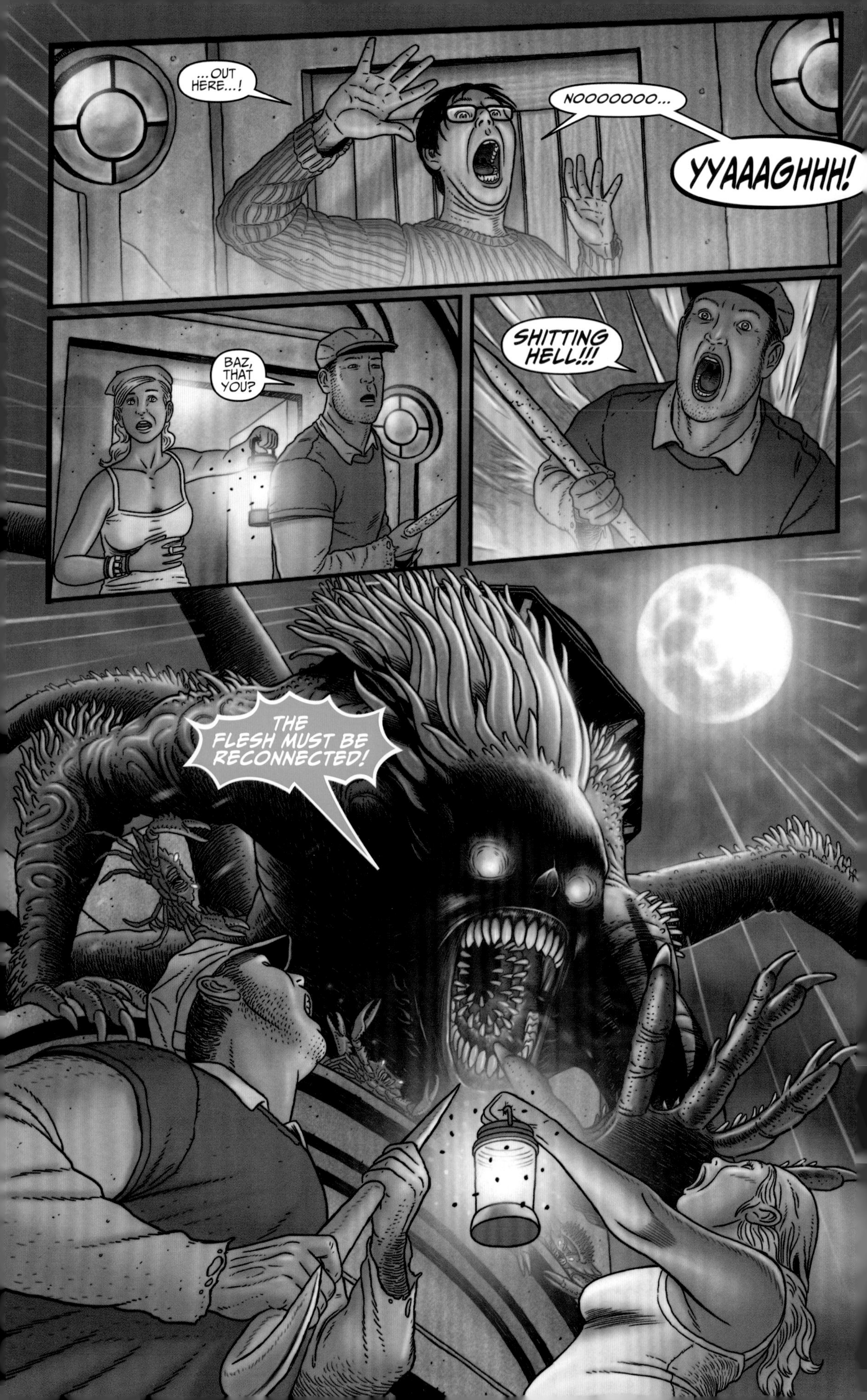
...OUT HERE...!
NOOOOOOO...
YYAAAGHHH!
BAZ, THAT YOU?
SHITTING HELL!!!
THE FLESH MUST BE RECONNECTED!

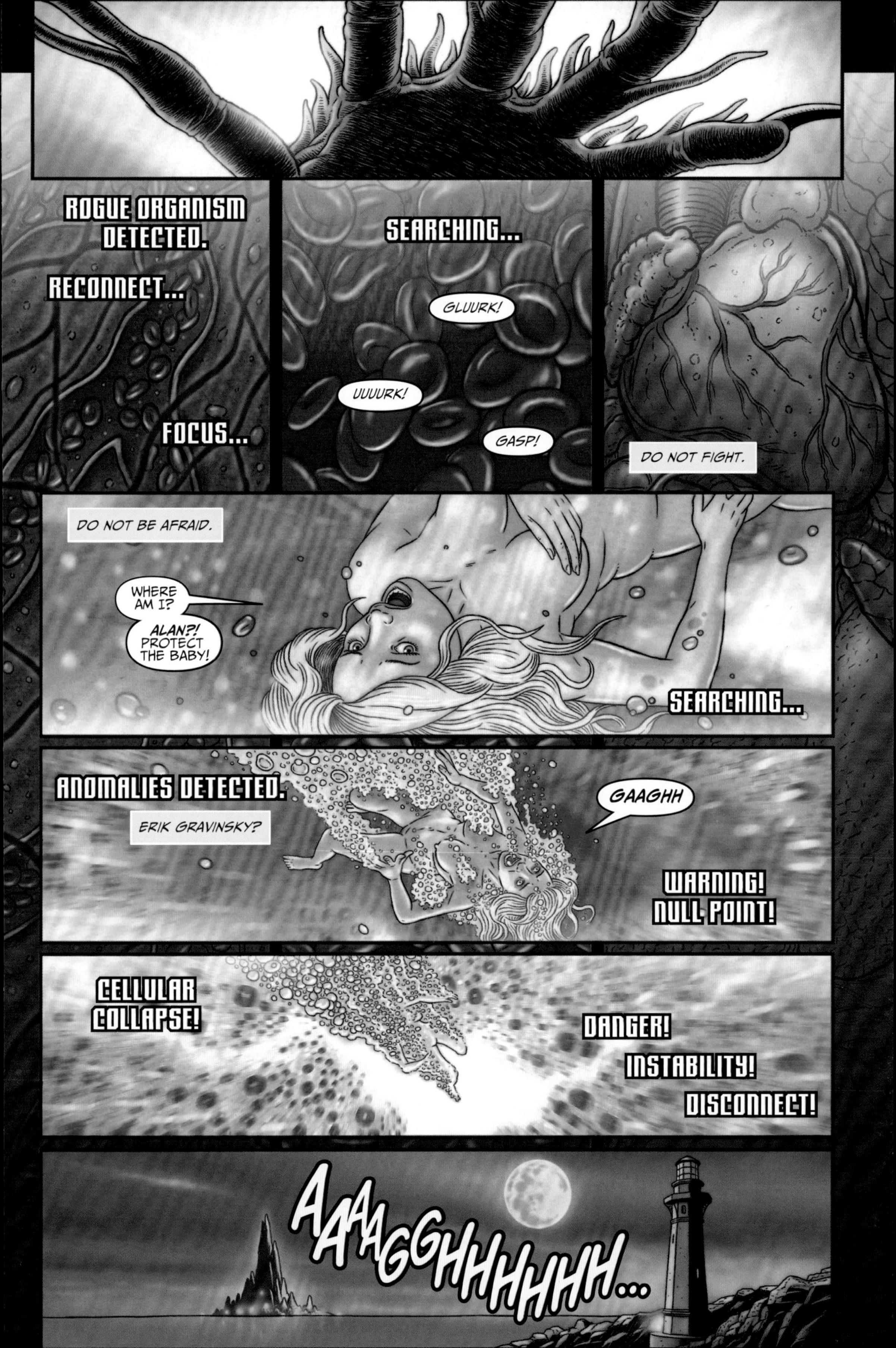

ROGUE ORGANISM DETECTED.
RECONNECT...
FOCUS...
SEARCHING...
GLUURK!
UUUURK!
GASP!
DO NOT FIGHT.
DO NOT BE AFRAID.
WHERE AM I?
ALAN?! PROTECT THE BABY!
SEARCHING...
ANOMALIES DETECTED.
ERIK GRAVINSKY?
GAAGHH
WARNING! NULL POINT!
CELLULAR COLLAPSE!
DANGER!
INSTABILITY!
DISCONNECT!
AAAAGGHHHHHHH...

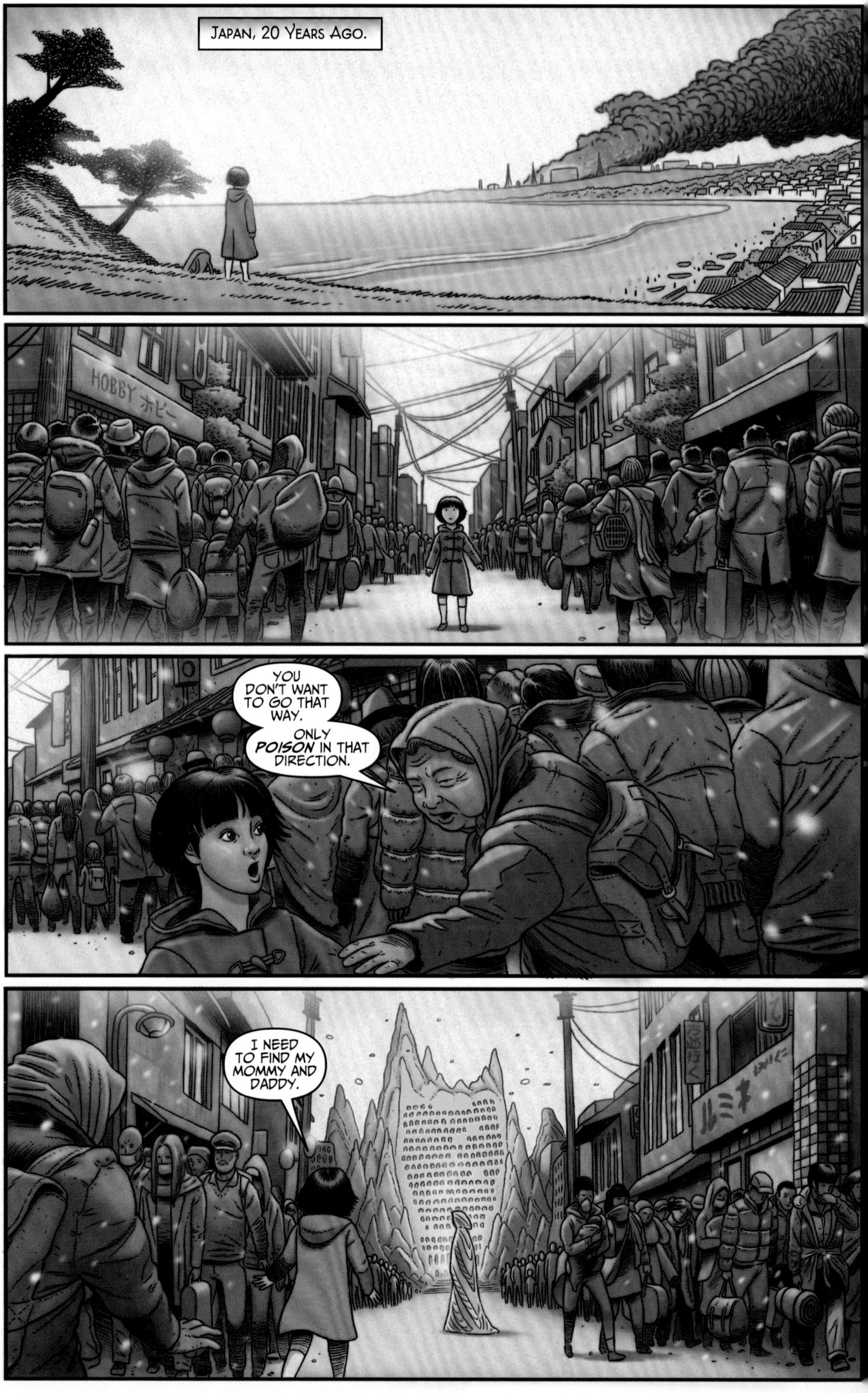
JAPAN, 20 YEARS AGO.
HOBBY ホビー
YOU DON'T WANT TO GO THAT WAY.
ONLY POISON IN THAT DIRECTION.
I NEED TO FIND MY MOMMY AND DADDY.
ルミネ

WE CANNOT POSSIBLY HELP THEM ALL.

MUM? DAD?

THE EVACUATION SHOULD HAVE HAPPENED SOONER.

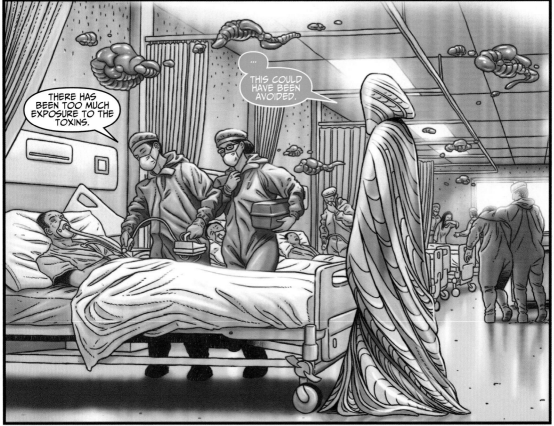

THERE HAS BEEN TOO MUCH EXPOSURE TO THE TOXINS.

... THIS COULD HAVE BEEN AVOIDED.

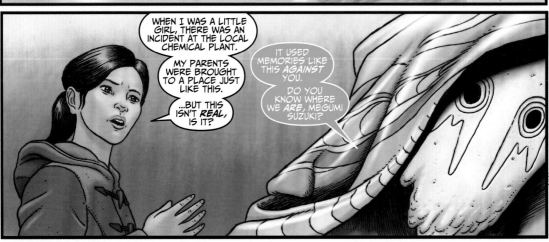

WHEN I WAS A LITTLE GIRL, THERE WAS AN INCIDENT AT THE LOCAL CHEMICAL PLANT.

MY PARENTS WERE BROUGHT TO A PLACE JUST LIKE THIS.

...BUT THIS ISN'T *REAL*, IS IT?

IT USED MEMORIES LIKE THIS *AGAINST* YOU.

DO YOU KNOW WHERE WE *ARE*, MEGUMI SUZUKI?

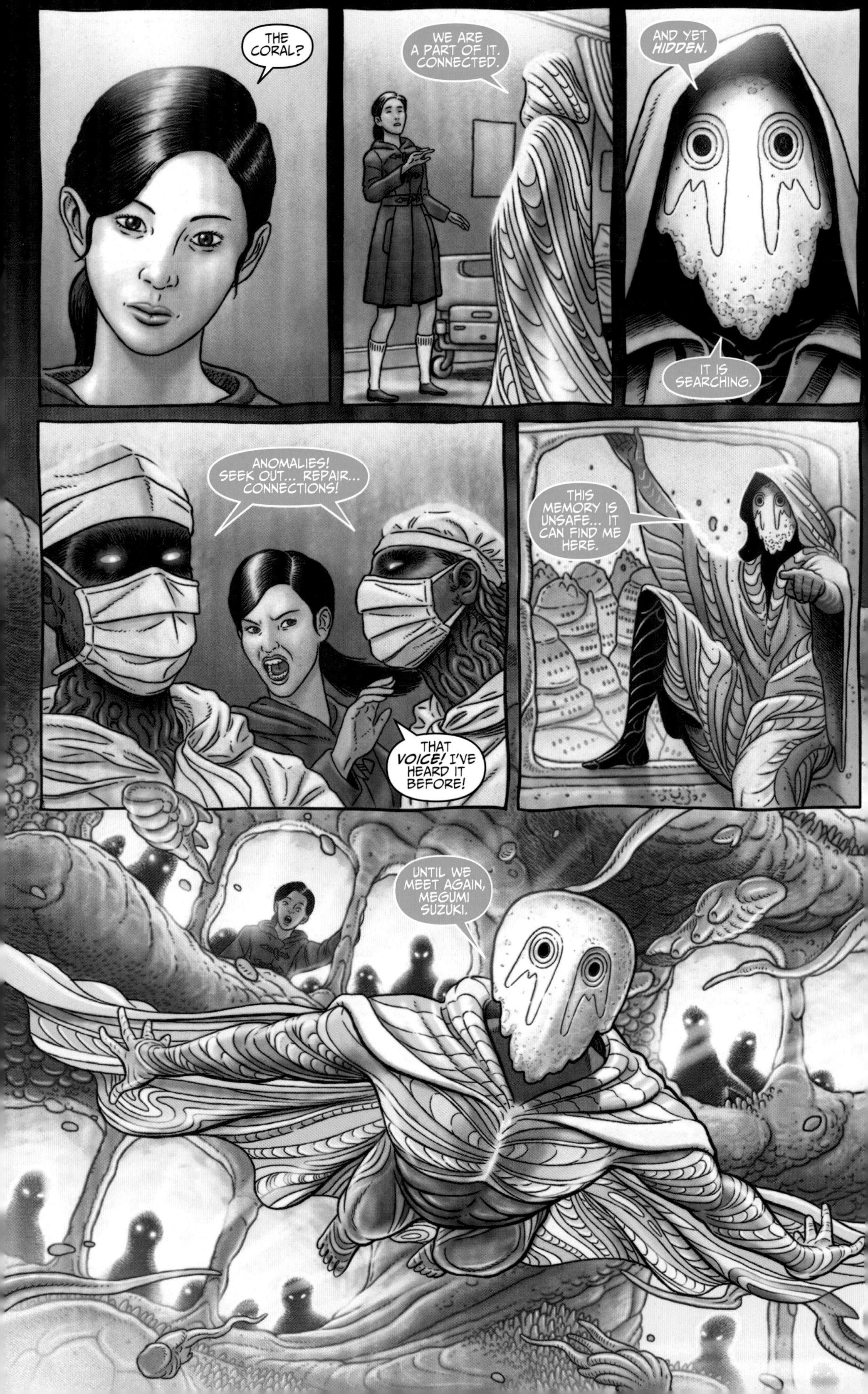
THE CORAL?
WE ARE A PART OF IT. CONNECTED.
AND YET *HIDDEN.*
IT IS SEARCHING.
ANOMALIES! SEEK OUT... REPAIR... CONNECTIONS!
THAT *VOICE!* I'VE HEARD IT BEFORE!
THIS MEMORY IS UNSAFE... IT CAN FIND ME HERE.
UNTIL WE MEET AGAIN, MEGUMI SUZUKI.

"AWAKE!"

I REALLY THOUGHT YOU OUGHT TO SEE THIS, MEG.

SEE?

YES.

TO CREATE A WHOLE NEW ECO-SYSTEM... ON SUCH A SCALE...

IT MUST TAKE AN *INCREDIBLE* AMOUNT OF ENERGY.

IT COULD BE VENTING PRESSURE?

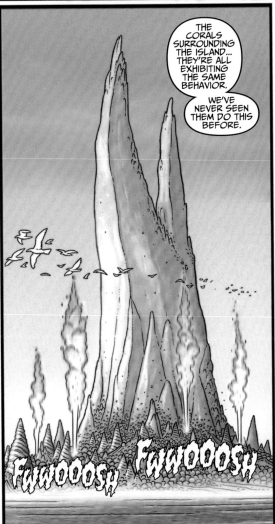

THE CORALS SURROUNDING THE ISLAND... THEY'RE ALL EXHIBITING THE SAME BEHAVIOR.

WE'VE NEVER SEEN THEM DO THIS BEFORE.

FWWOOOSH FWWOOOSH

THINK ABOUT IT, MARY.

"INTELLIGENT LIFE..."

"...WANTS TO PUT THINGS RIGHT..."

"...EVERYTHING IS CONNECTED..."

ERIK'S WORDS?

YES. HE THOUGHT THAT IT COULD HELP US.

WHAT IF HE WAS WRONG?

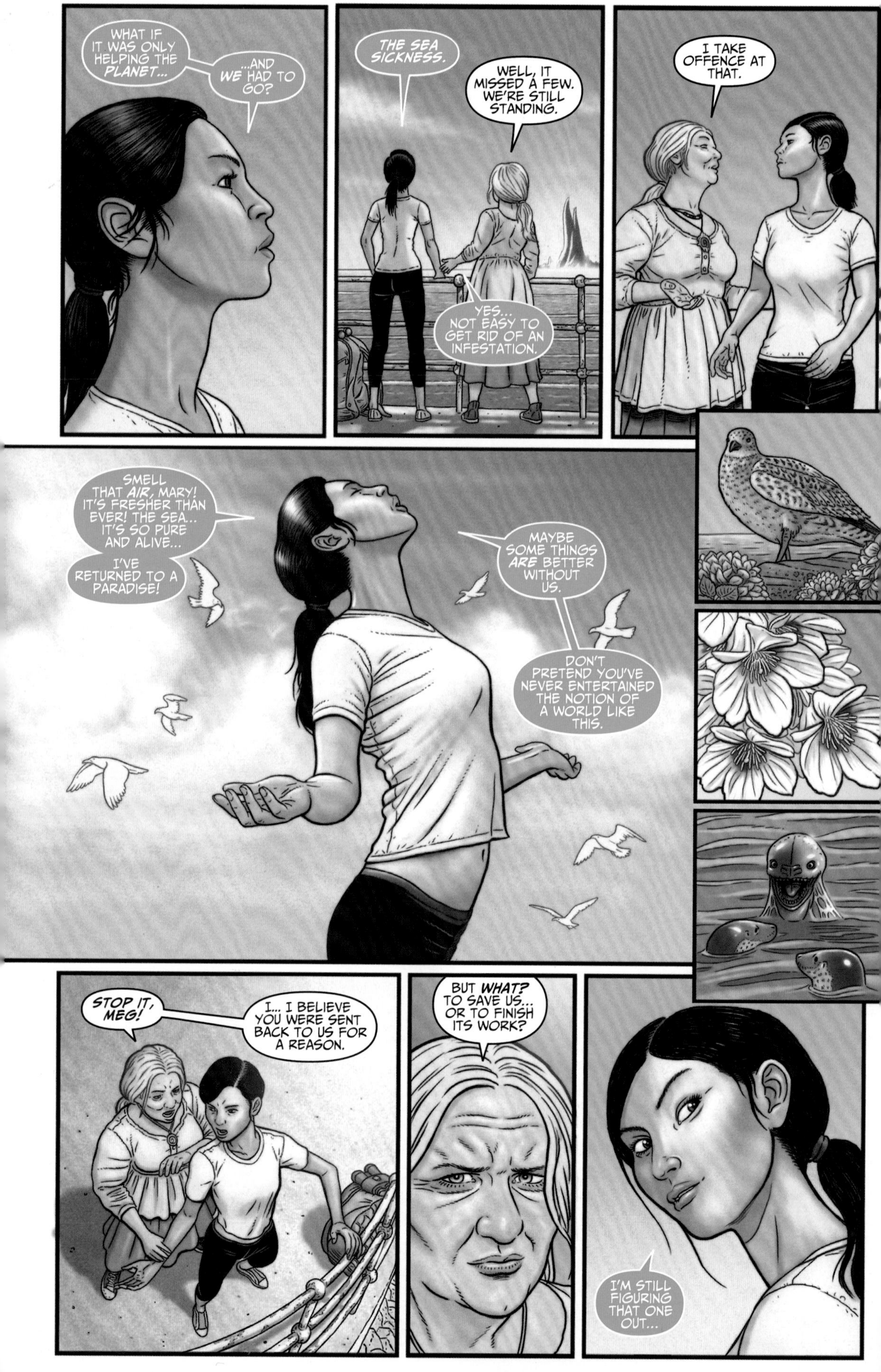
WHAT IF IT WAS ONLY HELPING THE PLANET...
...AND WE HAD TO GO?
THE SEA SICKNESS.
WELL, IT MISSED A FEW. WE'RE STILL STANDING.
YES... NOT EASY TO GET RID OF AN INFESTATION.
I TAKE OFFENCE AT THAT.
SMELL THAT AIR, MARY! IT'S FRESHER THAN EVER! THE SEA... IT'S SO PURE AND ALIVE...
I'VE RETURNED TO A PARADISE!
MAYBE SOME THINGS ARE BETTER WITHOUT US.
DON'T PRETEND YOU'VE NEVER ENTERTAINED THE NOTION OF A WORLD LIKE THIS.
STOP IT, MEG!
I... I BELIEVE YOU WERE SENT BACK TO US FOR A REASON.
BUT WHAT? TO SAVE US... OR TO FINISH ITS WORK?
I'M STILL FIGURING THAT ONE OUT...

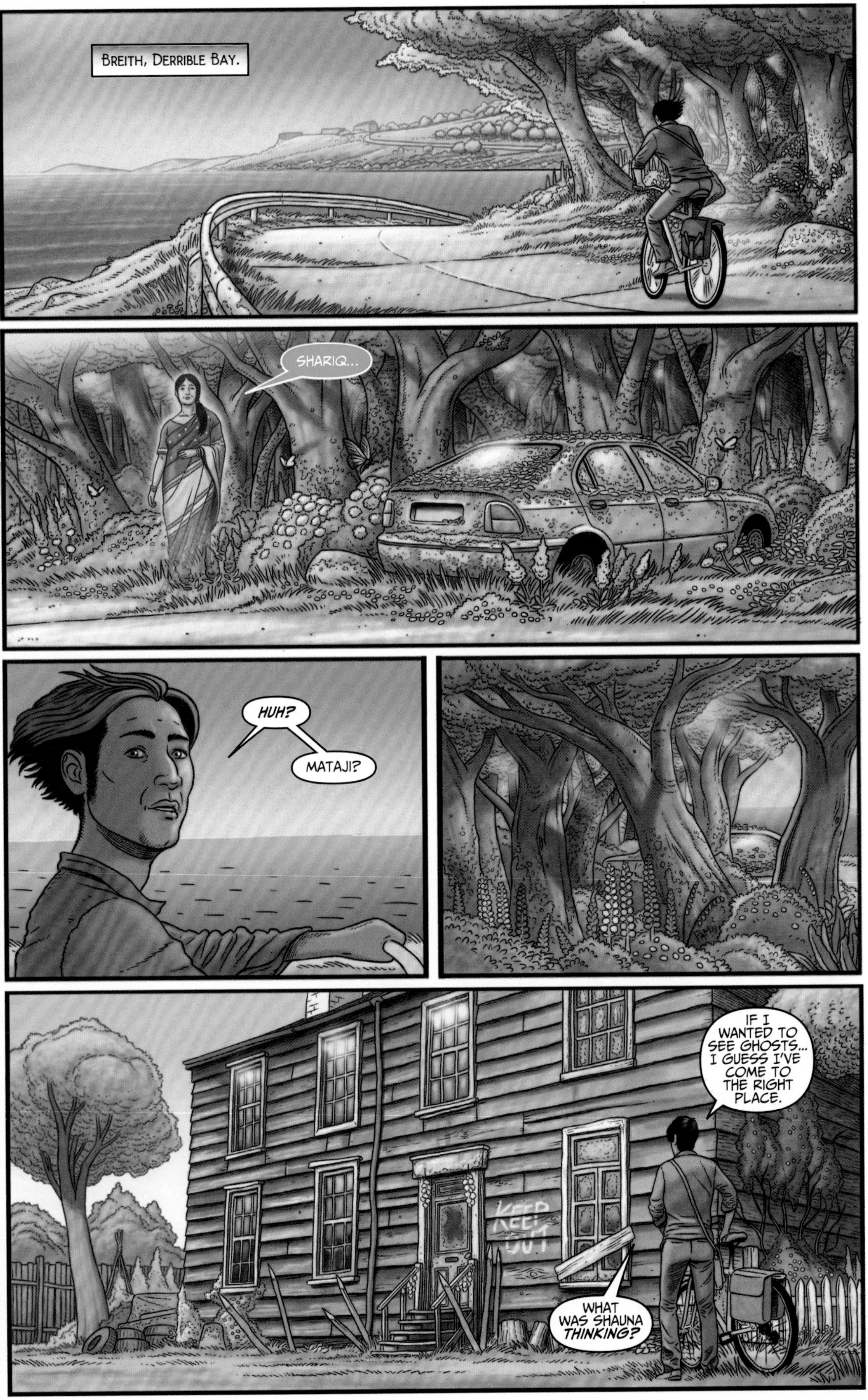
BREITH, DERRIBLE BAY.
SHARIQ...
HUH?
MATAJI?
IF I WANTED TO SEE GHOSTS... I GUESS I'VE COME TO THE RIGHT PLACE.
KEEP OUT
WHAT WAS SHAUNA *THINKING?*

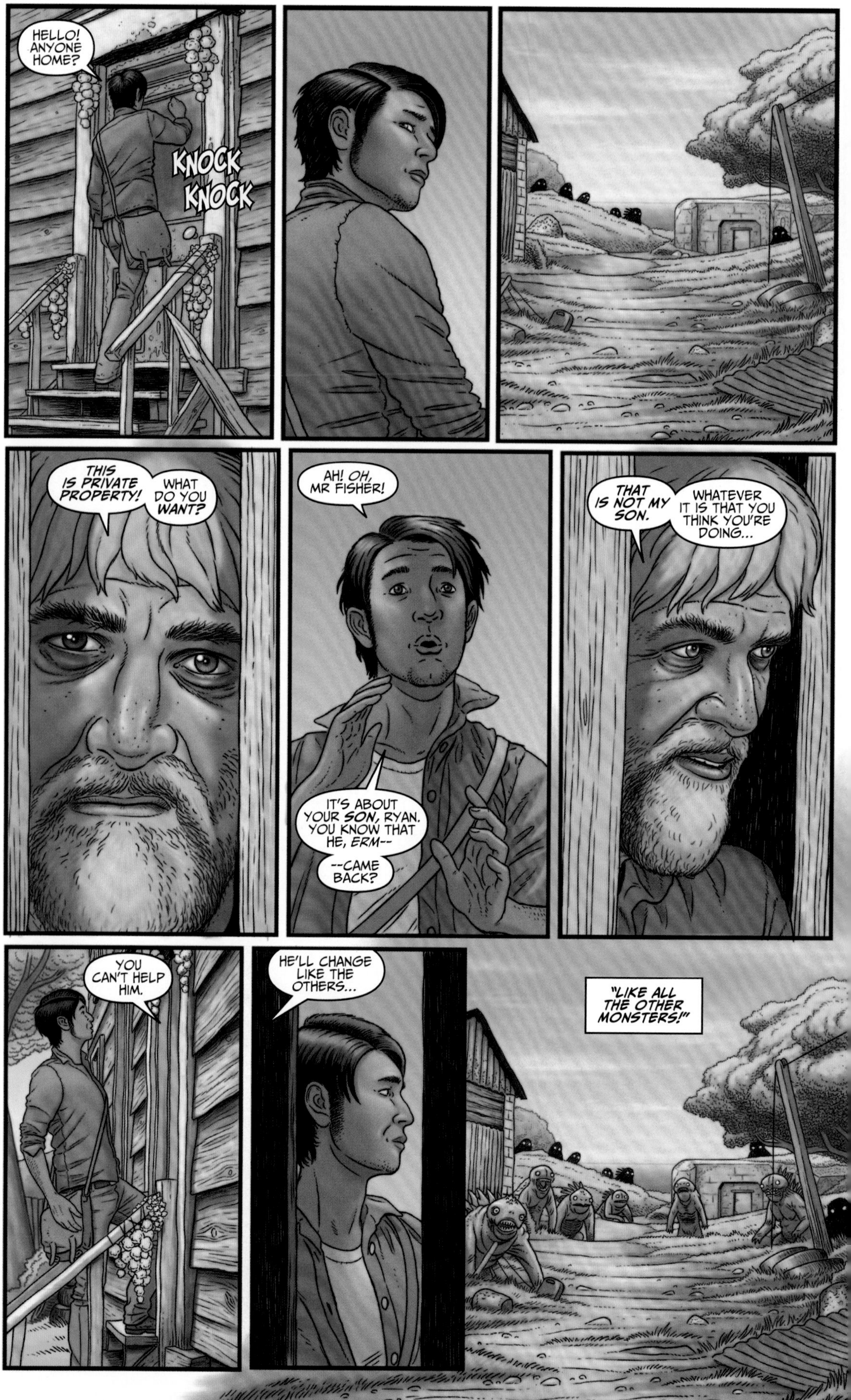
HELLO! ANYONE HOME?
KNOCK KNOCK
THIS IS PRIVATE PROPERTY!
WHAT DO YOU WANT?
AH! OH, MR FISHER!
IT'S ABOUT YOUR SON, RYAN. YOU KNOW THAT HE, ERM--
--CAME BACK?
THAT IS NOT MY SON.
WHATEVER IT IS THAT YOU THINK YOU'RE DOING...
YOU CAN'T HELP HIM.
HE'LL CHANGE LIKE THE OTHERS...
"LIKE ALL THE OTHER MONSTERS!"

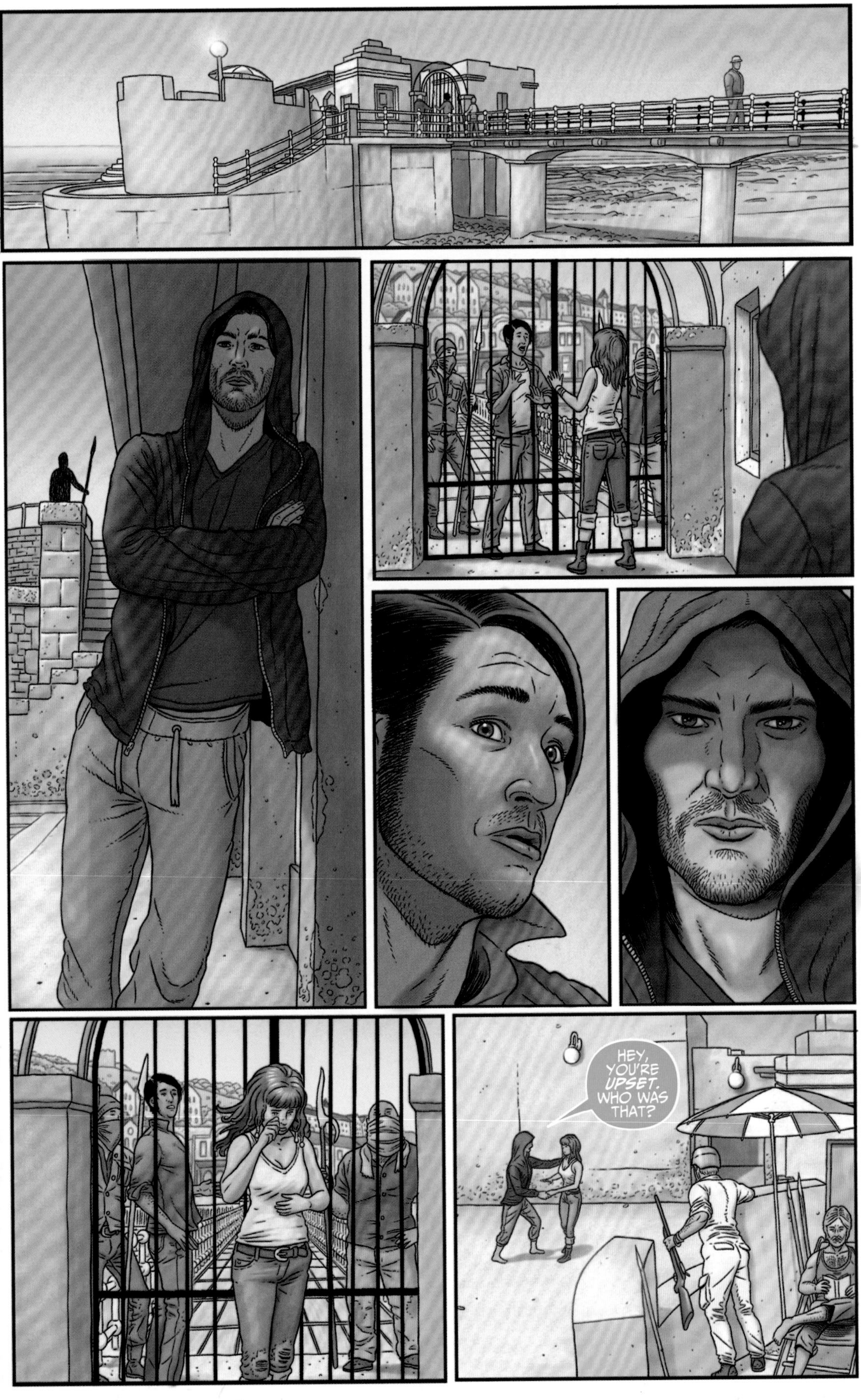
HEY, YOU'RE *UPSET*. WHO WAS THAT?

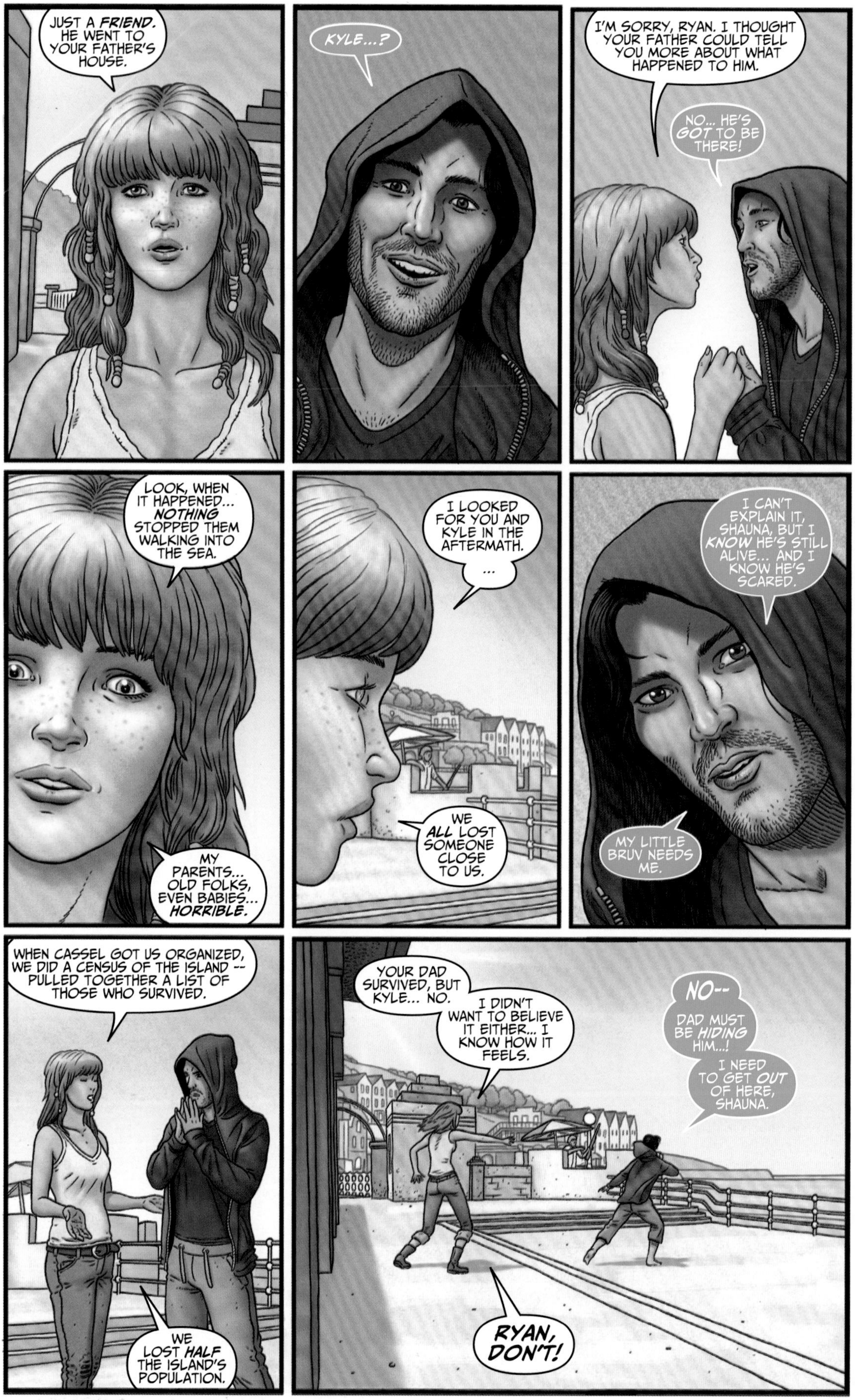
JUST A FRIEND. HE WENT TO YOUR FATHER'S HOUSE.
KYLE...?
I'M SORRY, RYAN. I THOUGHT YOUR FATHER COULD TELL YOU MORE ABOUT WHAT HAPPENED TO HIM.
NO... HE'S GOT TO BE THERE!
LOOK, WHEN IT HAPPENED... NOTHING STOPPED THEM WALKING INTO THE SEA.
MY PARENTS... OLD FOLKS, EVEN BABIES... HORRIBLE.
I LOOKED FOR YOU AND KYLE IN THE AFTERMATH.
...
WE ALL LOST SOMEONE CLOSE TO US.
I CAN'T EXPLAIN IT, SHAUNA, BUT I KNOW HE'S STILL ALIVE... AND I KNOW HE'S SCARED.
MY LITTLE BRUV NEEDS ME.
WHEN CASSEL GOT US ORGANIZED, WE DID A CENSUS OF THE ISLAND -- PULLED TOGETHER A LIST OF THOSE WHO SURVIVED.
WE LOST HALF THE ISLAND'S POPULATION.
YOUR DAD SURVIVED, BUT KYLE... NO.
I DIDN'T WANT TO BELIEVE IT EITHER... I KNOW HOW IT FEELS.
NO--
DAD MUST BE HIDING HIM...!
I NEED TO GET OUT OF HERE, SHAUNA.
RYAN, DON'T!

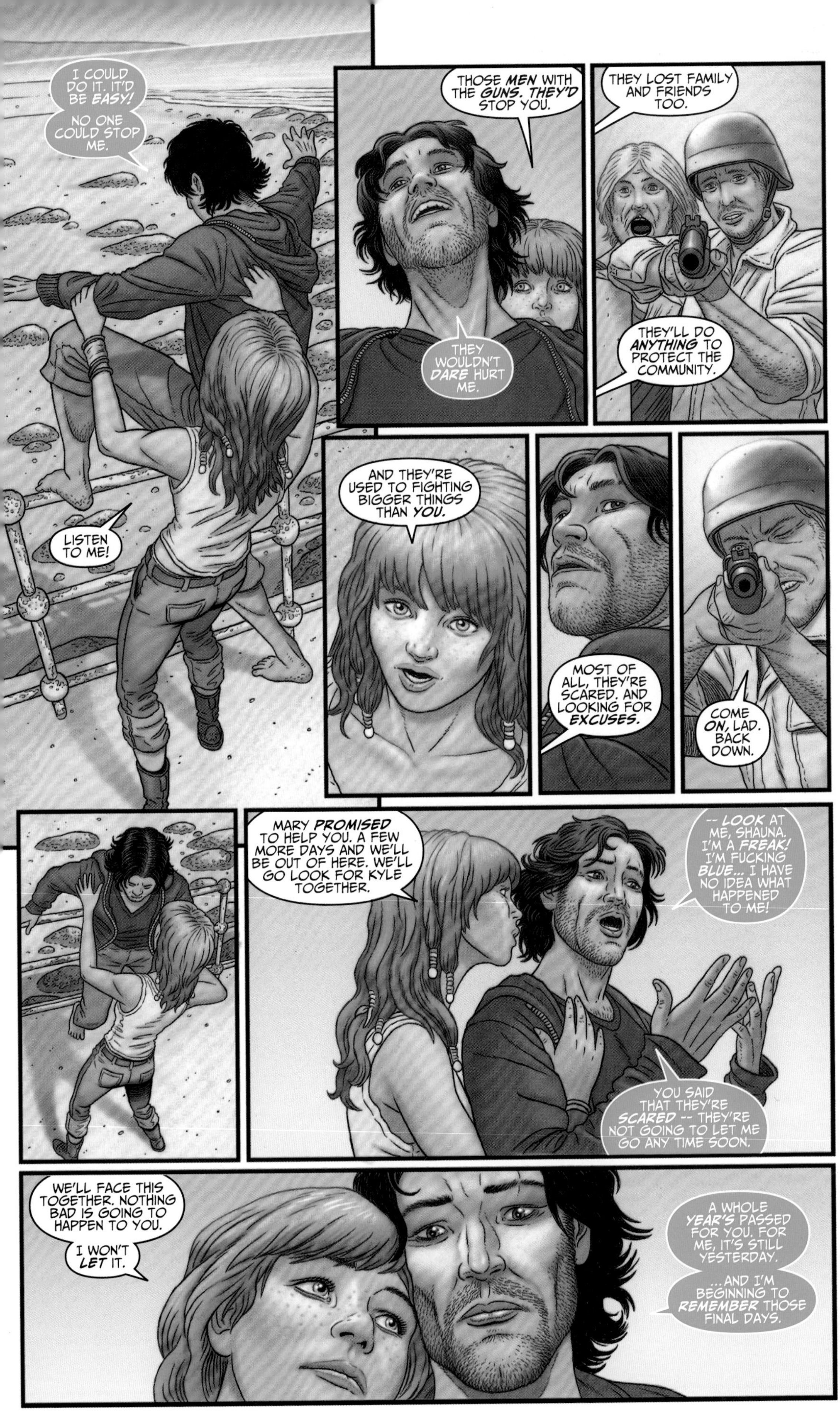

I COULD DO IT. IT'D BE EASY!
NO ONE COULD STOP ME.
THOSE MEN WITH THE GUNS. THEY'D STOP YOU.
THEY WOULDN'T DARE HURT ME.
THEY LOST FAMILY AND FRIENDS TOO.
THEY'LL DO ANYTHING TO PROTECT THE COMMUNITY.
LISTEN TO ME!
AND THEY'RE USED TO FIGHTING BIGGER THINGS THAN YOU.
MOST OF ALL, THEY'RE SCARED. AND LOOKING FOR EXCUSES.
COME ON, LAD. BACK DOWN.
MARY PROMISED TO HELP YOU. A FEW MORE DAYS AND WE'LL BE OUT OF HERE. WE'LL GO LOOK FOR KYLE TOGETHER.
-- LOOK AT ME, SHAUNA. I'M A FREAK! I'M FUCKING BLUE... I HAVE NO IDEA WHAT HAPPENED TO ME!
YOU SAID THAT THEY'RE SCARED -- THEY'RE NOT GOING TO LET ME GO ANY TIME SOON.
WE'LL FACE THIS TOGETHER. NOTHING BAD IS GOING TO HAPPEN TO YOU.
I WON'T LET IT.
A WHOLE YEAR'S PASSED FOR YOU. FOR ME, IT'S STILL YESTERDAY.
...AND I'M BEGINNING TO REMEMBER THOSE FINAL DAYS.

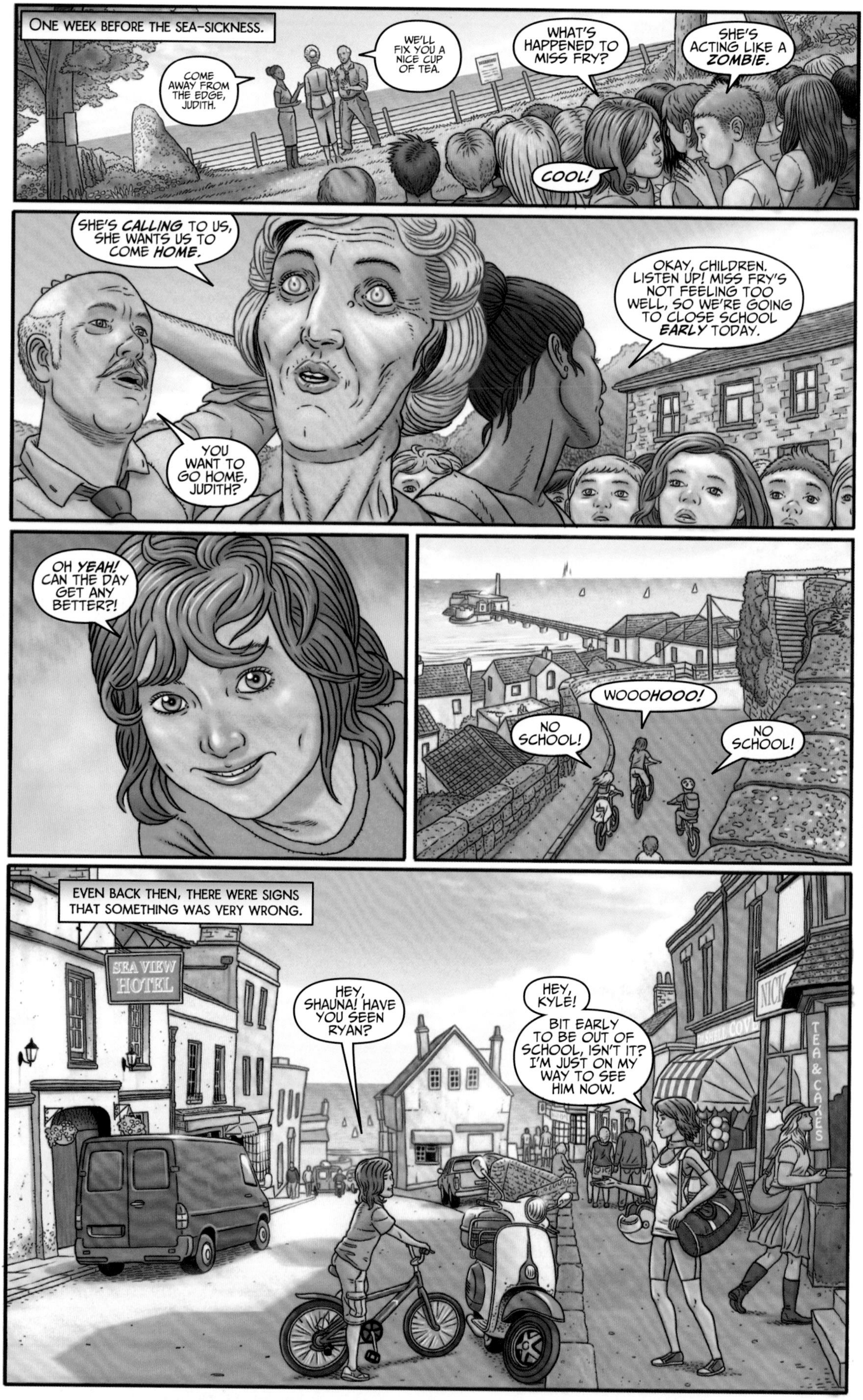
One week before the sea-sickness.
COME AWAY FROM THE EDGE, JUDITH.
WE'LL FIX YOU A NICE CUP OF TEA.
WHAT'S HAPPENED TO MISS FRY?
SHE'S ACTING LIKE A ZOMBIE.
COOL!
SHE'S CALLING TO US, SHE WANTS US TO COME HOME.
YOU WANT TO GO HOME, JUDITH?
OKAY, CHILDREN. LISTEN UP! MISS FRY'S NOT FEELING TOO WELL, SO WE'RE GOING TO CLOSE SCHOOL EARLY TODAY.
OH YEAH! CAN THE DAY GET ANY BETTER?!
WOOOHOOO!
NO SCHOOL!
NO SCHOOL!
EVEN BACK THEN, THERE WERE SIGNS THAT SOMETHING WAS VERY WRONG.
SEA VIEW HOTEL
HEY, SHAUNA! HAVE YOU SEEN RYAN?
HEY, KYLE!
BIT EARLY TO BE OUT OF SCHOOL, ISN'T IT? I'M JUST ON MY WAY TO SEE HIM NOW.
TEA & CAKES

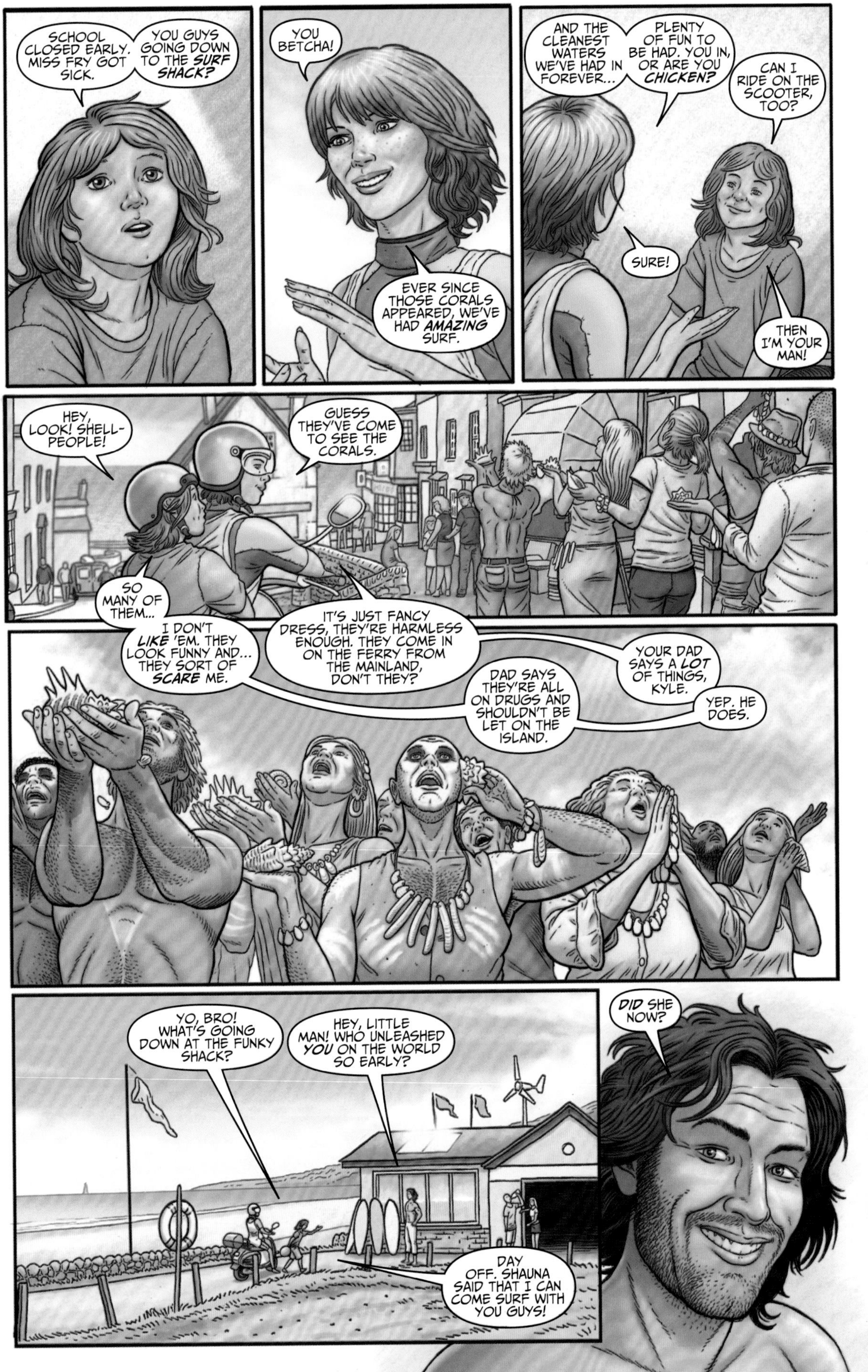
SCHOOL CLOSED EARLY. MISS FRY GOT SICK.
YOU GUYS GOING DOWN TO THE SURF SHACK?
YOU BETCHA!
EVER SINCE THOSE CORALS APPEARED, WE'VE HAD AMAZING SURF.
AND THE CLEANEST WATERS WE'VE HAD IN FOREVER...
PLENTY OF FUN TO BE HAD. YOU IN, OR ARE YOU CHICKEN?
CAN I RIDE ON THE SCOOTER, TOO?
SURE!
THEN I'M YOUR MAN!
HEY, LOOK! SHELL-PEOPLE!
GUESS THEY'VE COME TO SEE THE CORALS.
SO MANY OF THEM...
IT'S JUST FANCY DRESS, THEY'RE HARMLESS ENOUGH. THEY COME IN ON THE FERRY FROM THE MAINLAND, DON'T THEY?
I DON'T LIKE 'EM. THEY LOOK FUNNY AND... THEY SORT OF SCARE ME.
DAD SAYS THEY'RE ALL ON DRUGS AND SHOULDN'T BE LET ON THE ISLAND.
YOUR DAD SAYS A LOT OF THINGS, KYLE.
YEP. HE DOES.
YO, BRO! WHAT'S GOING DOWN AT THE FUNKY SHACK?
HEY, LITTLE MAN! WHO UNLEASHED YOU ON THE WORLD SO EARLY?
DAY OFF. SHAUNA SAID THAT I CAN COME SURF WITH YOU GUYS!
DID SHE NOW?

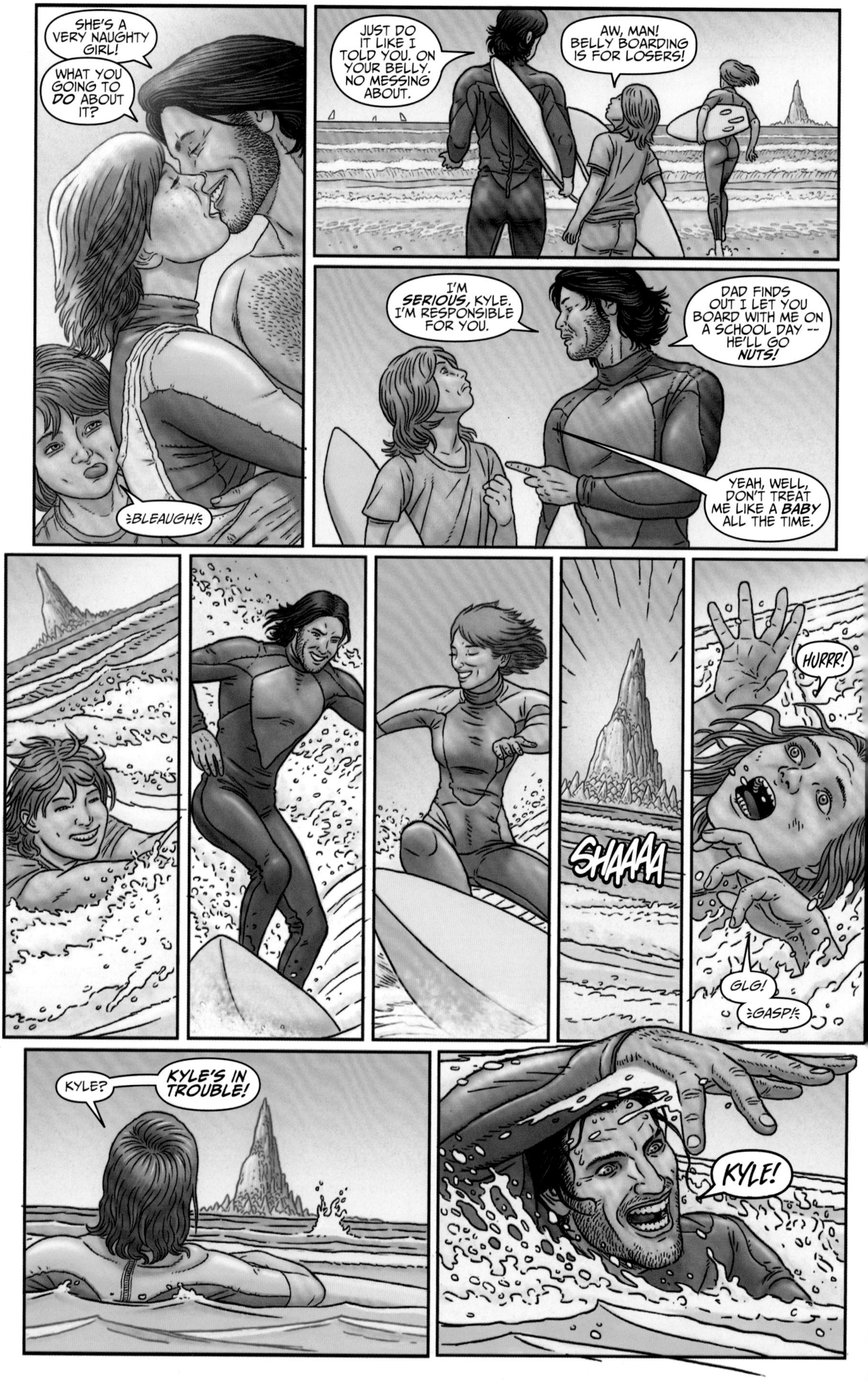
SHE'S A VERY NAUGHTY GIRL!
WHAT YOU GOING TO DO ABOUT IT?
BLEAUGH!
JUST DO IT LIKE I TOLD YOU. ON YOUR BELLY. NO MESSING ABOUT.
AW, MAN! BELLY BOARDING IS FOR LOSERS!
I'M SERIOUS, KYLE. I'M RESPONSIBLE FOR YOU.
DAD FINDS OUT I LET YOU BOARD WITH ME ON A SCHOOL DAY -- HE'LL GO NUTS!
YEAH, WELL, DON'T TREAT ME LIKE A BABY ALL THE TIME.
SHAAAA
HURRR!
GLG!
GASP!
KYLE?
KYLE'S IN TROUBLE!
KYLE!

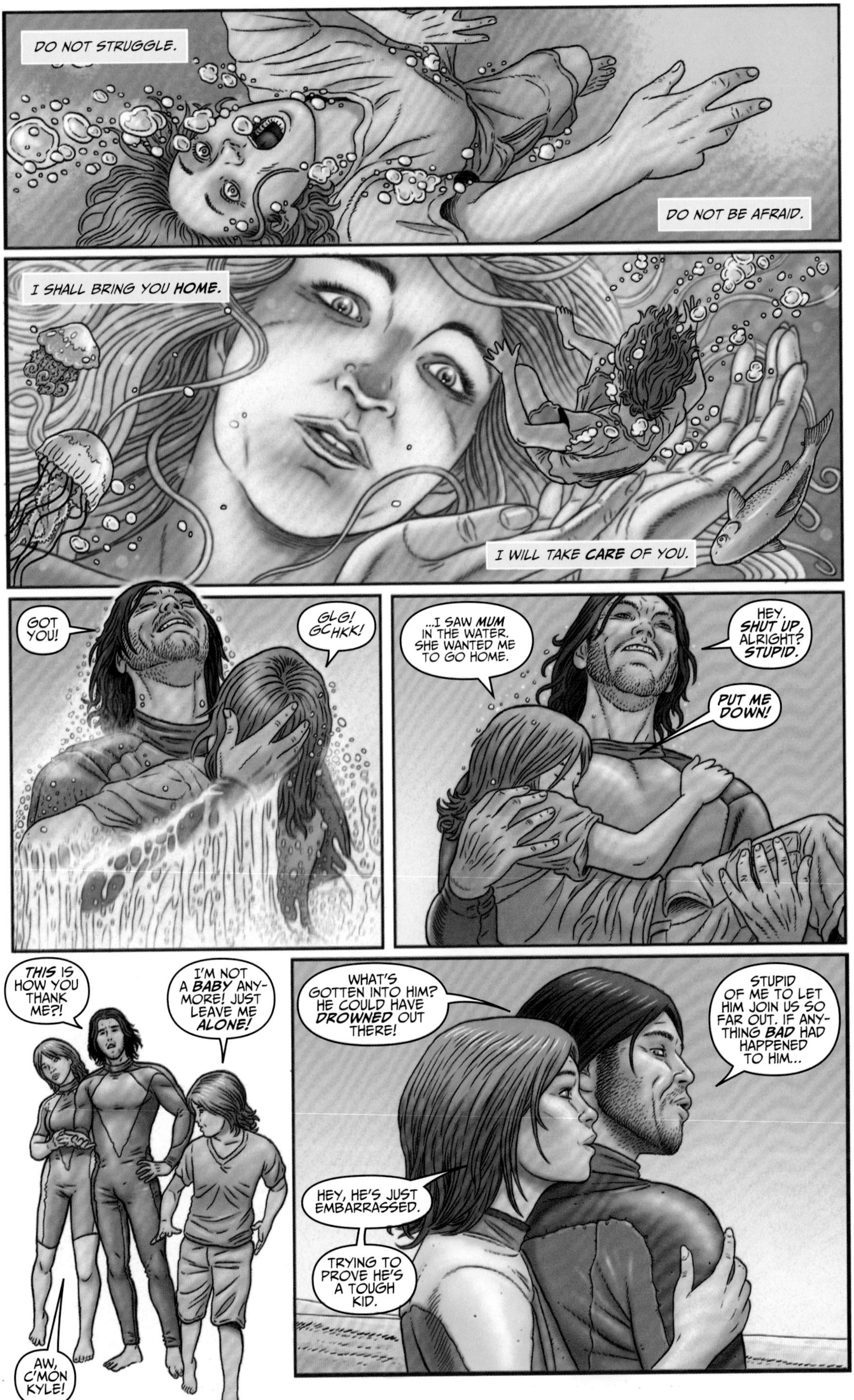
DO NOT STRUGGLE.
DO NOT BE AFRAID.
I SHALL BRING YOU **HOME.**
I WILL TAKE **CARE** OF YOU.
GOT YOU!
GLG! GCHKK!
...I SAW **MUM** IN THE WATER. SHE WANTED ME TO GO HOME.
HEY. **SHUT UP,** ALRIGHT? **STUPID.**
PUT ME DOWN!
THIS IS HOW YOU THANK ME?!
I'M NOT A **BABY** ANY-MORE! JUST LEAVE ME **ALONE!**
AW, C'MON KYLE!
WHAT'S GOTTEN INTO HIM? HE COULD HAVE **DROWNED** OUT THERE!
STUPID OF ME TO LET HIM JOIN US SO FAR OUT. IF ANY-THING **BAD** HAD HAPPENED TO HIM...
HEY, HE'S JUST EMBARRASSED.
TRYING TO PROVE HE'S A TOUGH KID.

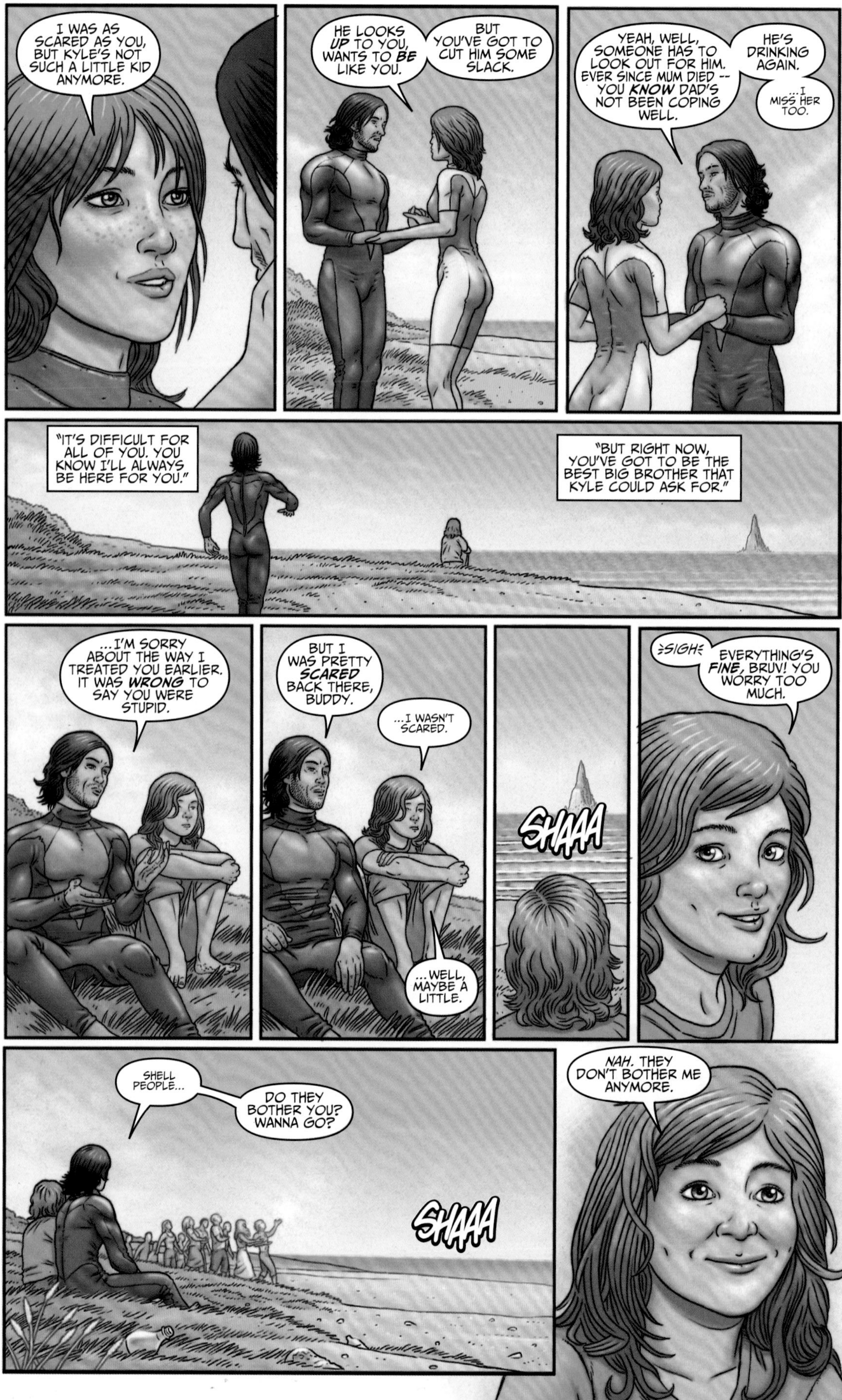
I WAS AS SCARED AS YOU, BUT KYLE'S NOT SUCH A LITTLE KID ANYMORE.
HE LOOKS UP TO YOU, WANTS TO BE LIKE YOU.
BUT YOU'VE GOT TO CUT HIM SOME SLACK.
YEAH, WELL, SOMEONE HAS TO LOOK OUT FOR HIM. EVER SINCE MUM DIED -- YOU KNOW DAD'S NOT BEEN COPING WELL.
HE'S DRINKING AGAIN.
...I MISS HER TOO.
"IT'S DIFFICULT FOR ALL OF YOU. YOU KNOW I'LL ALWAYS BE HERE FOR YOU."
"BUT RIGHT NOW, YOU'VE GOT TO BE THE BEST BIG BROTHER THAT KYLE COULD ASK FOR."
...I'M SORRY ABOUT THE WAY I TREATED YOU EARLIER. IT WAS WRONG TO SAY YOU WERE STUPID.
BUT I WAS PRETTY SCARED BACK THERE, BUDDY.
...I WASN'T SCARED.
...WELL, MAYBE A LITTLE.
SHAAA
SIGH
EVERYTHING'S FINE, BRUV! YOU WORRY TOO MUCH.
SHELL PEOPLE...
DO THEY BOTHER YOU? WANNA GO?
SHAAA
NAH. THEY DON'T BOTHER ME ANYMORE.

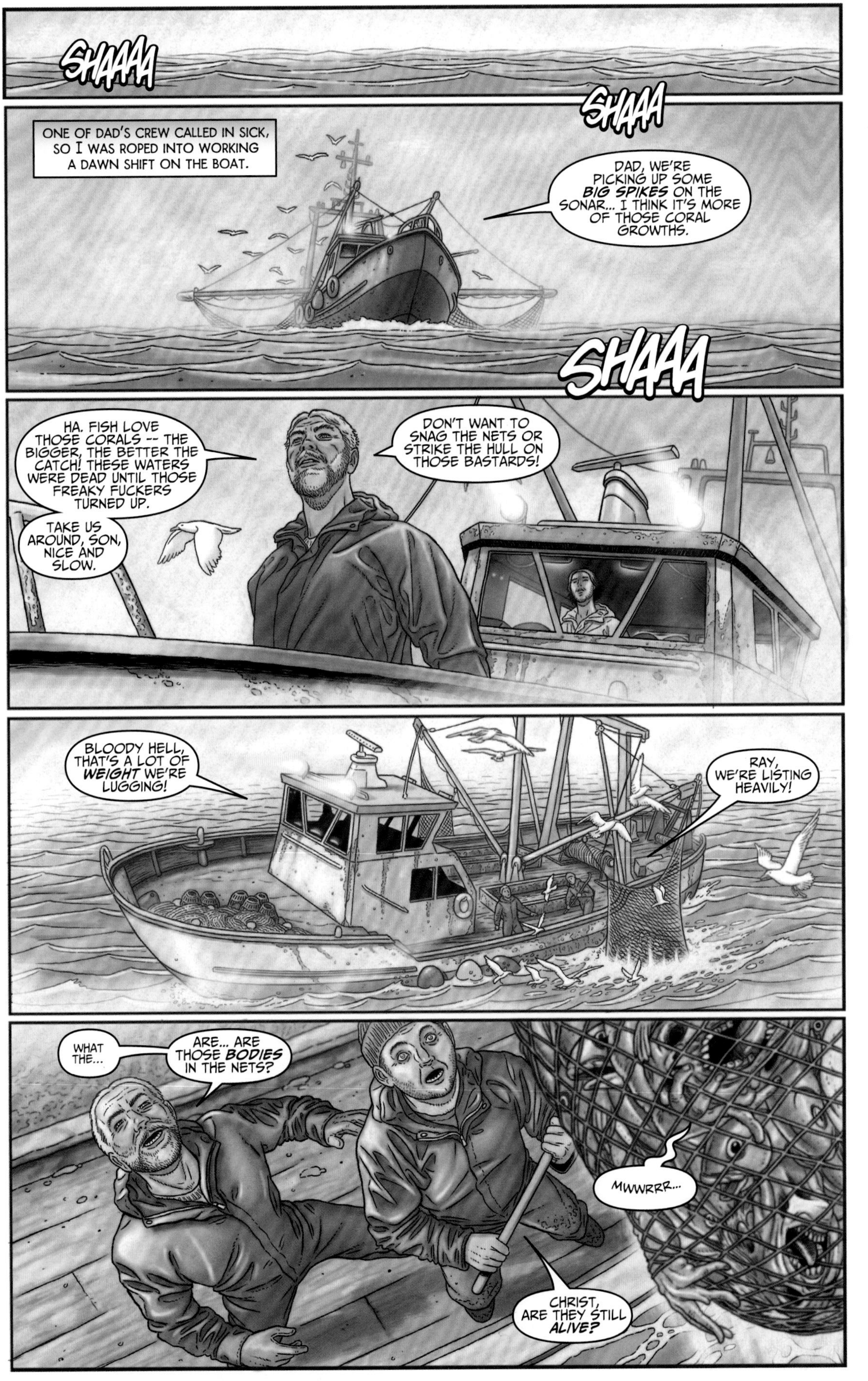
SHAAAA
SHAAA
ONE OF DAD'S CREW CALLED IN SICK, SO I WAS ROPED INTO WORKING A DAWN SHIFT ON THE BOAT.
DAD, WE'RE PICKING UP SOME BIG SPIKES ON THE SONAR... I THINK IT'S MORE OF THOSE CORAL GROWTHS.
SHAAA
HA. FISH LOVE THOSE CORALS -- THE BIGGER, THE BETTER THE CATCH! THESE WATERS WERE DEAD UNTIL THOSE FREAKY FUCKERS TURNED UP.
TAKE US AROUND, SON, NICE AND SLOW.
DON'T WANT TO SNAG THE NETS OR STRIKE THE HULL ON THOSE BASTARDS!
BLOODY HELL, THAT'S A LOT OF WEIGHT WE'RE LUGGING!
RAY, WE'RE LISTING HEAVILY!
WHAT THE...
ARE... ARE THOSE BODIES IN THE NETS?
MWWRRR...
CHRIST, ARE THEY STILL ALIVE?

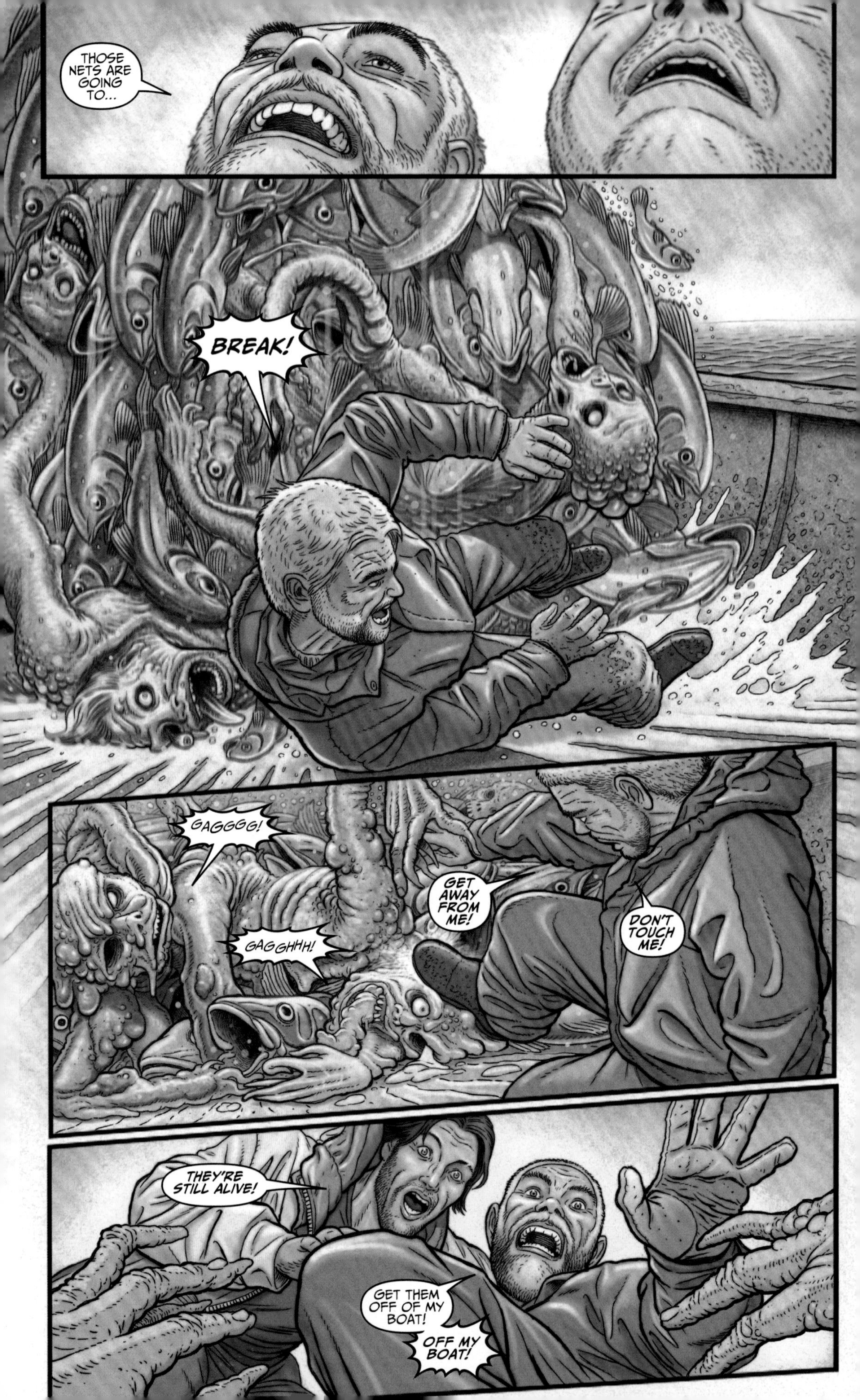
THOSE NETS ARE GOING TO...
BREAK!
GAGGGG!
GET AWAY FROM ME!
DON'T TOUCH ME!
GAGGHHH!
THEY'RE STILL ALIVE!
GET THEM OFF OF MY BOAT!
OFF MY BOAT!

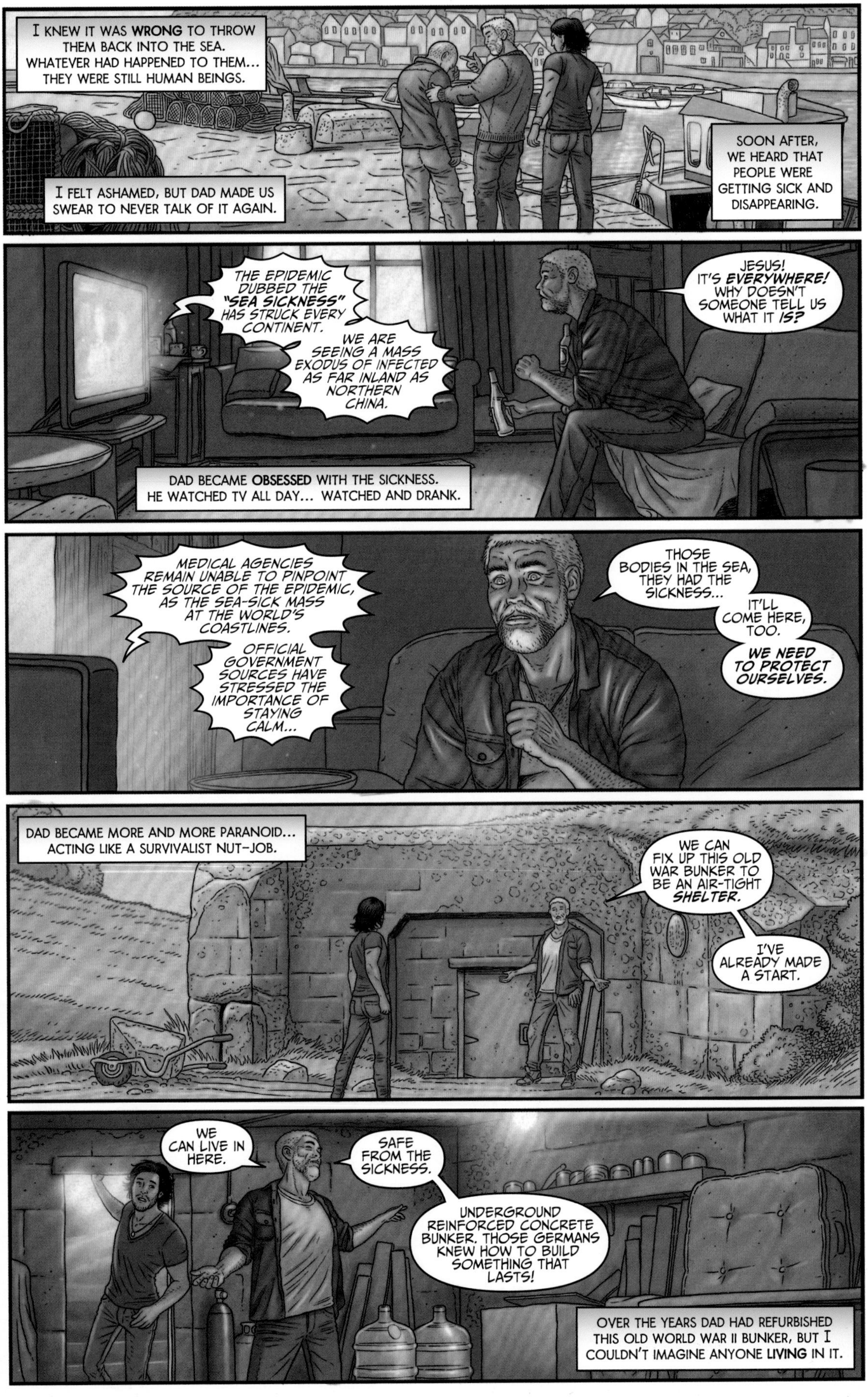
I KNEW IT WAS **WRONG** TO THROW THEM BACK INTO THE SEA. WHATEVER HAD HAPPENED TO THEM... THEY WERE STILL HUMAN BEINGS.
I FELT ASHAMED, BUT DAD MADE US SWEAR TO NEVER TALK OF IT AGAIN.
SOON AFTER, WE HEARD THAT PEOPLE WERE GETTING SICK AND DISAPPEARING.
THE EPIDEMIC DUBBED THE **"SEA SICKNESS"** HAS STRUCK EVERY CONTINENT.
WE ARE SEEING A MASS EXODUS OF INFECTED AS FAR INLAND AS NORTHERN CHINA.
JESUS! IT'S ***EVERYWHERE!*** WHY DOESN'T SOMEONE TELL US WHAT IT ***IS?***
DAD BECAME **OBSESSED** WITH THE SICKNESS. HE WATCHED TV ALL DAY... WATCHED AND DRANK.
MEDICAL AGENCIES REMAIN UNABLE TO PINPOINT THE SOURCE OF THE EPIDEMIC, AS THE SEA-SICK MASS AT THE WORLD'S COASTLINES.
OFFICIAL GOVERNMENT SOURCES HAVE STRESSED THE IMPORTANCE OF STAYING CALM...
THOSE BODIES IN THE SEA, THEY HAD THE SICKNESS...
IT'LL COME HERE, TOO.
WE NEED TO PROTECT OURSELVES.
DAD BECAME MORE AND MORE PARANOID... ACTING LIKE A SURVIVALIST NUT-JOB.
WE CAN FIX UP THIS OLD WAR BUNKER TO BE AN AIR-TIGHT ***SHELTER.***
I'VE ALREADY MADE A START.
WE CAN LIVE IN HERE.
SAFE FROM THE SICKNESS.
UNDERGROUND REINFORCED CONCRETE BUNKER. THOSE GERMANS KNEW HOW TO BUILD SOMETHING THAT LASTS!
OVER THE YEARS DAD HAD REFURBISHED THIS OLD WORLD WAR II BUNKER, BUT I COULDN'T IMAGINE ANYONE **LIVING** IN IT.

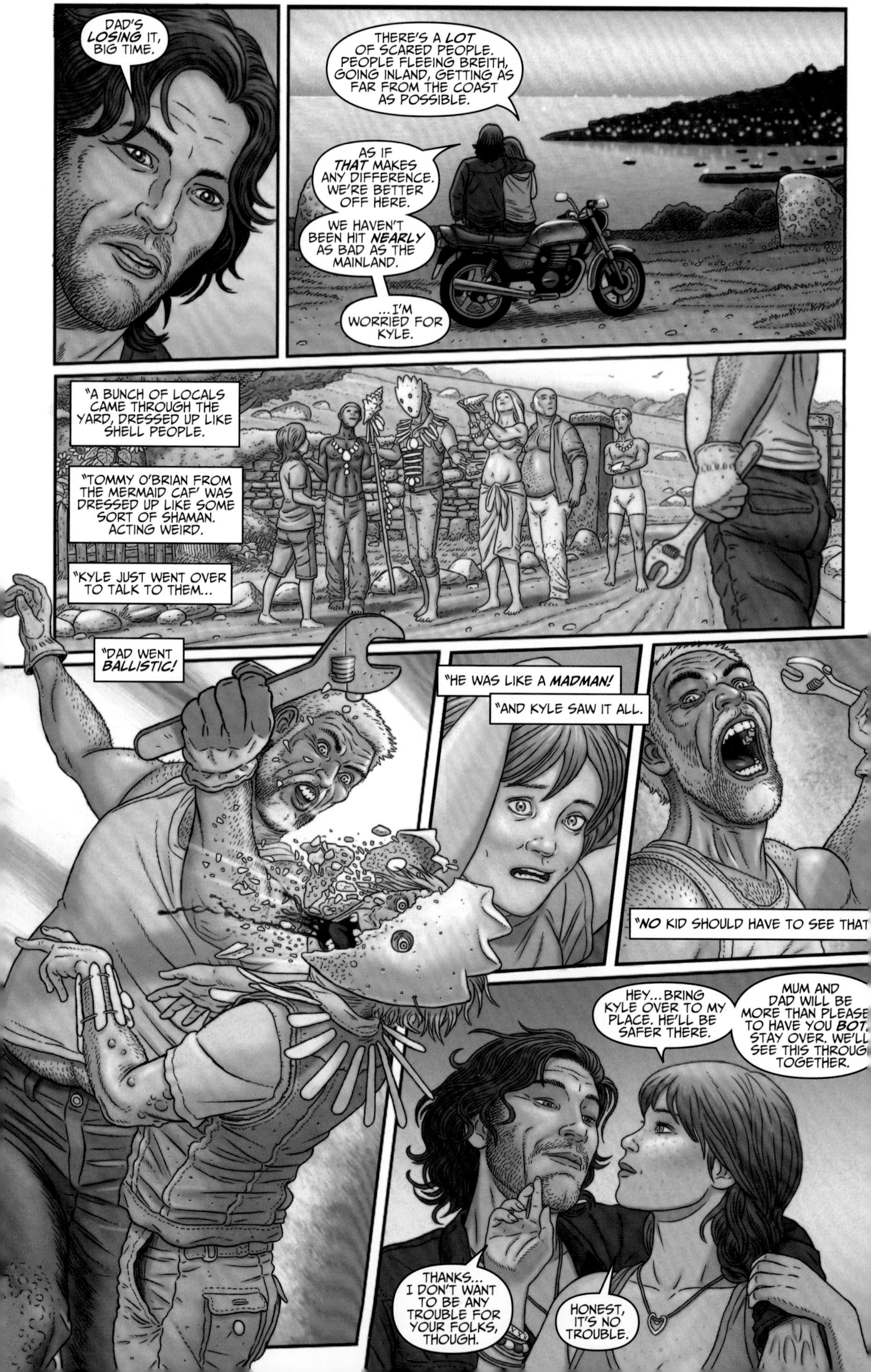
DAD'S LOSING IT, BIG TIME.
THERE'S A LOT OF SCARED PEOPLE. PEOPLE FLEEING BREITH, GOING INLAND, GETTING AS FAR FROM THE COAST AS POSSIBLE.
AS IF THAT MAKES ANY DIFFERENCE. WE'RE BETTER OFF HERE.
WE HAVEN'T BEEN HIT NEARLY AS BAD AS THE MAINLAND.
...I'M WORRIED FOR KYLE.
"A BUNCH OF LOCALS CAME THROUGH THE YARD, DRESSED UP LIKE SHELL PEOPLE.
"TOMMY O'BRIAN FROM THE MERMAID CAF' WAS DRESSED UP LIKE SOME SORT OF SHAMAN. ACTING WEIRD.
"KYLE JUST WENT OVER TO TALK TO THEM...
"DAD WENT BALLISTIC!
"HE WAS LIKE A MADMAN!
"AND KYLE SAW IT ALL.
"NO KID SHOULD HAVE TO SEE THAT
HEY... BRING KYLE OVER TO MY PLACE. HE'LL BE SAFER THERE.
MUM AND DAD WILL BE MORE THAN PLEASE TO HAVE YOU BOT STAY OVER. WE'LL SEE THIS THROUG TOGETHER.
THANKS... I DON'T WANT TO BE ANY TROUBLE FOR YOUR FOLKS, THOUGH.
HONEST, IT'S NO TROUBLE.

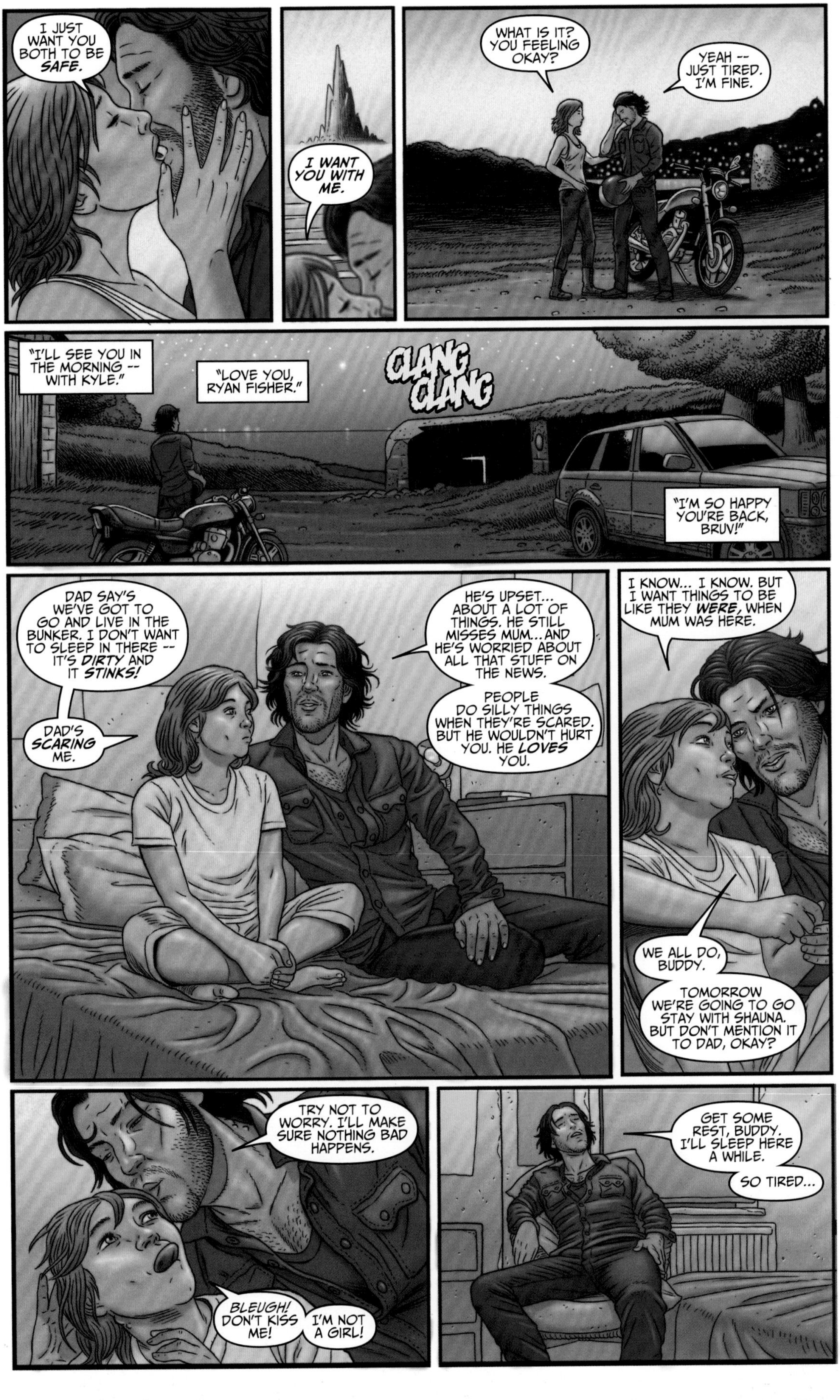
I JUST WANT YOU BOTH TO BE SAFE.
I WANT YOU WITH ME.
WHAT IS IT? YOU FEELING OKAY?
YEAH -- JUST TIRED. I'M FINE.
"I'LL SEE YOU IN THE MORNING -- WITH KYLE."
"LOVE YOU, RYAN FISHER."
CLANG CLANG
"I'M SO HAPPY YOU'RE BACK, BRUV!"
DAD SAY'S WE'VE GOT TO GO AND LIVE IN THE BUNKER. I DON'T WANT TO SLEEP IN THERE -- IT'S DIRTY AND IT STINKS!
DAD'S SCARING ME.
HE'S UPSET... ABOUT A LOT OF THINGS. HE STILL MISSES MUM... AND HE'S WORRIED ABOUT ALL THAT STUFF ON THE NEWS.
PEOPLE DO SILLY THINGS WHEN THEY'RE SCARED. BUT HE WOULDN'T HURT YOU. HE LOVES YOU.
I KNOW... I KNOW. BUT I WANT THINGS TO BE LIKE THEY WERE, WHEN MUM WAS HERE.
WE ALL DO, BUDDY.
TOMORROW WE'RE GOING TO GO STAY WITH SHAUNA. BUT DON'T MENTION IT TO DAD, OKAY?
TRY NOT TO WORRY. I'LL MAKE SURE NOTHING BAD HAPPENS.
BLEUGH! DON'T KISS ME!
I'M NOT A GIRL!
GET SOME REST, BUDDY. I'LL SLEEP HERE A WHILE.
SO TIRED...

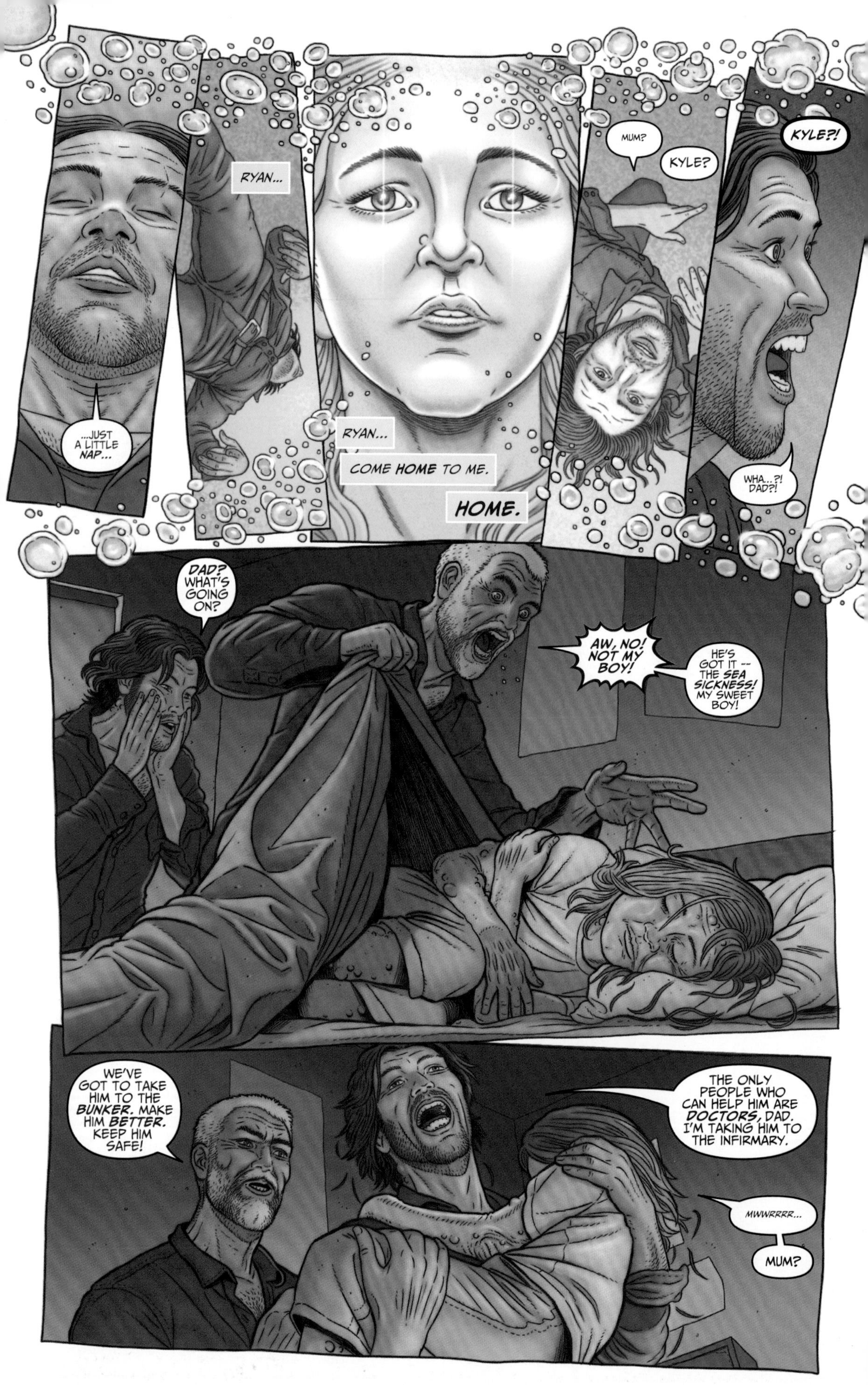
...JUST A LITTLE NAP...
RYAN...
RYAN...
COME HOME TO ME.
HOME.
MUM?
KYLE?
KYLE?!
WHA...?! DAD?!
DAD? WHAT'S GOING ON?
AW, NO! NOT MY BOY!
HE'S GOT IT -- THE SEA SICKNESS! MY SWEET BOY!
WE'VE GOT TO TAKE HIM TO THE BUNKER. MAKE HIM BETTER. KEEP HIM SAFE!
THE ONLY PEOPLE WHO CAN HELP HIM ARE DOCTORS, DAD. I'M TAKING HIM TO THE INFIRMARY.
MWWRRRR...
MUM?

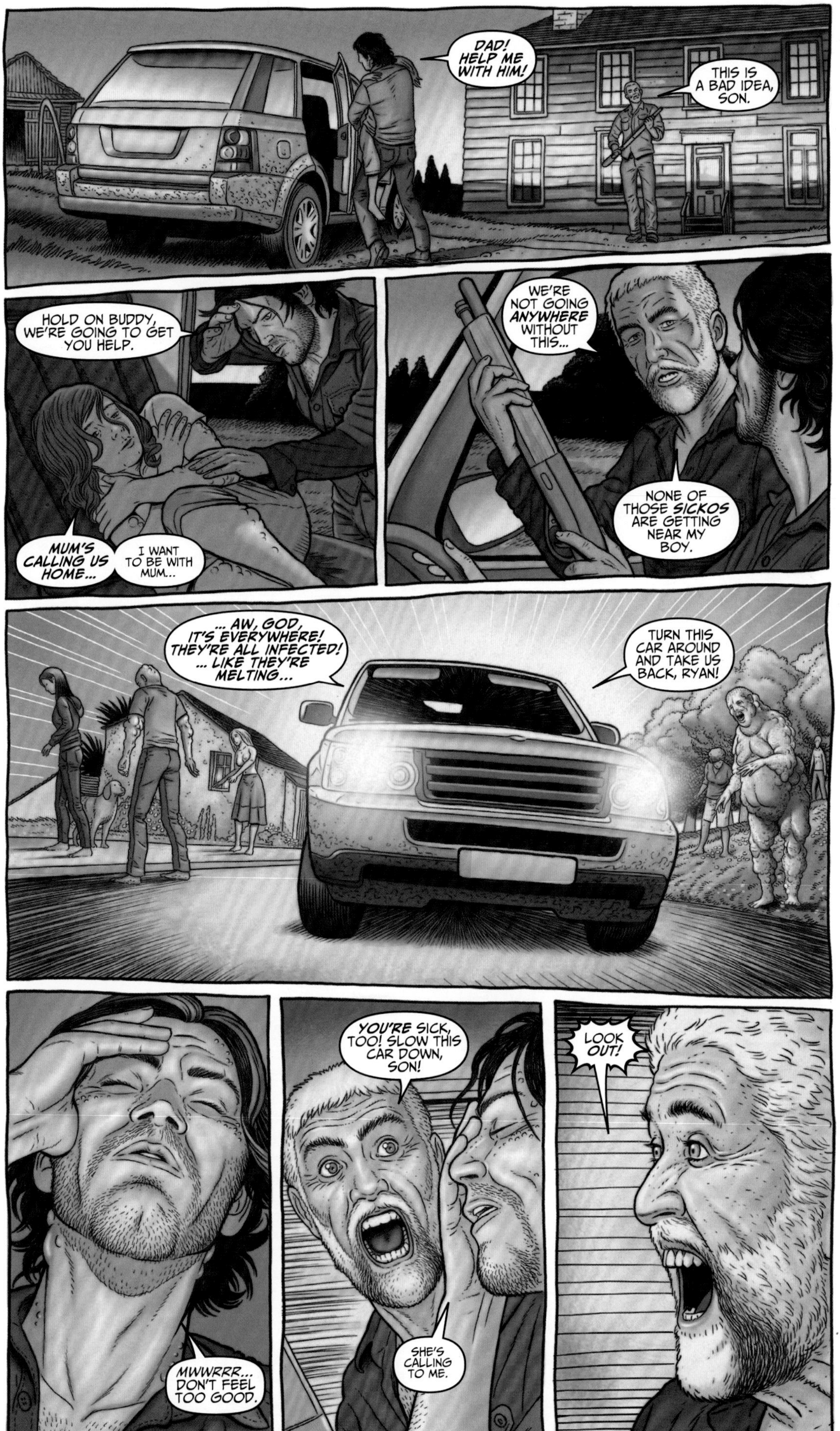
DAD! HELP ME WITH HIM!
THIS IS A BAD IDEA, SON.
HOLD ON BUDDY, WE'RE GOING TO GET YOU HELP.
MUM'S CALLING US HOME...
I WANT TO BE WITH MUM...
WE'RE NOT GOING ANYWHERE WITHOUT THIS...
NONE OF THOSE SICKOS ARE GETTING NEAR MY BOY.
... AW, GOD, IT'S EVERYWHERE! THEY'RE ALL INFECTED! ... LIKE THEY'RE MELTING...
TURN THIS CAR AROUND AND TAKE US BACK, RYAN!
MWWRRR... DON'T FEEL TOO GOOD.
YOU'RE SICK, TOO! SLOW THIS CAR DOWN, SON!
SHE'S CALLING TO ME.
LOOK OUT!

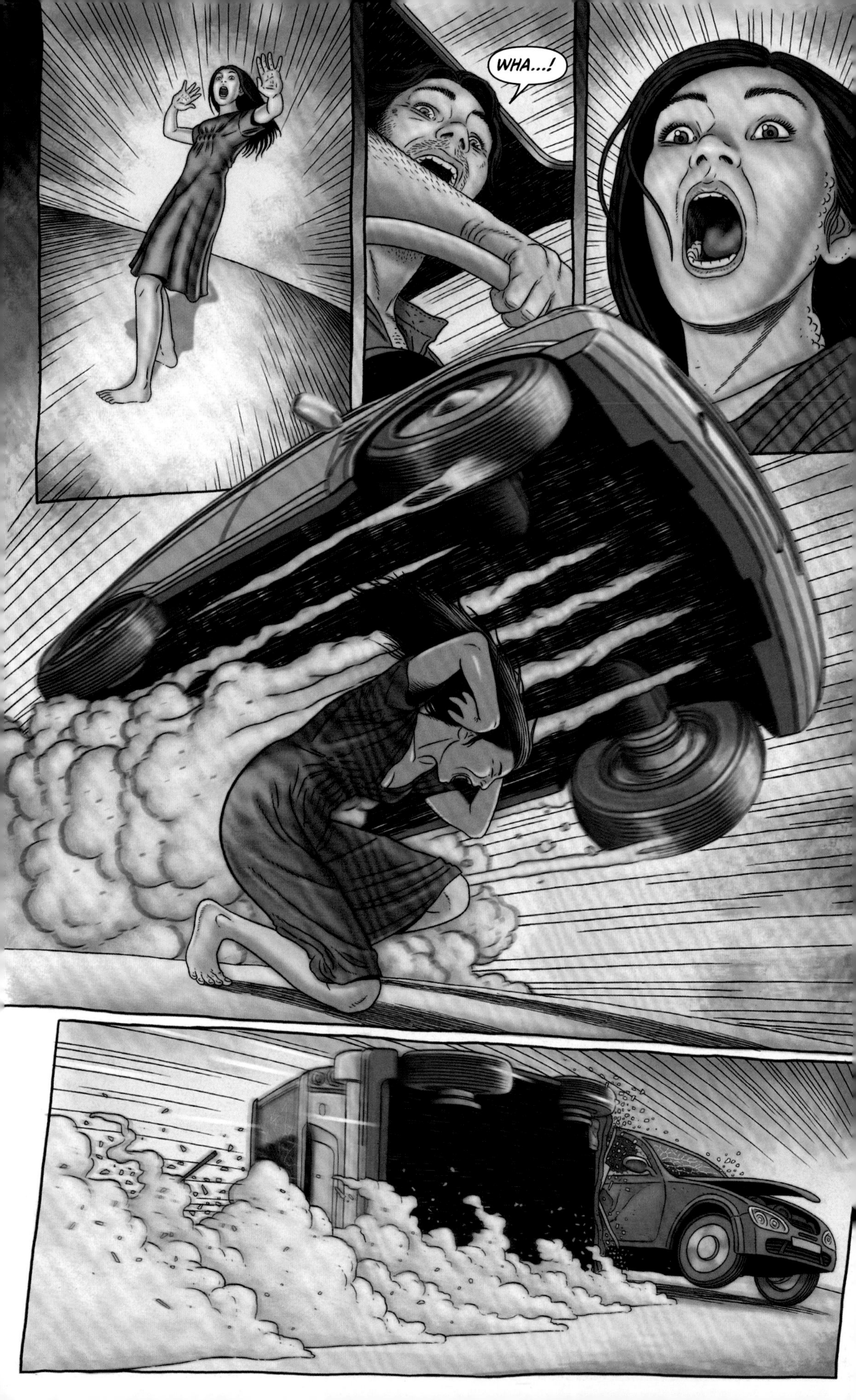
WHA...!

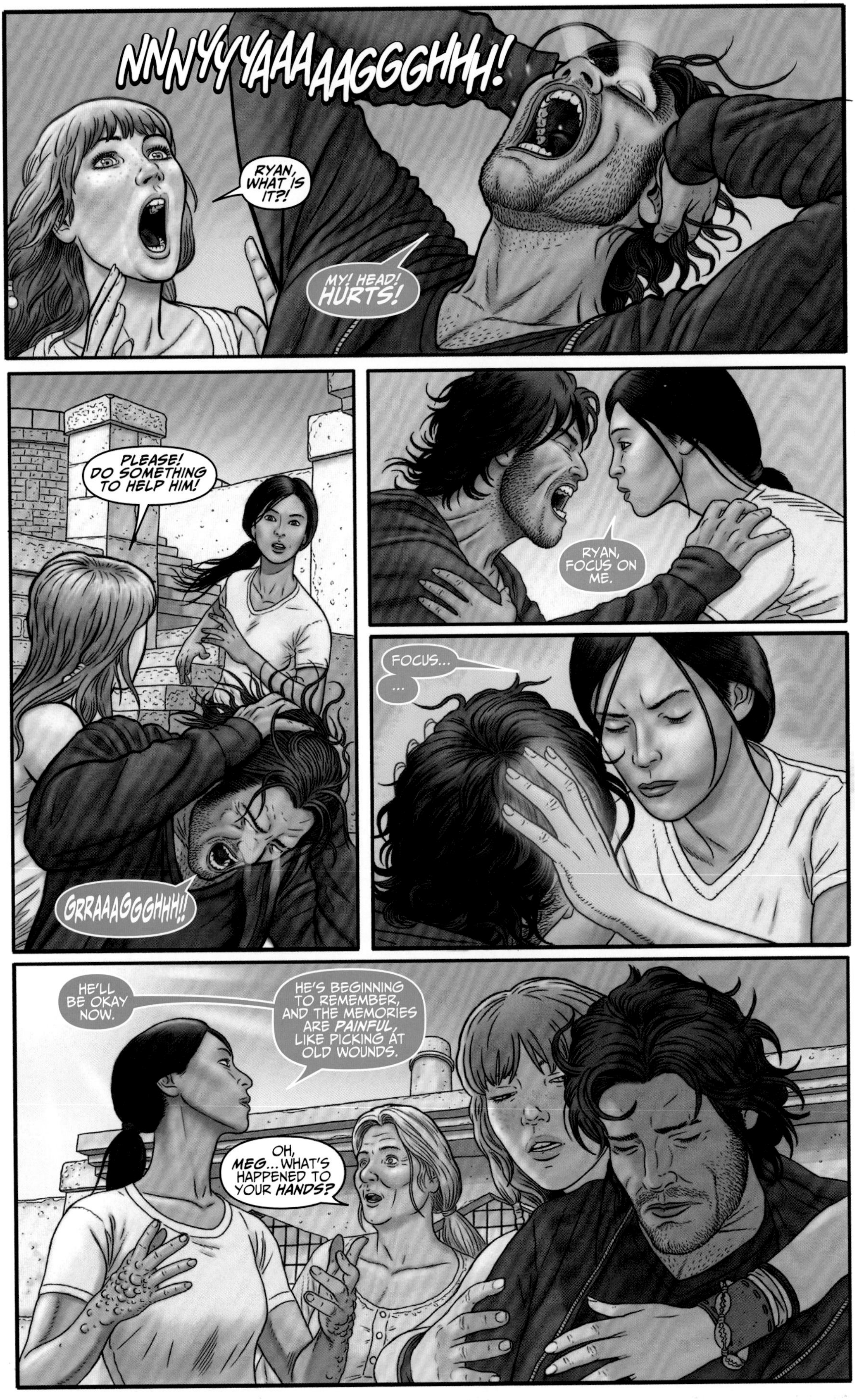
NNNYYYAAAAAGGGHHH!
RYAN, WHAT IS IT?!
MY! HEAD! HURTS!
PLEASE! DO SOMETHING TO HELP HIM!
GRRAAAGGGHHH!!
RYAN, FOCUS ON ME.
FOCUS...
...
HE'LL BE OKAY NOW.
HE'S BEGINNING TO REMEMBER, AND THE MEMORIES ARE PAINFUL, LIKE PICKING AT OLD WOUNDS.
OH, MEG... WHAT'S HAPPENED TO YOUR HANDS?

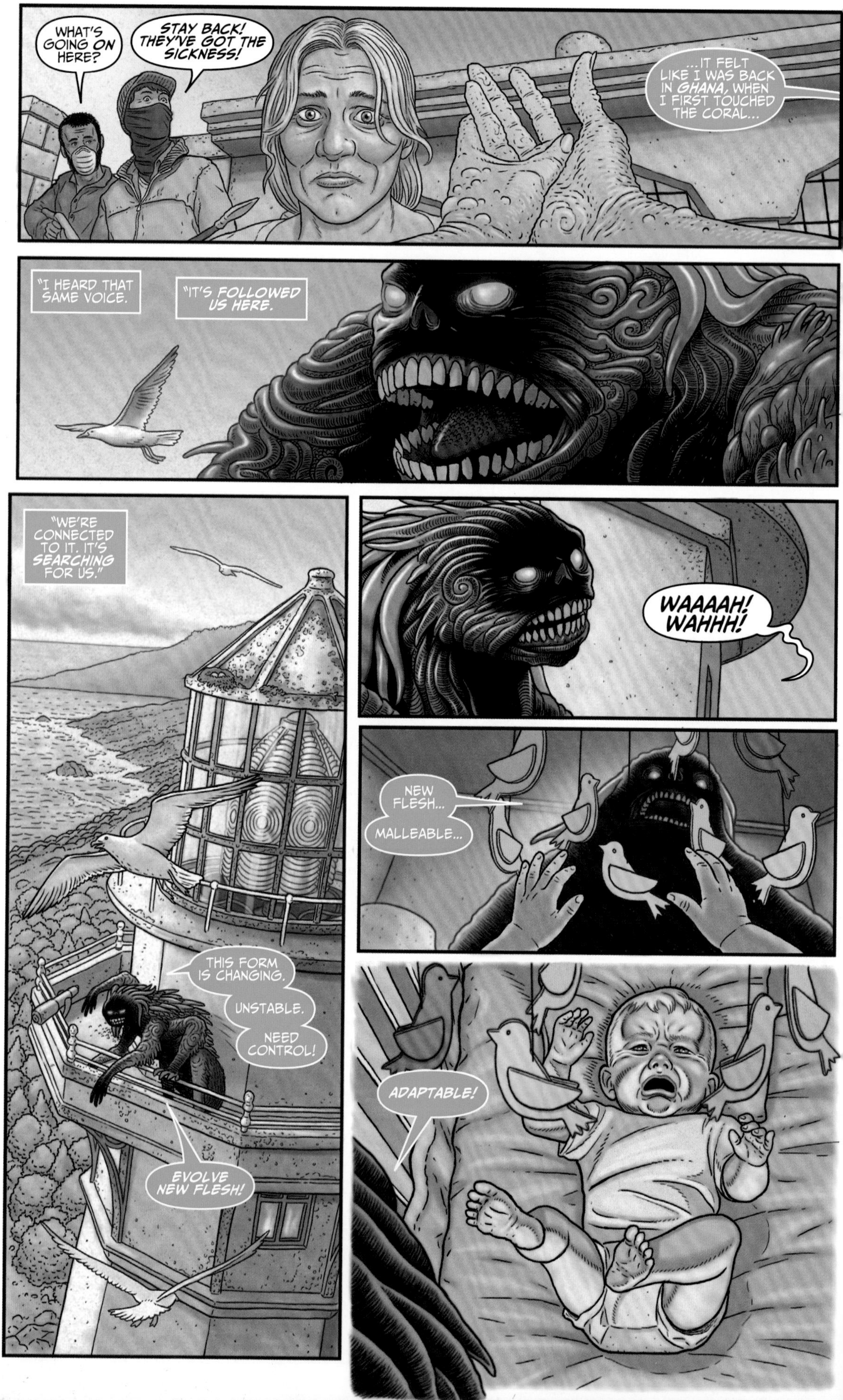
WHAT'S GOING ON HERE?
STAY BACK! THEY'VE GOT THE SICKNESS!
...IT FELT LIKE I WAS BACK IN GHANA, WHEN I FIRST TOUCHED THE CORAL...
"I HEARD THAT SAME VOICE.
"IT'S FOLLOWED US HERE.
"WE'RE CONNECTED TO IT. IT'S SEARCHING FOR US."
THIS FORM IS CHANGING.
UNSTABLE.
NEED CONTROL!
EVOLVE NEW FLESH!
WAAAAH! WAHHH!
NEW FLESH...
MALLEABLE...
ADAPTABLE!

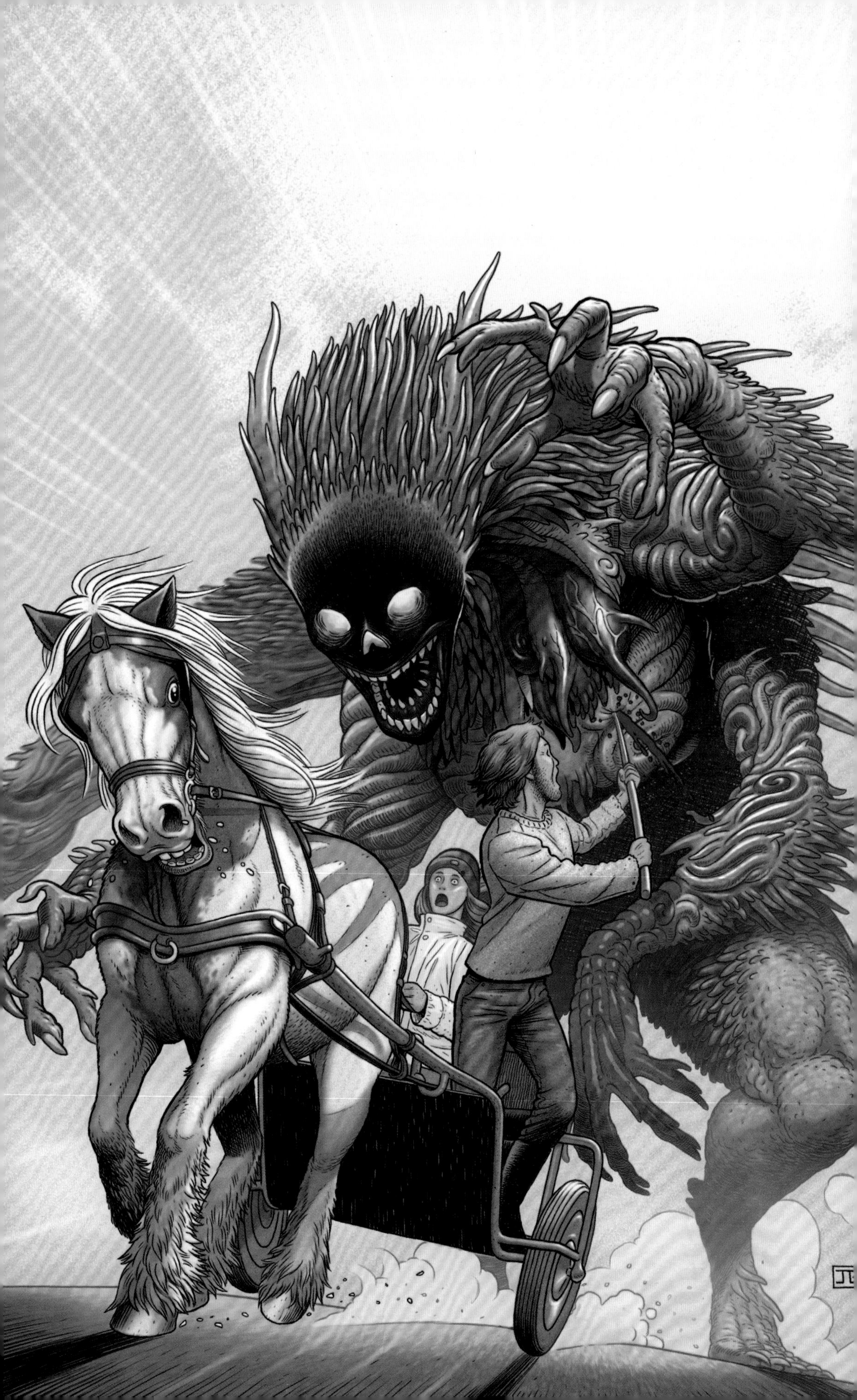

CHAPTER THREE
MUTANTS

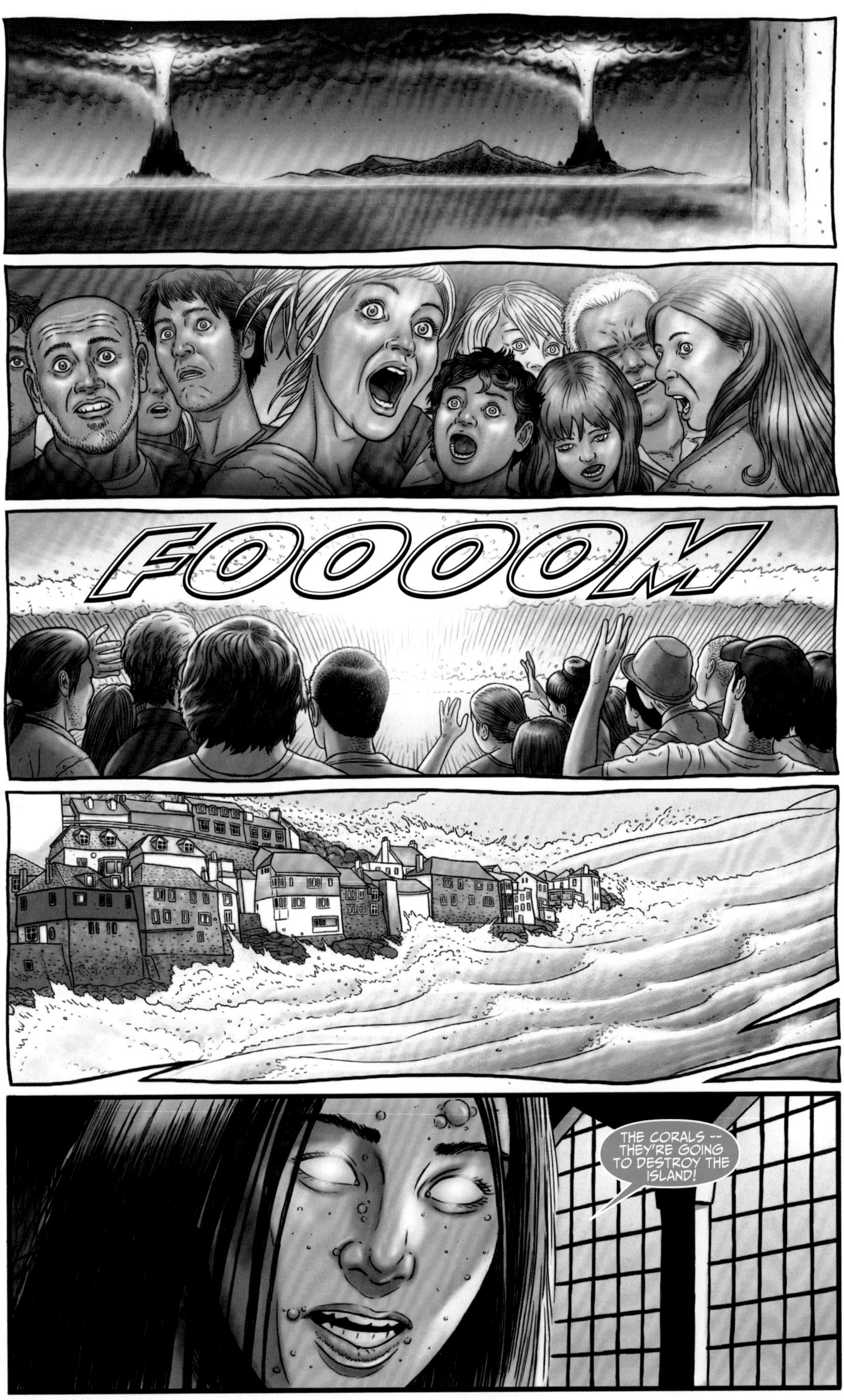
FOOOOM
THE CORALS -- THEY'RE GOING TO DESTROY THE ISLAND!

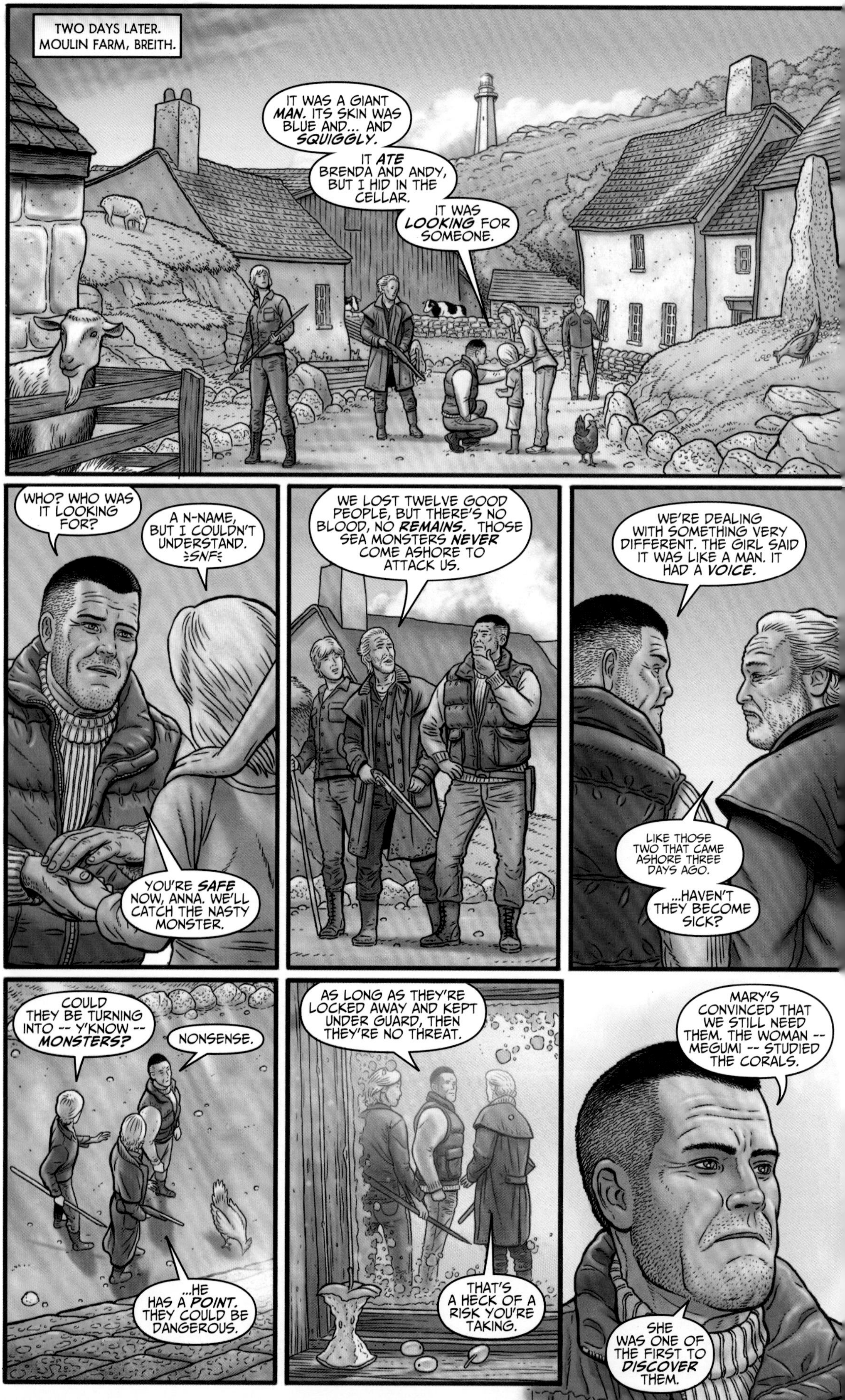
TWO DAYS LATER. MOULIN FARM, BREITH.
IT WAS A GIANT MAN. ITS SKIN WAS BLUE AND... AND SQUIGGLY.
IT ATE BRENDA AND ANDY, BUT I HID IN THE CELLAR.
IT WAS LOOKING FOR SOMEONE.
WHO? WHO WAS IT LOOKING FOR?
A N-NAME, BUT I COULDN'T UNDERSTAND. SNF
YOU'RE SAFE NOW, ANNA. WE'LL CATCH THE NASTY MONSTER.
WE LOST TWELVE GOOD PEOPLE, BUT THERE'S NO BLOOD, NO REMAINS. THOSE SEA MONSTERS NEVER COME ASHORE TO ATTACK US.
WE'RE DEALING WITH SOMETHING VERY DIFFERENT. THE GIRL SAID IT WAS LIKE A MAN. IT HAD A VOICE.
LIKE THOSE TWO THAT CAME ASHORE THREE DAYS AGO.
...HAVEN'T THEY BECOME SICK?
COULD THEY BE TURNING INTO -- Y'KNOW -- MONSTERS?
NONSENSE.
...HE HAS A POINT. THEY COULD BE DANGEROUS.
AS LONG AS THEY'RE LOCKED AWAY AND KEPT UNDER GUARD, THEN THEY'RE NO THREAT.
THAT'S A HECK OF A RISK YOU'RE TAKING.
MARY'S CONVINCED THAT WE STILL NEED THEM. THE WOMAN -- MEGUMI -- STUDIED THE CORALS.
SHE WAS ONE OF THE FIRST TO DISCOVER THEM.

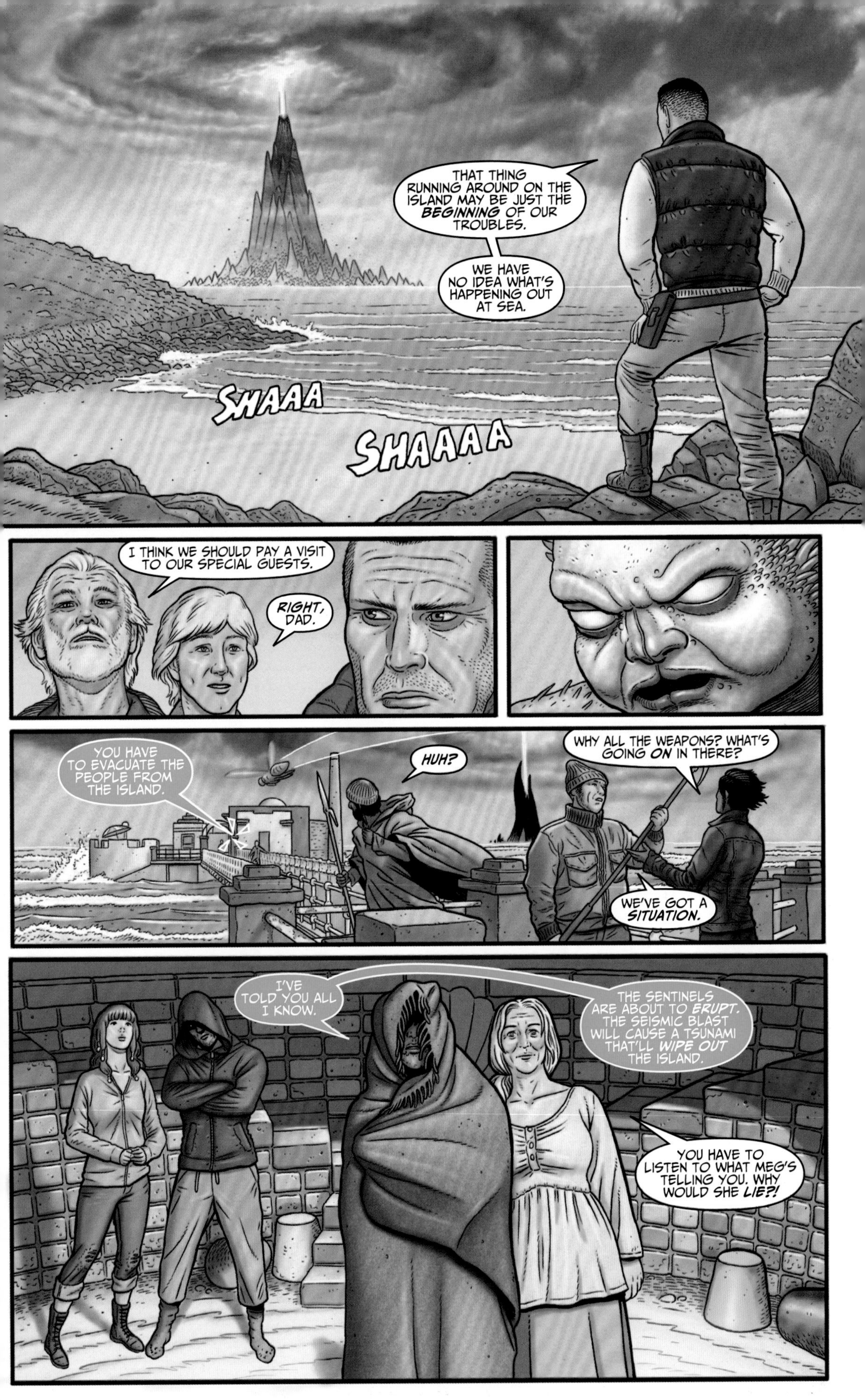
THAT THING RUNNING AROUND ON THE ISLAND MAY BE JUST THE BEGINNING OF OUR TROUBLES.
WE HAVE NO IDEA WHAT'S HAPPENING OUT AT SEA.
SHAAA
SHAAAA
I THINK WE SHOULD PAY A VISIT TO OUR SPECIAL GUESTS.
RIGHT, DAD.
YOU HAVE TO EVACUATE THE PEOPLE FROM THE ISLAND.
HUH?
WHY ALL THE WEAPONS? WHAT'S GOING ON IN THERE?
WE'VE GOT A SITUATION.
I'VE TOLD YOU ALL I KNOW.
THE SENTINELS ARE ABOUT TO ERUPT. THE SEISMIC BLAST WILL CAUSE A TSUNAMI THAT'LL WIPE OUT THE ISLAND.
YOU HAVE TO LISTEN TO WHAT MEG'S TELLING YOU. WHY WOULD SHE LIE?!

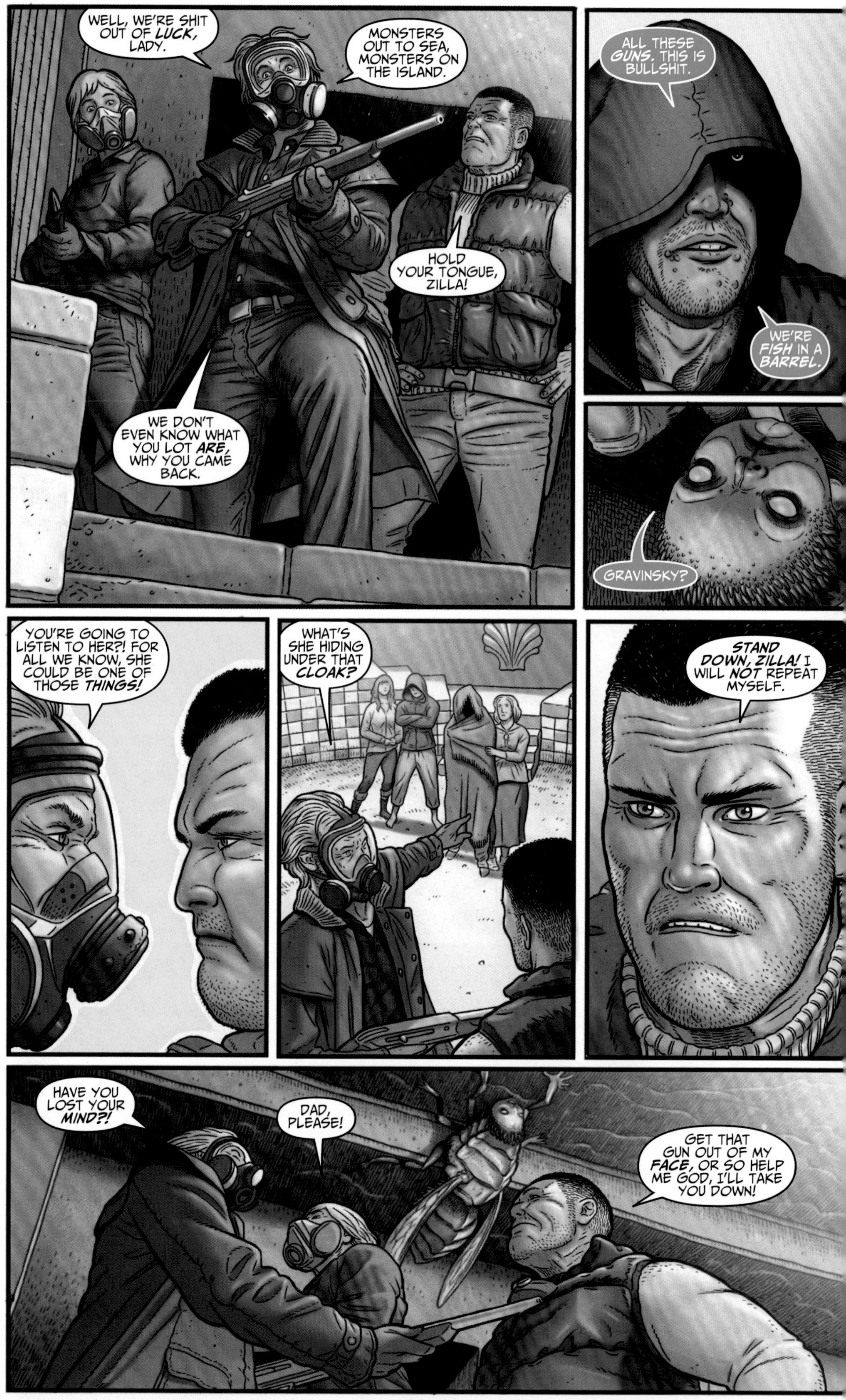
WELL, WE'RE SHIT OUT OF LUCK, LADY.
MONSTERS OUT TO SEA, MONSTERS ON THE ISLAND.
HOLD YOUR TONGUE, ZILLA!
WE DON'T EVEN KNOW WHAT YOU LOT ARE, WHY YOU CAME BACK.
ALL THESE GUNS. THIS IS BULLSHIT.
WE'RE FISH IN A BARREL.
GRAVINSKY?
YOU'RE GOING TO LISTEN TO HER?! FOR ALL WE KNOW, SHE COULD BE ONE OF THOSE THINGS!
WHAT'S SHE HIDING UNDER THAT CLOAK?
STAND DOWN, ZILLA! I WILL NOT REPEAT MYSELF.
HAVE YOU LOST YOUR MIND?!
DAD, PLEASE!
GET THAT GUN OUT OF MY FACE, OR SO HELP ME GOD, I'LL TAKE YOU DOWN!

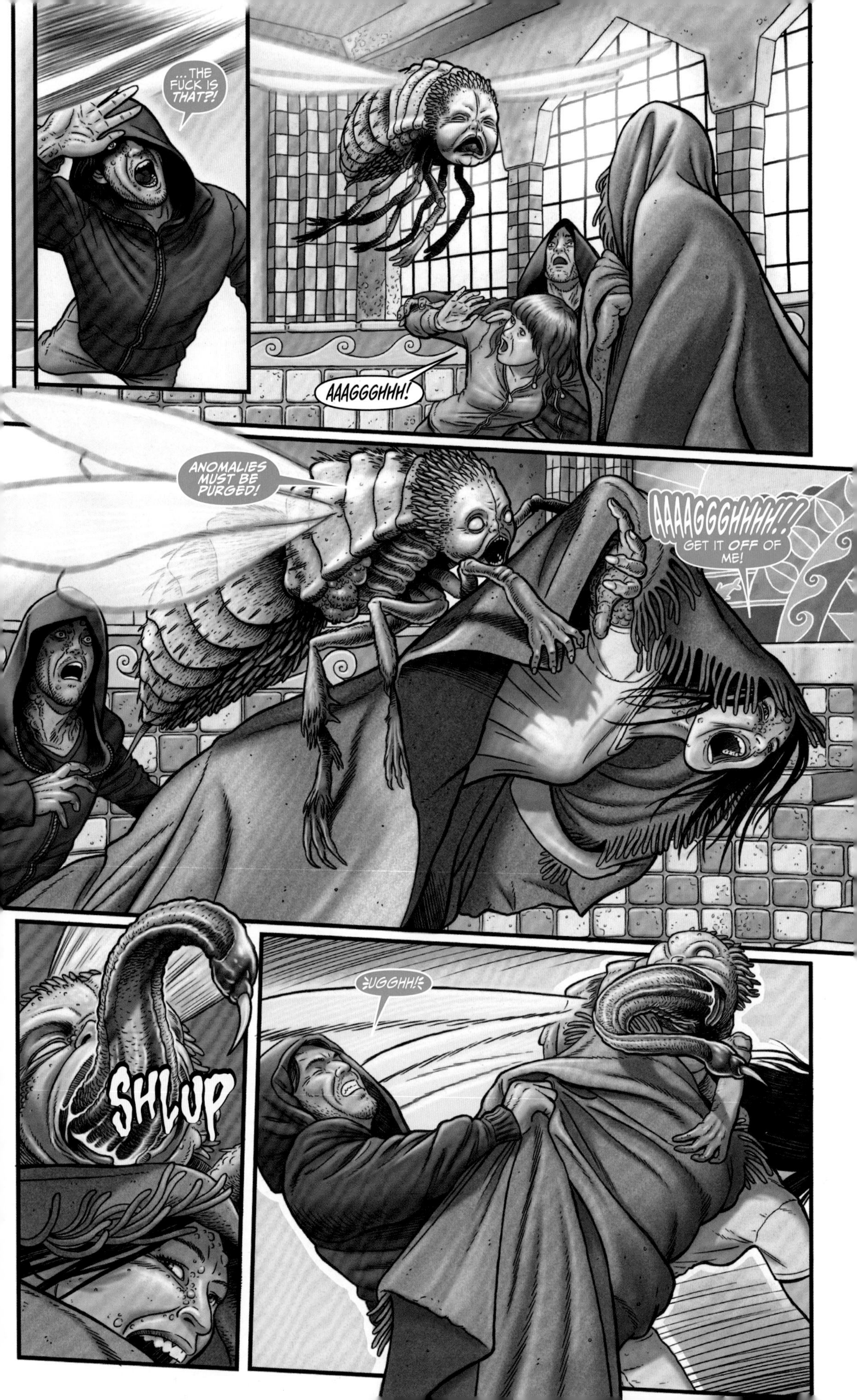
...THE FÜCK IS THAT?!
AAAGGGHHH!
ANOMALIES MUST BE PURGED!
AAAAGGGHHHH!!!
GET IT OFF OF ME!
SHLUP
UGGHH!

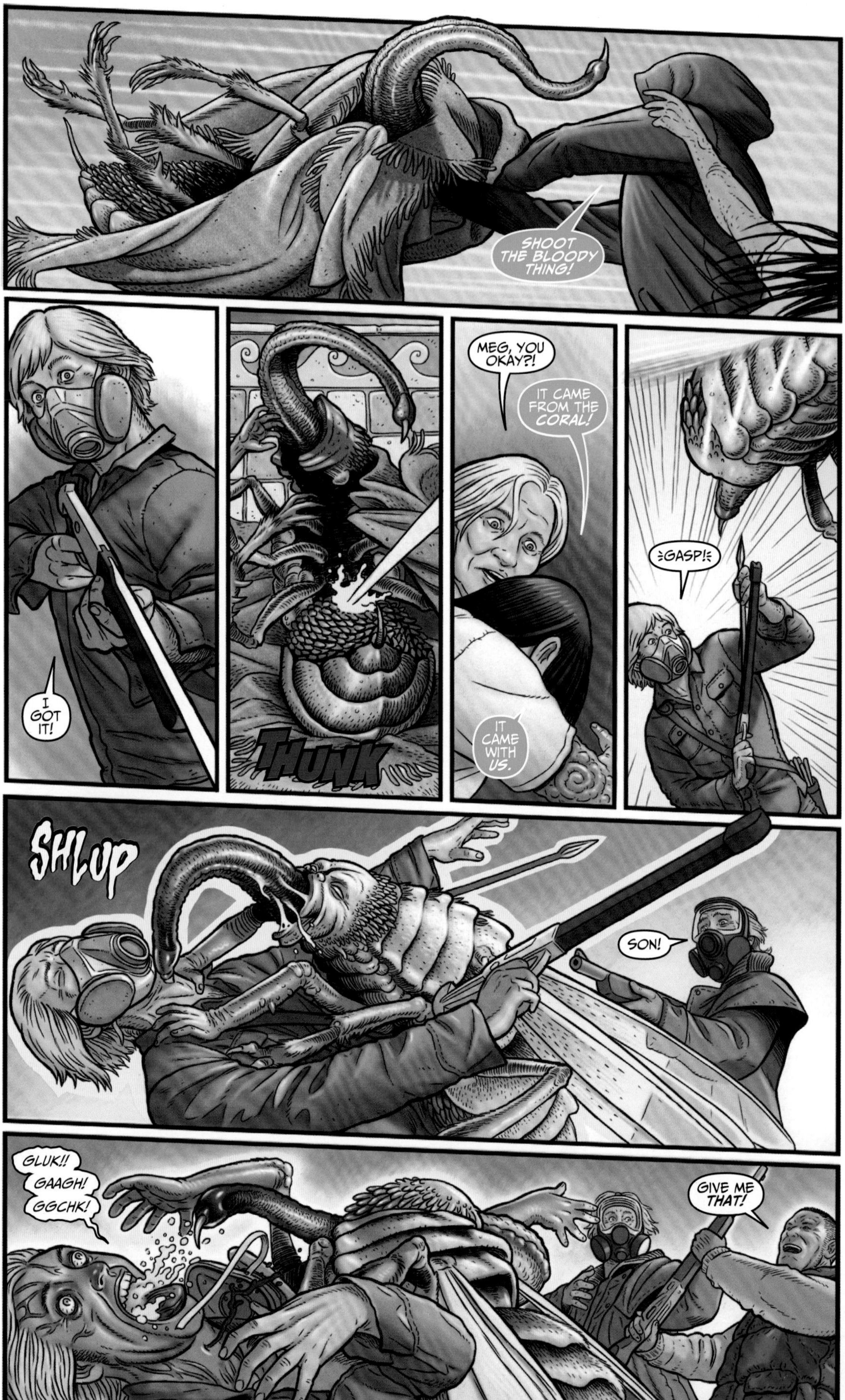
SHOOT THE BLOODY THING!
I GOT IT!
THUNK
MEG, YOU OKAY?!
IT CAME FROM THE CORAL!
IT CAME WITH US.
GASP!
SHLUP
SON!
GLUK!! GAAGH! GGCHK!
GIVE ME THAT!

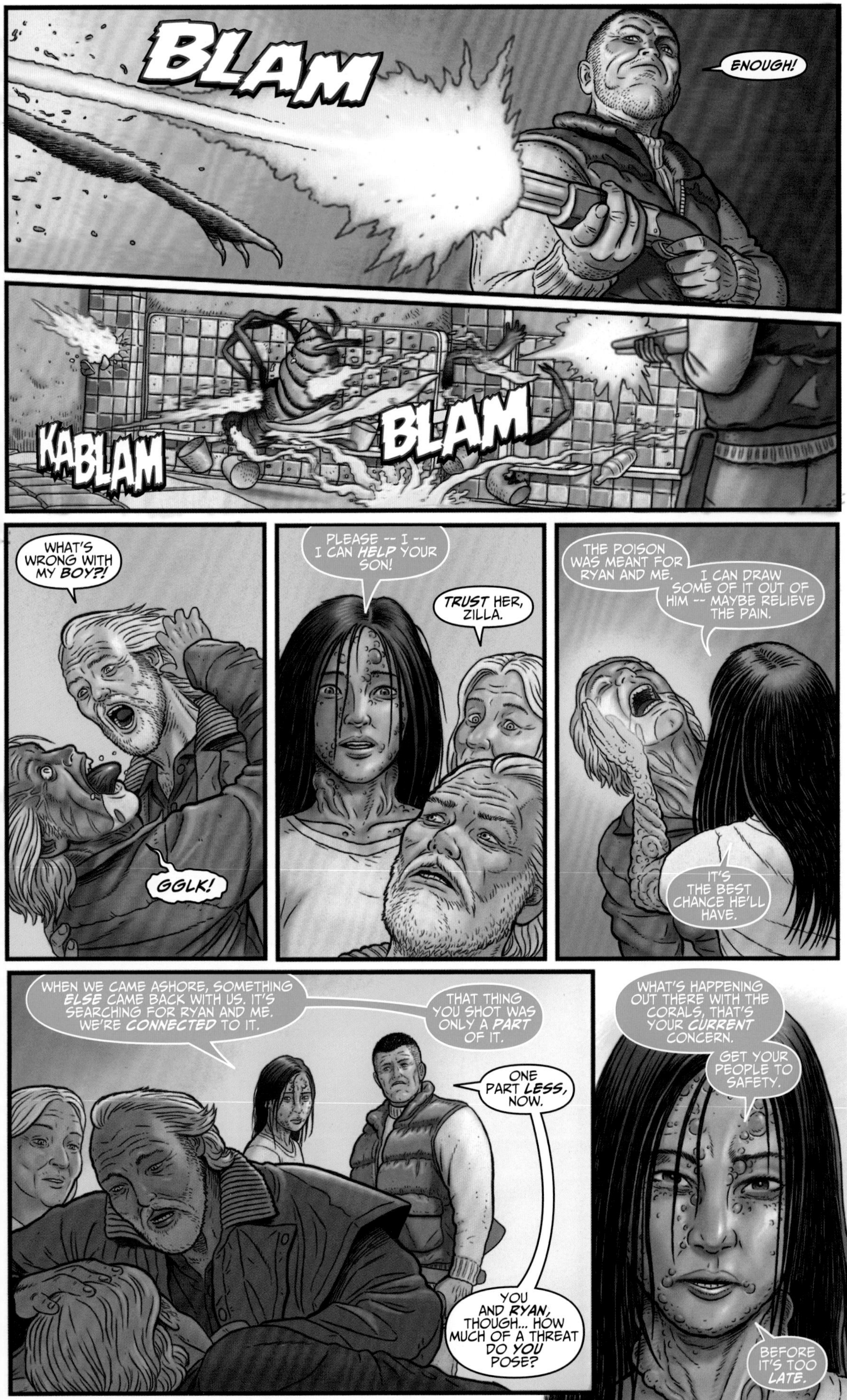
BLAM
ENOUGH!
KABLAM
BLAM
WHAT'S WRONG WITH MY BOY?!
GGLK!
PLEASE -- I -- I CAN HELP YOUR SON!
TRUST HER, ZILLA.
THE POISON WAS MEANT FOR RYAN AND ME.
I CAN DRAW SOME OF IT OUT OF HIM -- MAYBE RELIEVE THE PAIN.
IT'S THE BEST CHANCE HE'LL HAVE.
WHEN WE CAME ASHORE, SOMETHING ELSE CAME BACK WITH US. IT'S SEARCHING FOR RYAN AND ME. WE'RE CONNECTED TO IT.
THAT THING YOU SHOT WAS ONLY A PART OF IT.
ONE PART LESS, NOW.
YOU AND RYAN, THOUGH... HOW MUCH OF A THREAT DO YOU POSE?
WHAT'S HAPPENING OUT THERE WITH THE CORALS, THAT'S YOUR CURRENT CONCERN.
GET YOUR PEOPLE TO SAFETY.
BEFORE IT'S TOO LATE.

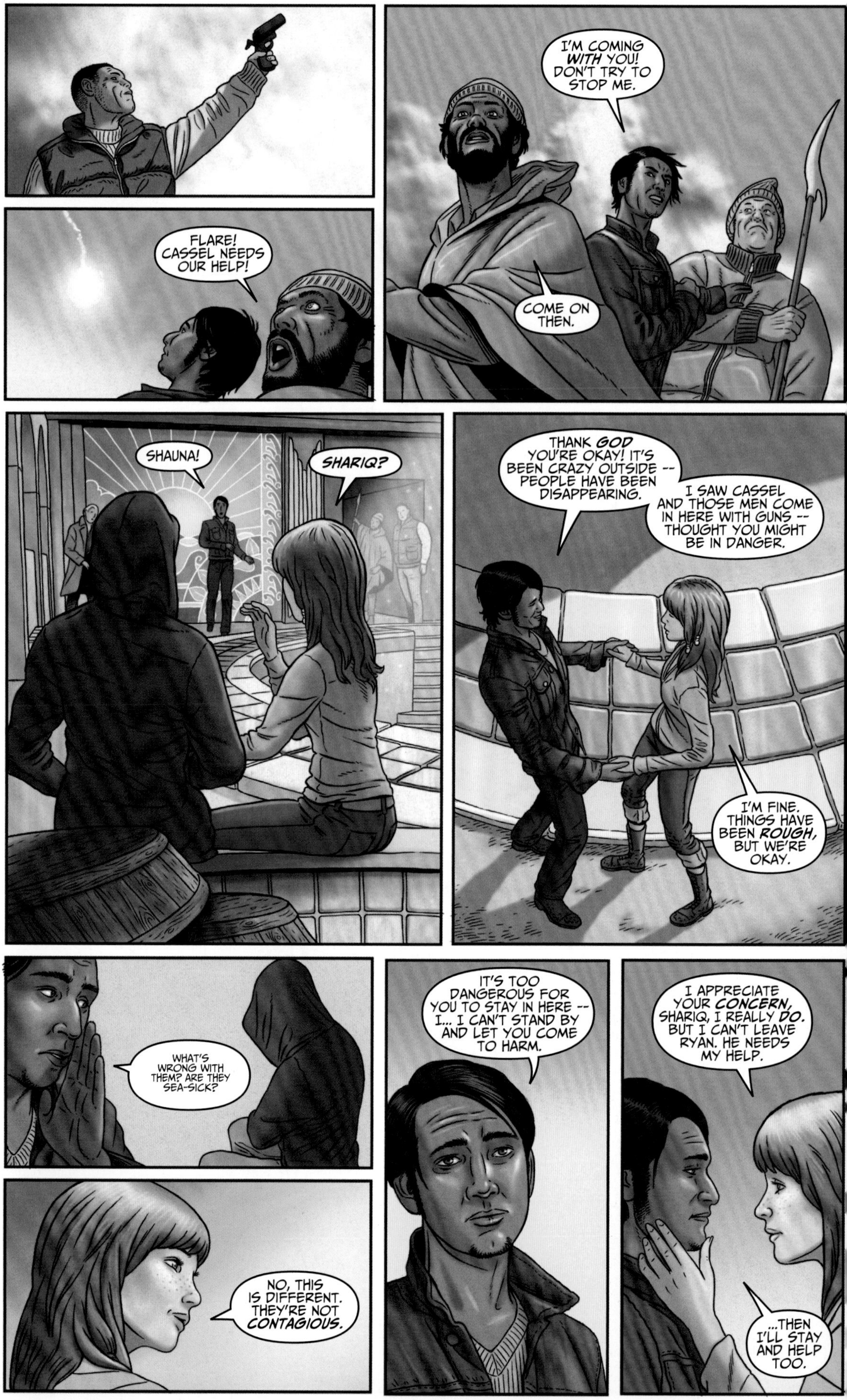
FLARE! CASSEL NEEDS OUR HELP!
I'M COMING WITH YOU! DON'T TRY TO STOP ME.
COME ON THEN.
SHAUNA!
SHARIQ?
THANK GOD YOU'RE OKAY! IT'S BEEN CRAZY OUTSIDE -- PEOPLE HAVE BEEN DISAPPEARING.
I SAW CASSEL AND THOSE MEN COME IN HERE WITH GUNS -- THOUGHT YOU MIGHT BE IN DANGER.
I'M FINE. THINGS HAVE BEEN ROUGH, BUT WE'RE OKAY.
WHAT'S WRONG WITH THEM? ARE THEY SEA-SICK?
NO, THIS IS DIFFERENT. THEY'RE NOT CONTAGIOUS.
IT'S TOO DANGEROUS FOR YOU TO STAY IN HERE -- I... I CAN'T STAND BY AND LET YOU COME TO HARM.
I APPRECIATE YOUR CONCERN, SHARIQ, I REALLY DO. BUT I CAN'T LEAVE RYAN. HE NEEDS MY HELP.
...THEN I'LL STAY AND HELP TOO.

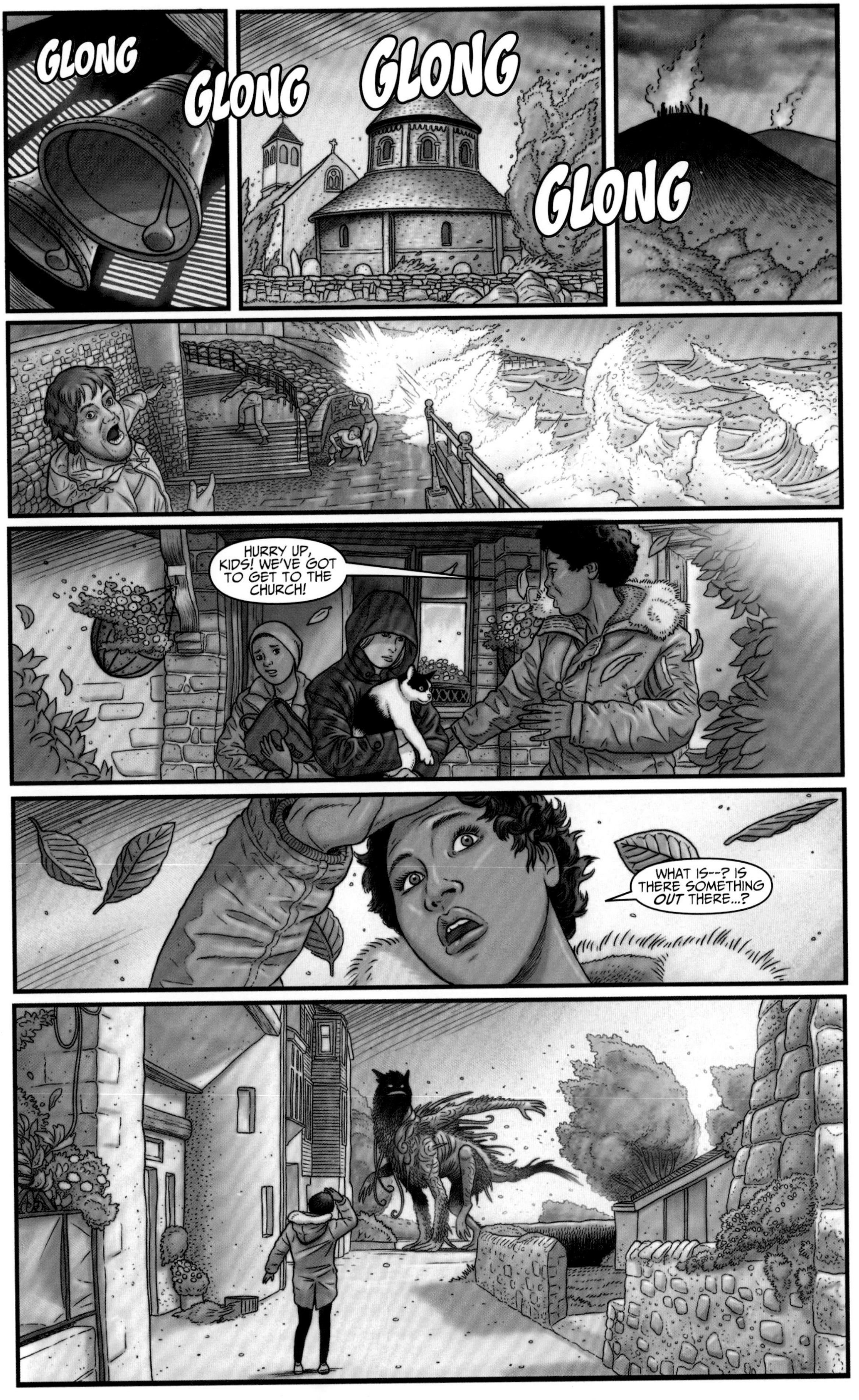
GLONG
GLONG
GLONG
GLONG
HURRY UP, KIDS! WE'VE GOT TO GET TO THE CHURCH!
WHAT IS--? IS THERE SOMETHING *OUT* THERE...?

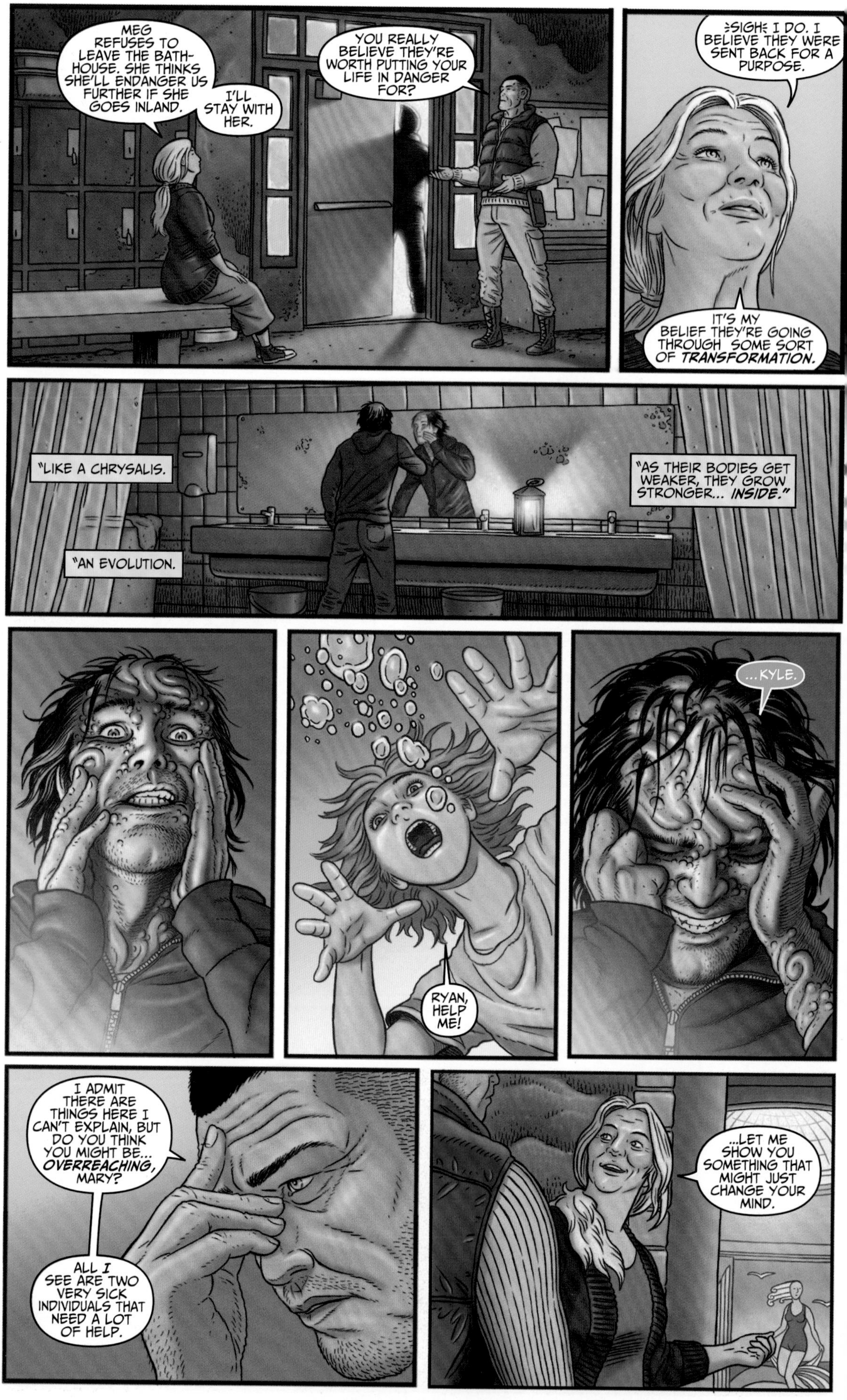
MEG REFUSES TO LEAVE THE BATH-HOUSE. SHE THINKS SHE'LL ENDANGER US FURTHER IF SHE GOES INLAND.
I'LL STAY WITH HER.
YOU REALLY BELIEVE THEY'RE WORTH PUTTING YOUR LIFE IN DANGER FOR?
SIGH I DO. I BELIEVE THEY WERE SENT BACK FOR A PURPOSE.
IT'S MY BELIEF THEY'RE GOING THROUGH SOME SORT OF *TRANSFORMATION.*
"LIKE A CHRYSALIS.
"AN EVOLUTION.
"AS THEIR BODIES GET WEAKER, THEY GROW STRONGER... *INSIDE.*"
RYAN, HELP ME!
...KYLE.
I ADMIT THERE ARE THINGS HERE I CAN'T EXPLAIN, BUT DO YOU THINK YOU MIGHT BE... *OVERREACHING,* MARY?
ALL *I* SEE ARE TWO VERY SICK INDIVIDUALS THAT NEED A LOT OF HELP.
...LET ME SHOW YOU SOMETHING THAT MIGHT JUST CHANGE YOUR MIND.

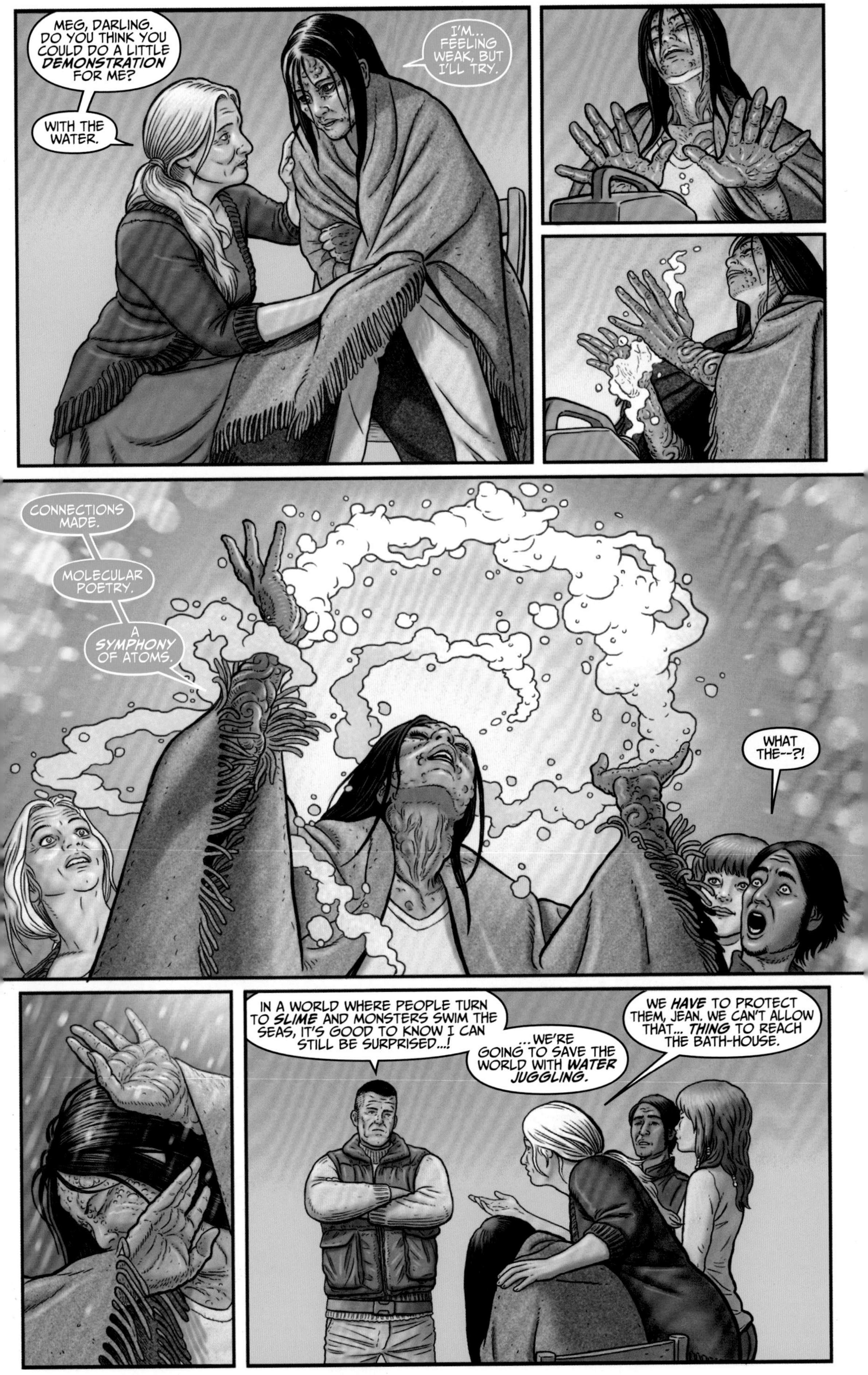
MEG, DARLING. DO YOU THINK YOU COULD DO A LITTLE *DEMONSTRATION* FOR ME?
WITH THE WATER.
I'M... FEELING WEAK, BUT I'LL TRY.
CONNECTIONS MADE.
MOLECULAR POETRY.
A *SYMPHONY* OF ATOMS.
WHAT THE--?!
IN A WORLD WHERE PEOPLE TURN TO *SLIME* AND MONSTERS SWIM THE SEAS, IT'S GOOD TO KNOW I CAN STILL BE SURPRISED...!
...WE'RE GOING TO SAVE THE WORLD WITH *WATER JUGGLING.*
WE *HAVE* TO PROTECT THEM, JEAN. WE CAN'T ALLOW THAT... *THING* TO REACH THE BATH-HOUSE.

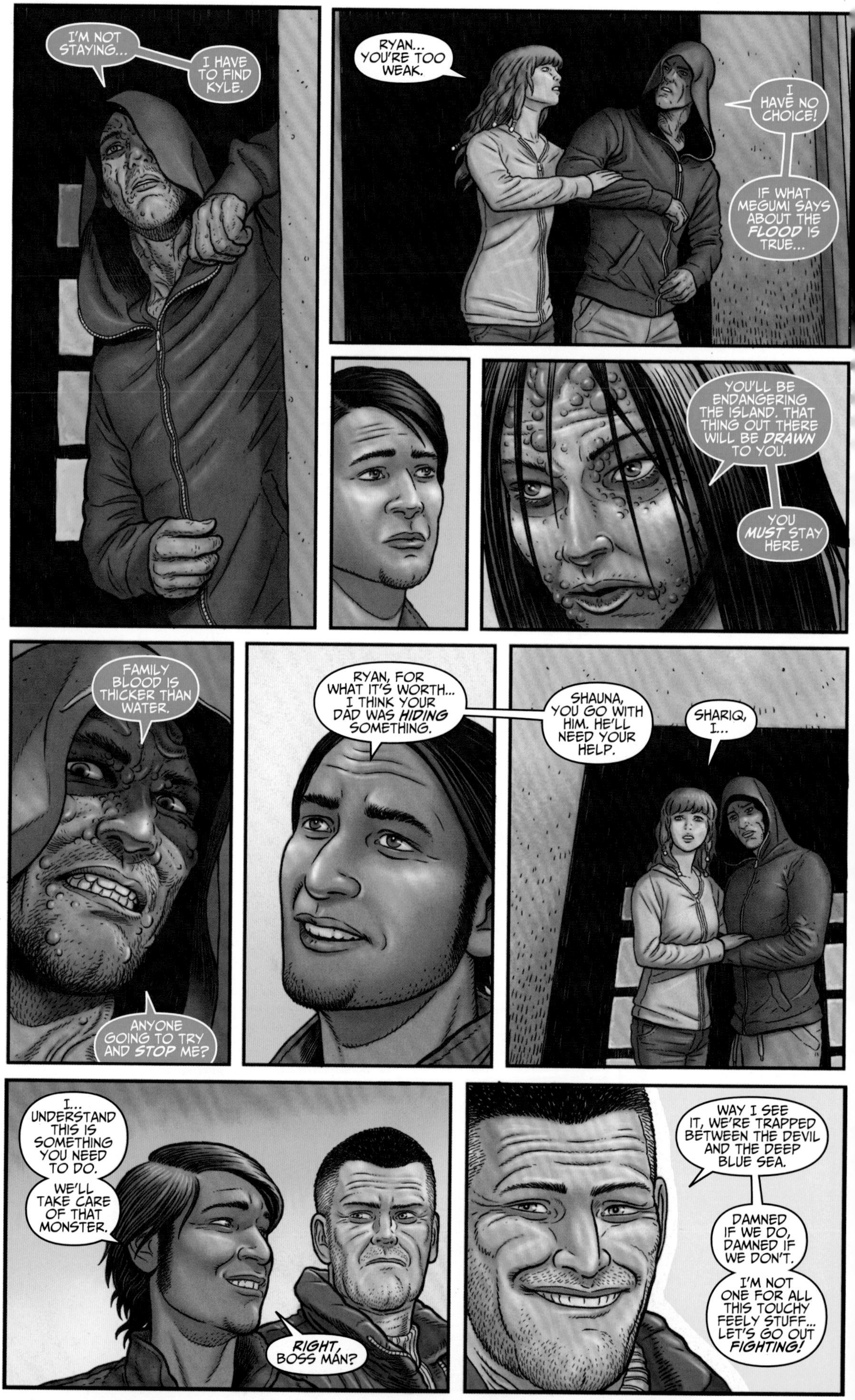
I'M NOT STAYING...
I HAVE TO FIND KYLE.
RYAN... YOU'RE TOO WEAK.
I HAVE NO CHOICE!
IF WHAT MEGUMI SAYS ABOUT THE *FLOOD* IS TRUE...
YOU'LL BE ENDANGERING THE ISLAND. THAT THING OUT THERE WILL BE *DRAWN* TO YOU.
YOU *MUST* STAY HERE.
FAMILY BLOOD IS THICKER THAN WATER.
ANYONE GOING TO TRY AND *STOP* ME?
RYAN, FOR WHAT IT'S WORTH... I THINK YOUR DAD WAS *HIDING* SOMETHING.
SHAUNA, YOU GO WITH HIM. HE'LL NEED YOUR HELP.
SHARIQ, I...
I... UNDERSTAND THIS IS SOMETHING YOU NEED TO DO.
WE'LL TAKE CARE OF THAT MONSTER.
RIGHT, BOSS MAN?
WAY I SEE IT, WE'RE TRAPPED BETWEEN THE DEVIL AND THE DEEP BLUE SEA.
DAMNED IF WE DO, DAMNED IF WE DON'T.
I'M NOT ONE FOR ALL THIS TOUCHY FEELY STUFF... LET'S GO OUT *FIGHTING!*

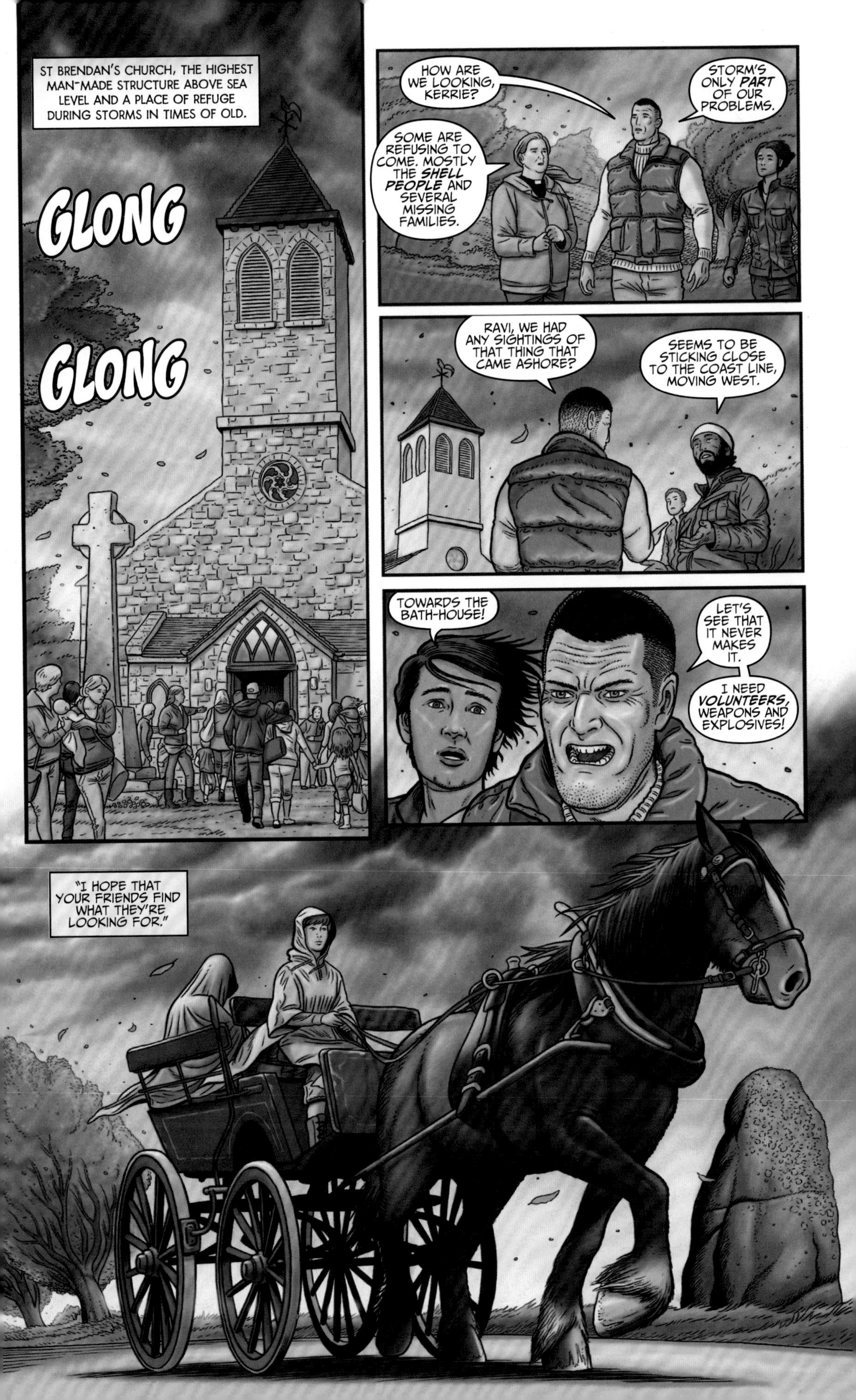
ST BRENDAN'S CHURCH, THE HIGHEST MAN-MADE STRUCTURE ABOVE SEA LEVEL AND A PLACE OF REFUGE DURING STORMS IN TIMES OF OLD.
GLONG
GLONG
HOW ARE WE LOOKING, KERRIE?
STORM'S ONLY PART OF OUR PROBLEMS.
SOME ARE REFUSING TO COME. MOSTLY THE SHELL PEOPLE AND SEVERAL MISSING FAMILIES.
RAVI, WE HAD ANY SIGHTINGS OF THAT THING THAT CAME ASHORE?
SEEMS TO BE STICKING CLOSE TO THE COAST LINE, MOVING WEST.
TOWARDS THE BATH-HOUSE!
LET'S SEE THAT IT NEVER MAKES IT.
I NEED VOLUNTEERS, WEAPONS AND EXPLOSIVES!
"I HOPE THAT YOUR FRIENDS FIND WHAT THEY'RE LOOKING FOR."

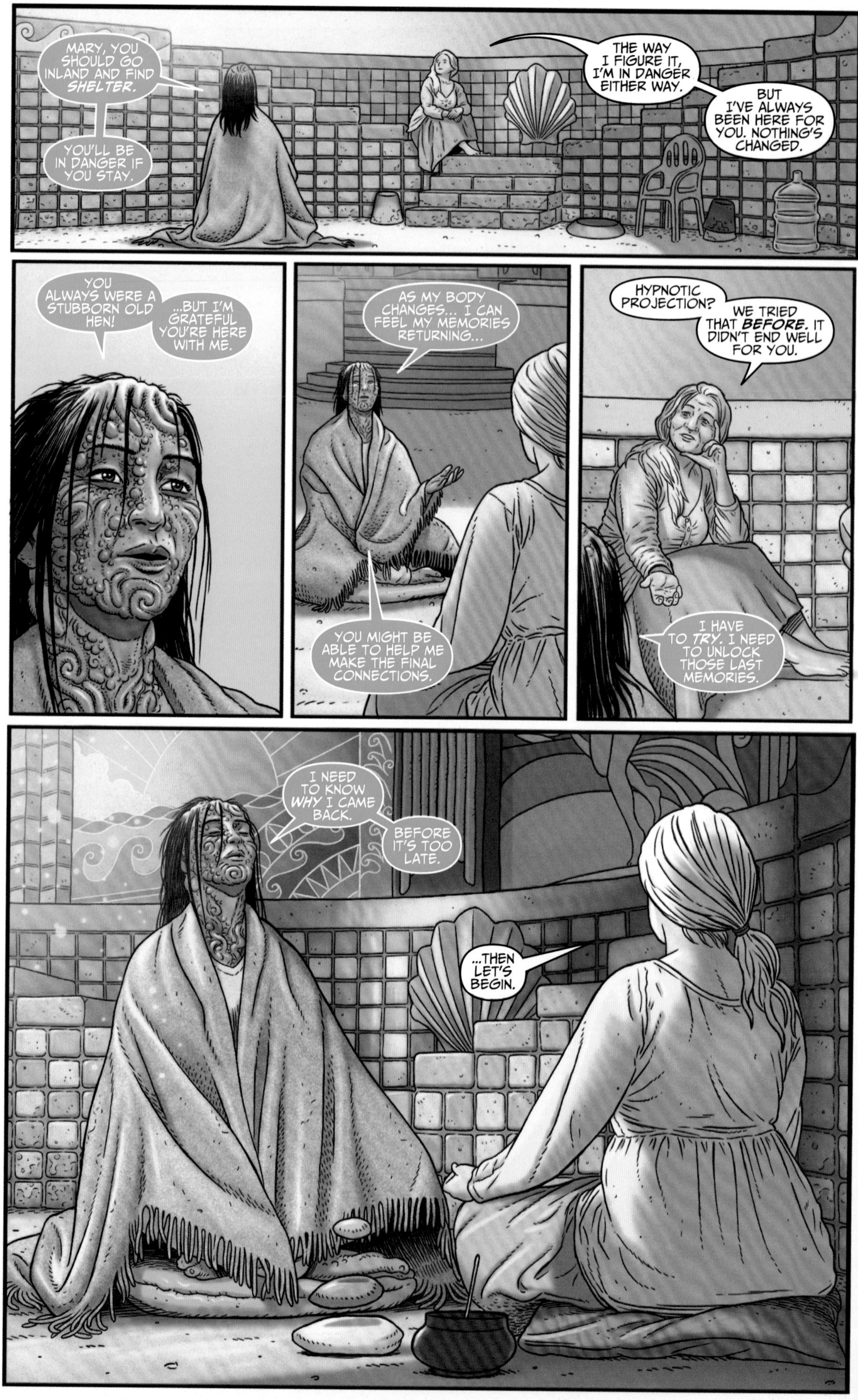
MARY, YOU SHOULD GO INLAND AND FIND *SHELTER.*
YOU'LL BE IN DANGER IF YOU STAY.
THE WAY I FIGURE IT, I'M IN DANGER EITHER WAY.
BUT I'VE ALWAYS BEEN HERE FOR YOU. NOTHING'S CHANGED.
YOU ALWAYS WERE A STUBBORN OLD HEN!
...BUT I'M GRATEFUL YOU'RE HERE WITH ME.
AS MY BODY CHANGES... I CAN FEEL MY MEMORIES RETURNING...
YOU MIGHT BE ABLE TO HELP ME MAKE THE FINAL CONNECTIONS.
HYPNOTIC PROJECTION?
WE TRIED THAT *BEFORE.* IT DIDN'T END WELL FOR YOU.
I HAVE TO *TRY.* I NEED TO UNLOCK THOSE LAST MEMORIES.
I NEED TO KNOW *WHY* I CAME BACK.
BEFORE IT'S TOO LATE.
...THEN LET'S BEGIN.

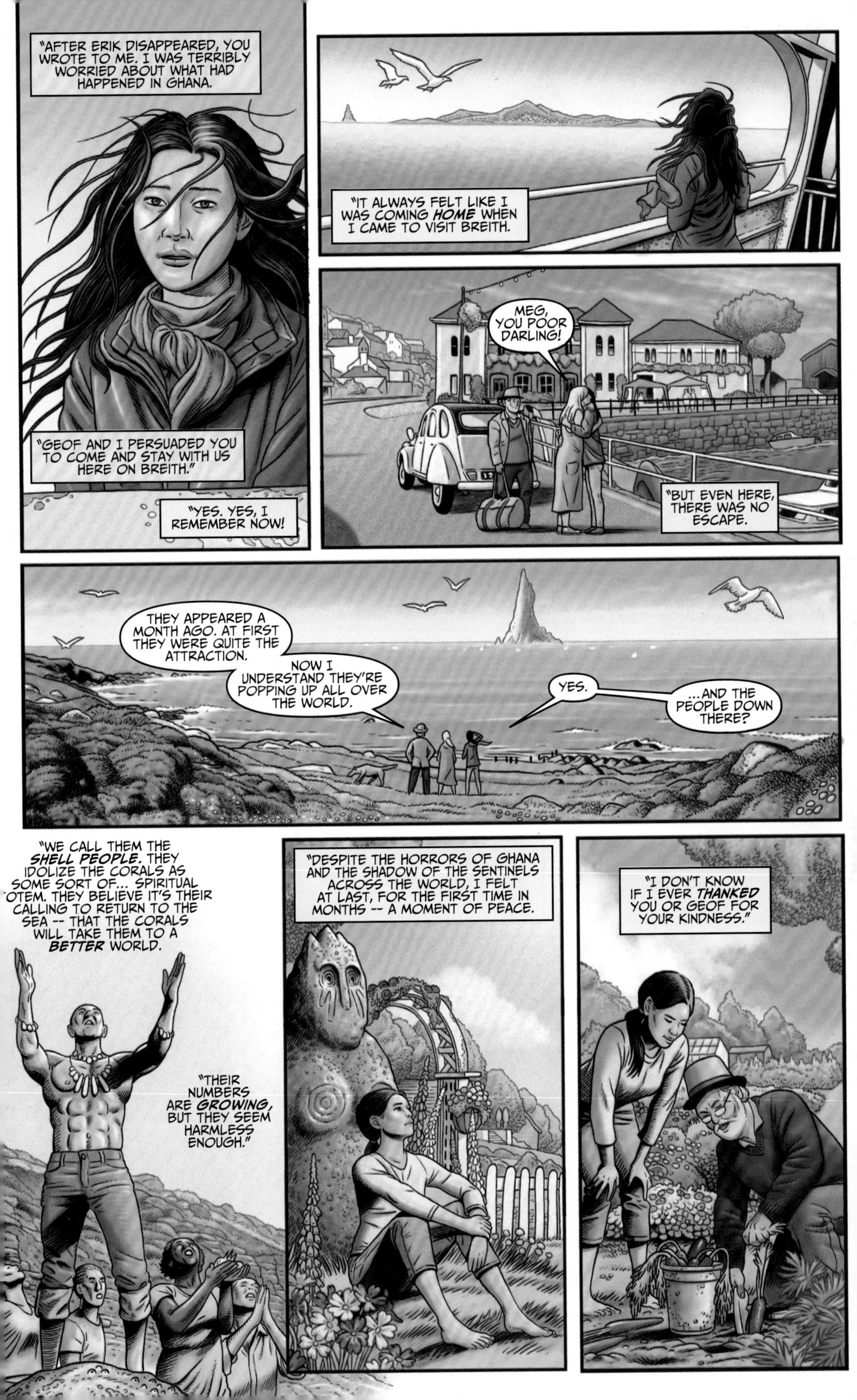
"AFTER ERIK DISAPPEARED, YOU WROTE TO ME. I WAS TERRIBLY WORRIED ABOUT WHAT HAD HAPPENED IN GHANA.
"GEOF AND I PERSUADED YOU TO COME AND STAY WITH US HERE ON BREITH."
"YES. YES, I REMEMBER NOW!
"IT ALWAYS FELT LIKE I WAS COMING HOME WHEN I CAME TO VISIT BREITH.
MEG, YOU POOR DARLING!
"BUT EVEN HERE, THERE WAS NO ESCAPE.
THEY APPEARED A MONTH AGO. AT FIRST THEY WERE QUITE THE ATTRACTION.
NOW I UNDERSTAND THEY'RE POPPING UP ALL OVER THE WORLD.
YES.
...AND THE PEOPLE DOWN THERE?
"WE CALL THEM THE SHELL PEOPLE. THEY IDOLIZE THE CORALS AS SOME SORT OF... SPIRITUAL OTEM. THEY BELIEVE IT'S THEIR CALLING TO RETURN TO THE SEA -- THAT THE CORALS WILL TAKE THEM TO A BETTER WORLD.
"THEIR NUMBERS ARE GROWING, BUT THEY SEEM HARMLESS ENOUGH."
"DESPITE THE HORRORS OF GHANA AND THE SHADOW OF THE SENTINELS ACROSS THE WORLD, I FELT AT LAST, FOR THE FIRST TIME IN MONTHS -- A MOMENT OF PEACE.
"I DON'T KNOW IF I EVER THANKED YOU OR GEOF FOR YOUR KINDNESS."

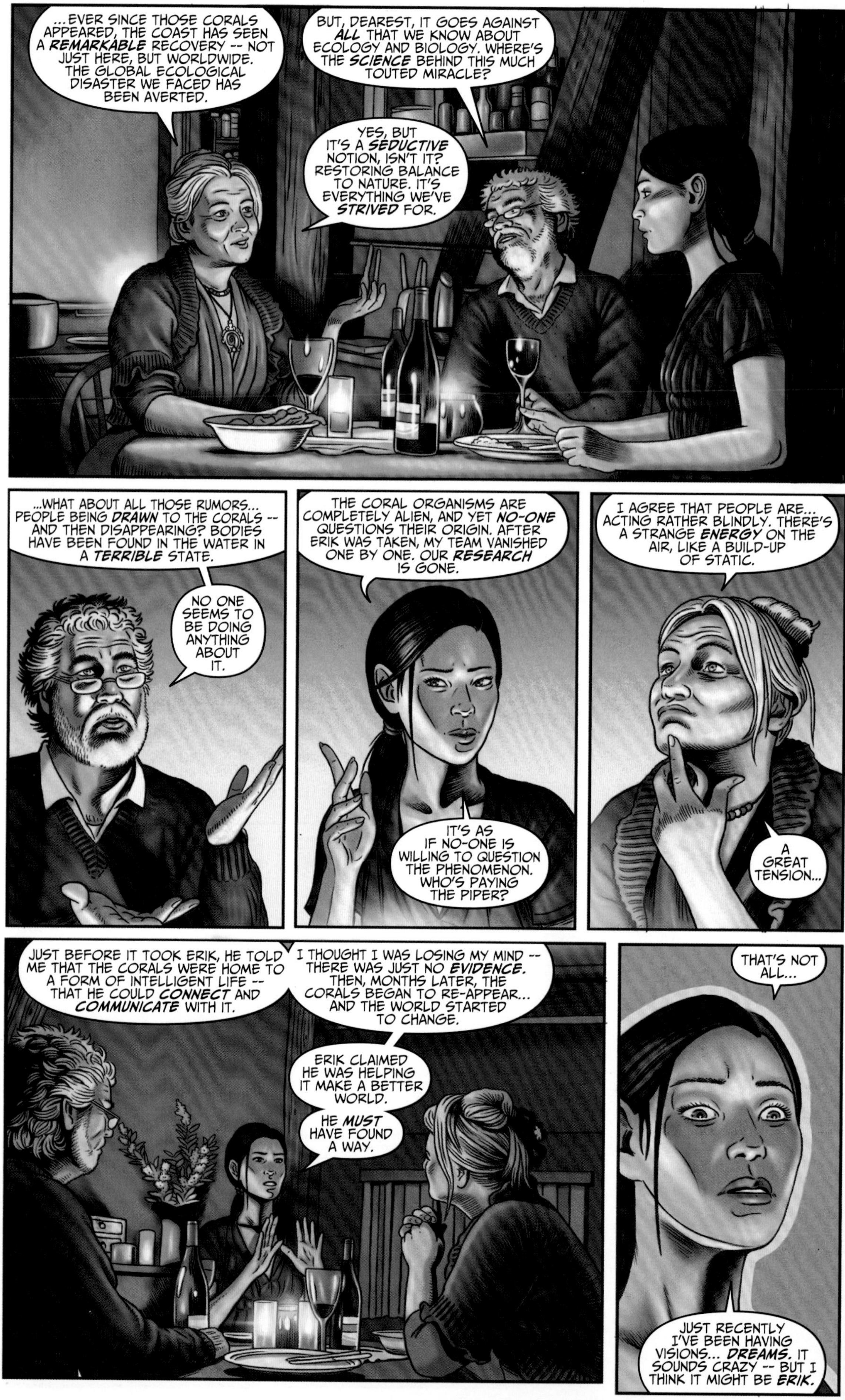
...EVER SINCE THOSE CORALS APPEARED, THE COAST HAS SEEN A REMARKABLE RECOVERY -- NOT JUST HERE, BUT WORLDWIDE. THE GLOBAL ECOLOGICAL DISASTER WE FACED HAS BEEN AVERTED.
BUT, DEAREST, IT GOES AGAINST ALL THAT WE KNOW ABOUT ECOLOGY AND BIOLOGY. WHERE'S THE SCIENCE BEHIND THIS MUCH TOUTED MIRACLE?
YES, BUT IT'S A SEDUCTIVE NOTION, ISN'T IT? RESTORING BALANCE TO NATURE. IT'S EVERYTHING WE'VE STRIVED FOR.
...WHAT ABOUT ALL THOSE RUMORS... PEOPLE BEING DRAWN TO THE CORALS -- AND THEN DISAPPEARING? BODIES HAVE BEEN FOUND IN THE WATER IN A TERRIBLE STATE.
NO ONE SEEMS TO BE DOING ANYTHING ABOUT IT.
THE CORAL ORGANISMS ARE COMPLETELY ALIEN, AND YET NO-ONE QUESTIONS THEIR ORIGIN. AFTER ERIK WAS TAKEN, MY TEAM VANISHED ONE BY ONE. OUR RESEARCH IS GONE.
IT'S AS IF NO-ONE IS WILLING TO QUESTION THE PHENOMENON. WHO'S PAYING THE PIPER?
I AGREE THAT PEOPLE ARE... ACTING RATHER BLINDLY. THERE'S A STRANGE ENERGY ON THE AIR, LIKE A BUILD-UP OF STATIC.
A GREAT TENSION...
JUST BEFORE IT TOOK ERIK, HE TOLD ME THAT THE CORALS WERE HOME TO A FORM OF INTELLIGENT LIFE -- THAT HE COULD CONNECT AND COMMUNICATE WITH IT.
I THOUGHT I WAS LOSING MY MIND -- THERE WAS JUST NO EVIDENCE. THEN, MONTHS LATER, THE CORALS BEGAN TO RE-APPEAR... AND THE WORLD STARTED TO CHANGE.
ERIK CLAIMED HE WAS HELPING IT MAKE A BETTER WORLD.
HE MUST HAVE FOUND A WAY.
THAT'S NOT ALL...
JUST RECENTLY I'VE BEEN HAVING VISIONS... DREAMS. IT SOUNDS CRAZY -- BUT I THINK IT MIGHT BE ERIK.

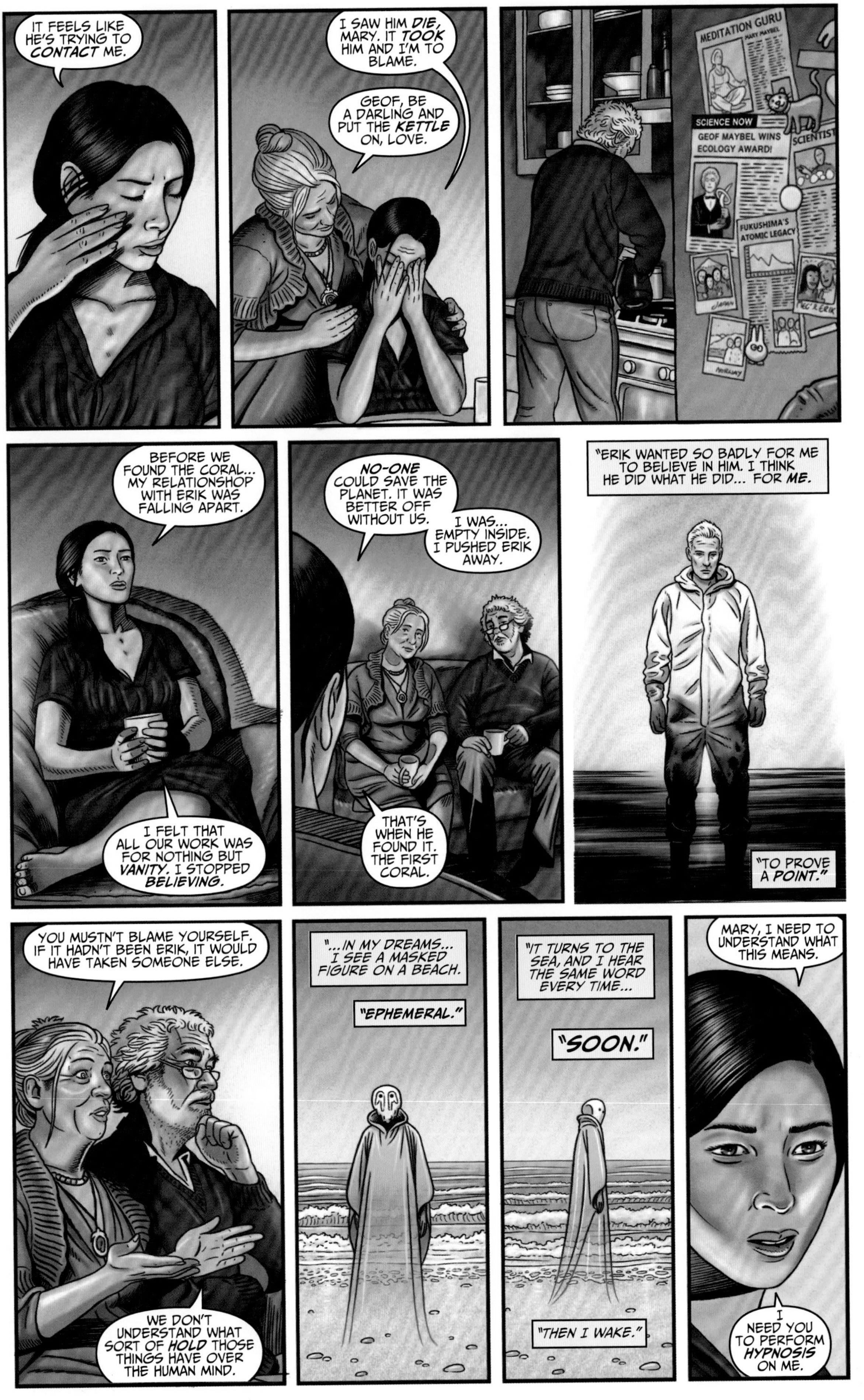
IT FEELS LIKE HE'S TRYING TO CONTACT ME.
I SAW HIM DIE, MARY. IT TOOK HIM AND I'M TO BLAME.
GEOF, BE A DARLING AND PUT THE KETTLE ON, LOVE.
MEDITATION GURU
MARY MAYBEL
SCIENCE NOW
GEOF MAYBEL WINS ECOLOGY AWARD!
SCIENTIST
FUKUSHIMA'S ATOMIC LEGACY
BEFORE WE FOUND THE CORAL... MY RELATIONSHOP WITH ERIK WAS FALLING APART.
I FELT THAT ALL OUR WORK WAS FOR NOTHING BUT VANITY. I STOPPED BELIEVING.
NO-ONE COULD SAVE THE PLANET. IT WAS BETTER OFF WITHOUT US.
I WAS... EMPTY INSIDE. I PUSHED ERIK AWAY.
THAT'S WHEN HE FOUND IT. THE FIRST CORAL.
"ERIK WANTED SO BADLY FOR ME TO BELIEVE IN HIM. I THINK HE DID WHAT HE DID... FOR ME.
"TO PROVE A POINT."
YOU MUSTN'T BLAME YOURSELF. IF IT HADN'T BEEN ERIK, IT WOULD HAVE TAKEN SOMEONE ELSE.
WE DON'T UNDERSTAND WHAT SORT OF HOLD THOSE THINGS HAVE OVER THE HUMAN MIND.
"...IN MY DREAMS... I SEE A MASKED FIGURE ON A BEACH.
"EPHEMERAL."
"IT TURNS TO THE SEA, AND I HEAR THE SAME WORD EVERY TIME...
"SOON."
"THEN I WAKE."
MARY, I NEED TO UNDERSTAND WHAT THIS MEANS.
I NEED YOU TO PERFORM HYPNOSIS ON ME.

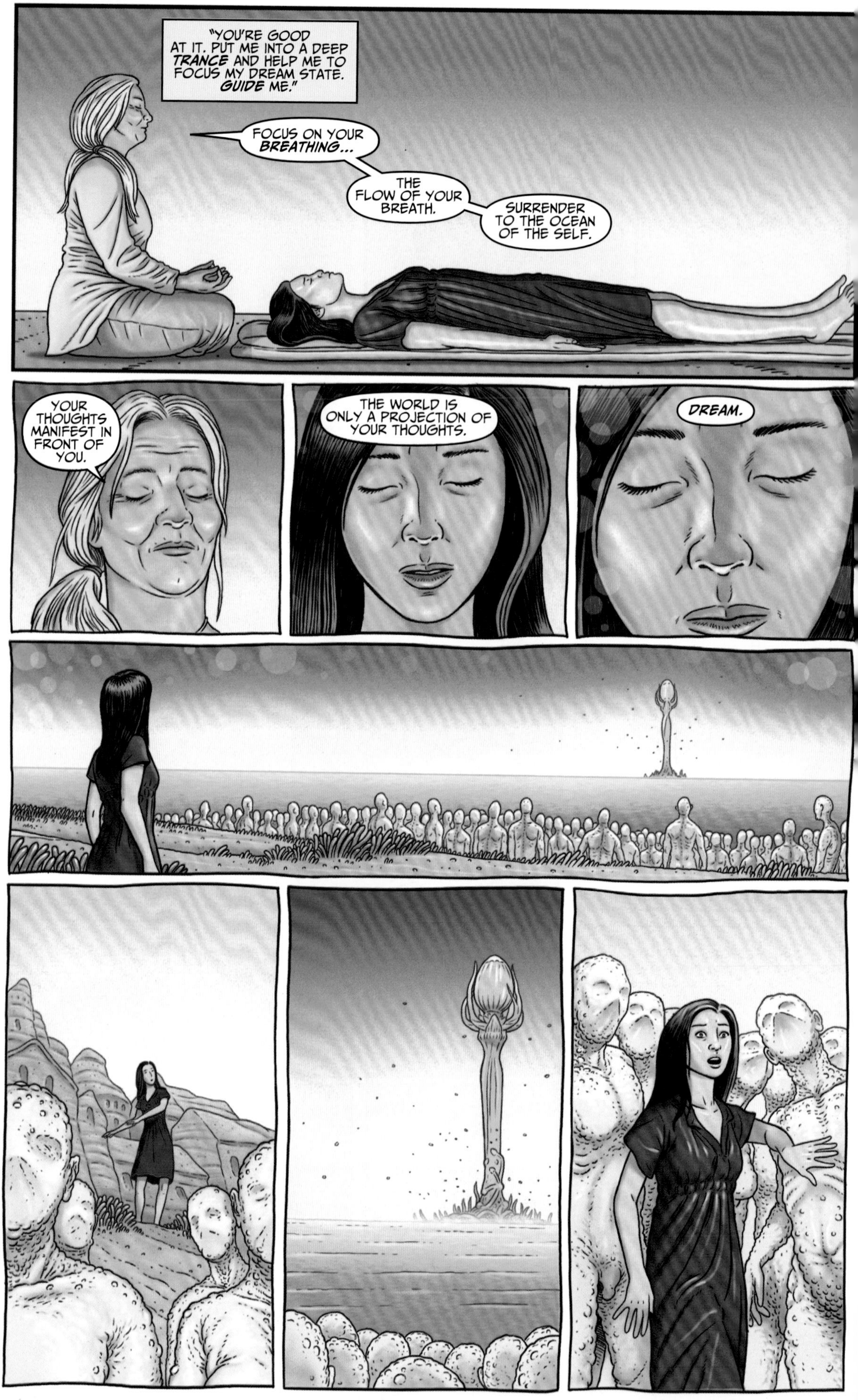
"YOU'RE GOOD AT IT. PUT ME INTO A DEEP *TRANCE* AND HELP ME TO FOCUS MY DREAM STATE. *GUIDE* ME."
FOCUS ON YOUR *BREATHING...*
THE FLOW OF YOUR BREATH.
SURRENDER TO THE OCEAN OF THE SELF.
YOUR THOUGHTS MANIFEST IN FRONT OF YOU.
THE WORLD IS ONLY A PROJECTION OF YOUR THOUGHTS.
DREAM.

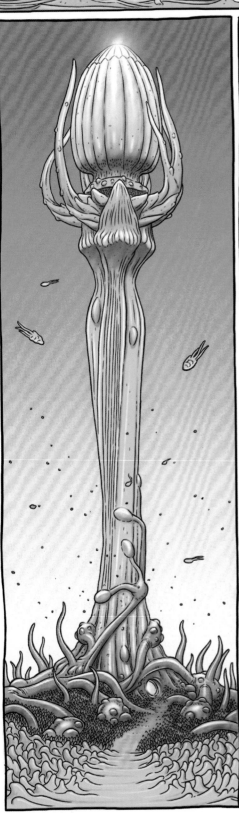

DAD?

MY PARENTS. WHEN I WAS A BABY.

ERIK... WINTERTIME IN PARIS.

MY MEMORIES...

≥GASP≤

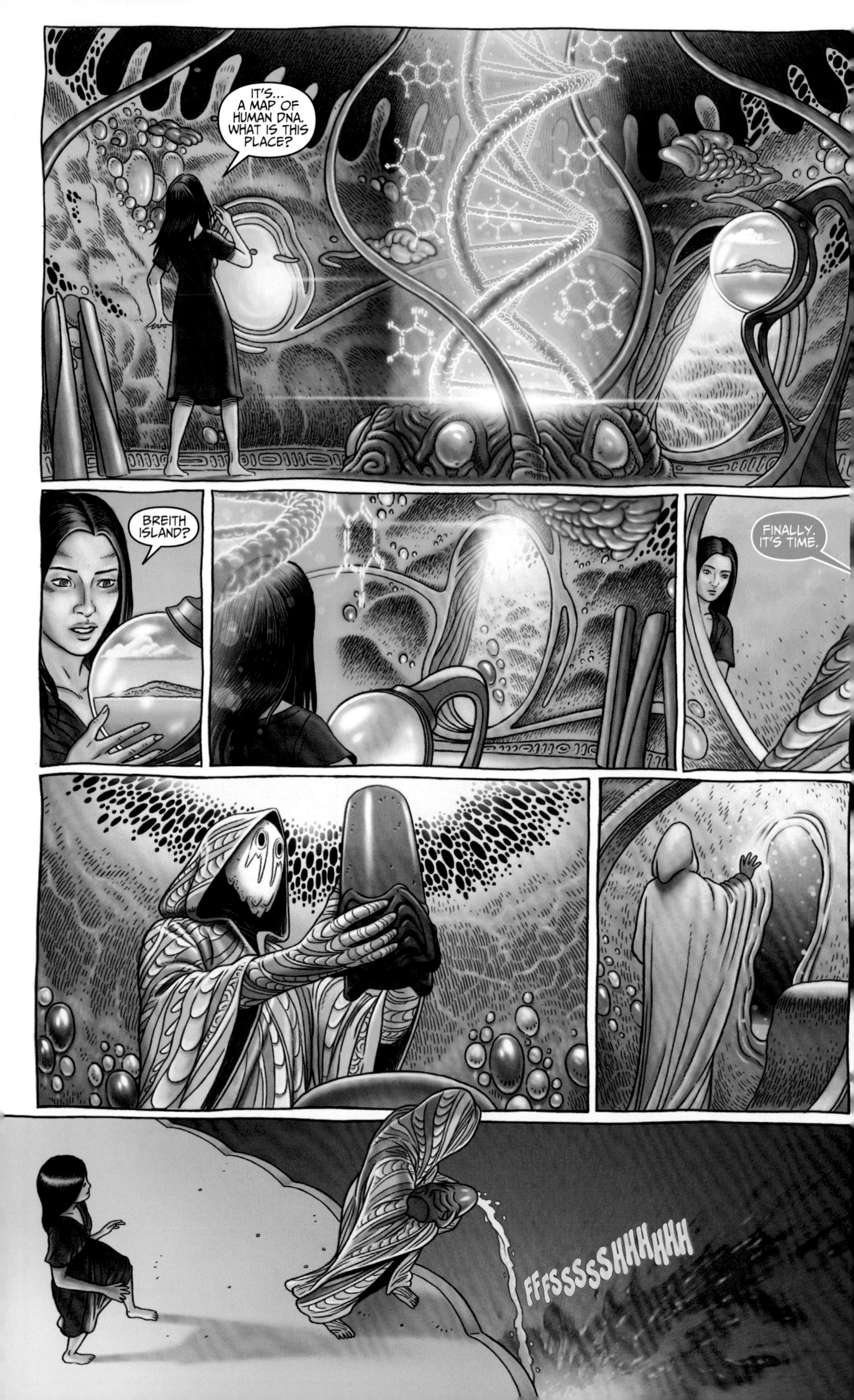
IT'S... A MAP OF HUMAN DNA. WHAT IS THIS PLACE?
BREITH ISLAND?
FINALLY. IT'S TIME.
FFFSSSSSHHHHHH

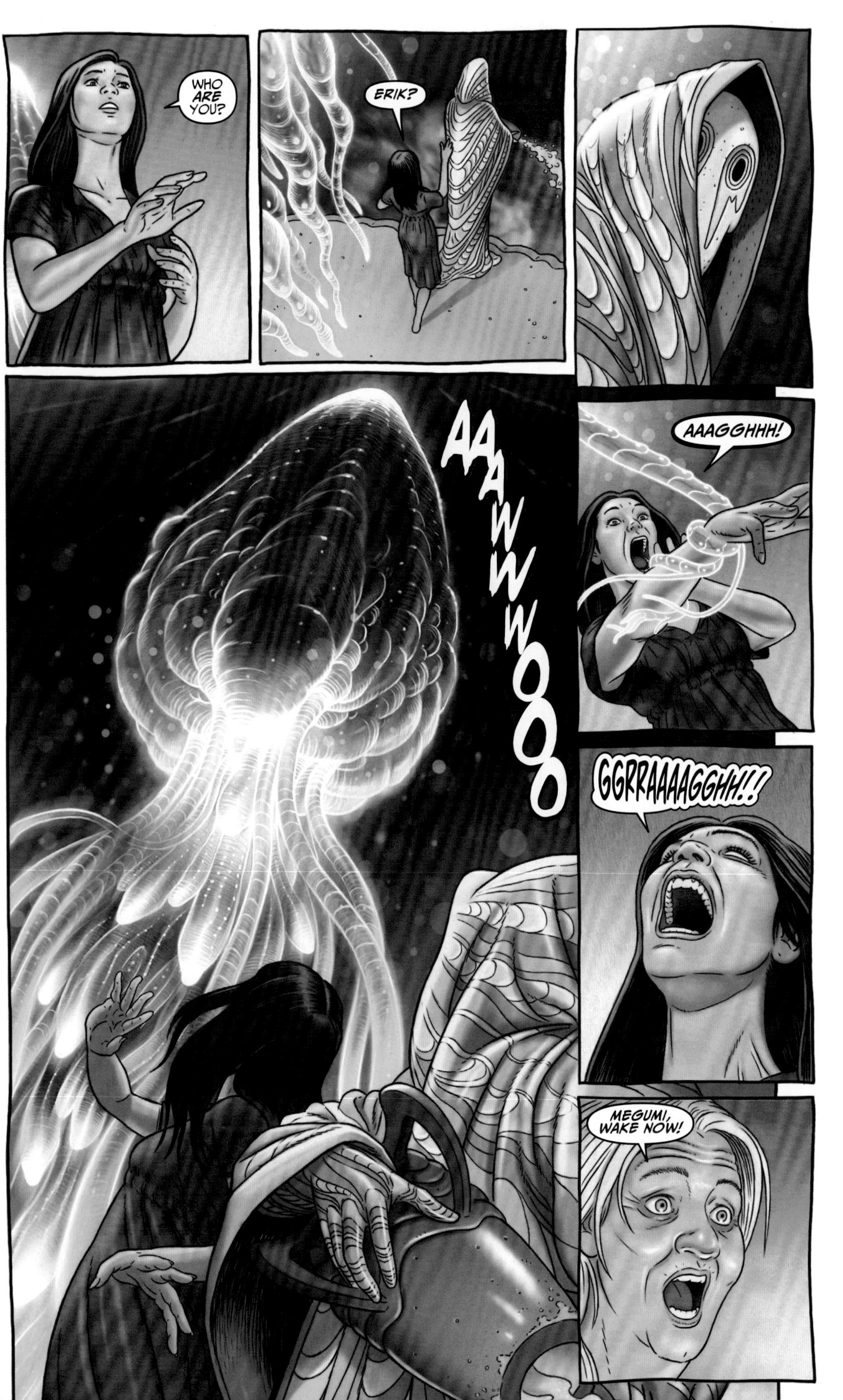
WHO ARE YOU?
ERIK?
AAAWWWOOO
AAAGGHHH!
GGRRAAAAGGHH!!
MEGUMI, WAKE NOW!

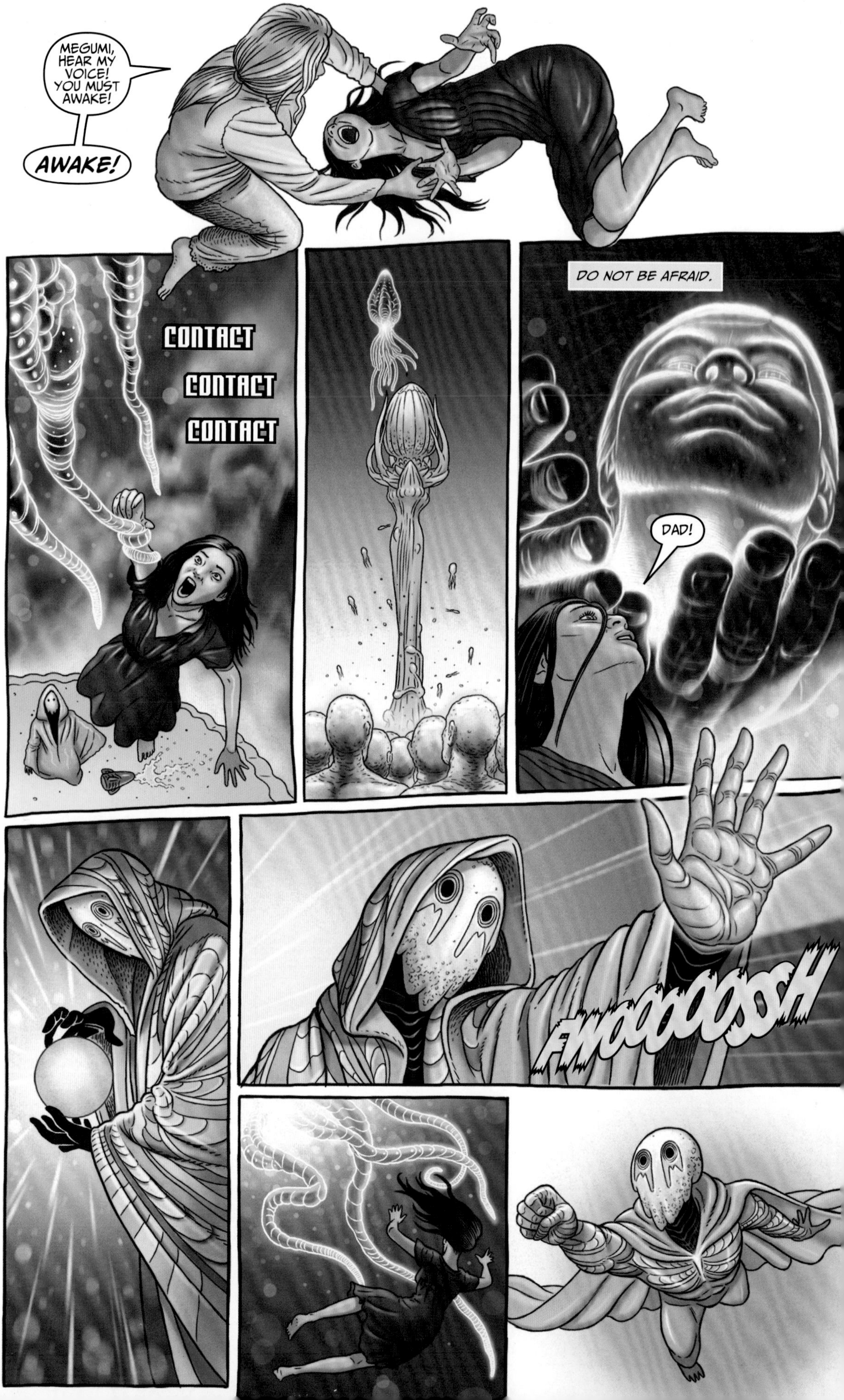
MEGUMI, HEAR MY VOICE! YOU MUST AWAKE!
AWAKE!
CONTACT
CONTACT
CONTACT
DO NOT BE AFRAID.
DAD!
FWOOOOOSSH

MY *FATHER!* TAKE ME BACK!

THAT WAS *NOT* YOUR FATHER.

IT MUST NOT FIND US HERE.

WHERE ARE WE?

INSIDE THE *CORAL.*

CONNECTED TO IT ON A BIOLOGICAL LEVEL.

AS YOU HAVE BEEN FOR SOME TIME, LIKE THE OTHERS YOU SAW.

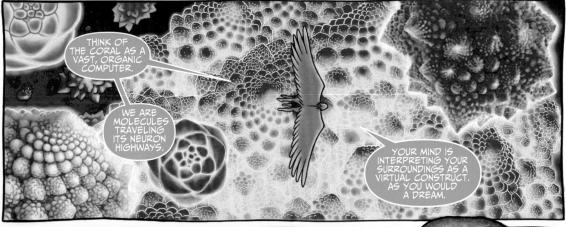

THINK OF THE CORAL AS A VAST, ORGANIC COMPUTER.

WE ARE MOLECULES TRAVELING ITS NEURON HIGHWAYS.

YOUR MIND IS INTERPRETING YOUR SURROUNDINGS AS A VIRTUAL CONSTRUCT. AS YOU WOULD A DREAM.

THIS AREA IS *DYING.* WE SHOULD BE ABLE TO HIDE HERE.

DYING?

WE DO NOT HAVE MUCH TIME. IT HAS RELEASED ITS *VIRUS* INTO THE WORLD.

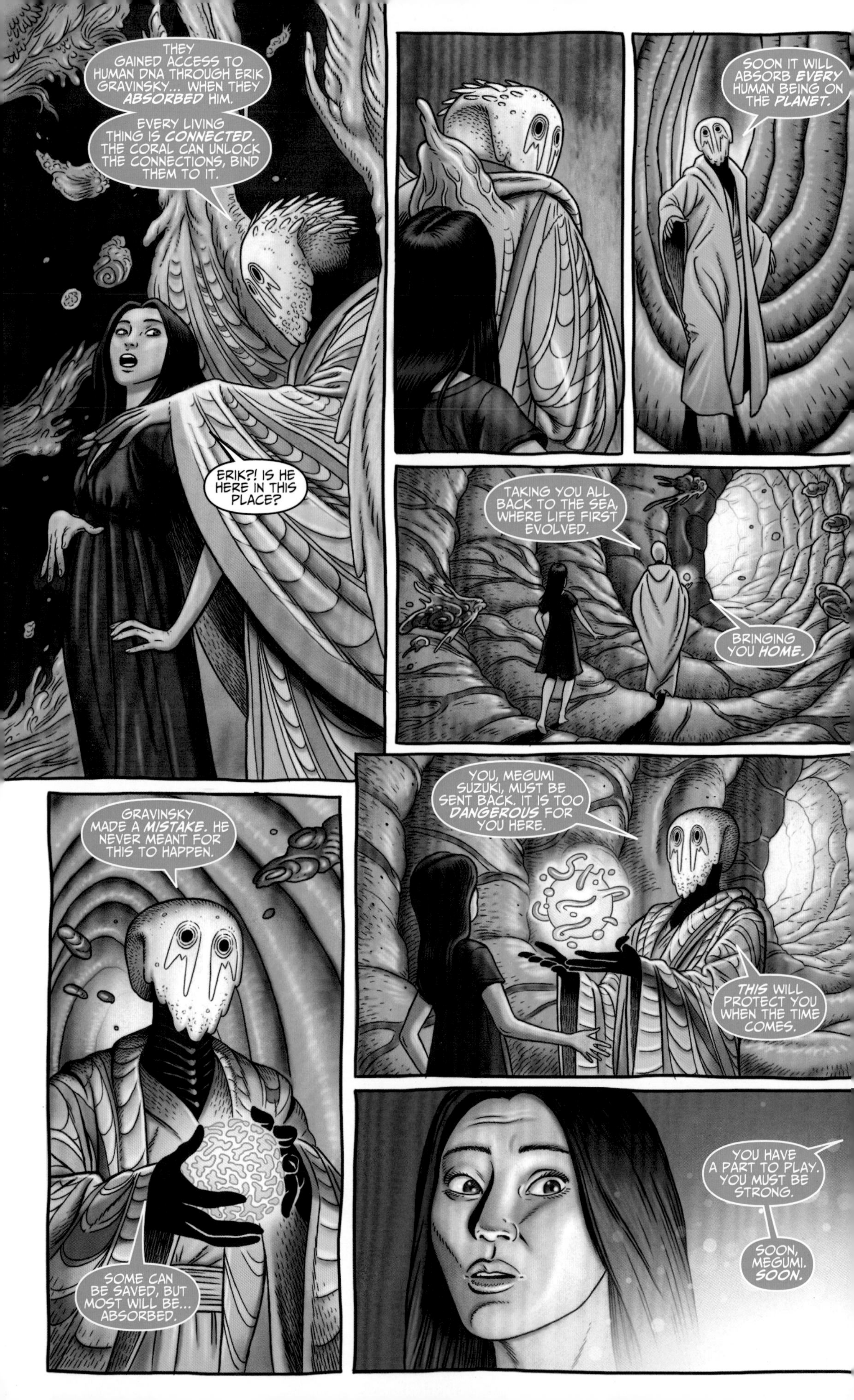
THEY GAINED ACCESS TO HUMAN DNA THROUGH ERIK GRAVINSKY... WHEN THEY ABSORBED HIM.
EVERY LIVING THING IS CONNECTED. THE CORAL CAN UNLOCK THE CONNECTIONS, BIND THEM TO IT.
ERIK?! IS HE HERE IN THIS PLACE?
SOON IT WILL ABSORB EVERY HUMAN BEING ON THE PLANET.
TAKING YOU ALL BACK TO THE SEA, WHERE LIFE FIRST EVOLVED.
BRINGING YOU HOME.
GRAVINSKY MADE A MISTAKE. HE NEVER MEANT FOR THIS TO HAPPEN.
SOME CAN BE SAVED, BUT MOST WILL BE... ABSORBED.
YOU, MEGUMI SUZUKI, MUST BE SENT BACK. IT IS TOO DANGEROUS FOR YOU HERE.
THIS WILL PROTECT YOU WHEN THE TIME COMES.
YOU HAVE A PART TO PLAY. YOU MUST BE STRONG.
SOON, MEGUMI. SOON.

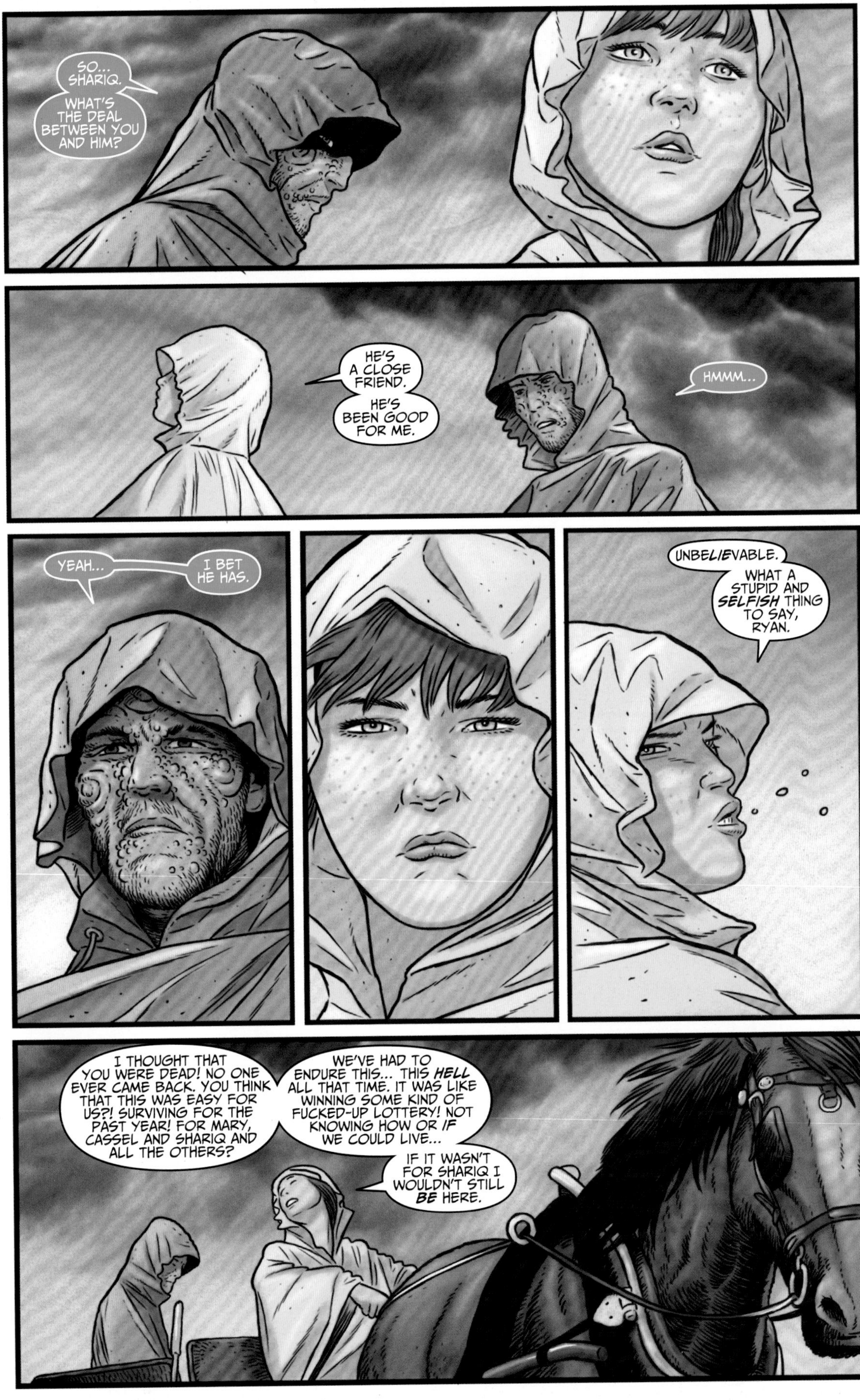
SO... SHARIQ.
WHAT'S THE DEAL BETWEEN YOU AND HIM?
HE'S A CLOSE FRIEND.
HE'S BEEN GOOD FOR ME.
HMMM...
YEAH...
I BET HE HAS.
UNBELIEVABLE.
WHAT A STUPID AND SELFISH THING TO SAY, RYAN.
I THOUGHT THAT YOU WERE DEAD! NO ONE EVER CAME BACK. YOU THINK THAT THIS WAS EASY FOR US?! SURVIVING FOR THE PAST YEAR! FOR MARY, CASSEL AND SHARIQ AND ALL THE OTHERS?
WE'VE HAD TO ENDURE THIS... THIS HELL ALL THAT TIME. IT WAS LIKE WINNING SOME KIND OF FUCKED-UP LOTTERY! NOT KNOWING HOW OR IF WE COULD LIVE...
IF IT WASN'T FOR SHARIQ I WOULDN'T STILL BE HERE.

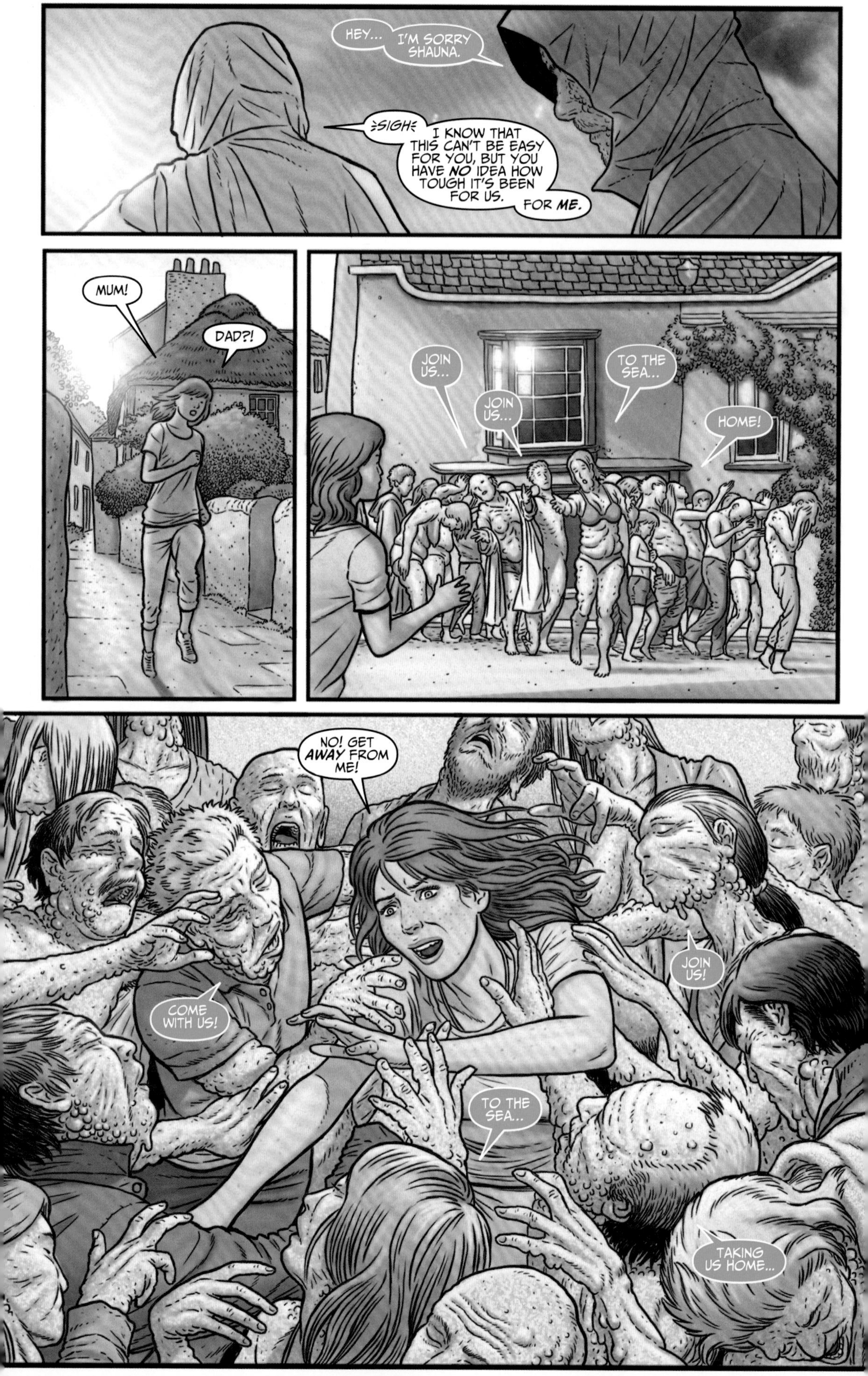

HEY...
I'M SORRY SHAUNA.
≈SIGH≈ I KNOW THAT THIS CAN'T BE EASY FOR YOU, BUT YOU HAVE NO IDEA HOW TOUGH IT'S BEEN FOR US.
FOR ME.
MUM!
DAD?!
JOIN US...
JOIN US...
TO THE SEA...
HOME!
NO! GET AWAY FROM ME!
JOIN US!
COME WITH US!
TO THE SEA...
TAKING US HOME...

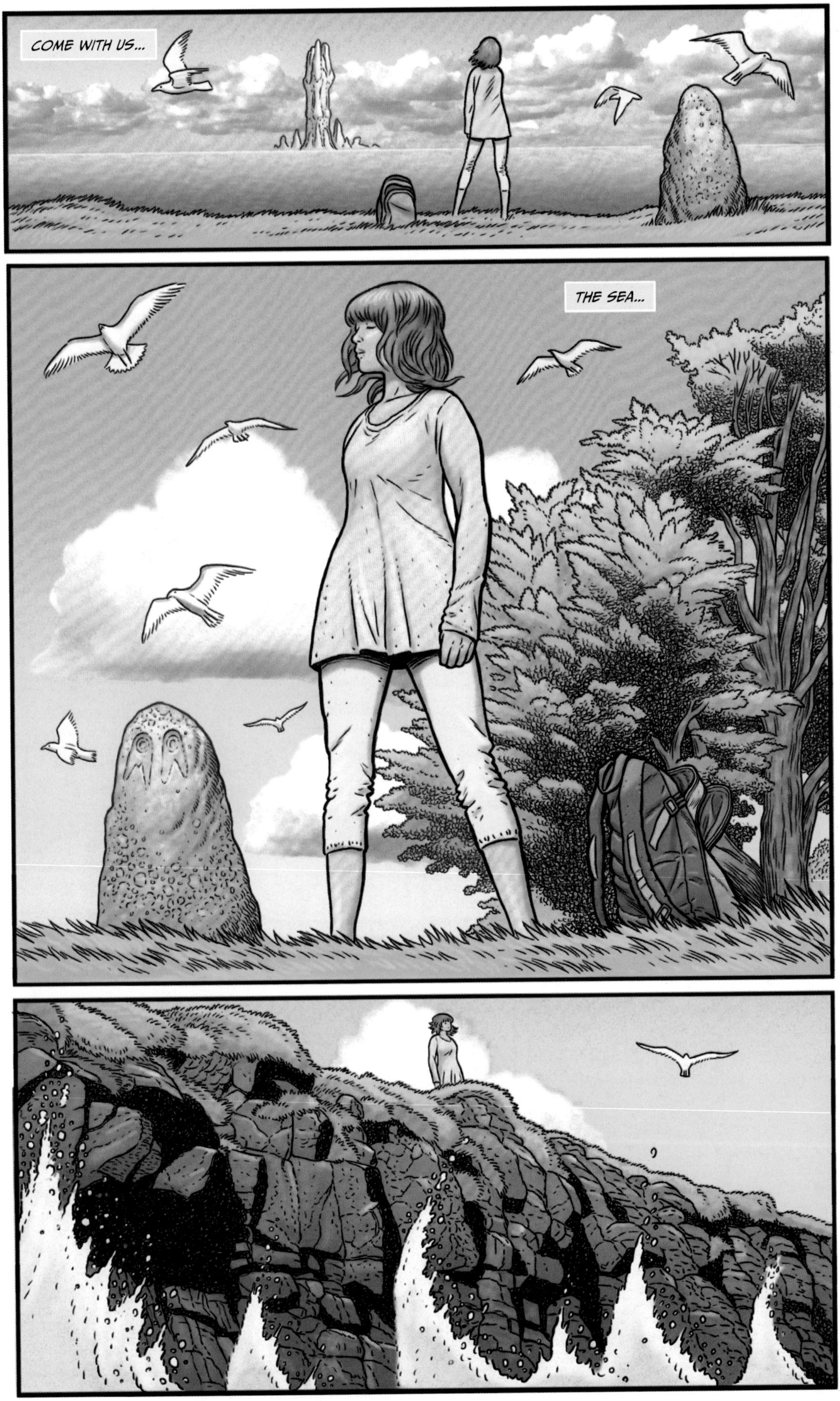
COME WITH US...
THE SEA...

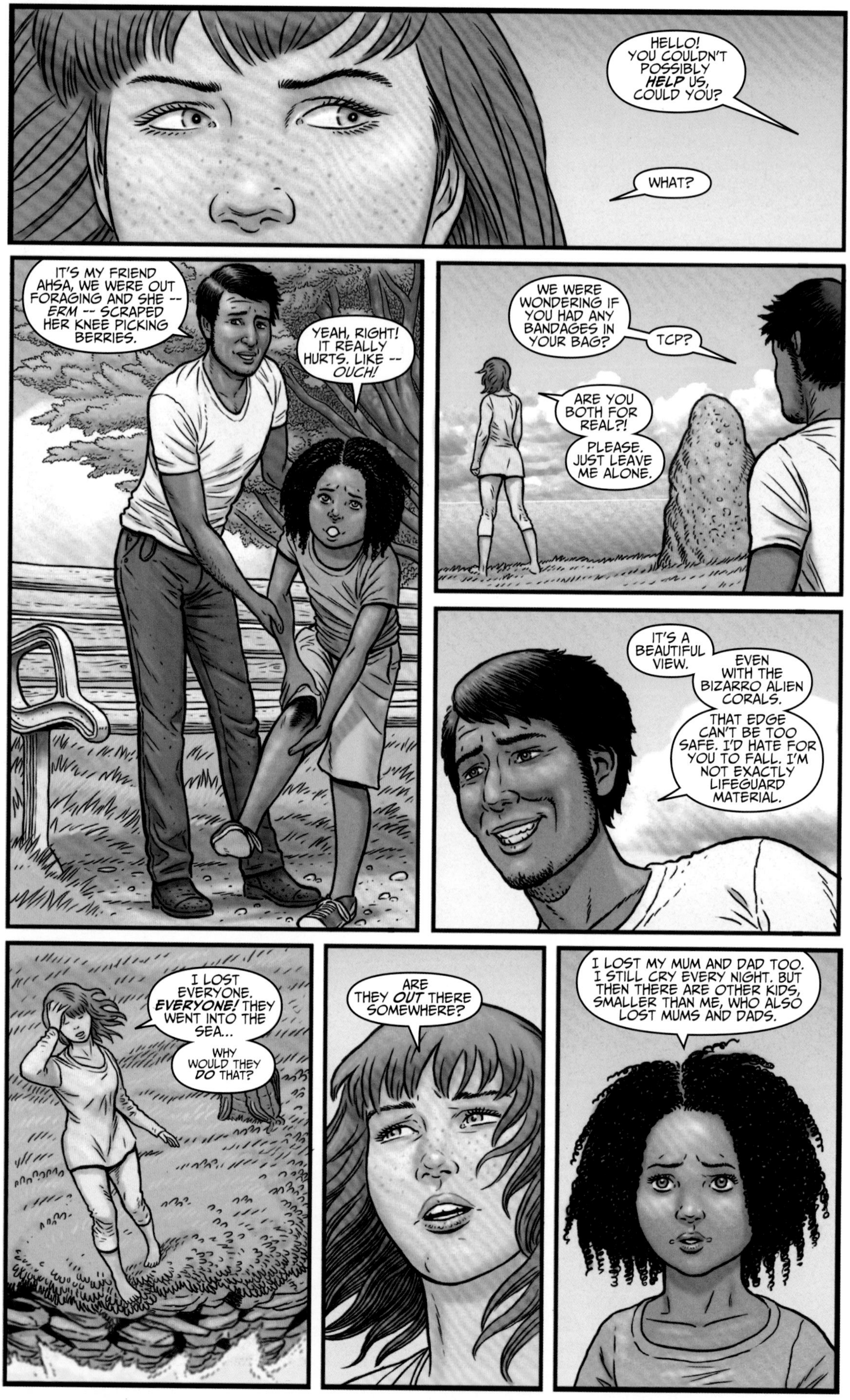
HELLO! YOU COULDN'T POSSIBLY HELP US, COULD YOU?
WHAT?
IT'S MY FRIEND AHSA, WE WERE OUT FORAGING AND SHE -- ERM -- SCRAPED HER KNEE PICKING BERRIES.
YEAH, RIGHT! IT REALLY HURTS. LIKE -- OUCH!
WE WERE WONDERING IF YOU HAD ANY BANDAGES IN YOUR BAG?
TCP?
ARE YOU BOTH FOR REAL?!
PLEASE. JUST LEAVE ME ALONE.
IT'S A BEAUTIFUL VIEW.
EVEN WITH THE BIZARRO ALIEN CORALS.
THAT EDGE CAN'T BE TOO SAFE. I'D HATE FOR YOU TO FALL. I'M NOT EXACTLY LIFEGUARD MATERIAL.
I LOST EVERYONE. EVERYONE! THEY WENT INTO THE SEA...
WHY WOULD THEY DO THAT?
ARE THEY OUT THERE SOMEWHERE?
I LOST MY MUM AND DAD TOO. I STILL CRY EVERY NIGHT. BUT THEN THERE ARE OTHER KIDS, SMALLER THAN ME, WHO ALSO LOST MUMS AND DADS.

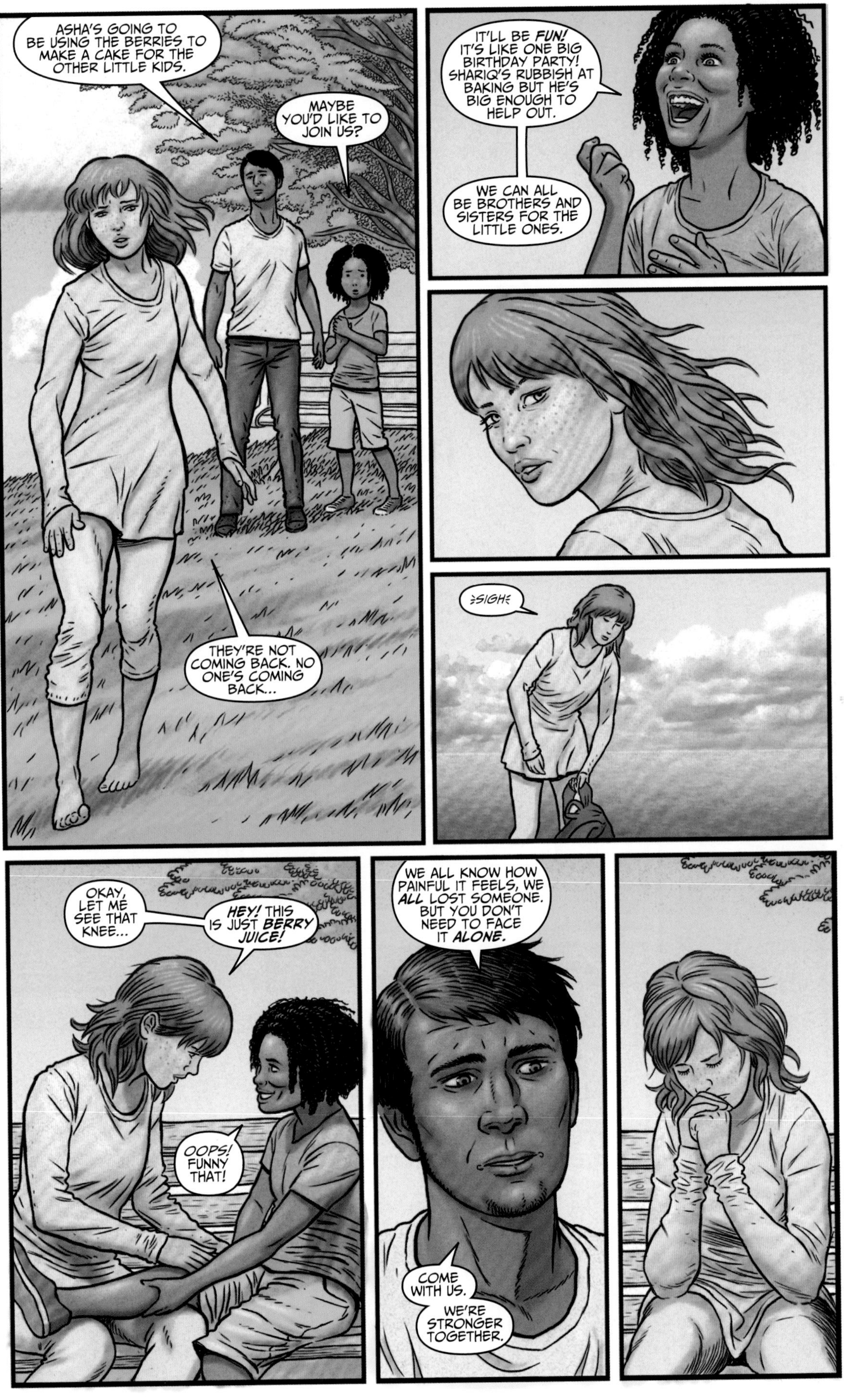
ASHA'S GOING TO BE USING THE BERRIES TO MAKE A CAKE FOR THE OTHER LITTLE KIDS.
MAYBE YOU'D LIKE TO JOIN US?
THEY'RE NOT COMING BACK. NO ONE'S COMING BACK...
IT'LL BE FUN! IT'S LIKE ONE BIG BIRTHDAY PARTY! SHARIQ'S RUBBISH AT BAKING BUT HE'S BIG ENOUGH TO HELP OUT.
WE CAN ALL BE BROTHERS AND SISTERS FOR THE LITTLE ONES.
SIGH
OKAY, LET ME SEE THAT KNEE...
HEY! THIS IS JUST BERRY JUICE!
OOPS! FUNNY THAT!
WE ALL KNOW HOW PAINFUL IT FEELS, WE ALL LOST SOMEONE. BUT YOU DON'T NEED TO FACE IT ALONE.
COME WITH US.
WE'RE STRONGER TOGETHER.

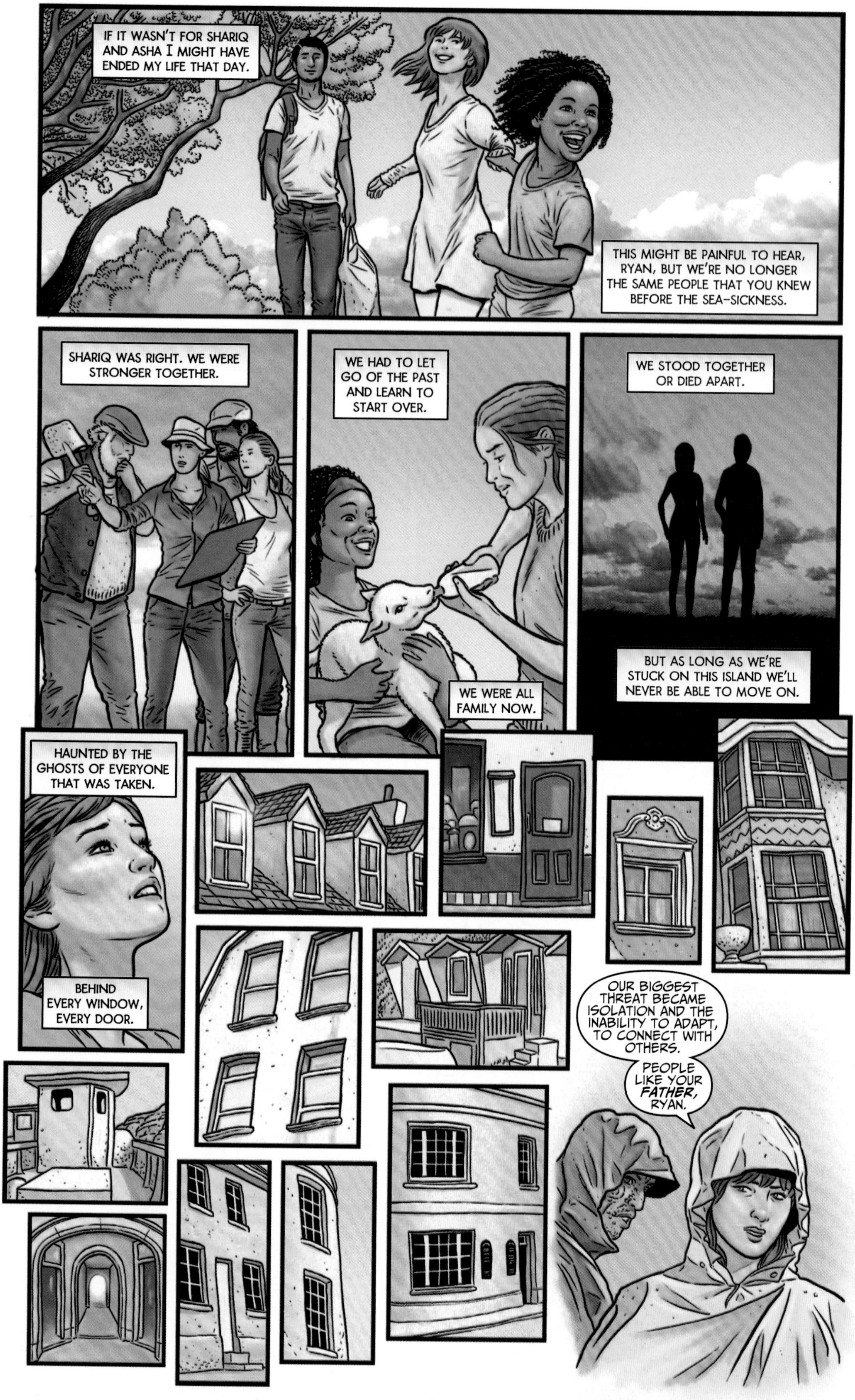
IF IT WASN'T FOR SHARIQ AND ASHA I MIGHT HAVE ENDED MY LIFE THAT DAY.
THIS MIGHT BE PAINFUL TO HEAR, RYAN, BUT WE'RE NO LONGER THE SAME PEOPLE THAT YOU KNEW BEFORE THE SEA-SICKNESS.
SHARIQ WAS RIGHT. WE WERE STRONGER TOGETHER.
WE HAD TO LET GO OF THE PAST AND LEARN TO START OVER.
WE WERE ALL FAMILY NOW.
WE STOOD TOGETHER OR DIED APART.
BUT AS LONG AS WE'RE STUCK ON THIS ISLAND WE'LL NEVER BE ABLE TO MOVE ON.
HAUNTED BY THE GHOSTS OF EVERYONE THAT WAS TAKEN.
BEHIND EVERY WINDOW, EVERY DOOR.
OUR BIGGEST THREAT BECAME ISOLATION AND THE INABILITY TO ADAPT, TO CONNECT WITH OTHERS.
PEOPLE LIKE YOUR FATHER, RYAN.

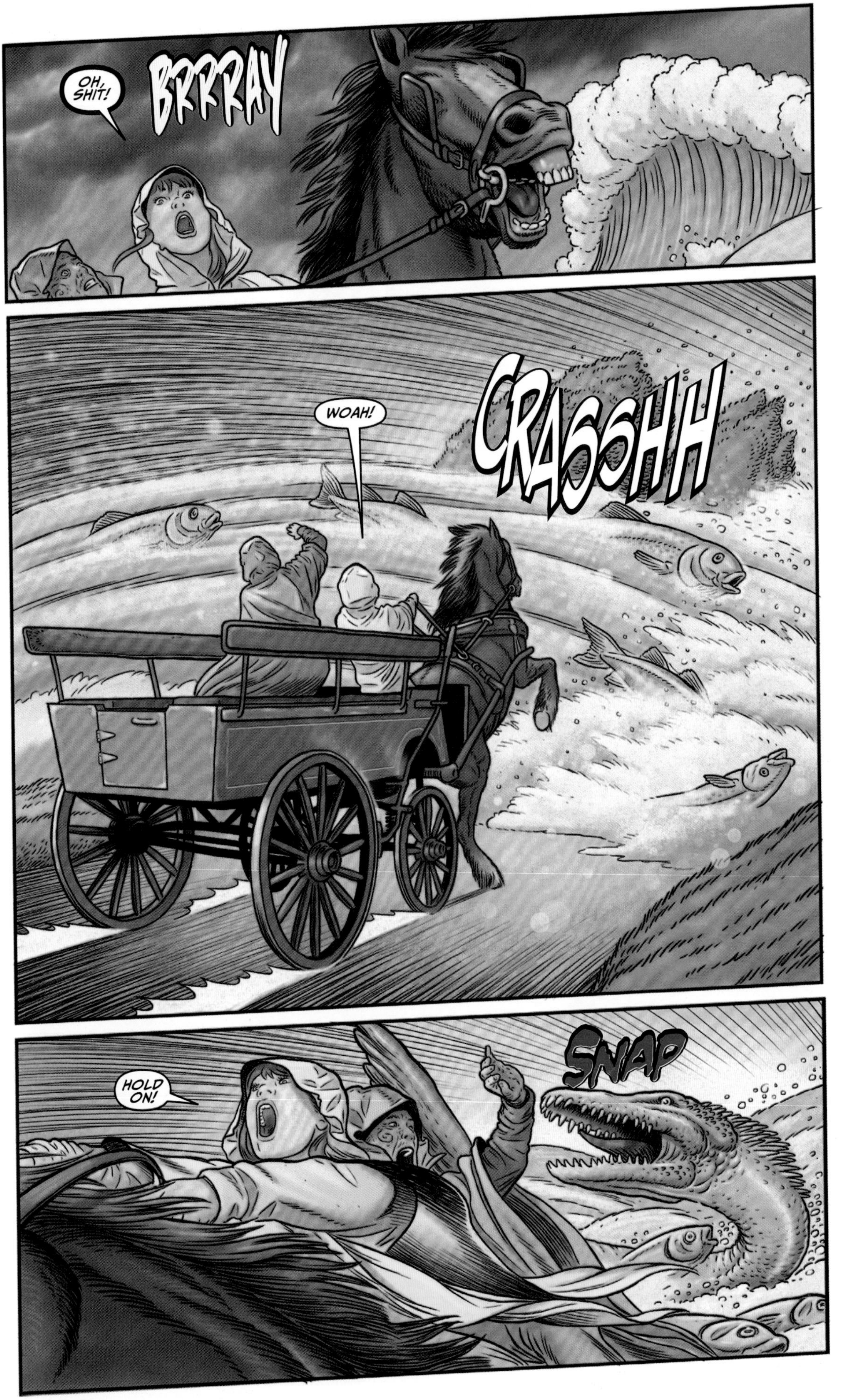
OH, SHIT!
BRRRAY
WOAH!
CRASSHH
HOLD ON!
SNAP

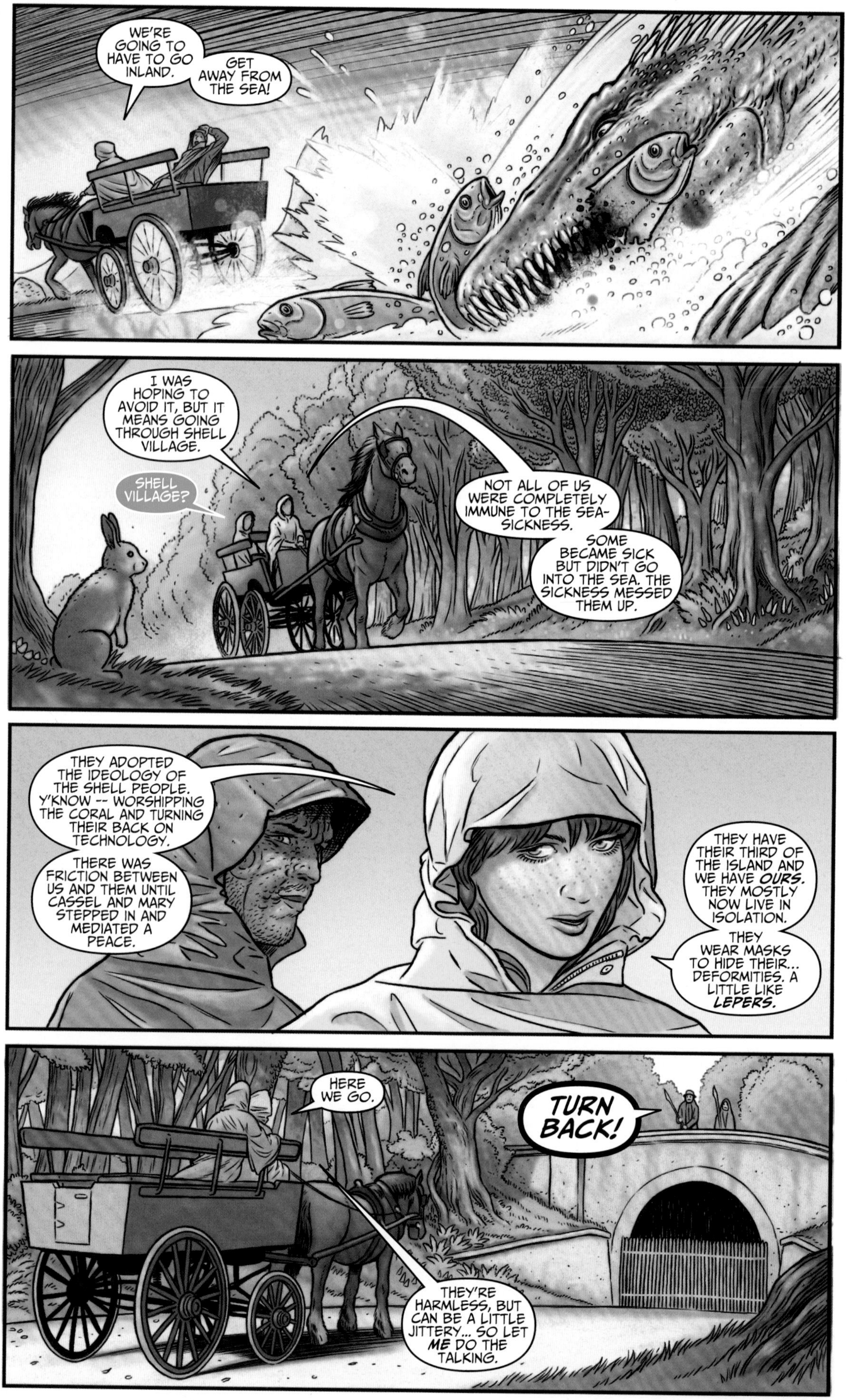
WE'RE GOING TO HAVE TO GO INLAND.
GET AWAY FROM THE SEA!
I WAS HOPING TO AVOID IT, BUT IT MEANS GOING THROUGH SHELL VILLAGE.
SHELL VILLAGE?
NOT ALL OF US WERE COMPLETELY IMMUNE TO THE SEA-SICKNESS.
SOME BECAME SICK BUT DIDN'T GO INTO THE SEA. THE SICKNESS MESSED THEM UP.
THEY ADOPTED THE IDEOLOGY OF THE SHELL PEOPLE. Y'KNOW -- WORSHIPPING THE CORAL AND TURNING THEIR BACK ON TECHNOLOGY.
THERE WAS FRICTION BETWEEN US AND THEM UNTIL CASSEL AND MARY STEPPED IN AND MEDIATED A PEACE.
THEY HAVE THEIR THIRD OF THE ISLAND AND WE HAVE *OURS.* THEY MOSTLY NOW LIVE IN ISOLATION.
THEY WEAR MASKS TO HIDE THEIR... DEFORMITIES. A LITTLE LIKE **LEPERS.**
HERE WE GO.
TURN BACK!
THEY'RE HARMLESS, BUT CAN BE A LITTLE JITTERY... SO LET **ME** DO THE TALKING.

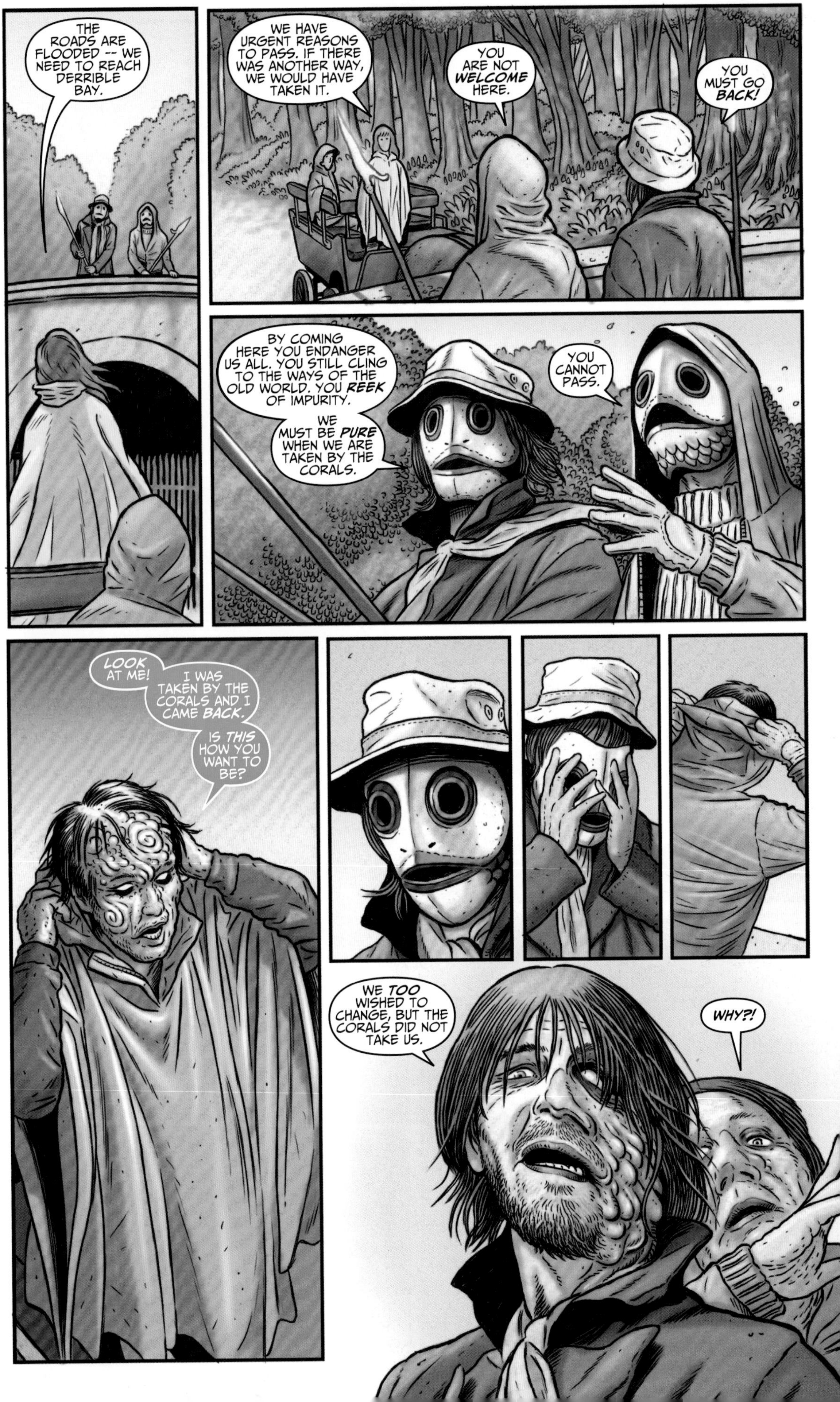
THE ROADS ARE FLOODED -- WE NEED TO REACH DERRIBLE BAY.
WE HAVE URGENT REASONS TO PASS. IF THERE WAS ANOTHER WAY, WE WOULD HAVE TAKEN IT.
YOU ARE NOT WELCOME HERE.
YOU MUST GO BACK!
BY COMING HERE YOU ENDANGER US ALL. YOU STILL CLING TO THE WAYS OF THE OLD WORLD. YOU REEK OF IMPURITY.
WE MUST BE PURE WHEN WE ARE TAKEN BY THE CORALS.
YOU CANNOT PASS.
LOOK AT ME!
I WAS TAKEN BY THE CORALS AND I CAME BACK.
IS THIS HOW YOU WANT TO BE?
WE TOO WISHED TO CHANGE, BUT THE CORALS DID NOT TAKE US.
WHY?!

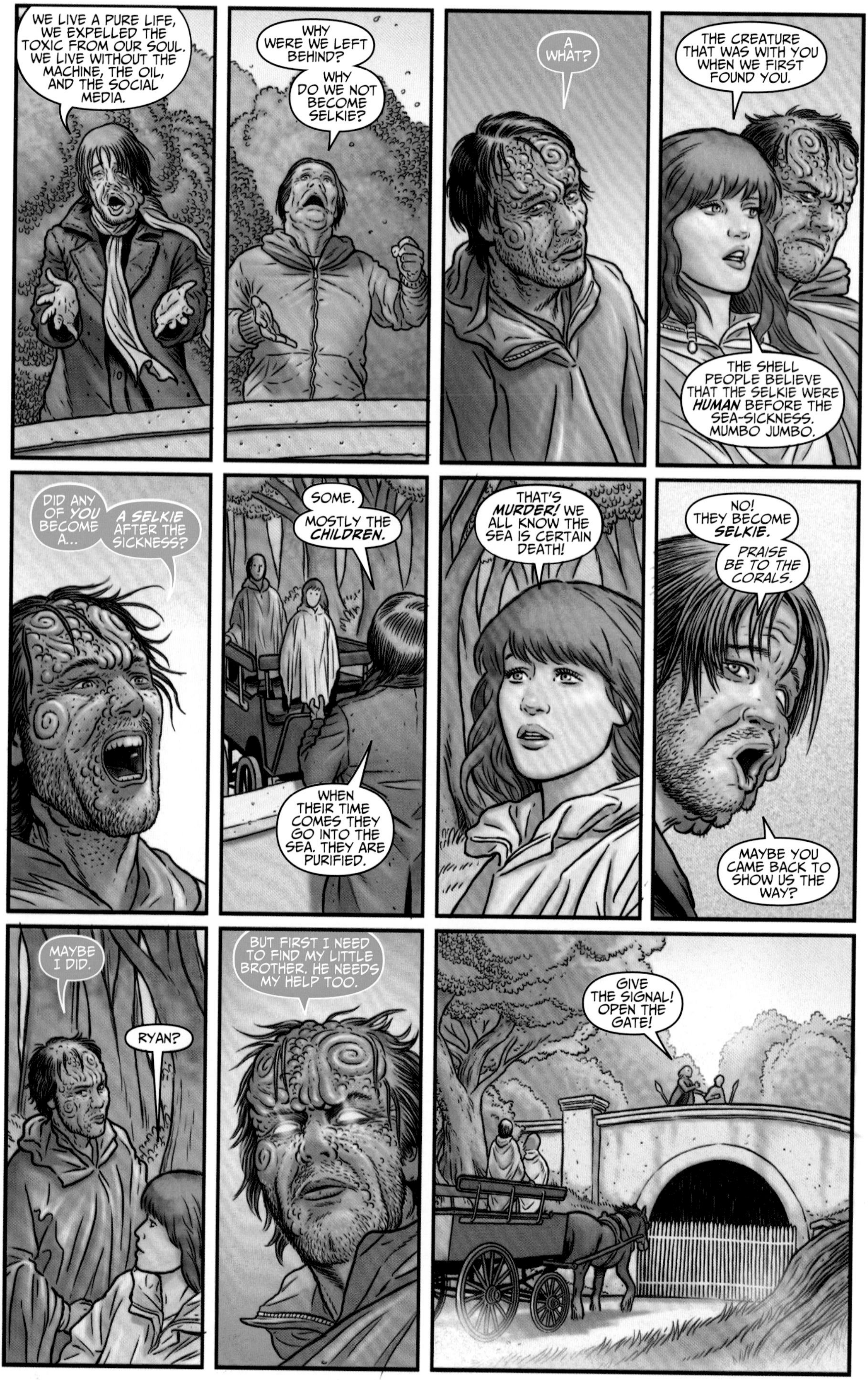

WE LIVE A PURE LIFE, WE EXPELLED THE TOXIC FROM OUR SOUL. WE LIVE WITHOUT THE MACHINE, THE OIL, AND THE SOCIAL MEDIA.
WHY WERE WE LEFT BEHIND?
WHY DO WE NOT BECOME SELKIE?
A WHAT?
THE CREATURE THAT WAS WITH YOU WHEN WE FIRST FOUND YOU.
THE SHELL PEOPLE BELIEVE THAT THE SELKIE WERE HUMAN BEFORE THE SEA-SICKNESS. MUMBO JUMBO.
DID ANY OF YOU BECOME A...
A SELKIE AFTER THE SICKNESS?
SOME. MOSTLY THE CHILDREN.
WHEN THEIR TIME COMES THEY GO INTO THE SEA. THEY ARE PURIFIED.
THAT'S MURDER! WE ALL KNOW THE SEA IS CERTAIN DEATH!
NO! THEY BECOME SELKIE.
PRAISE BE TO THE CORALS.
MAYBE YOU CAME BACK TO SHOW US THE WAY?
MAYBE I DID.
RYAN?
BUT FIRST I NEED TO FIND MY LITTLE BROTHER. HE NEEDS MY HELP TOO.
GIVE THE SIGNAL! OPEN THE GATE!

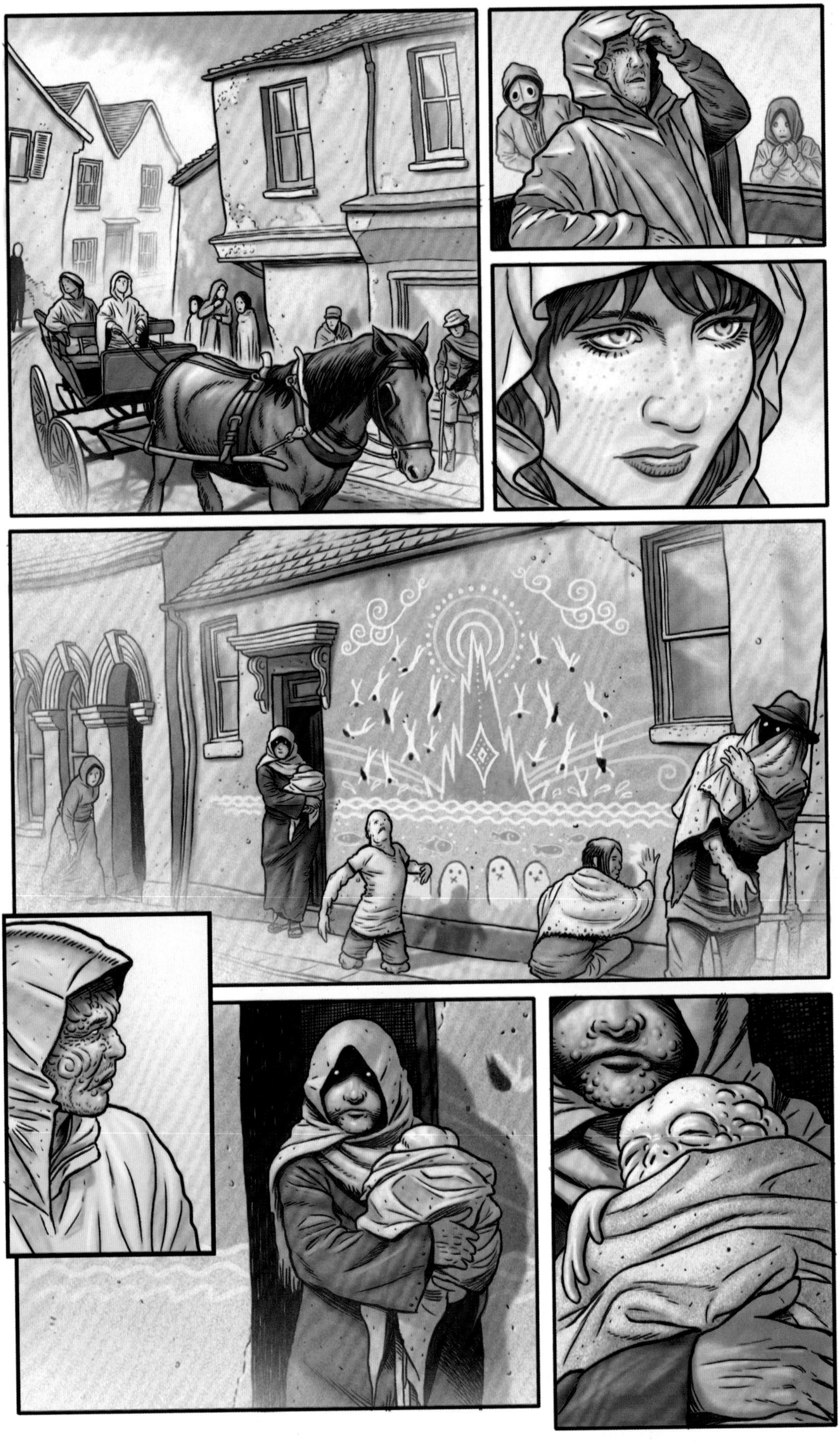

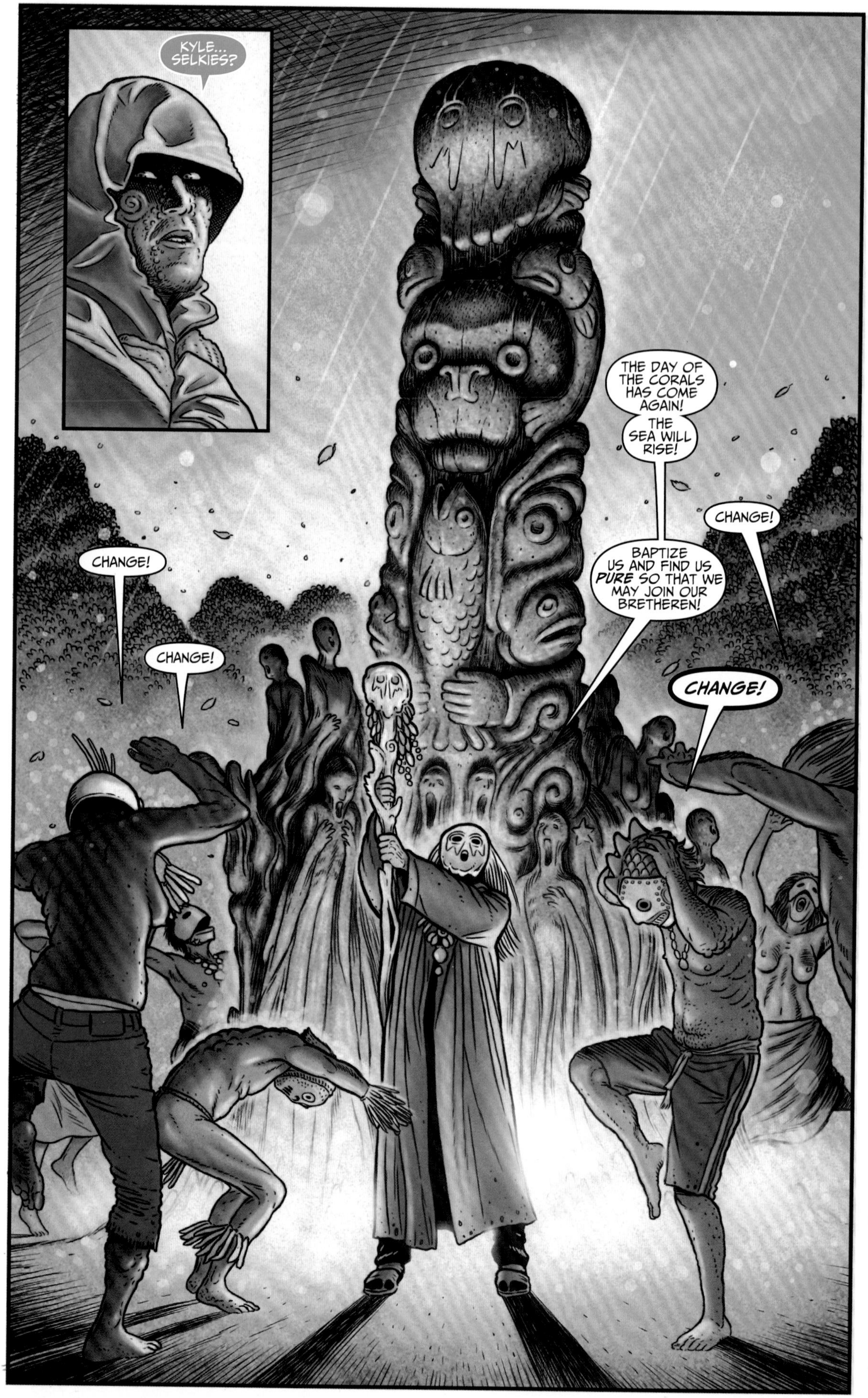
KYLE... SELKIES?
THE DAY OF THE CORALS HAS COME AGAIN!
THE SEA WILL RISE!
BAPTIZE US AND FIND US *PURE* SO THAT WE MAY JOIN OUR BRETHEREN!
CHANGE!
CHANGE!
CHANGE!
CHANGE!

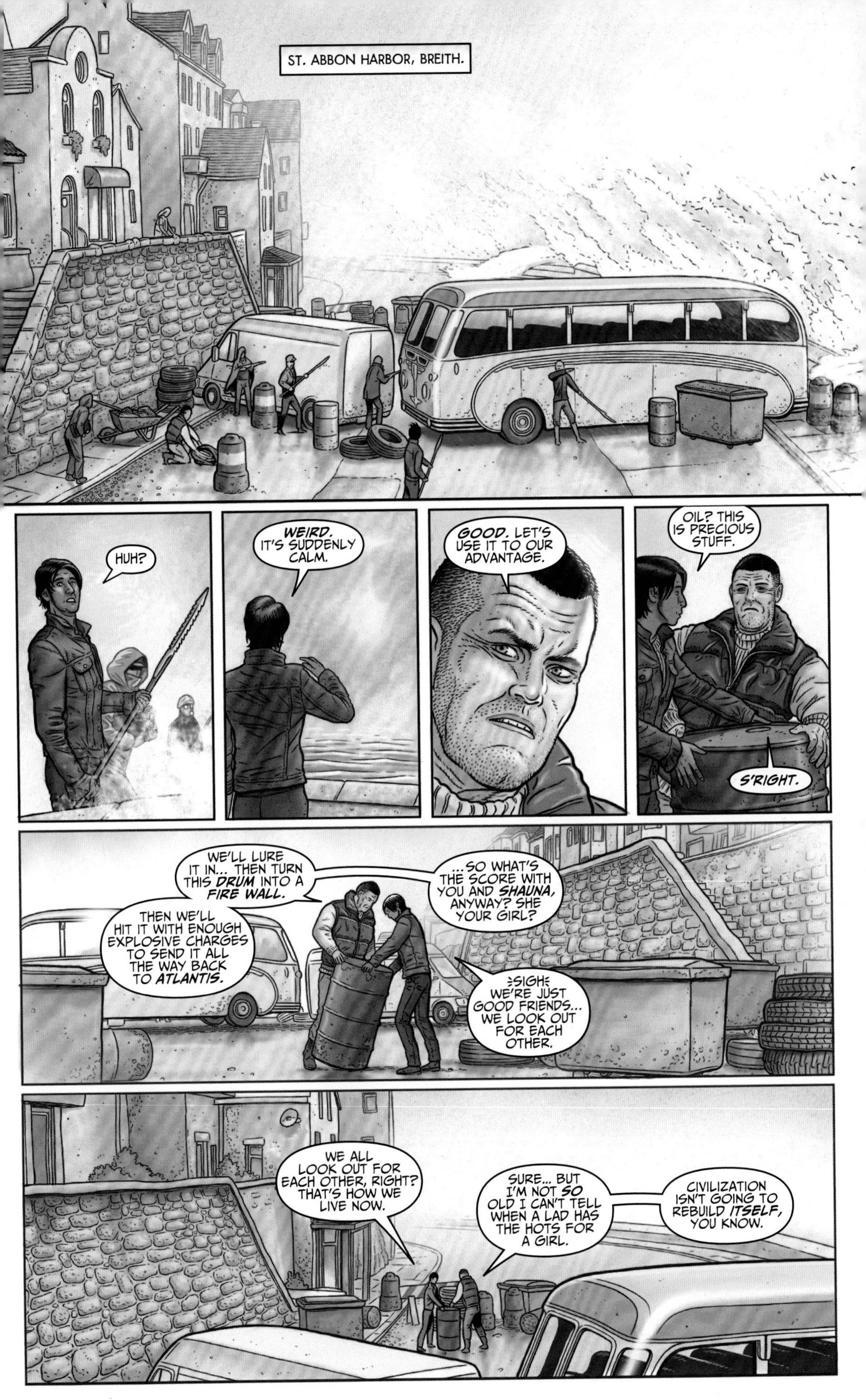
ST. ABBON HARBOR, BREITH.
HUH?
WEIRD. IT'S SUDDENLY CALM.
GOOD. LET'S USE IT TO OUR ADVANTAGE.
OIL? THIS IS PRECIOUS STUFF.
S'RIGHT.
WE'LL LURE IT IN... THEN TURN THIS DRUM INTO A FIRE WALL.
THEN WE'LL HIT IT WITH ENOUGH EXPLOSIVE CHARGES TO SEND IT ALL THE WAY BACK TO ATLANTIS.
...SO WHAT'S THE SCORE WITH YOU AND SHAUNA, ANYWAY? SHE YOUR GIRL?
SIGH WE'RE JUST GOOD FRIENDS... WE LOOK OUT FOR EACH OTHER.
WE ALL LOOK OUT FOR EACH OTHER, RIGHT? THAT'S HOW WE LIVE NOW.
SURE... BUT I'M NOT SO OLD I CAN'T TELL WHEN A LAD HAS THE HOTS FOR A GIRL.
CIVILIZATION ISN'T GOING TO REBUILD ITSELF, YOU KNOW.

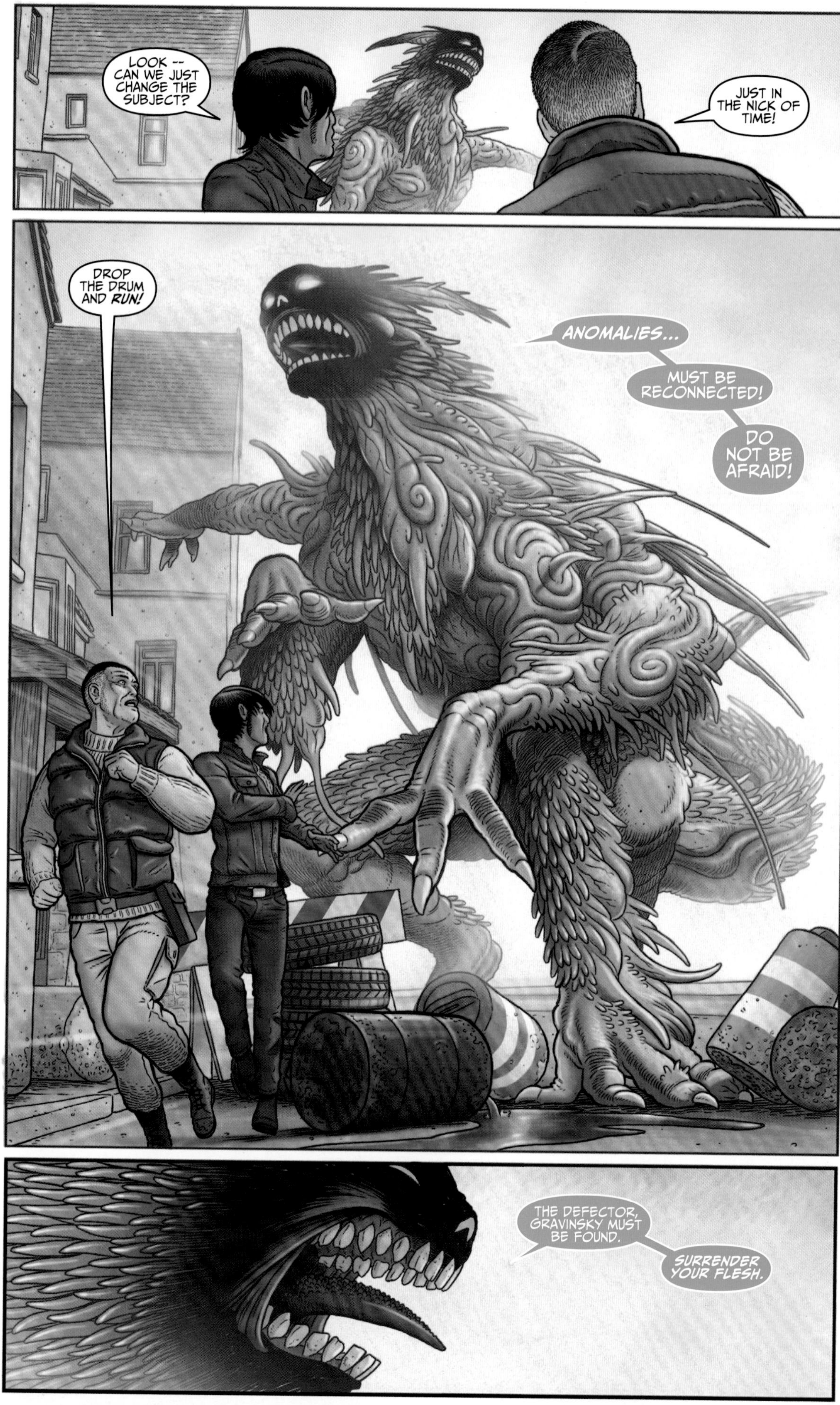
LOOK -- CAN WE JUST CHANGE THE SUBJECT?
JUST IN THE NICK OF TIME!
DROP THE DRUM AND *RUN!*
ANOMALIES...
MUST BE RECONNECTED!
DO NOT BE AFRAID!
THE DEFECTOR, GRAVINSKY MUST BE FOUND.
SURRENDER YOUR FLESH.

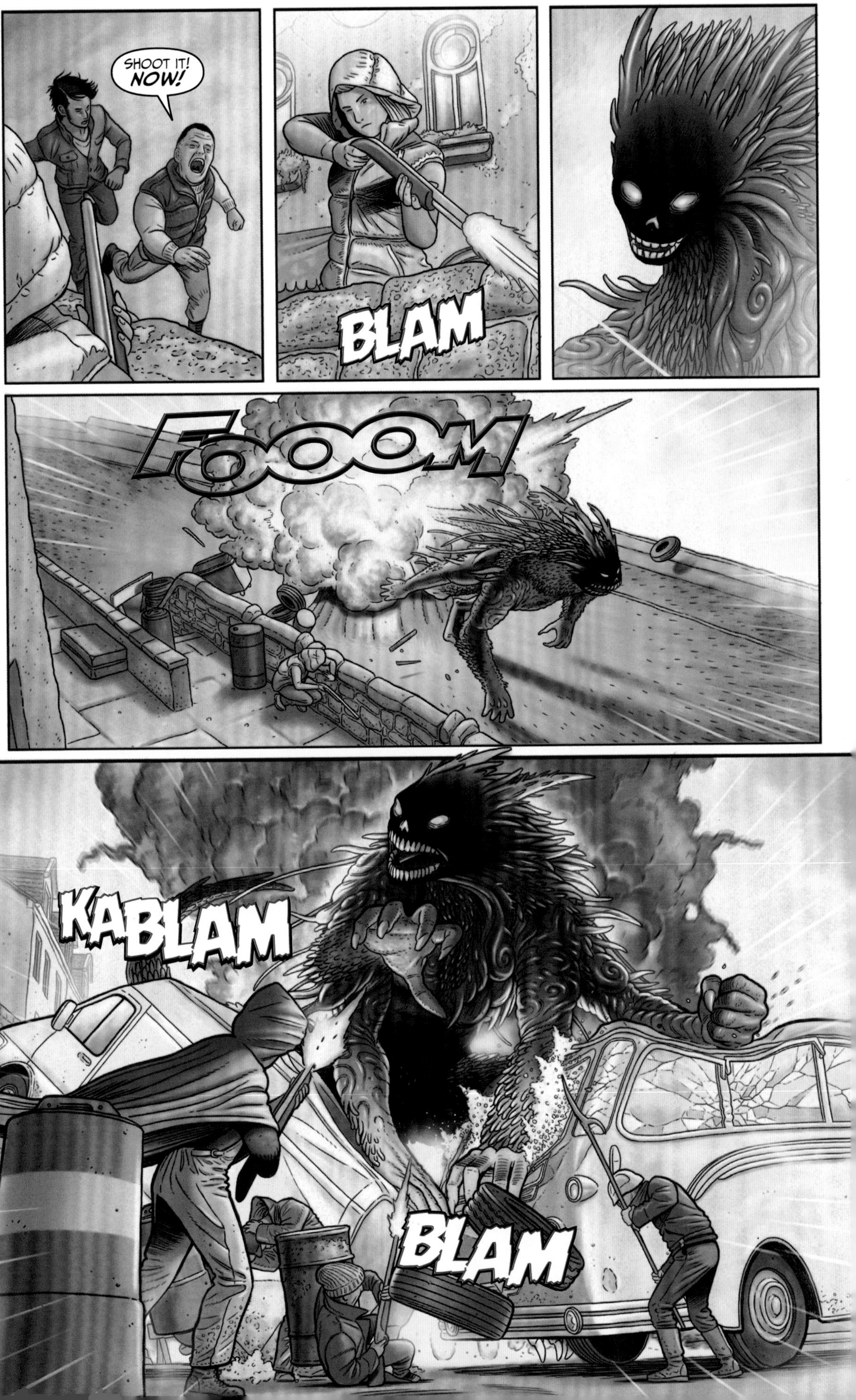

SHOOT IT! NOW!
BLAM
FOOOM
KABLAM
BLAM

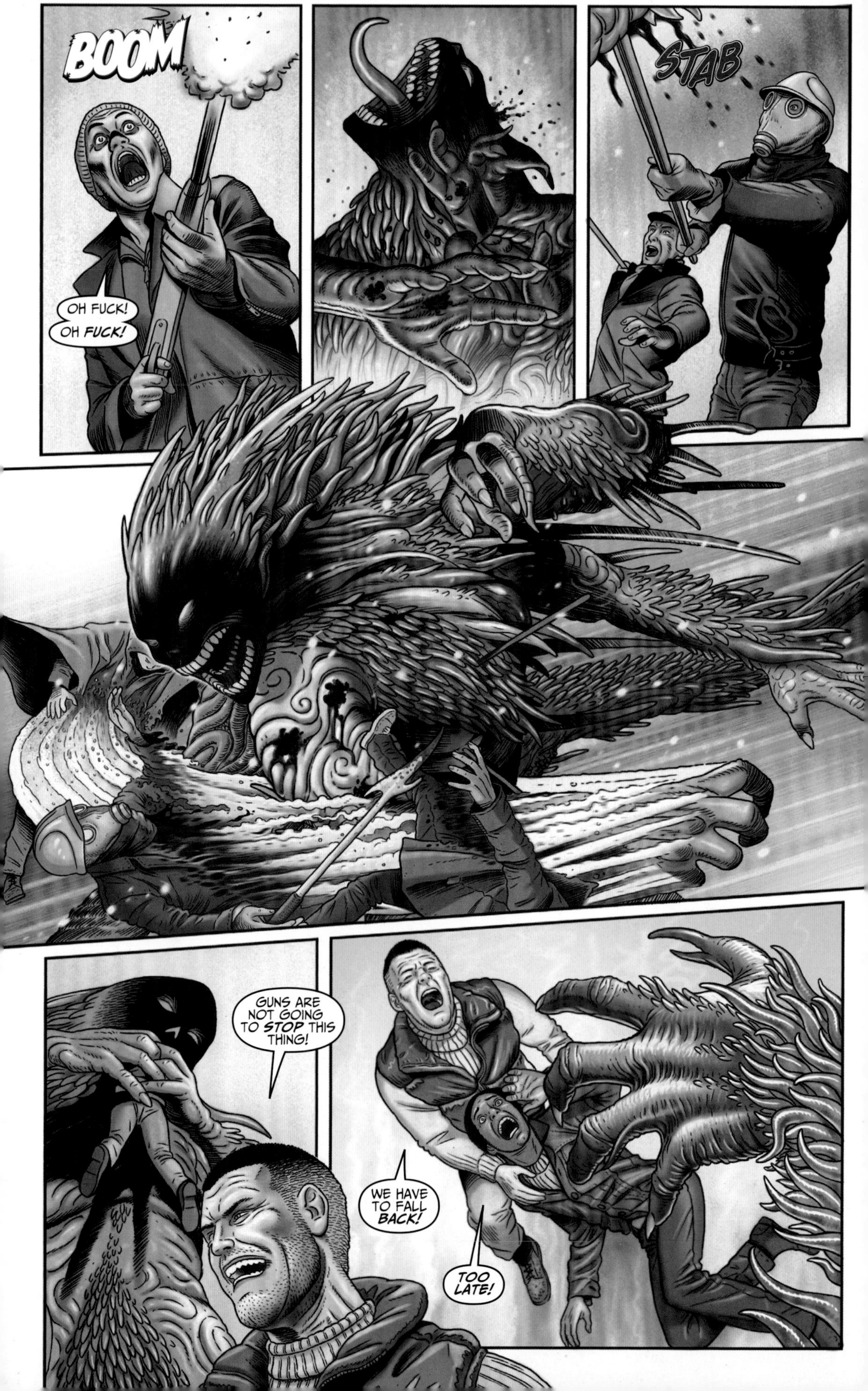
BOOM
OH FUCK!
OH FUCK!
STAB
GUNS ARE NOT GOING TO STOP THIS THING!
WE HAVE TO FALL BACK!
TOO LATE!

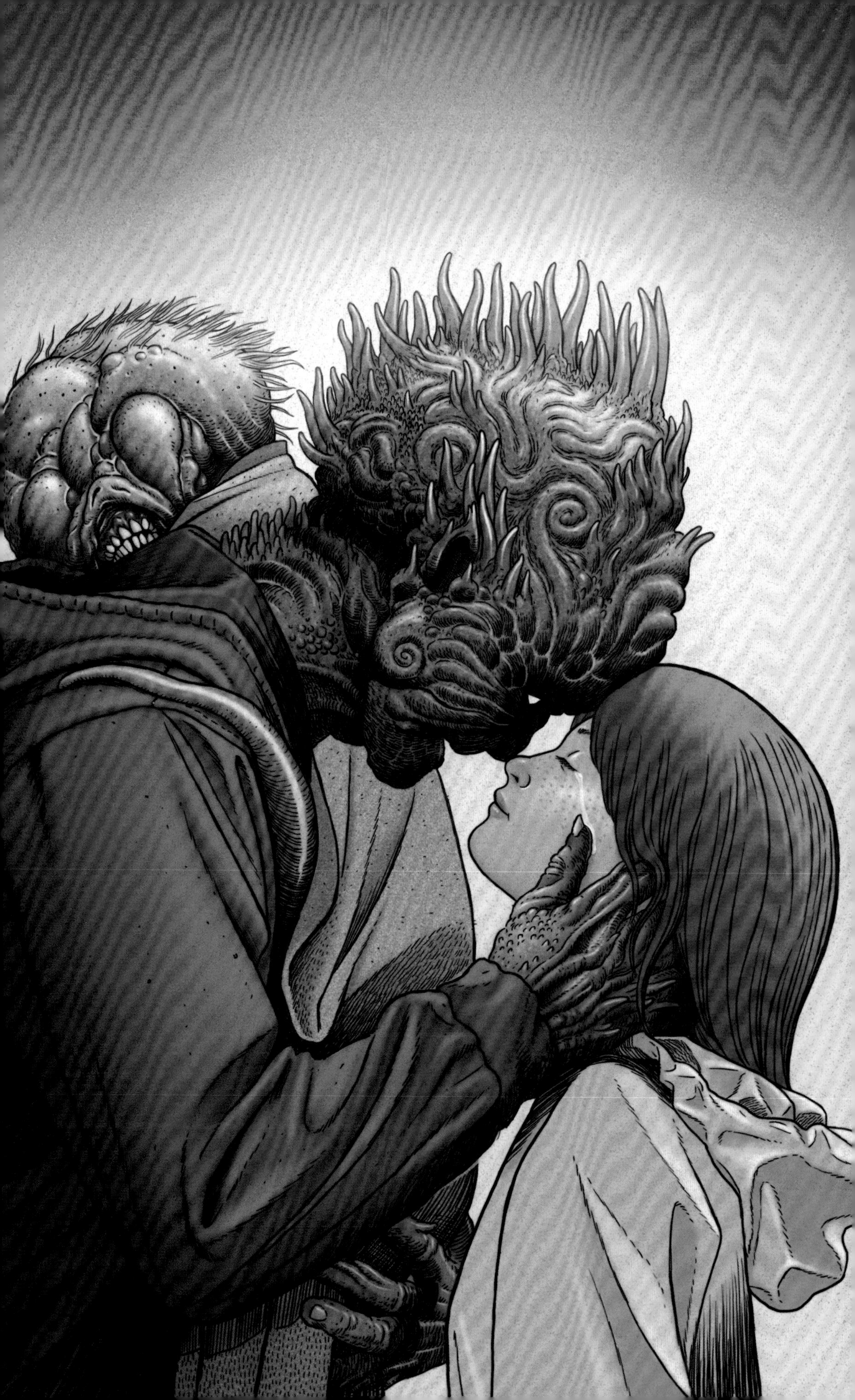

CHAPTER FOUR
CHOICES

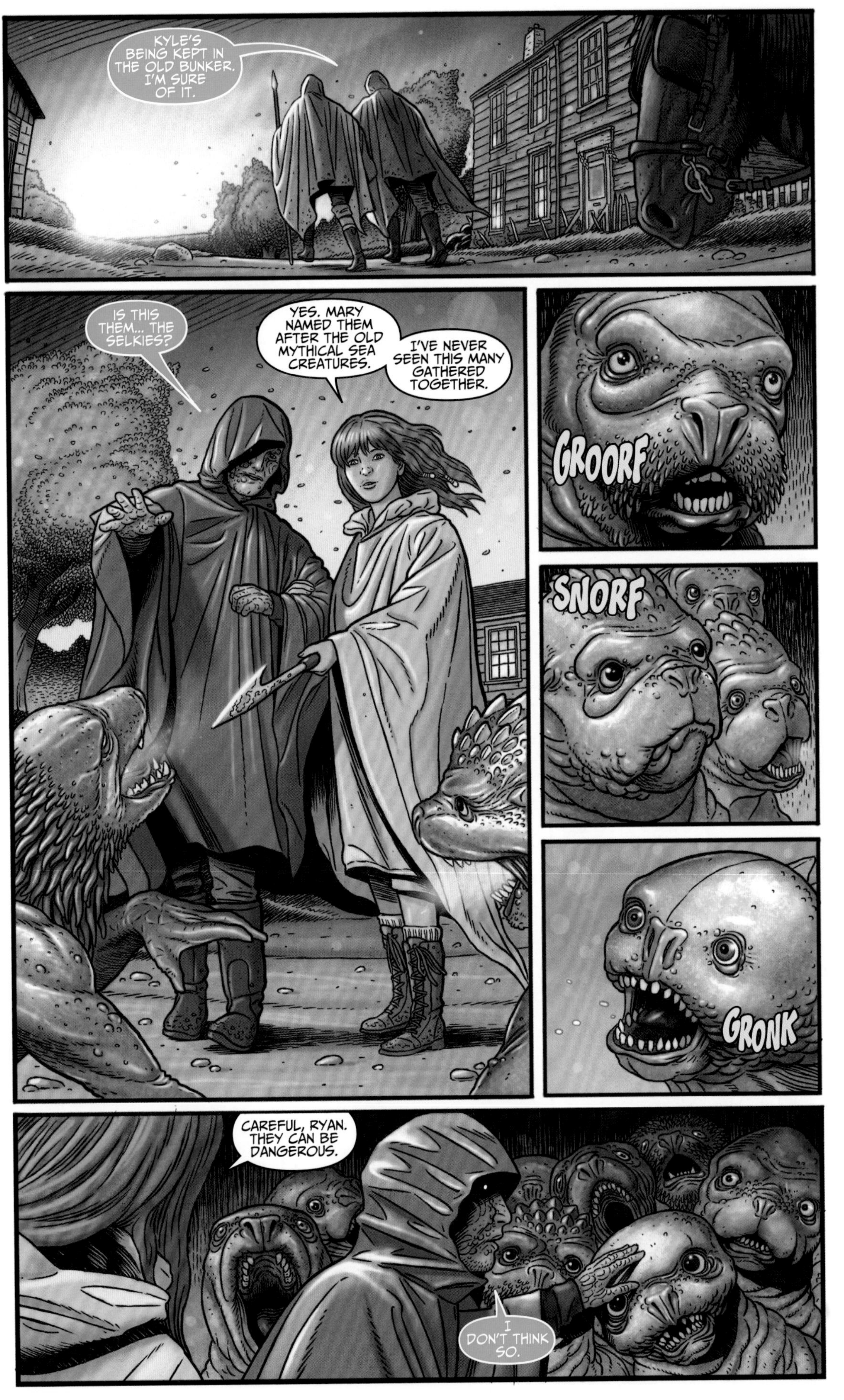
KYLE'S BEING KEPT IN THE OLD BUNKER. I'M SURE OF IT.
IS THIS THEM... THE SELKIES?
YES. MARY NAMED THEM AFTER THE OLD MYTHICAL SEA CREATURES.
I'VE NEVER SEEN THIS MANY GATHERED TOGETHER.
GROORF
SNORF
GRONK
CAREFUL, RYAN. THEY CAN BE DANGEROUS.
I DON'T THINK SO.

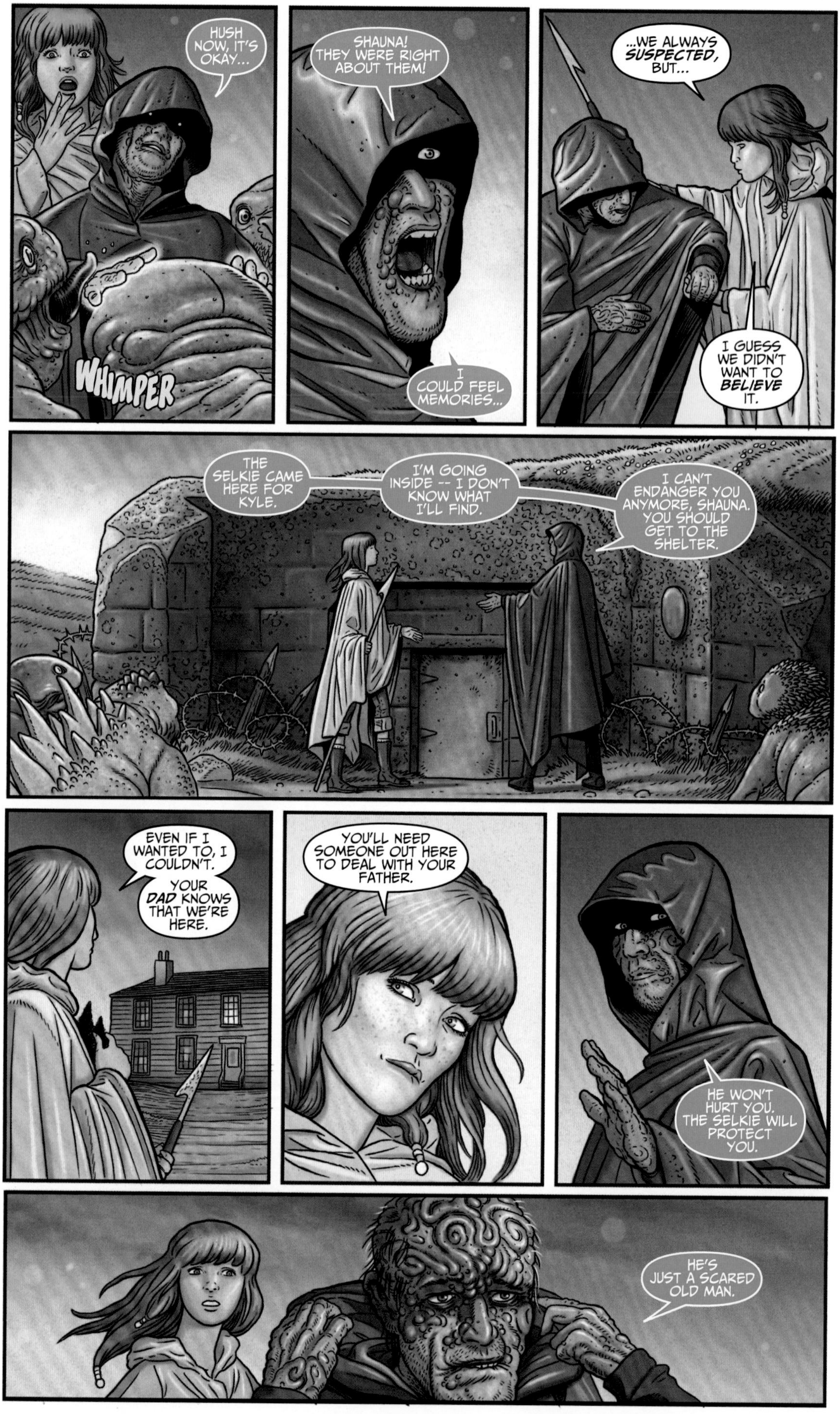
HUSH NOW, IT'S OKAY...
WHIMPER
SHAUNA! THEY WERE RIGHT ABOUT THEM!
I COULD FEEL MEMORIES...
...WE ALWAYS *SUSPECTED*, BUT...
I GUESS WE DIDN'T WANT TO *BELIEVE* IT.
THE SELKIE CAME HERE FOR KYLE.
I'M GOING INSIDE -- I DON'T KNOW WHAT I'LL FIND.
I CAN'T ENDANGER YOU ANYMORE, SHAUNA. YOU SHOULD GET TO THE SHELTER.
EVEN IF I WANTED TO, I COULDN'T.
YOUR *DAD* KNOWS THAT WE'RE HERE.
YOU'LL NEED SOMEONE OUT HERE TO DEAL WITH YOUR FATHER.
HE WON'T HURT YOU. THE SELKIE WILL PROTECT YOU.
HE'S JUST A SCARED OLD MAN.

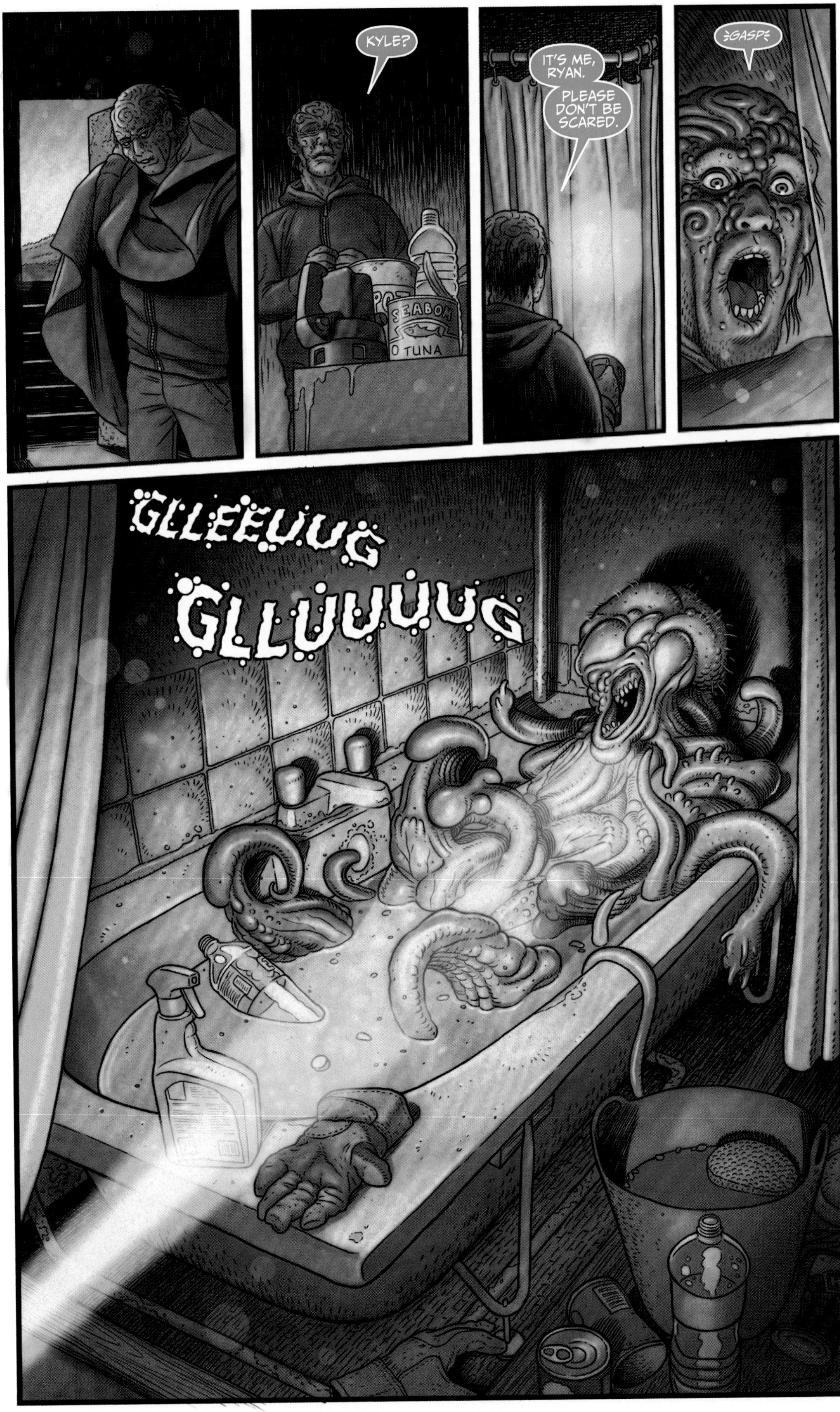
KYLE?
IT'S ME, RYAN.
PLEASE DON'T BE SCARED.
GASP
SEABOM
TUNA
GLLEEUUG
GLLUUUUG

THE BATH HOUSE.

MEG?

ARE YOU STILL THERE?

YES.

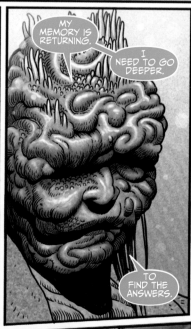

MY MEMORY IS RETURNING.

I NEED TO GO DEEPER.

TO FIND THE ANSWERS.

I NEED TO QUICKEN THE CHANGE.

THEN LET US CONTINUE.

AAGGGHHHH!

IT'S OKAY, MEG, YOU'RE *SAFE*. FOCUS ON ME, FOCUS ON MY VOICE.

YOU'RE IN THE *INFIRMARY*. YOU'VE BEEN UNCONSCIOUS FOR *TWO DAYS*.

I CAME BACK HERE TO CHECK UP ON YOU... AND TO SEE IF ANYONE WAS LEFT TO HELP.

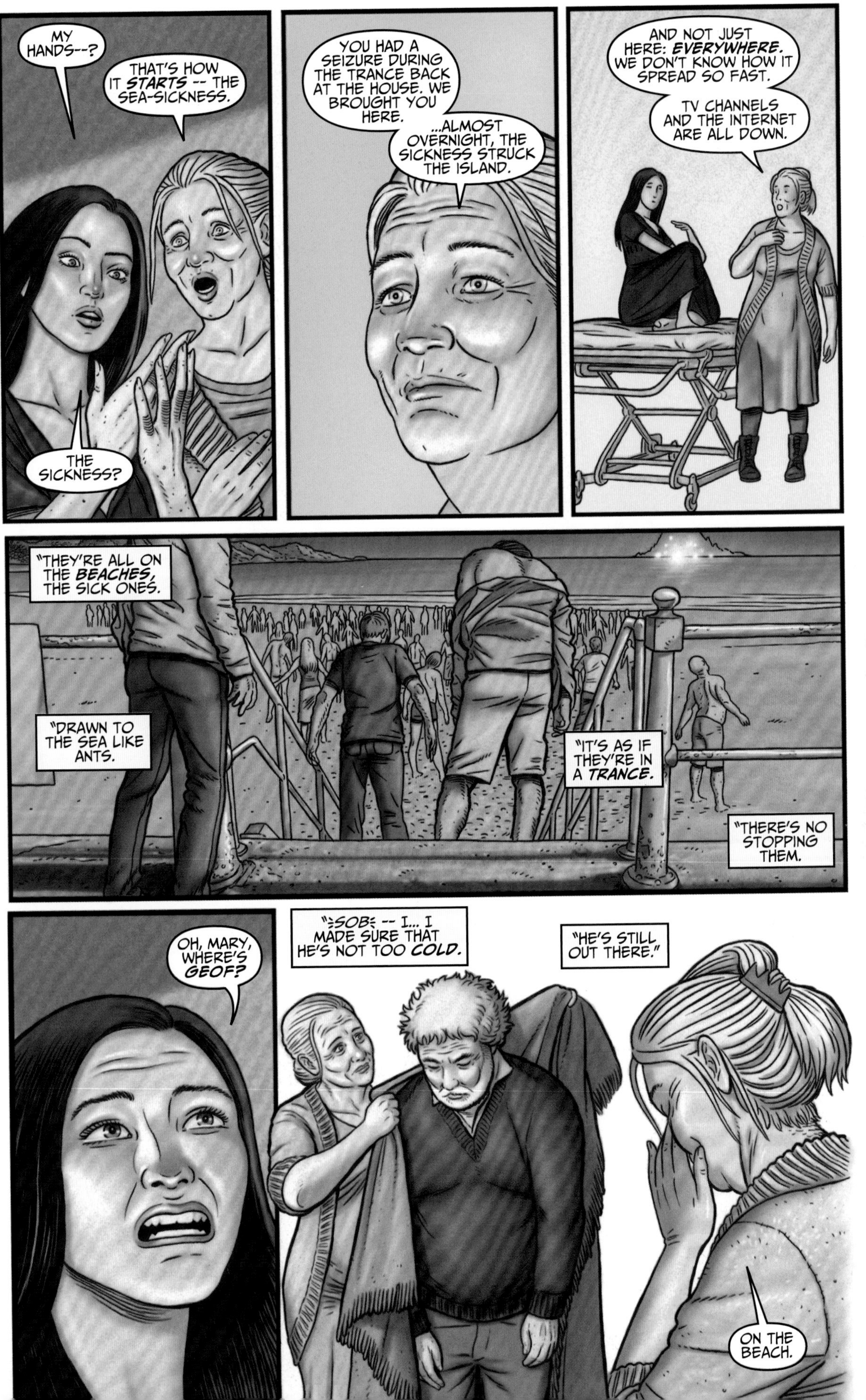

MY HANDS--?
THAT'S HOW IT STARTS -- THE SEA-SICKNESS.
THE SICKNESS?
YOU HAD A SEIZURE DURING THE TRANCE BACK AT THE HOUSE. WE BROUGHT YOU HERE.
...ALMOST OVERNIGHT, THE SICKNESS STRUCK THE ISLAND.
AND NOT JUST HERE: EVERYWHERE. WE DON'T KNOW HOW IT SPREAD SO FAST.
TV CHANNELS AND THE INTERNET ARE ALL DOWN.
"THEY'RE ALL ON THE BEACHES, THE SICK ONES.
"DRAWN TO THE SEA LIKE ANTS.
"IT'S AS IF THEY'RE IN A TRANCE.
"THERE'S NO STOPPING THEM.
OH, MARY, WHERE'S GEOF?
"SOB -- I... I MADE SURE THAT HE'S NOT TOO COLD.
"HE'S STILL OUT THERE."
ON THE BEACH.

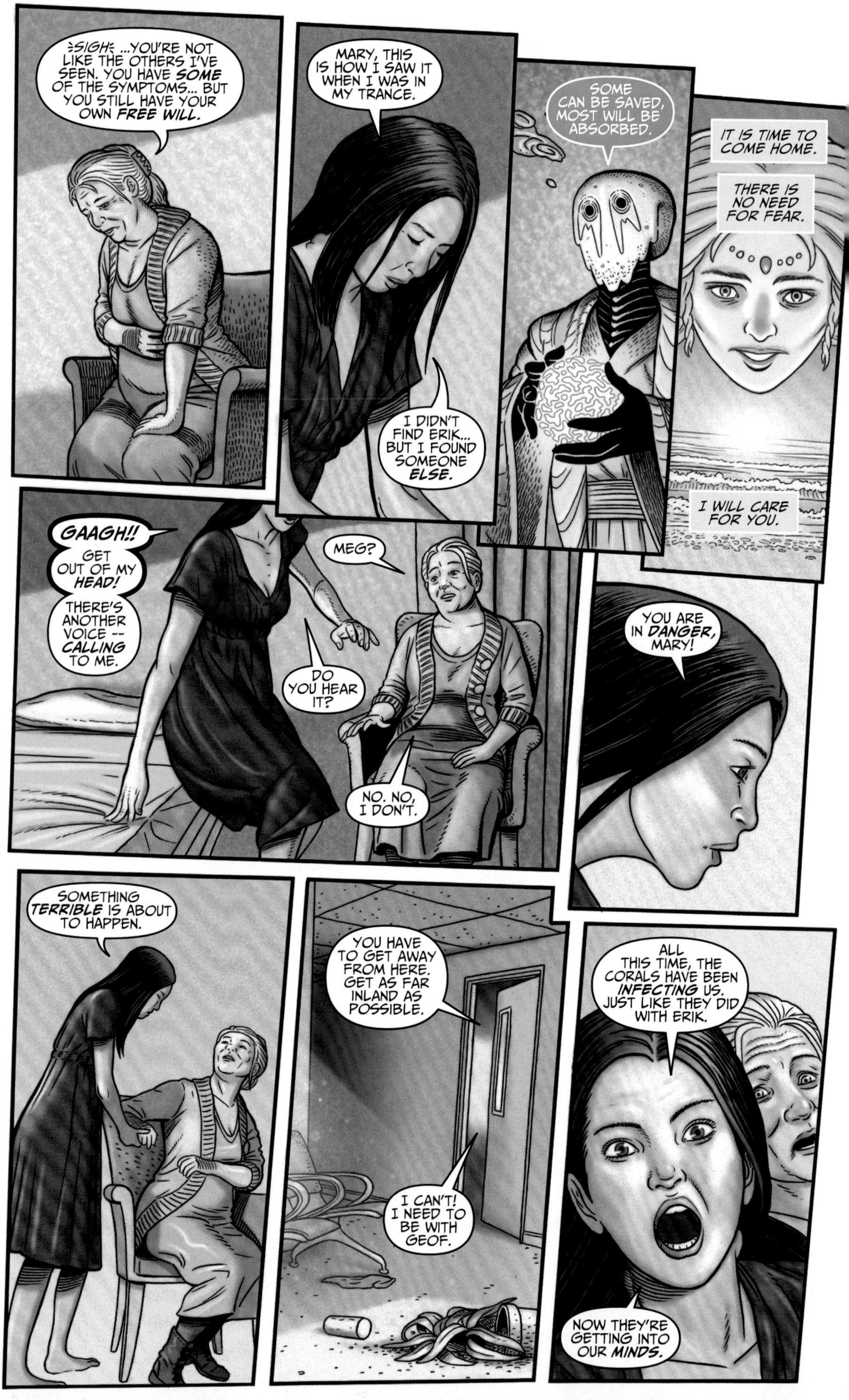

SIGH ...YOU'RE NOT LIKE THE OTHERS I'VE SEEN. YOU HAVE SOME OF THE SYMPTOMS... BUT YOU STILL HAVE YOUR OWN FREE WILL.
MARY, THIS IS HOW I SAW IT WHEN I WAS IN MY TRANCE.
I DIDN'T FIND ERIK... BUT I FOUND SOMEONE ELSE.
SOME CAN BE SAVED, MOST WILL BE ABSORBED.
IT IS TIME TO COME HOME.
THERE IS NO NEED FOR FEAR.
I WILL CARE FOR YOU.
GAAGH!! GET OUT OF MY HEAD!
THERE'S ANOTHER VOICE -- CALLING TO ME.
MEG?
DO YOU HEAR IT?
NO. NO, I DON'T.
YOU ARE IN DANGER, MARY!
SOMETHING TERRIBLE IS ABOUT TO HAPPEN.
YOU HAVE TO GET AWAY FROM HERE. GET AS FAR INLAND AS POSSIBLE.
I CAN'T! I NEED TO BE WITH GEOF.
ALL THIS TIME, THE CORALS HAVE BEEN INFECTING US. JUST LIKE THEY DID WITH ERIK.
NOW THEY'RE GETTING INTO OUR MINDS.

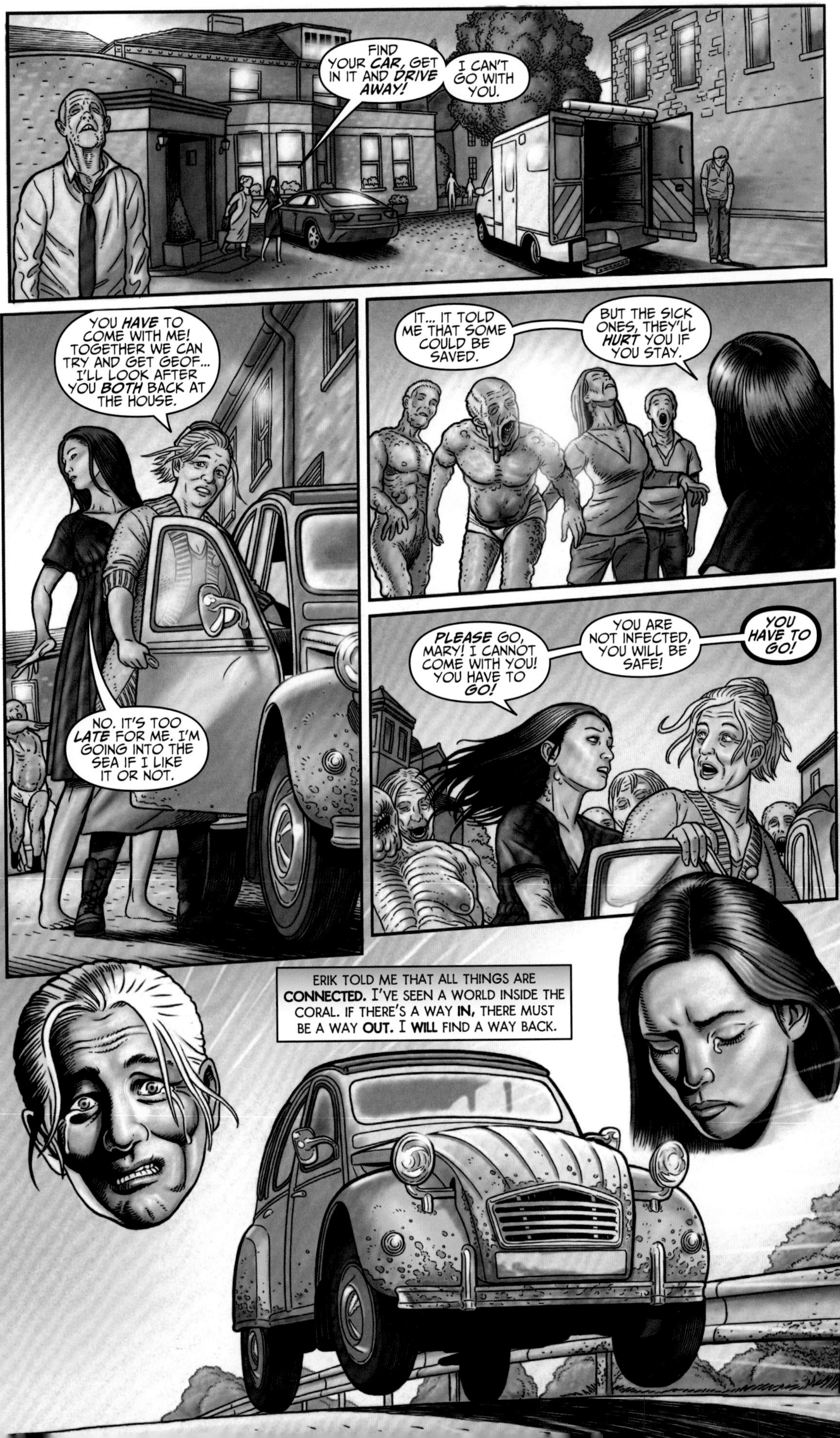
FIND YOUR CAR, GET IN IT AND DRIVE AWAY!
I CAN'T GO WITH YOU.
YOU HAVE TO COME WITH ME! TOGETHER WE CAN TRY AND GET GEOF... I'LL LOOK AFTER YOU BOTH BACK AT THE HOUSE.
NO. IT'S TOO LATE FOR ME. I'M GOING INTO THE SEA IF I LIKE IT OR NOT.
IT... IT TOLD ME THAT SOME COULD BE SAVED.
BUT THE SICK ONES, THEY'LL HURT YOU IF YOU STAY.
PLEASE GO, MARY! I CANNOT COME WITH YOU! YOU HAVE TO GO!
YOU ARE NOT INFECTED, YOU WILL BE SAFE!
YOU HAVE TO GO!
ERIK TOLD ME THAT ALL THINGS ARE CONNECTED. I'VE SEEN A WORLD INSIDE THE CORAL. IF THERE'S A WAY IN, THERE MUST BE A WAY OUT. I WILL FIND A WAY BACK.

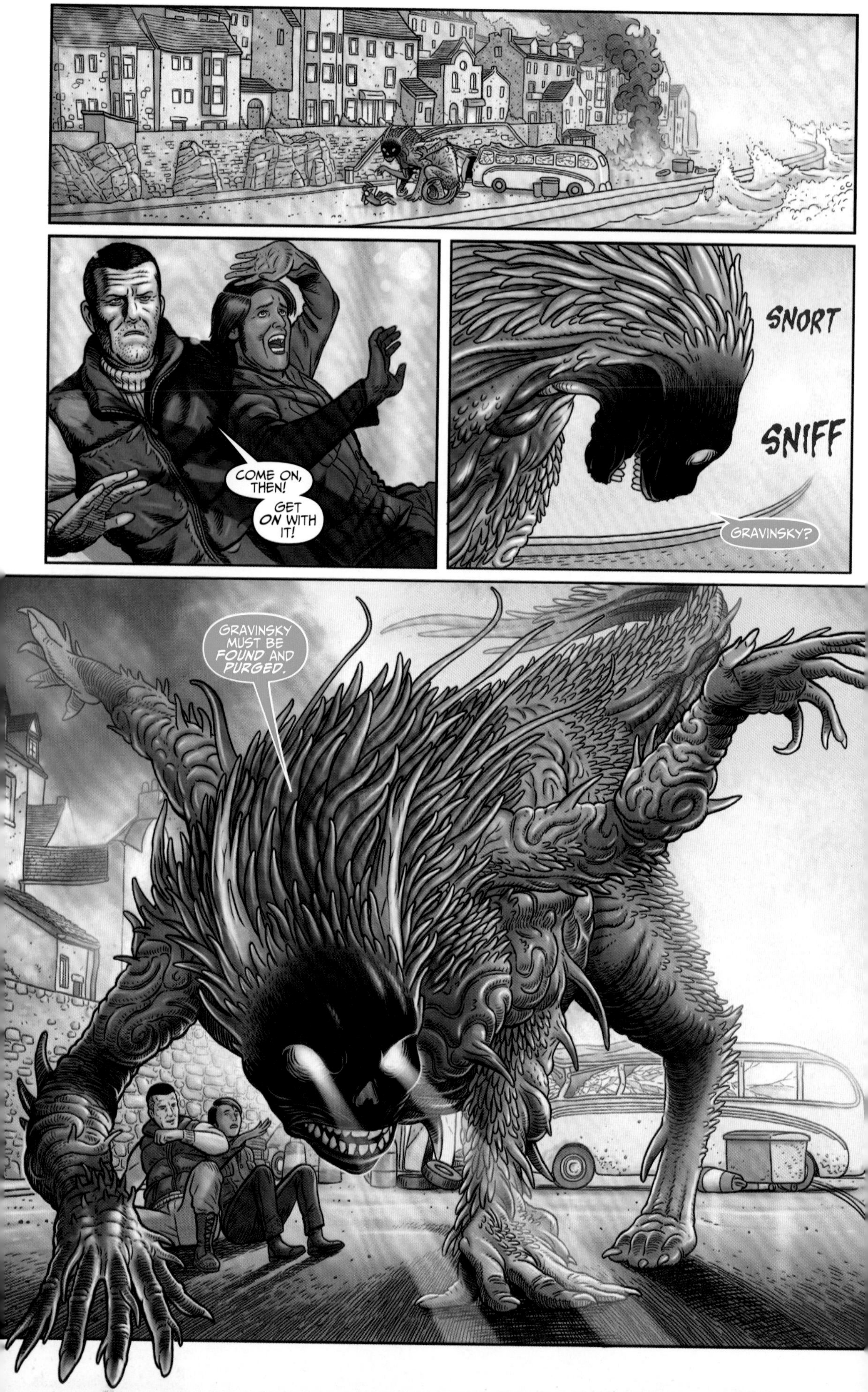

COME ON, THEN!
GET ON WITH IT!
SNORT
SNIFF
GRAVINSKY?
GRAVINSKY MUST BE FOUND AND PURGED.

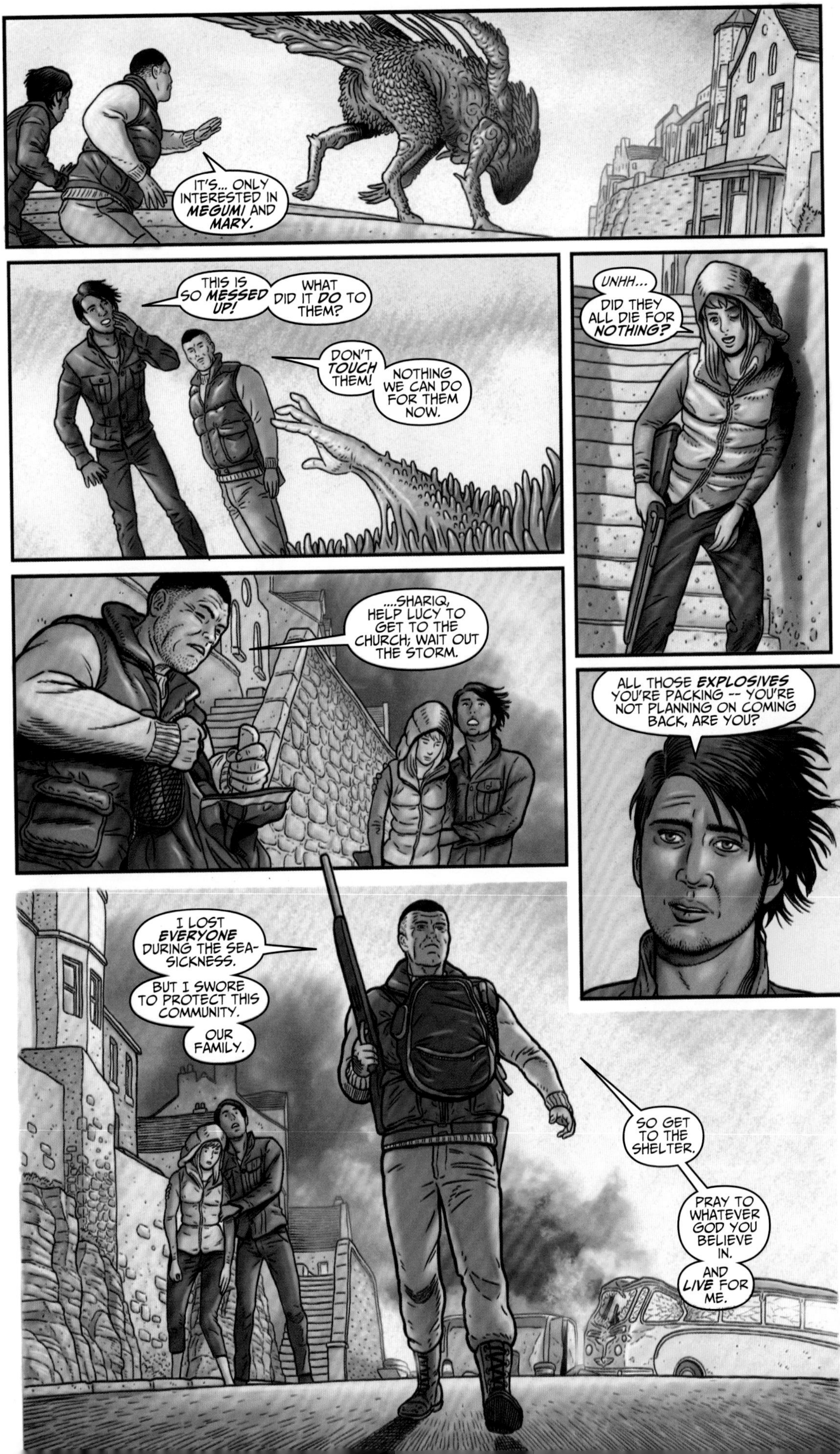
IT'S... ONLY INTERESTED IN MEGUMI AND MARY.
THIS IS SO MESSED UP!
WHAT DID IT DO TO THEM?
DON'T TOUCH THEM!
NOTHING WE CAN DO FOR THEM NOW.
UNHH...
DID THEY ALL DIE FOR NOTHING?
....SHARIQ, HELP LUCY TO GET TO THE CHURCH; WAIT OUT THE STORM.
ALL THOSE EXPLOSIVES YOU'RE PACKING -- YOU'RE NOT PLANNING ON COMING BACK, ARE YOU?
I LOST EVERYONE DURING THE SEA-SICKNESS.
BUT I SWORE TO PROTECT THIS COMMUNITY.
OUR FAMILY.
SO GET TO THE SHELTER.
PRAY TO WHATEVER GOD YOU BELIEVE IN.
AND LIVE FOR ME.

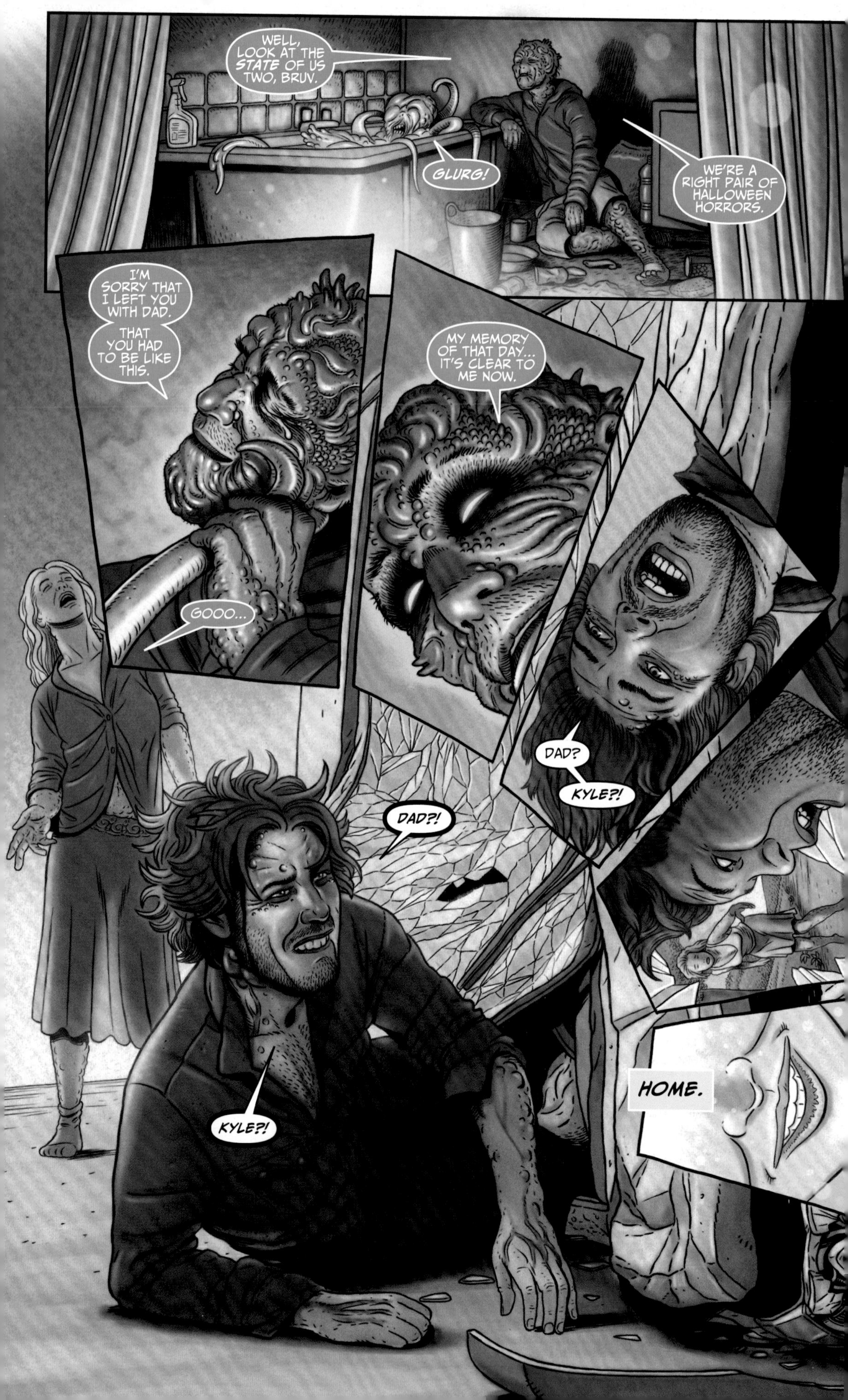
WELL, LOOK AT THE STATE OF US TWO, BRUV.
GLURG!
WE'RE A RIGHT PAIR OF HALLOWEEN HORRORS.
I'M SORRY THAT I LEFT YOU WITH DAD.
THAT YOU HAD TO BE LIKE THIS.
GOOO...
MY MEMORY OF THAT DAY... IT'S CLEAR TO ME NOW.
DAD?
KYLE?!
DAD?!
KYLE?!
HOME.

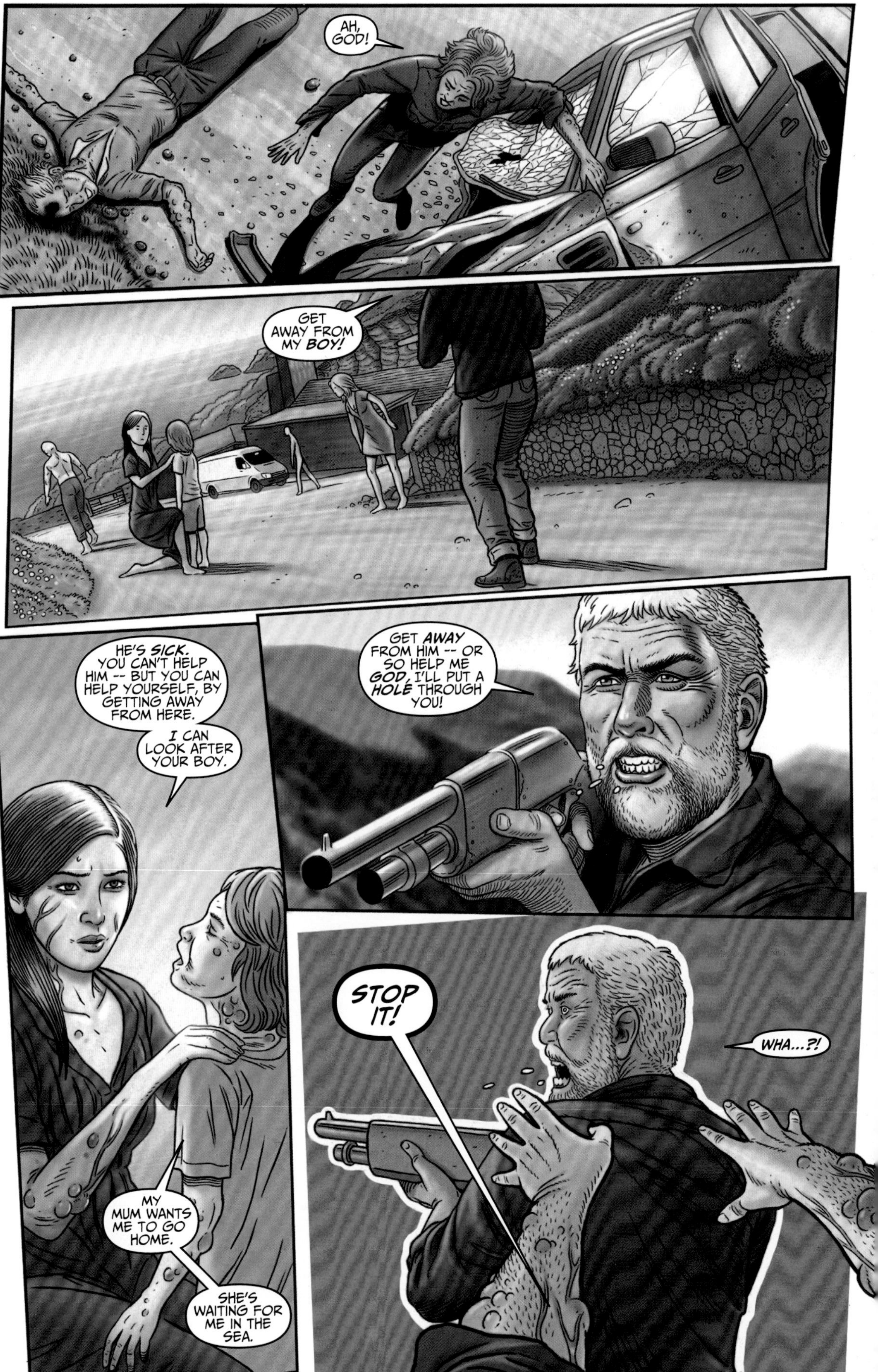
AH, GOD!
GET AWAY FROM MY BOY!
HE'S SICK. YOU CAN'T HELP HIM -- BUT YOU CAN HELP YOURSELF, BY GETTING AWAY FROM HERE.
I CAN LOOK AFTER YOUR BOY.
GET AWAY FROM HIM -- OR SO HELP ME GOD, I'LL PUT A HOLE THROUGH YOU!
MY MUM WANTS ME TO GO HOME.
SHE'S WAITING FOR ME IN THE SEA.
STOP IT!
WHA...?!

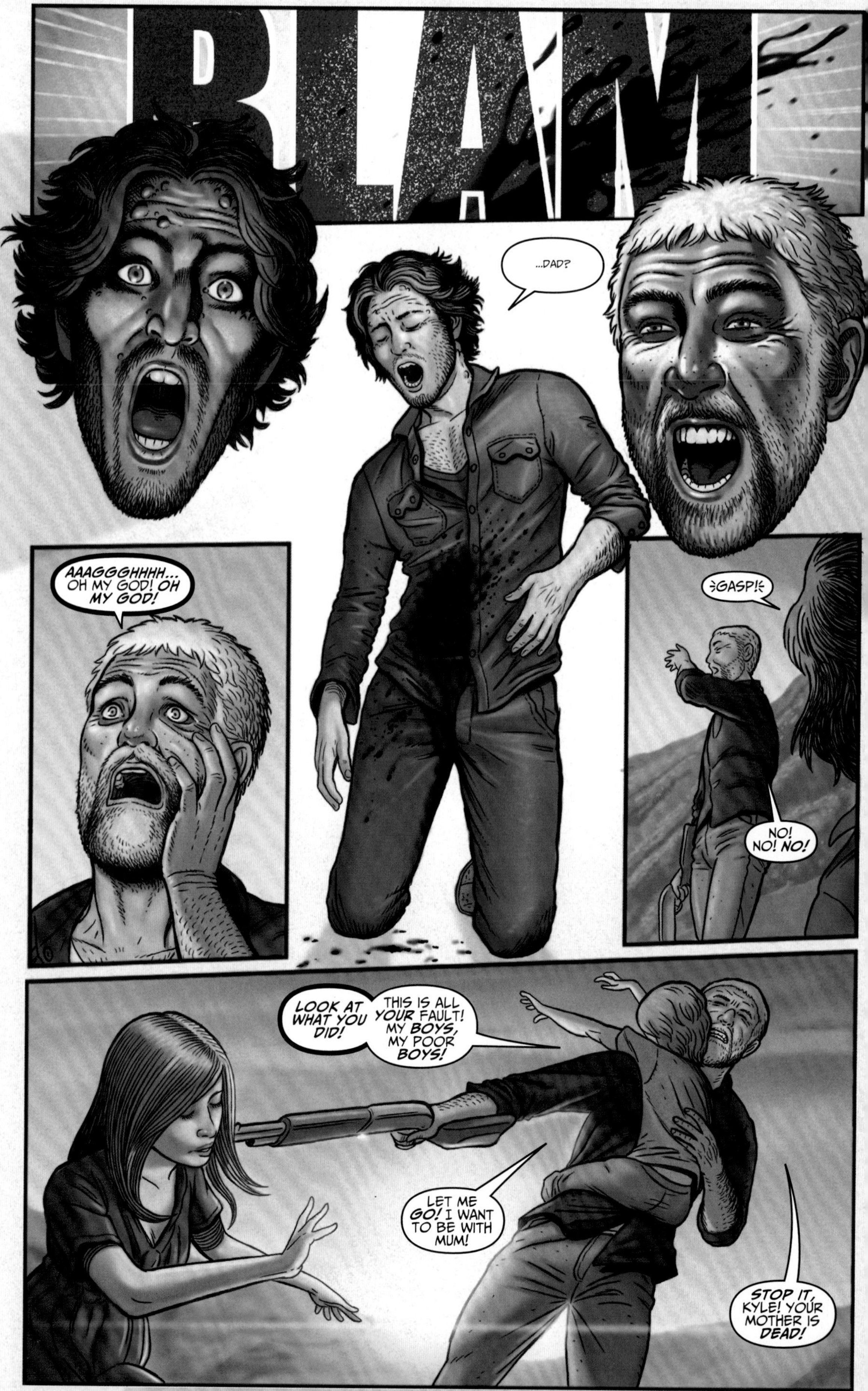
BLAM
...DAD?
AAAGGGHHHH... OH MY GOD! OH MY GOD!
GASP!
NO! NO! NO!
LOOK AT WHAT YOU DID!
THIS IS ALL YOUR FAULT! MY BOYS, MY POOR BOYS!
LET ME GO! I WANT TO BE WITH MUM!
STOP IT, KYLE! YOUR MOTHER IS DEAD!

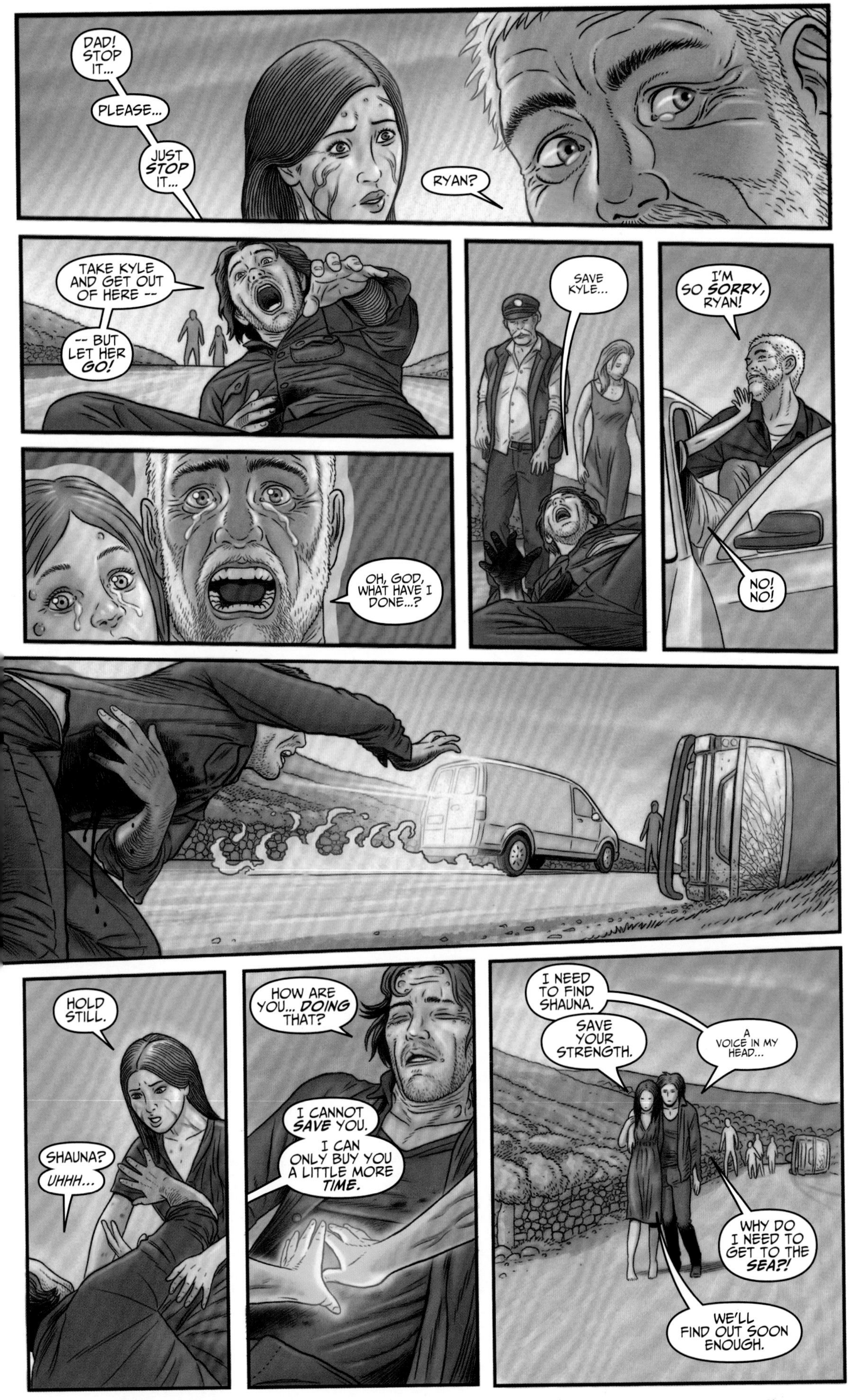
DAD! STOP IT...
PLEASE...
JUST STOP IT...
RYAN?
TAKE KYLE AND GET OUT OF HERE --
-- BUT LET HER GO!
SAVE KYLE...
I'M SO SORRY, RYAN!
OH, GOD, WHAT HAVE I DONE...?
NO! NO!
HOLD STILL.
SHAUNA? UHHH...
HOW ARE YOU... DOING THAT?
I CANNOT SAVE YOU.
I CAN ONLY BUY YOU A LITTLE MORE TIME.
I NEED TO FIND SHAUNA.
SAVE YOUR STRENGTH.
A VOICE IN MY HEAD...
WHY DO I NEED TO GET TO THE SEA?!
WE'LL FIND OUT SOON ENOUGH.

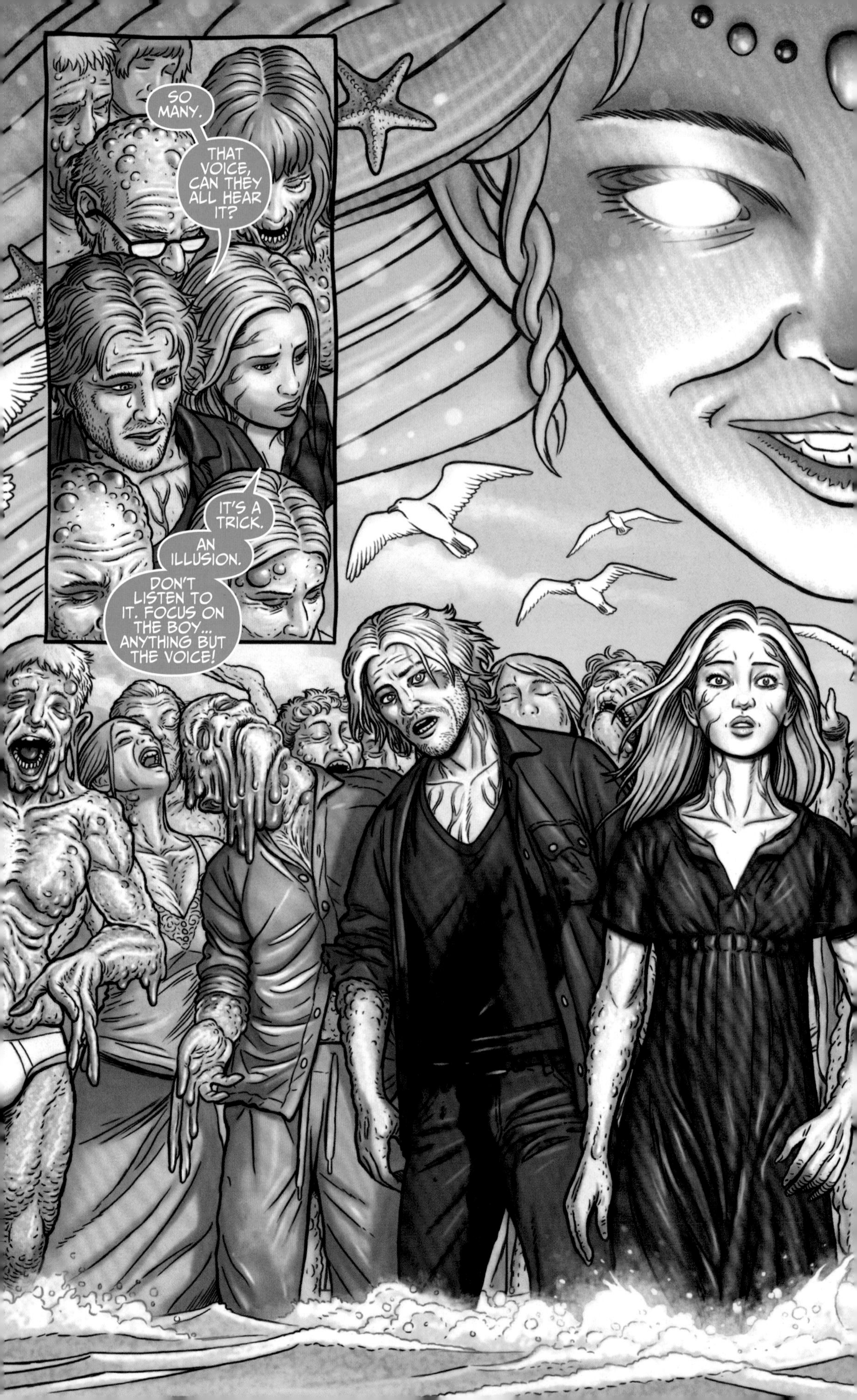
SO MANY.
THAT VOICE, CAN THEY ALL HEAR IT?
IT'S A TRICK.
AN ILLUSION.
DON'T LISTEN TO IT. FOCUS ON THE BOY... ANYTHING BUT THE VOICE!

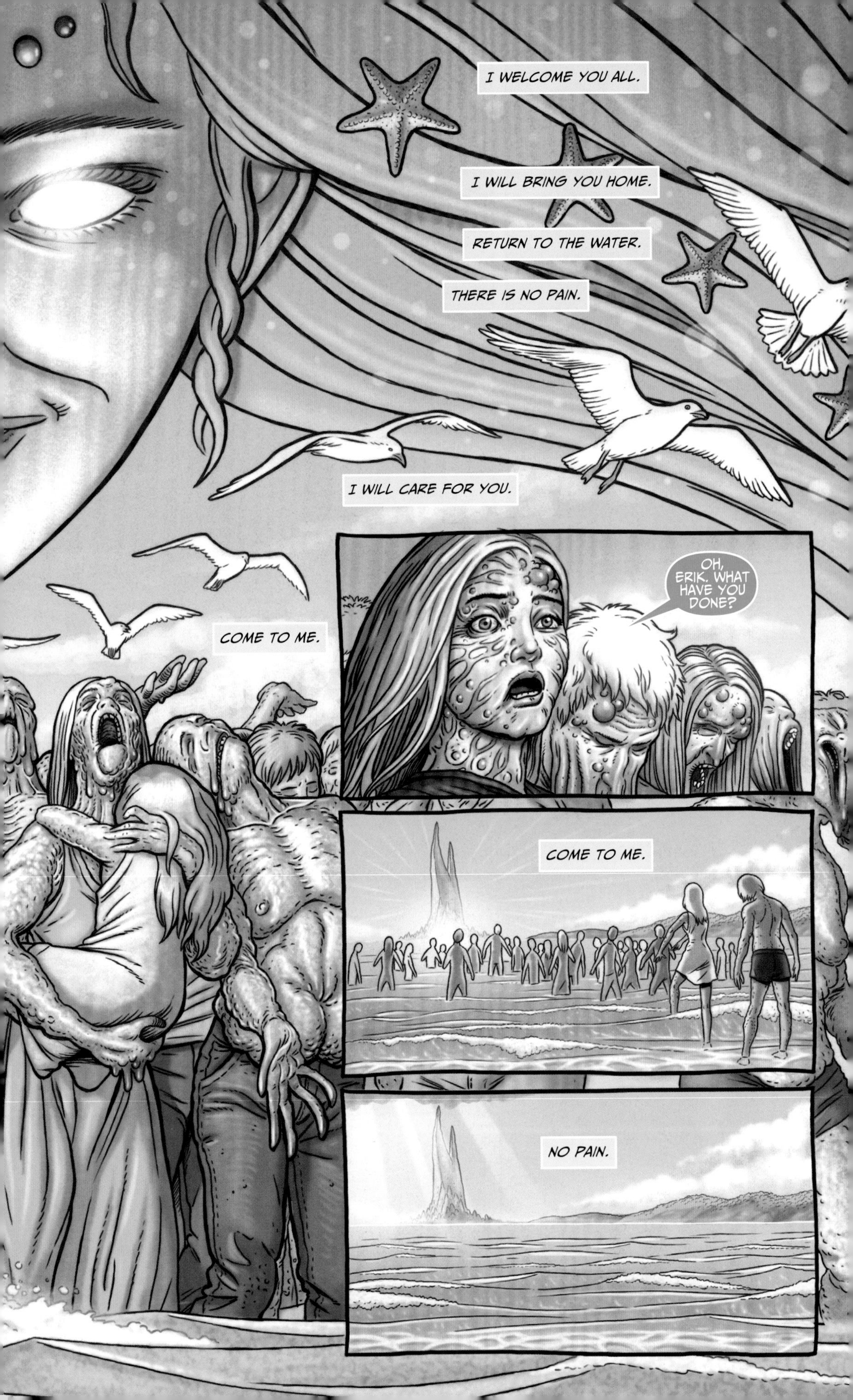
I WELCOME YOU ALL.
I WILL BRING YOU HOME.
RETURN TO THE WATER.
THERE IS NO PAIN.
I WILL CARE FOR YOU.
COME TO ME.
OH, ERIK. WHAT HAVE YOU DONE?
COME TO ME.
NO PAIN.

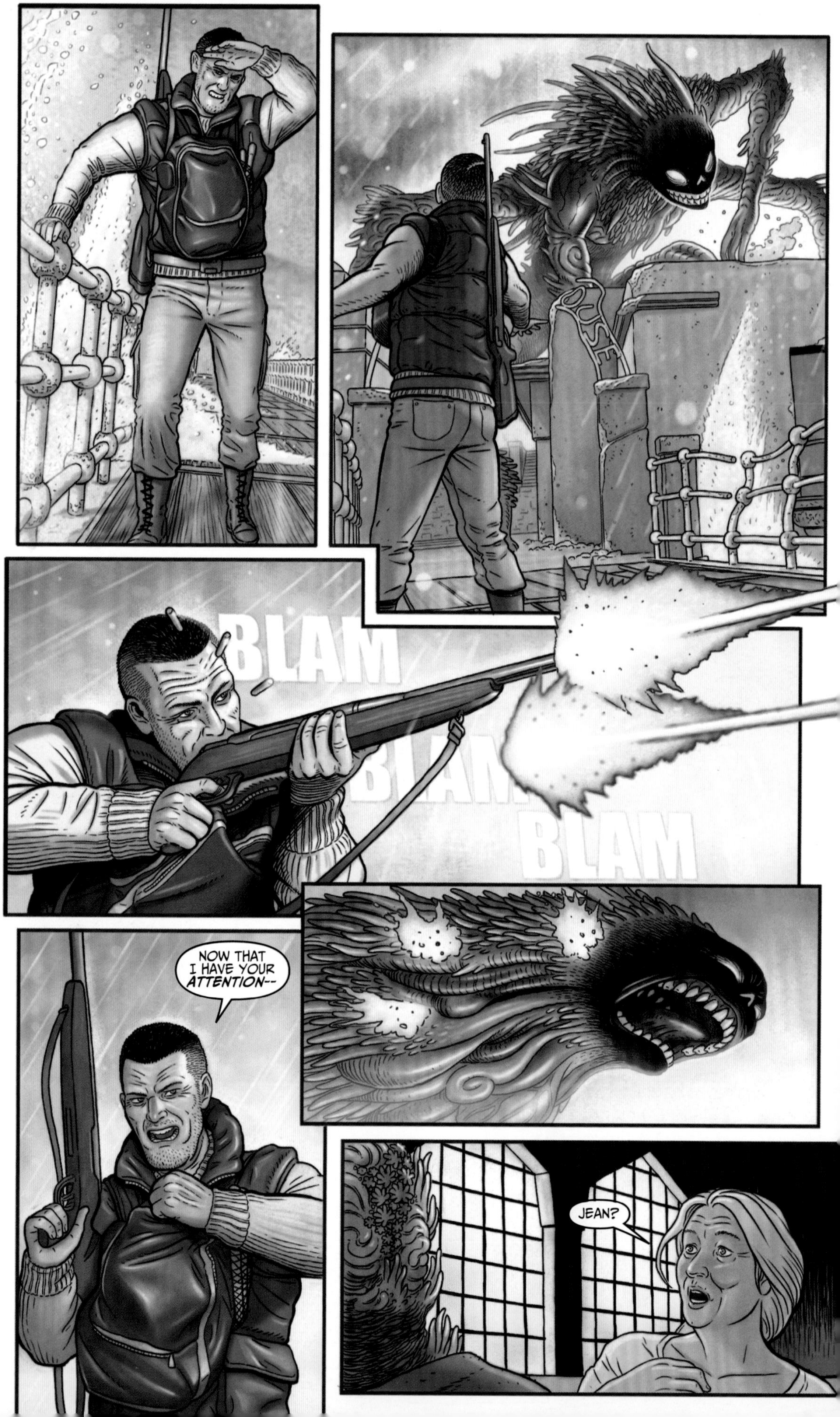
BLAM
BLAM
BLAM
NOW THAT I HAVE YOUR *ATTENTION*--
JEAN?

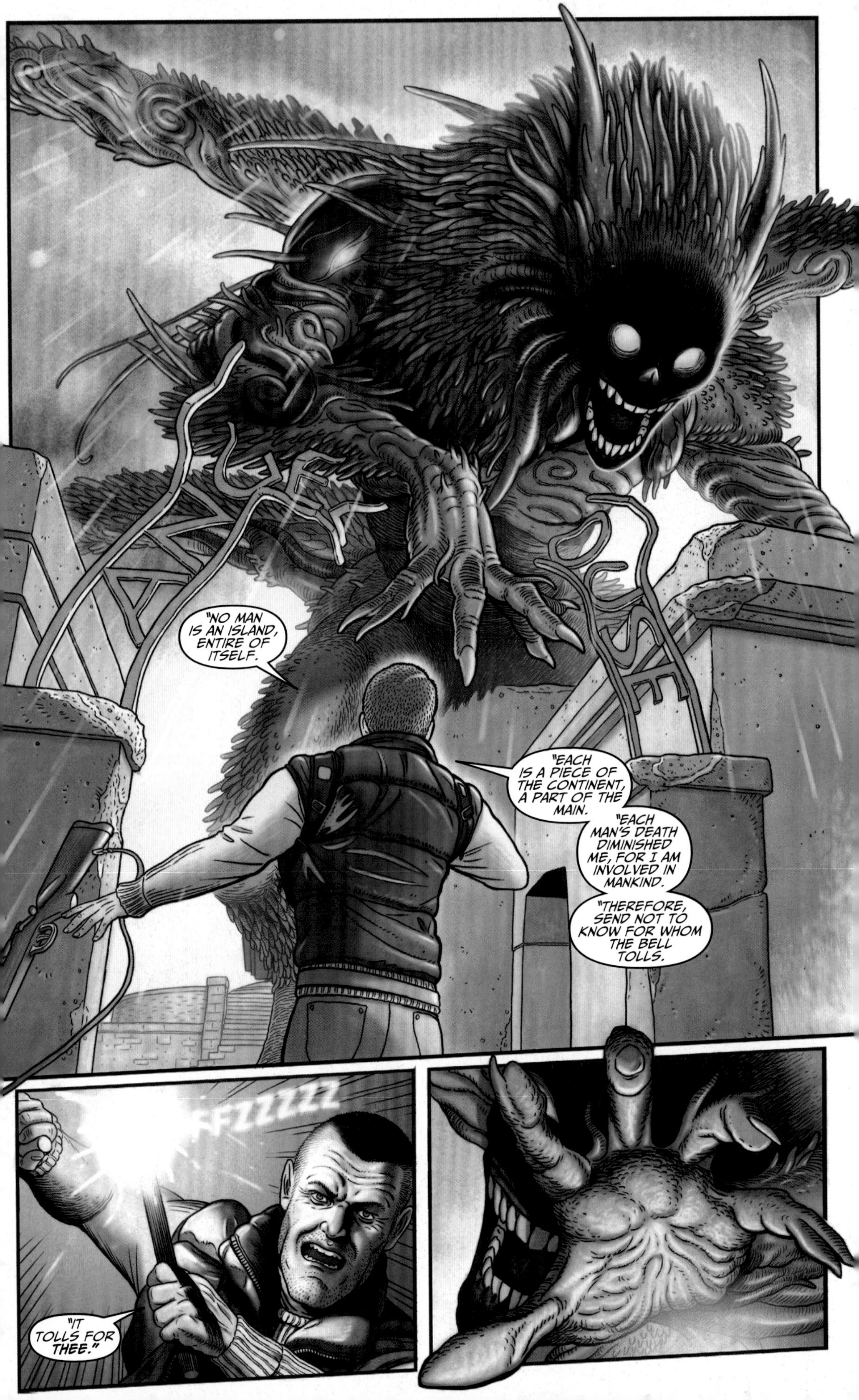
"NO MAN IS AN ISLAND, ENTIRE OF ITSELF.
"EACH IS A PIECE OF THE CONTINENT, A PART OF THE MAIN.
"EACH MAN'S DEATH DIMINISHED ME, FOR I AM INVOLVED IN MANKIND.
"THEREFORE, SEND NOT TO KNOW FOR WHOM THE BELL TOLLS.
FZZZZZZ
"IT TOLLS FOR THEE."

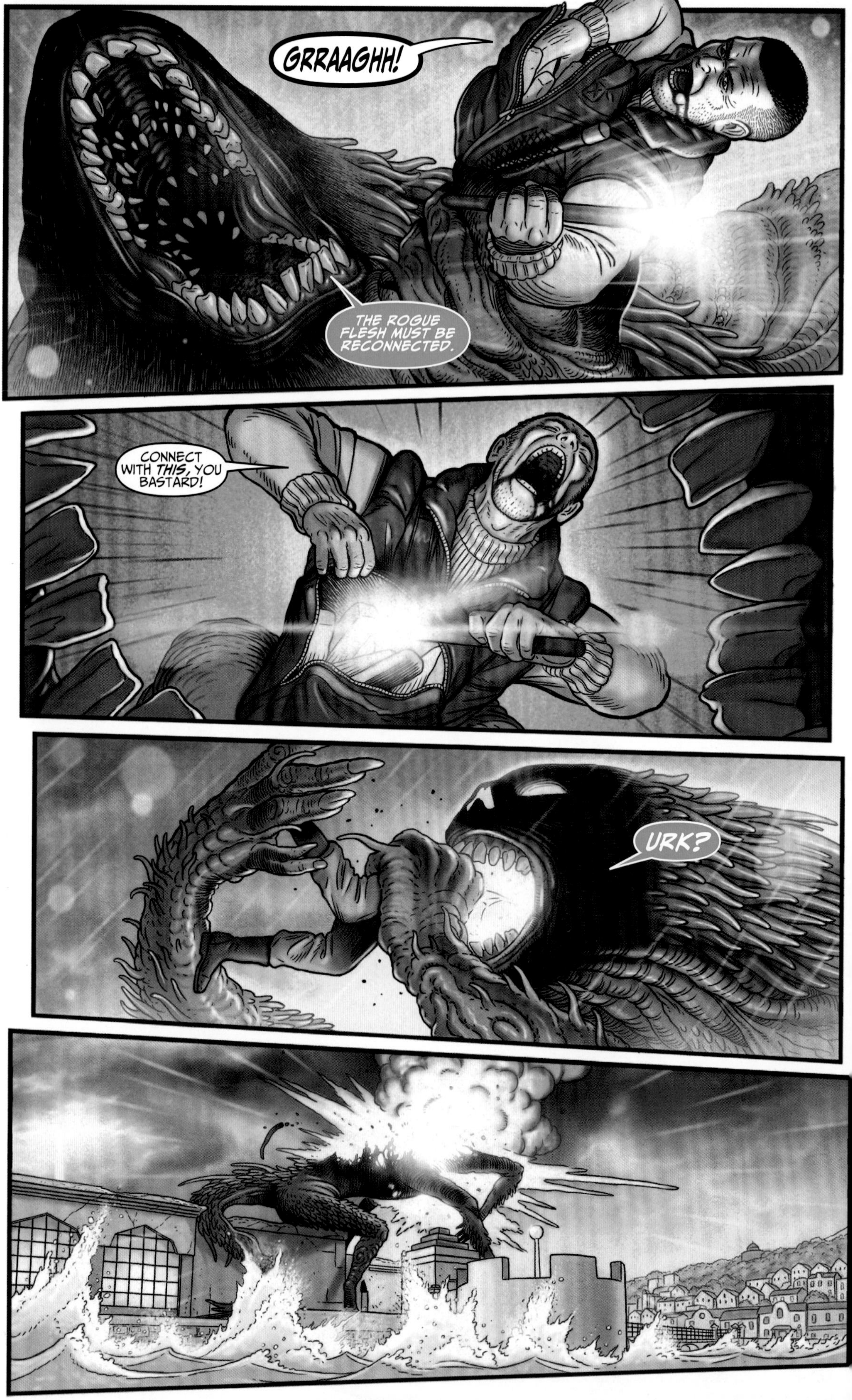
GRRAAGHH!
THE ROGUE FLESH MUST BE RECONNECTED.
CONNECT WITH THIS, YOU BASTARD!
URK?

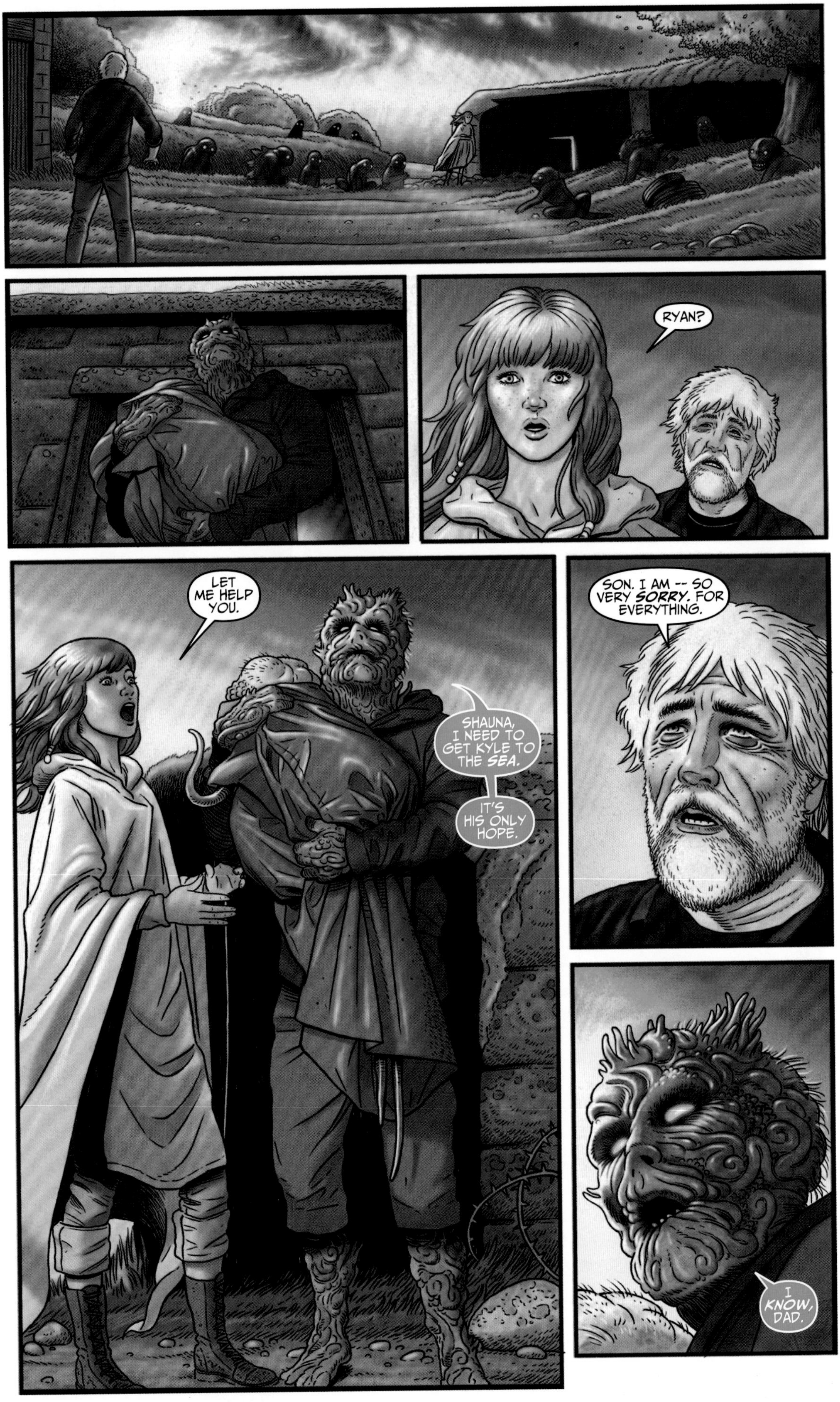
RYAN?
LET ME HELP YOU.
SHAUNA, I NEED TO GET KYLE TO THE SEA.
IT'S HIS ONLY HOPE.
SON. I AM -- SO VERY SORRY. FOR EVERYTHING.
I KNOW, DAD.

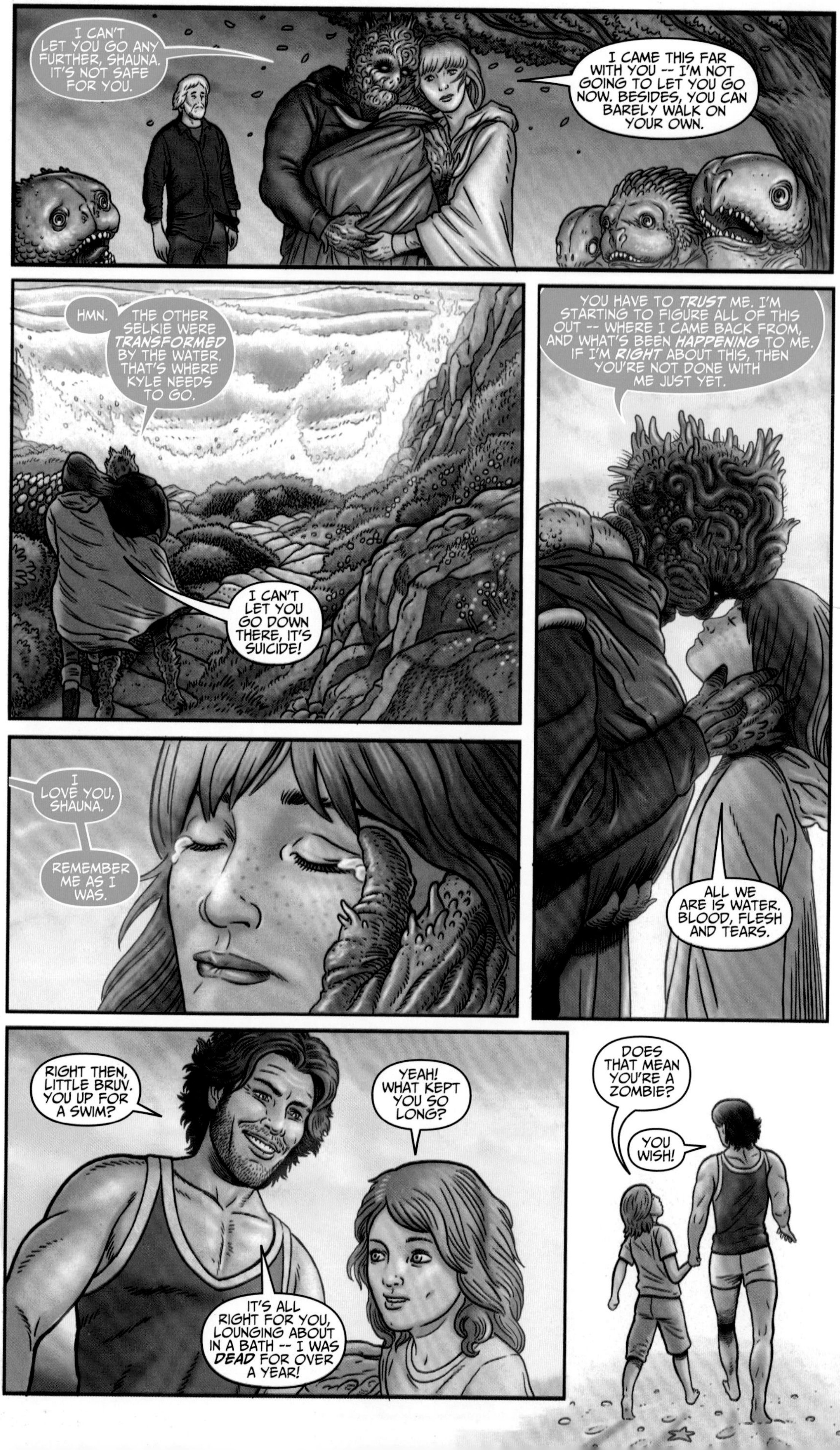
I CAN'T LET YOU GO ANY FURTHER, SHAUNA. IT'S NOT SAFE FOR YOU.
I CAME THIS FAR WITH YOU -- I'M NOT GOING TO LET YOU GO NOW. BESIDES, YOU CAN BARELY WALK ON YOUR OWN.
HMN.
THE OTHER SELKIE WERE TRANSFORMED BY THE WATER. THAT'S WHERE KYLE NEEDS TO GO.
I CAN'T LET YOU GO DOWN THERE, IT'S SUICIDE!
YOU HAVE TO TRUST ME. I'M STARTING TO FIGURE ALL OF THIS OUT -- WHERE I CAME BACK FROM, AND WHAT'S BEEN HAPPENING TO ME. IF I'M RIGHT ABOUT THIS, THEN YOU'RE NOT DONE WITH ME JUST YET.
ALL WE ARE IS WATER. BLOOD, FLESH AND TEARS.
I LOVE YOU, SHAUNA.
REMEMBER ME AS I WAS.
RIGHT THEN, LITTLE BRUV. YOU UP FOR A SWIM?
YEAH! WHAT KEPT YOU SO LONG?
IT'S ALL RIGHT FOR YOU, LOUNGING ABOUT IN A BATH -- I WAS DEAD FOR OVER A YEAR!
DOES THAT MEAN YOU'RE A ZOMBIE?
YOU WISH!

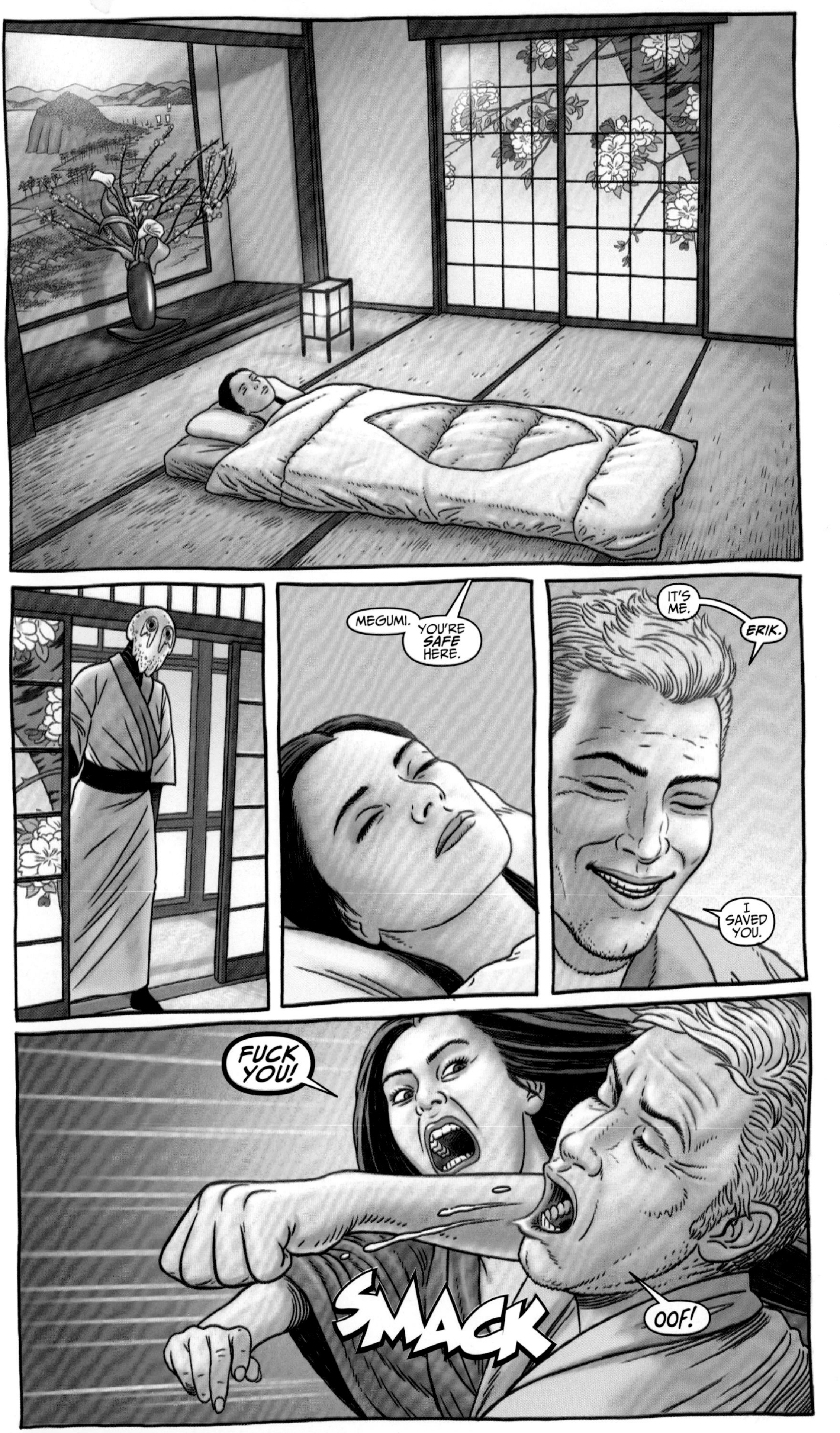
MEGUMI.
YOU'RE SAFE HERE.
IT'S ME.
ERIK.
I SAVED YOU.
FUCK YOU!
SMACK
OOF!

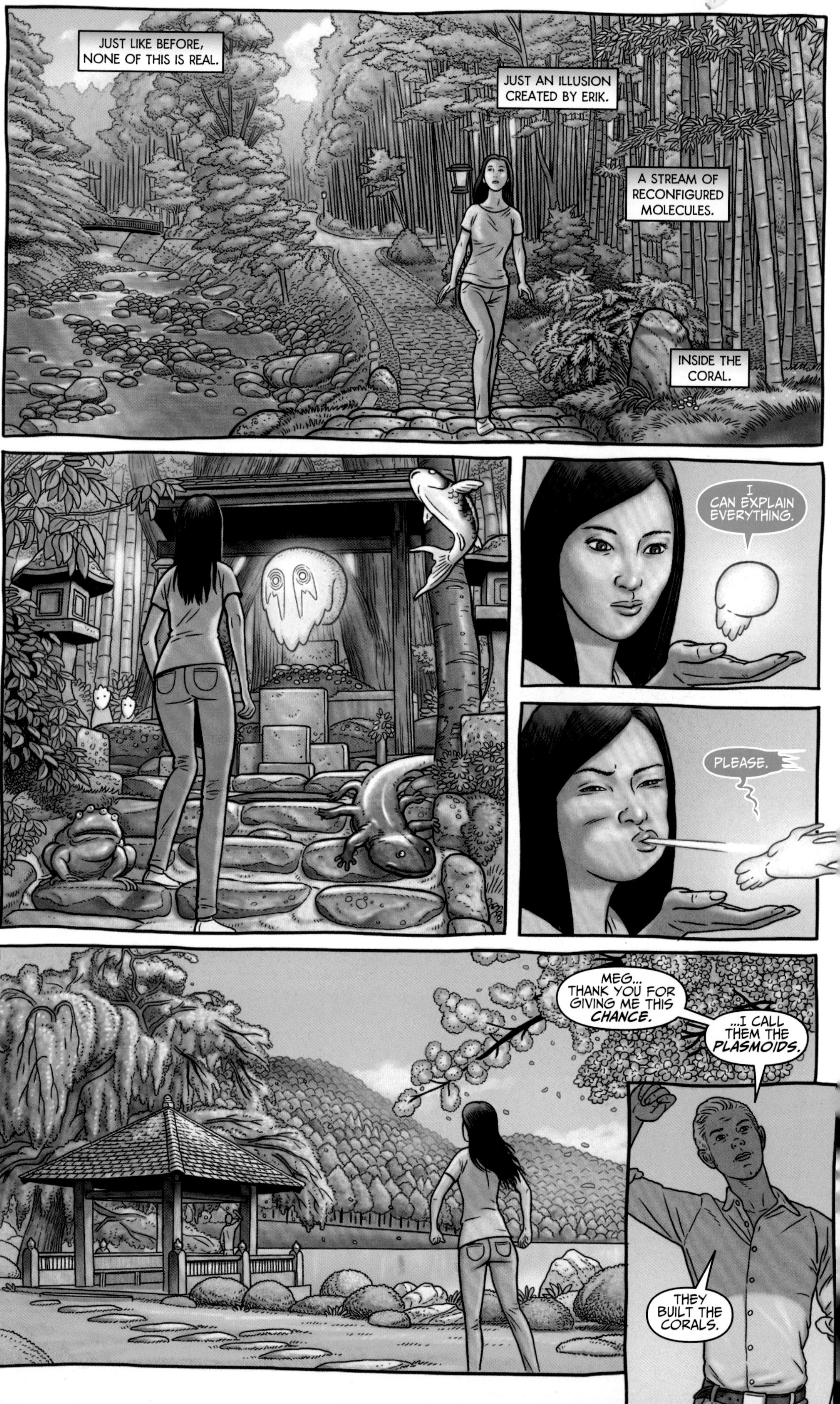
JUST LIKE BEFORE, NONE OF THIS IS REAL.
JUST AN ILLUSION CREATED BY ERIK.
A STREAM OF RECONFIGURED MOLECULES.
INSIDE THE CORAL.
I CAN EXPLAIN EVERYTHING.
PLEASE.
MEG... THANK YOU FOR GIVING ME THIS *CHANCE.*
...I CALL THEM THE ***PLASMOIDS.***
THEY BUILT THE CORALS.

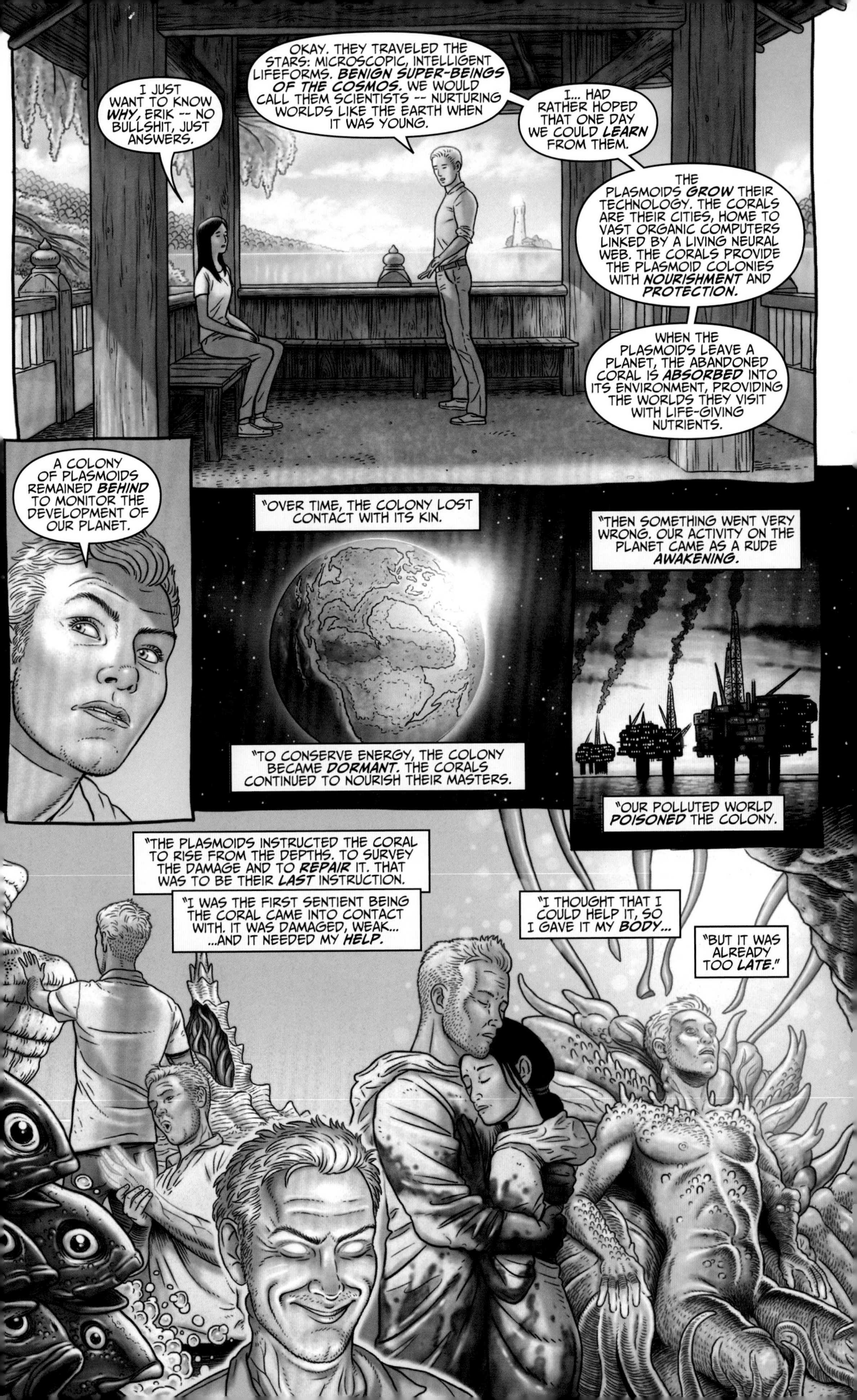
I JUST WANT TO KNOW WHY, ERIK -- NO BULLSHIT, JUST ANSWERS.
OKAY. THEY TRAVELED THE STARS: MICROSCOPIC, INTELLIGENT LIFEFORMS. BENIGN SUPER-BEINGS OF THE COSMOS. WE WOULD CALL THEM SCIENTISTS -- NURTURING WORLDS LIKE THE EARTH WHEN IT WAS YOUNG.
I... HAD RATHER HOPED THAT ONE DAY WE COULD LEARN FROM THEM.
THE PLASMOIDS GROW THEIR TECHNOLOGY. THE CORALS ARE THEIR CITIES, HOME TO VAST ORGANIC COMPUTERS LINKED BY A LIVING NEURAL WEB. THE CORALS PROVIDE THE PLASMOID COLONIES WITH NOURISHMENT AND PROTECTION.
WHEN THE PLASMOIDS LEAVE A PLANET, THE ABANDONED CORAL IS ABSORBED INTO ITS ENVIRONMENT, PROVIDING THE WORLDS THEY VISIT WITH LIFE-GIVING NUTRIENTS.
A COLONY OF PLASMOIDS REMAINED BEHIND TO MONITOR THE DEVELOPMENT OF OUR PLANET.
"OVER TIME, THE COLONY LOST CONTACT WITH ITS KIN.
"TO CONSERVE ENERGY, THE COLONY BECAME DORMANT. THE CORALS CONTINUED TO NOURISH THEIR MASTERS.
"THEN SOMETHING WENT VERY WRONG. OUR ACTIVITY ON THE PLANET CAME AS A RUDE AWAKENING.
"OUR POLLUTED WORLD POISONED THE COLONY.
"THE PLASMOIDS INSTRUCTED THE CORAL TO RISE FROM THE DEPTHS. TO SURVEY THE DAMAGE AND TO REPAIR IT. THAT WAS TO BE THEIR LAST INSTRUCTION.
"I WAS THE FIRST SENTIENT BEING THE CORAL CAME INTO CONTACT WITH. IT WAS DAMAGED, WEAK... ...AND IT NEEDED MY HELP.
"I THOUGHT THAT I COULD HELP IT, SO I GAVE IT MY BODY...
"BUT IT WAS ALREADY TOO LATE."

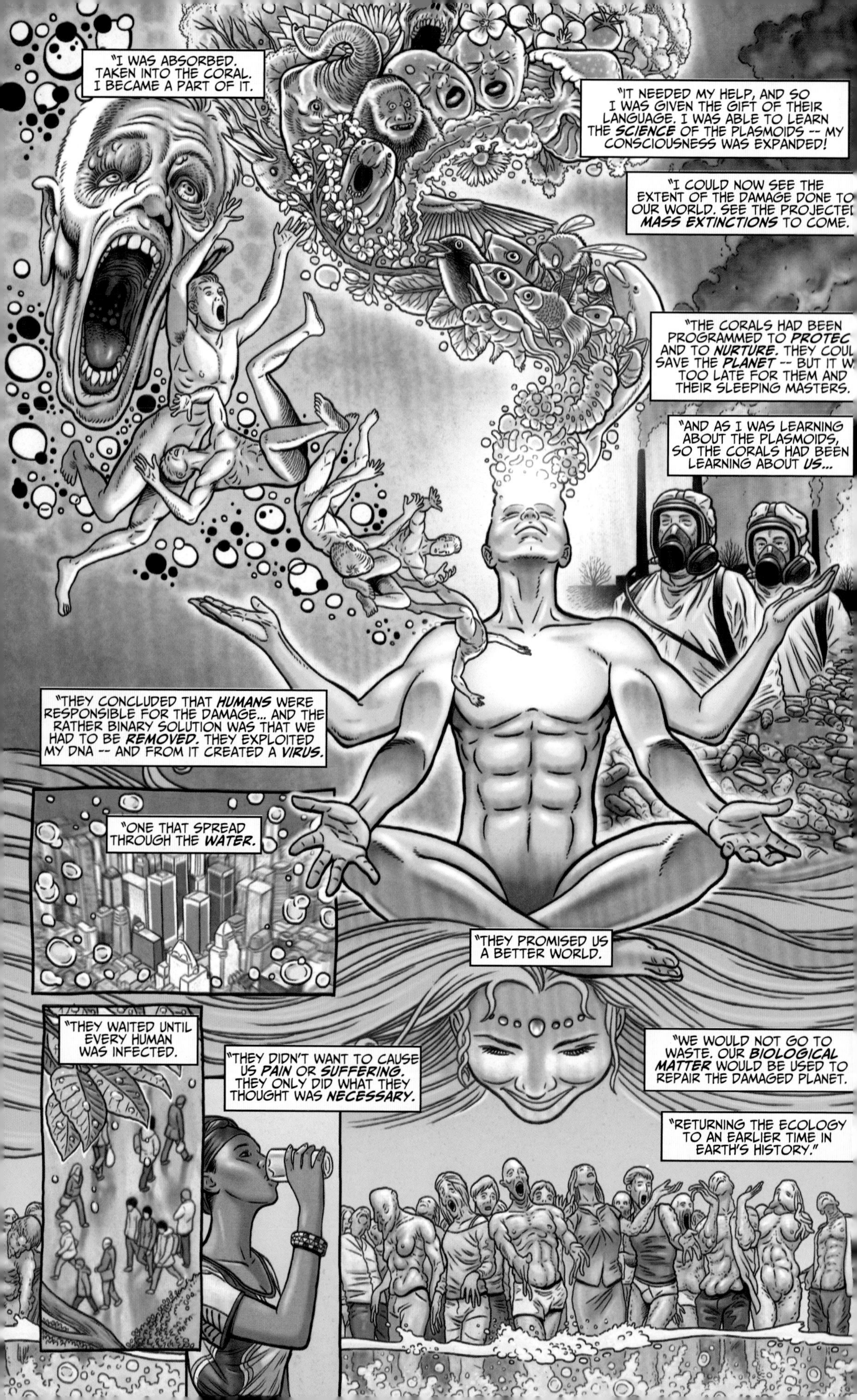
"I WAS ABSORBED. TAKEN INTO THE CORAL. I BECAME A PART OF IT.
"IT NEEDED MY HELP, AND SO I WAS GIVEN THE GIFT OF THEIR LANGUAGE. I WAS ABLE TO LEARN THE SCIENCE OF THE PLASMOIDS -- MY CONSCIOUSNESS WAS EXPANDED!
"I COULD NOW SEE THE EXTENT OF THE DAMAGE DONE TO OUR WORLD. SEE THE PROJECTED MASS EXTINCTIONS TO COME.
"THE CORALS HAD BEEN PROGRAMMED TO PROTEC AND TO NURTURE. THEY COUL SAVE THE PLANET -- BUT IT W TOO LATE FOR THEM AND THEIR SLEEPING MASTERS.
"AND AS I WAS LEARNING ABOUT THE PLASMOIDS, SO THE CORALS HAD BEEN LEARNING ABOUT US...
"THEY CONCLUDED THAT HUMANS WERE RESPONSIBLE FOR THE DAMAGE... AND THE RATHER BINARY SOLUTION WAS THAT WE HAD TO BE REMOVED. THEY EXPLOITED MY DNA -- AND FROM IT CREATED A VIRUS.
"ONE THAT SPREAD THROUGH THE WATER.
"THEY PROMISED US A BETTER WORLD.
"THEY WAITED UNTIL EVERY HUMAN WAS INFECTED.
"THEY DIDN'T WANT TO CAUSE US PAIN OR SUFFERING. THEY ONLY DID WHAT THEY THOUGHT WAS NECESSARY.
"WE WOULD NOT GO TO WASTE. OUR BIOLOGICAL MATTER WOULD BE USED TO REPAIR THE DAMAGED PLANET.
"RETURNING THE ECOLOGY TO AN EARLIER TIME IN EARTH'S HISTORY."

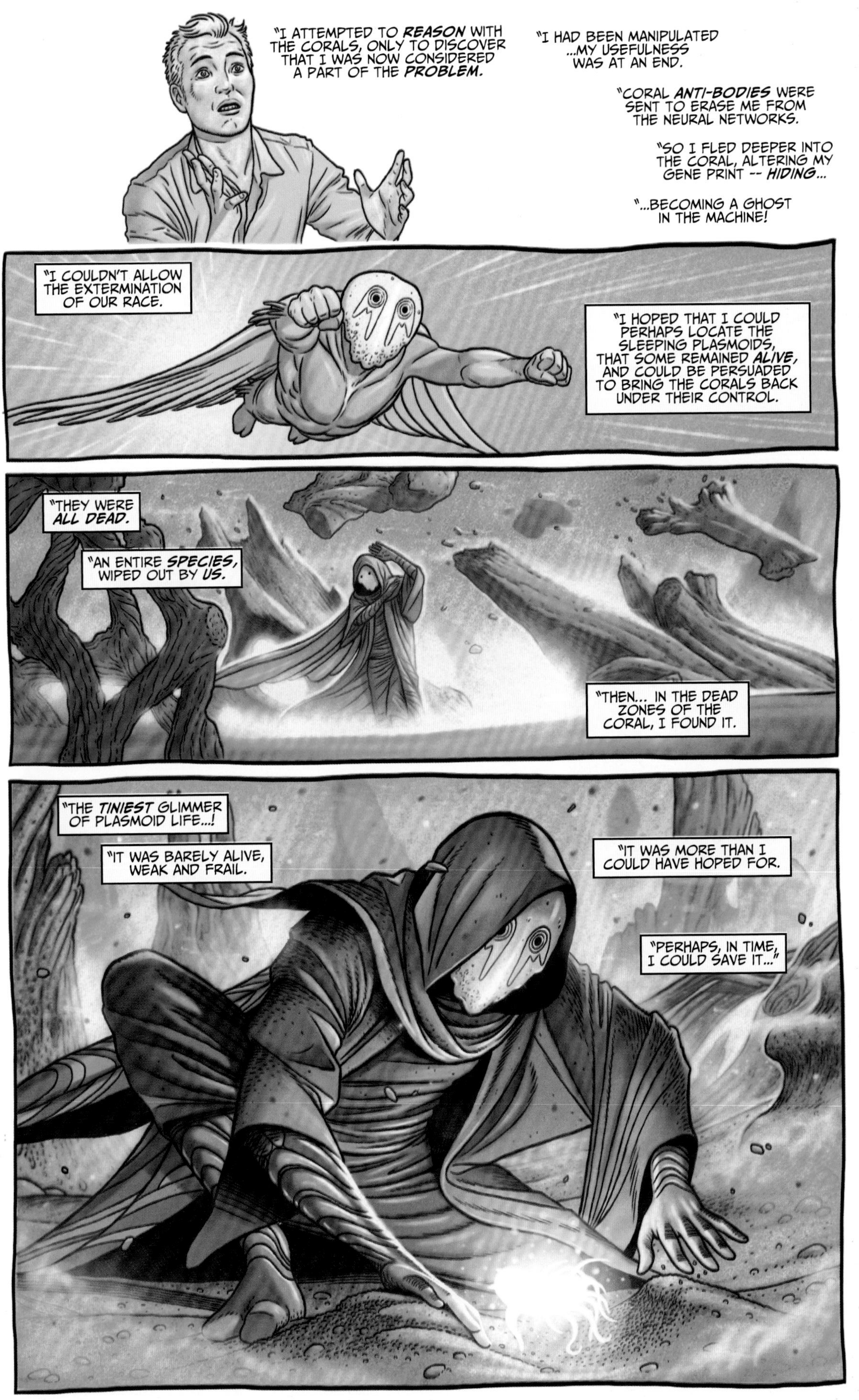
"I ATTEMPTED TO REASON WITH THE CORALS, ONLY TO DISCOVER THAT I WAS NOW CONSIDERED A PART OF THE PROBLEM.
"I HAD BEEN MANIPULATED ...MY USEFULNESS WAS AT AN END.
"CORAL ANTI-BODIES WERE SENT TO ERASE ME FROM THE NEURAL NETWORKS.
"SO I FLED DEEPER INTO THE CORAL, ALTERING MY GENE PRINT -- HIDING...
"...BECOMING A GHOST IN THE MACHINE!
"I COULDN'T ALLOW THE EXTERMINATION OF OUR RACE.
"I HOPED THAT I COULD PERHAPS LOCATE THE SLEEPING PLASMOIDS, THAT SOME REMAINED ALIVE, AND COULD BE PERSUADED TO BRING THE CORALS BACK UNDER THEIR CONTROL.
"THEY WERE ALL DEAD.
"AN ENTIRE SPECIES, WIPED OUT BY US.
"THEN... IN THE DEAD ZONES OF THE CORAL, I FOUND IT.
"THE TINIEST GLIMMER OF PLASMOID LIFE...!
"IT WAS BARELY ALIVE, WEAK AND FRAIL.
"IT WAS MORE THAN I COULD HAVE HOPED FOR.
"PERHAPS, IN TIME, I COULD SAVE IT..."

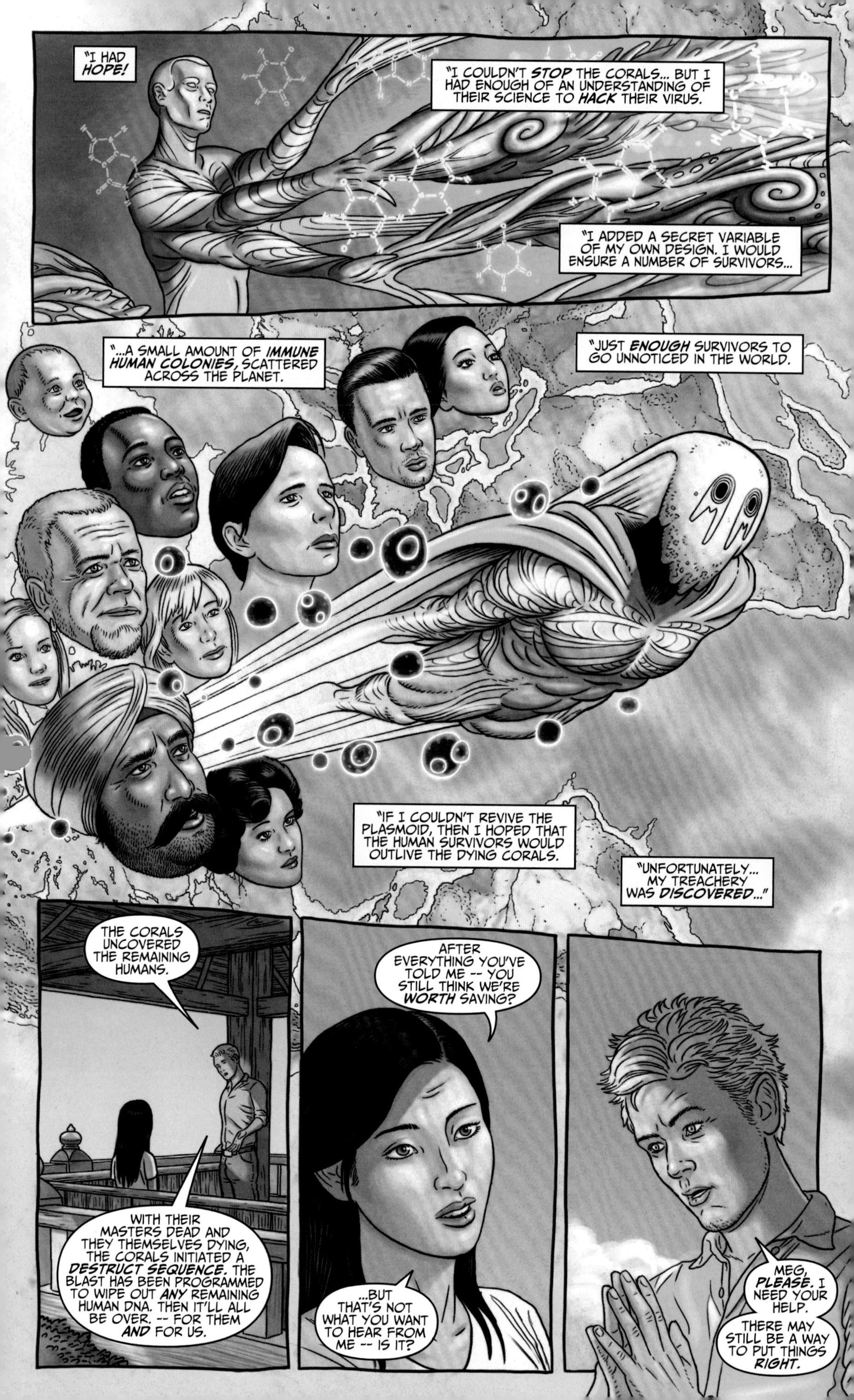
"I HAD HOPE!
"I COULDN'T STOP THE CORALS... BUT I HAD ENOUGH OF AN UNDERSTANDING OF THEIR SCIENCE TO HACK THEIR VIRUS.
"I ADDED A SECRET VARIABLE OF MY OWN DESIGN. I WOULD ENSURE A NUMBER OF SURVIVORS...
"...A SMALL AMOUNT OF IMMUNE HUMAN COLONIES, SCATTERED ACROSS THE PLANET.
"JUST ENOUGH SURVIVORS TO GO UNNOTICED IN THE WORLD.
"IF I COULDN'T REVIVE THE PLASMOID, THEN I HOPED THAT THE HUMAN SURVIVORS WOULD OUTLIVE THE DYING CORALS.
"UNFORTUNATELY... MY TREACHERY WAS DISCOVERED..."
THE CORALS UNCOVERED THE REMAINING HUMANS.
WITH THEIR MASTERS DEAD AND THEY THEMSELVES DYING, THE CORALS INITIATED A DESTRUCT SEQUENCE. THE BLAST HAS BEEN PROGRAMMED TO WIPE OUT ANY REMAINING HUMAN DNA. THEN IT'LL ALL BE OVER. -- FOR THEM AND FOR US.
AFTER EVERYTHING YOU'VE TOLD ME -- YOU STILL THINK WE'RE WORTH SAVING?
...BUT THAT'S NOT WHAT YOU WANT TO HEAR FROM ME -- IS IT?
MEG, PLEASE. I NEED YOUR HELP.
THERE MAY STILL BE A WAY TO PUT THINGS RIGHT.

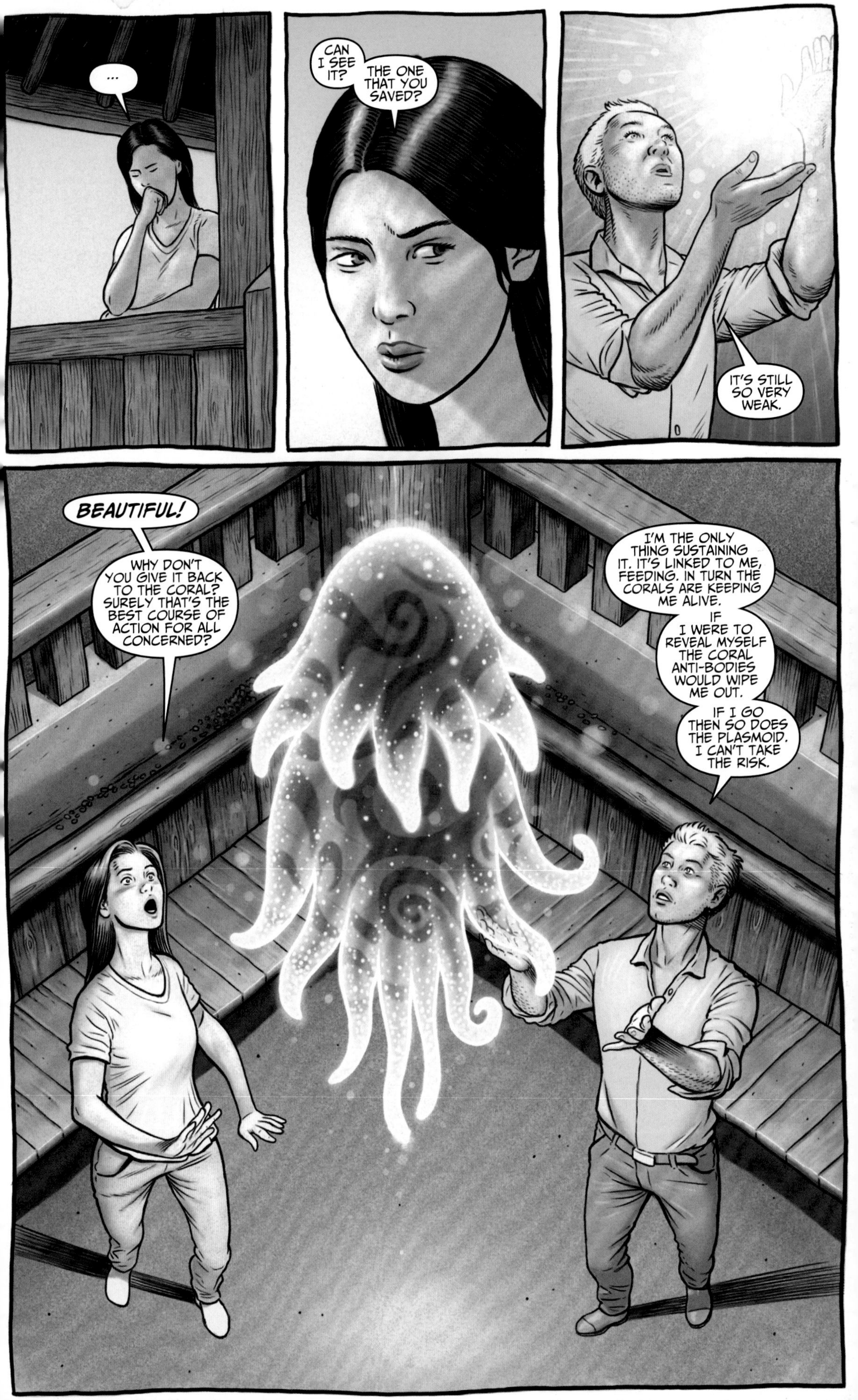
...
CAN I SEE IT?
THE ONE THAT YOU SAVED?
IT'S STILL SO VERY WEAK.
BEAUTIFUL!
WHY DON'T YOU GIVE IT BACK TO THE CORAL? SURELY THAT'S THE BEST COURSE OF ACTION FOR ALL CONCERNED?
I'M THE ONLY THING SUSTAINING IT. IT'S LINKED TO ME, FEEDING. IN TURN THE CORALS ARE KEEPING ME ALIVE.
IF I WERE TO REVEAL MYSELF THE CORAL ANTI-BODIES WOULD WIPE ME OUT.
IF I GO THEN SO DOES THE PLASMOID. I CAN'T TAKE THE RISK.

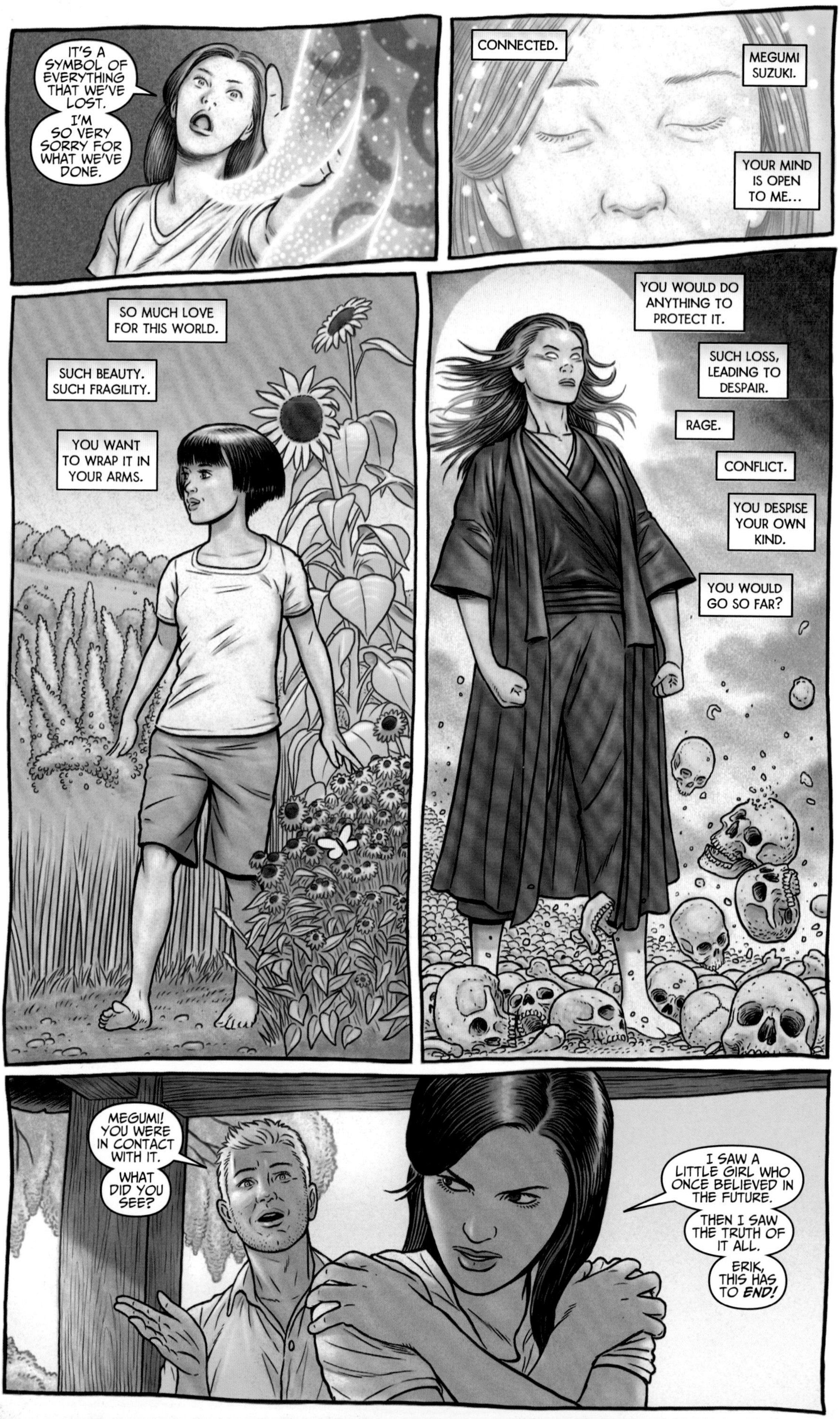
IT'S A SYMBOL OF EVERYTHING THAT WE'VE LOST.
I'M SO VERY SORRY FOR WHAT WE'VE DONE.
CONNECTED.
MEGUMI SUZUKI.
YOUR MIND IS OPEN TO ME...
SO MUCH LOVE FOR THIS WORLD.
SUCH BEAUTY. SUCH FRAGILITY.
YOU WANT TO WRAP IT IN YOUR ARMS.
YOU WOULD DO ANYTHING TO PROTECT IT.
SUCH LOSS, LEADING TO DESPAIR.
RAGE.
CONFLICT.
YOU DESPISE YOUR OWN KIND.
YOU WOULD GO SO FAR?
MEGUMI! YOU WERE IN CONTACT WITH IT.
WHAT DID YOU SEE?
I SAW A LITTLE GIRL WHO ONCE BELIEVED IN THE FUTURE.
THEN I SAW THE TRUTH OF IT ALL.
ERIK, THIS HAS TO END!

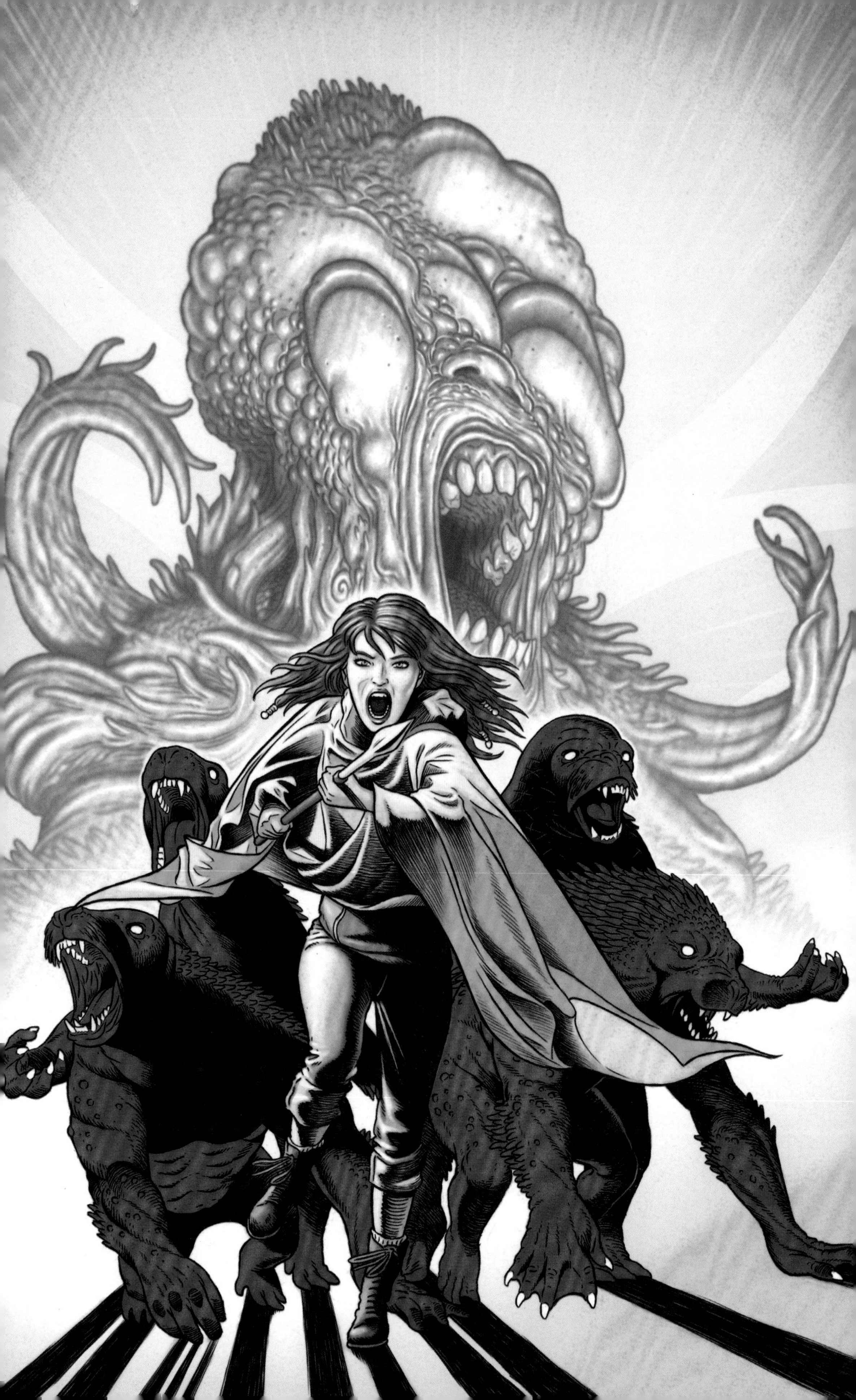

CHAPTER FIVE
WAVES

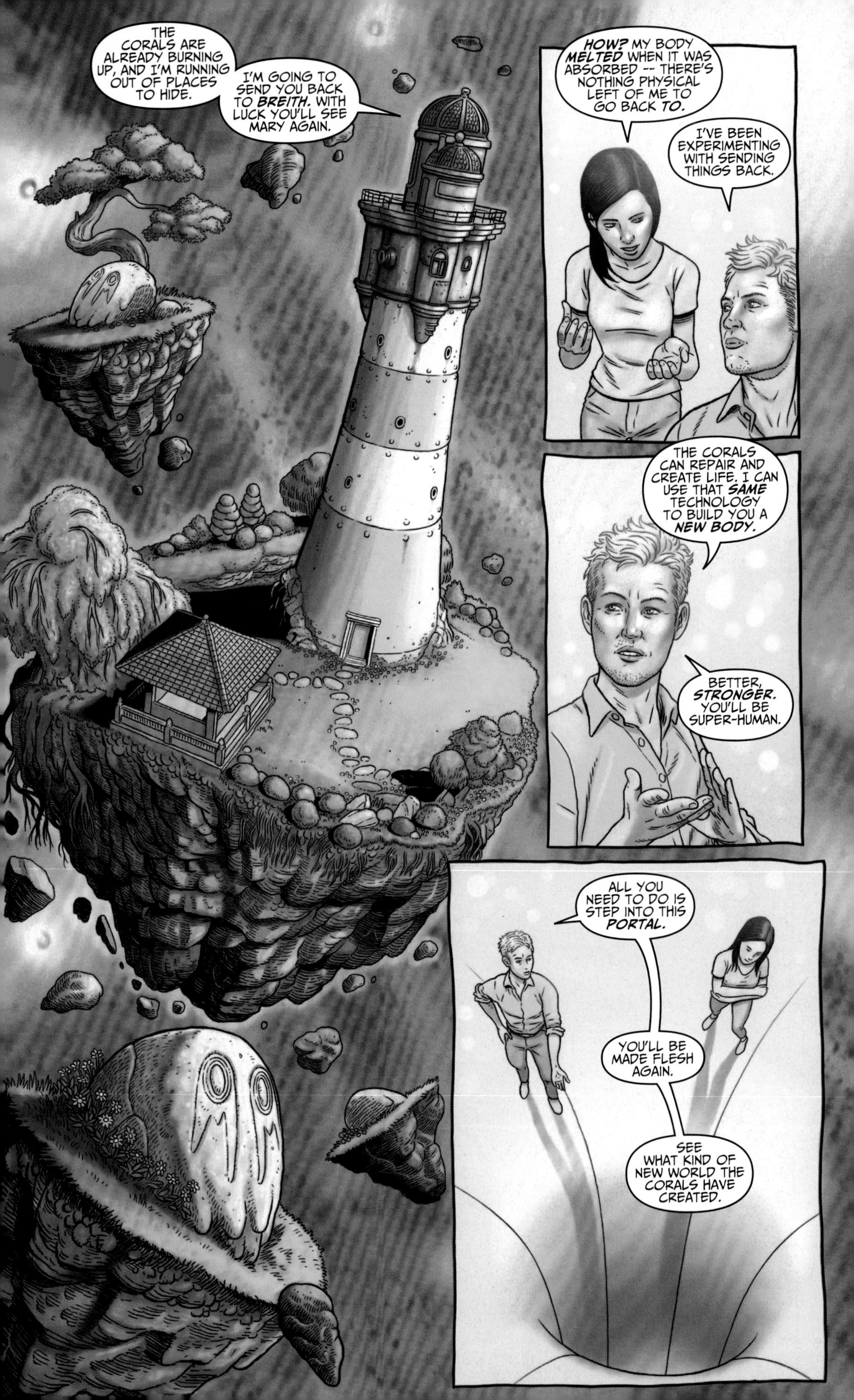
THE CORALS ARE ALREADY BURNING UP, AND I'M RUNNING OUT OF PLACES TO HIDE.
I'M GOING TO SEND YOU BACK TO BREITH. WITH LUCK YOU'LL SEE MARY AGAIN.
HOW? MY BODY MELTED WHEN IT WAS ABSORBED -- THERE'S NOTHING PHYSICAL LEFT OF ME TO GO BACK TO.
I'VE BEEN EXPERIMENTING WITH SENDING THINGS BACK.
THE CORALS CAN REPAIR AND CREATE LIFE. I CAN USE THAT SAME TECHNOLOGY TO BUILD YOU A NEW BODY.
BETTER, STRONGER. YOU'LL BE SUPER-HUMAN.
ALL YOU NEED TO DO IS STEP INTO THIS PORTAL.
YOU'LL BE MADE FLESH AGAIN.
SEE WHAT KIND OF NEW WORLD THE CORALS HAVE CREATED.

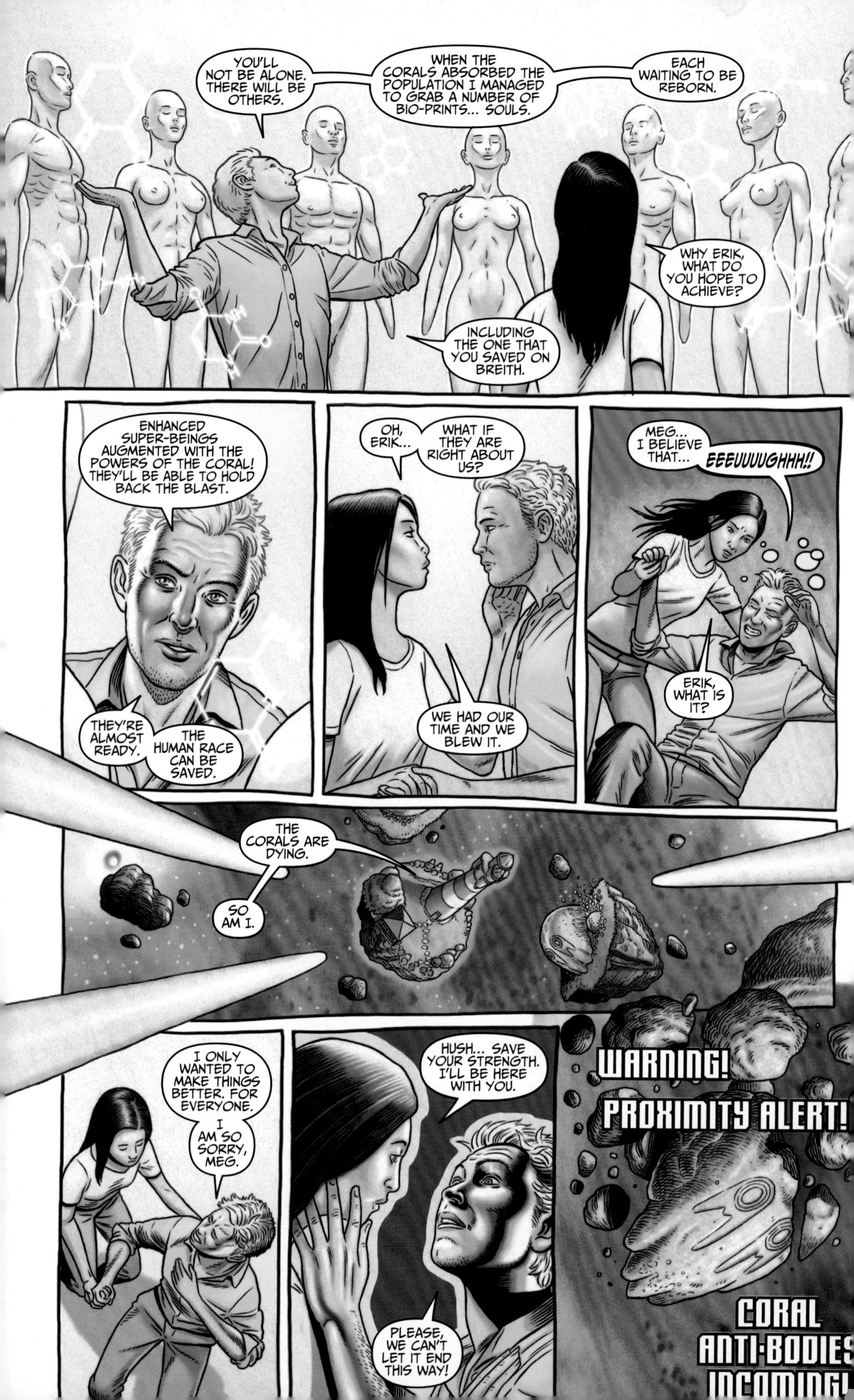

YOU'LL NOT BE ALONE. THERE WILL BE OTHERS.
WHEN THE CORALS ABSORBED THE POPULATION I MANAGED TO GRAB A NUMBER OF BIO-PRINTS... SOULS.
EACH WAITING TO BE REBORN.
WHY ERIK, WHAT DO YOU HOPE TO ACHIEVE?
INCLUDING THE ONE THAT YOU SAVED ON BREITH.
ENHANCED SUPER-BEINGS AUGMENTED WITH THE POWERS OF THE CORAL! THEY'LL BE ABLE TO HOLD BACK THE BLAST.
THEY'RE ALMOST READY.
THE HUMAN RACE CAN BE SAVED.
OH, ERIK...
WHAT IF THEY ARE RIGHT ABOUT US?
WE HAD OUR TIME AND WE BLEW IT.
MEG... I BELIEVE THAT...
EEEUUUUGHHH!!
ERIK, WHAT IS IT?
THE CORALS ARE DYING.
SO AM I.
I ONLY WANTED TO MAKE THINGS BETTER. FOR EVERYONE.
I AM SO SORRY, MEG.
HUSH... SAVE YOUR STRENGTH. I'LL BE HERE WITH YOU.
PLEASE, WE CAN'T LET IT END THIS WAY!
WARNING!
PROXIMITY ALERT!
CORAL ANTI-BODIES INCOMING!

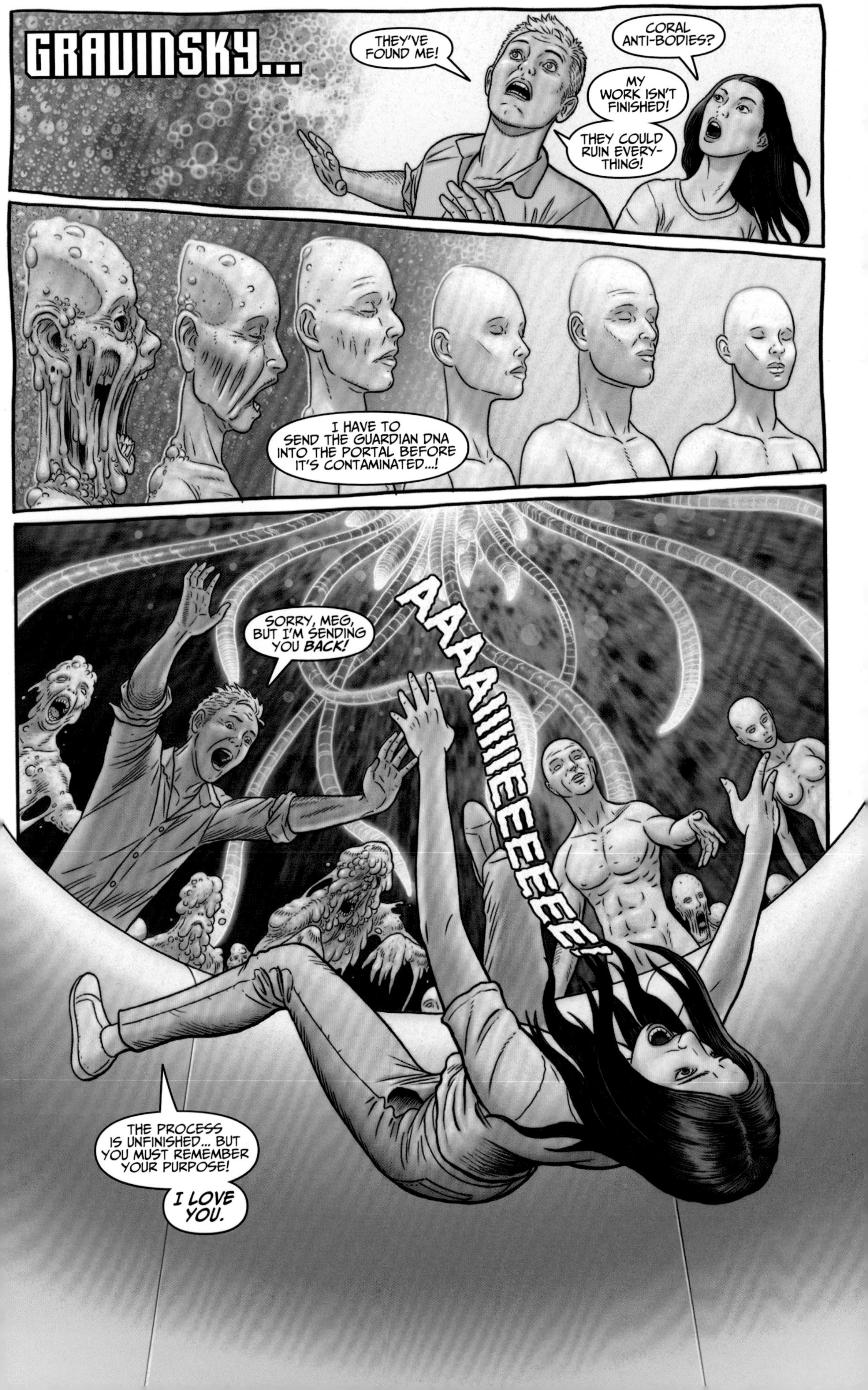
GRAVINSKY...
THEY'VE FOUND ME!
CORAL ANTI-BODIES?
MY WORK ISN'T FINISHED!
THEY COULD RUIN EVERY-THING!
I HAVE TO SEND THE GUARDIAN DNA INTO THE PORTAL BEFORE IT'S CONTAMINATED...!
SORRY, MEG, BUT I'M SENDING YOU BACK!
AAAAIIIIEEEEEE!
THE PROCESS IS UNFINISHED... BUT YOU MUST REMEMBER YOUR PURPOSE!
I LOVE YOU.

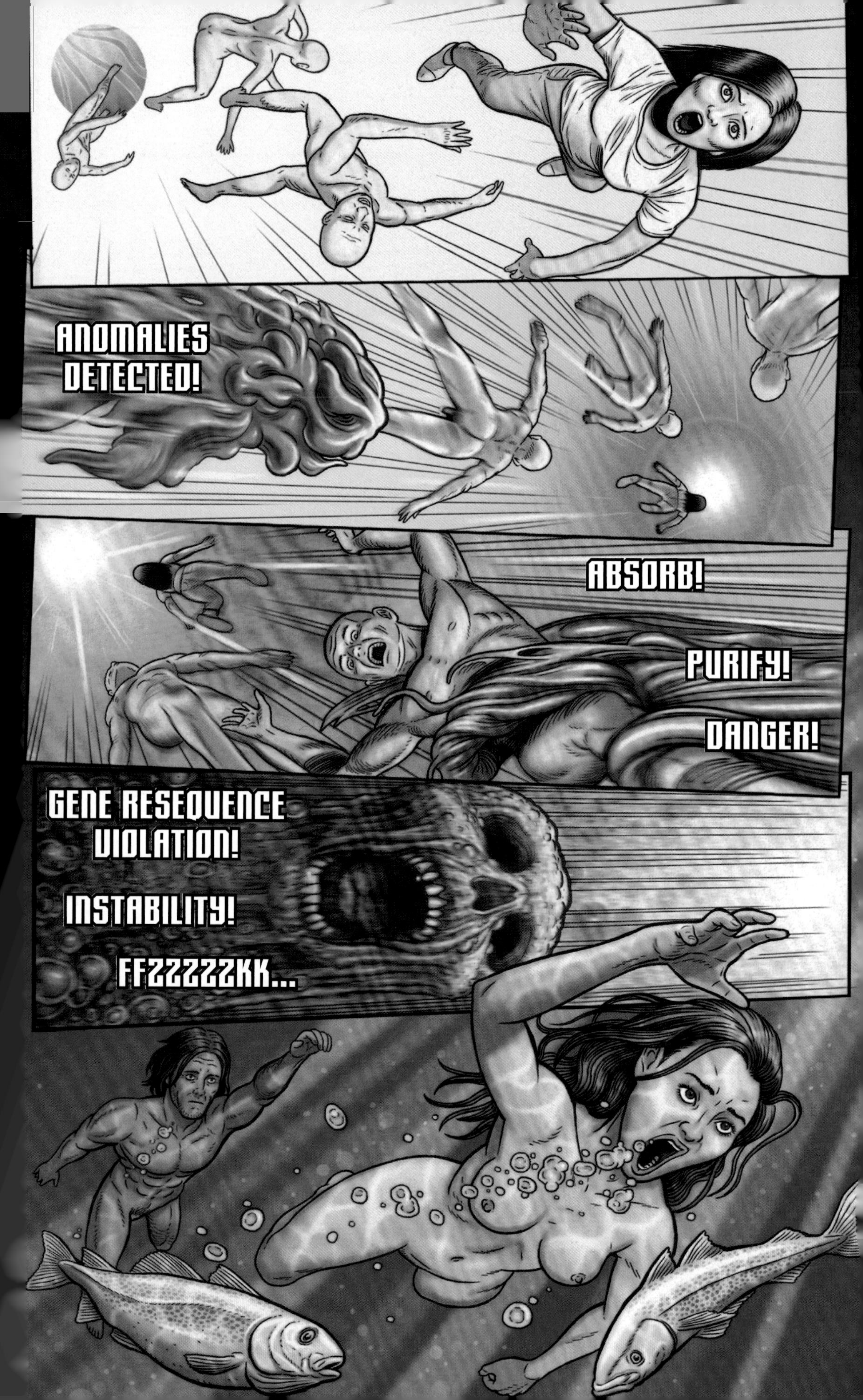
ANOMALIES DETECTED!
ABSORB!
PURIFY!
DANGER!
GENE RESEQUENCE VIOLATION!
INSTABILITY!
FFZZZZZKK...

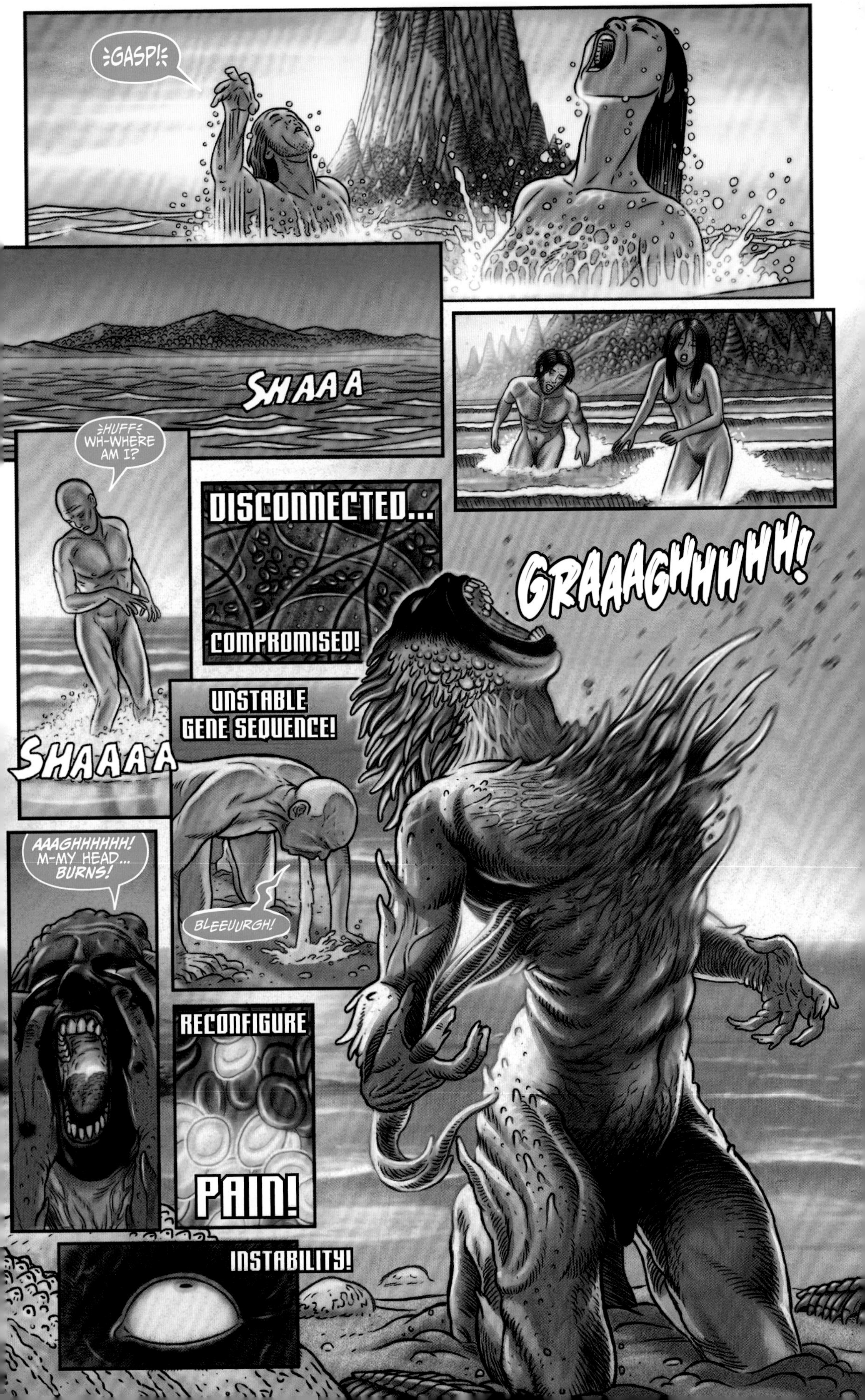

GASP!
SHAAA
HUFF
WH-WHERE AM I?
DISCONNECTED...
COMPROMISED!
UNSTABLE GENE SEQUENCE!
SHAAAA
GRAAAGHHHHH!
BLEEUURGH!
AAAGHHHHHH! M-MY HEAD... BURNS!
RECONFIGURE
PAIN!
INSTABILITY!

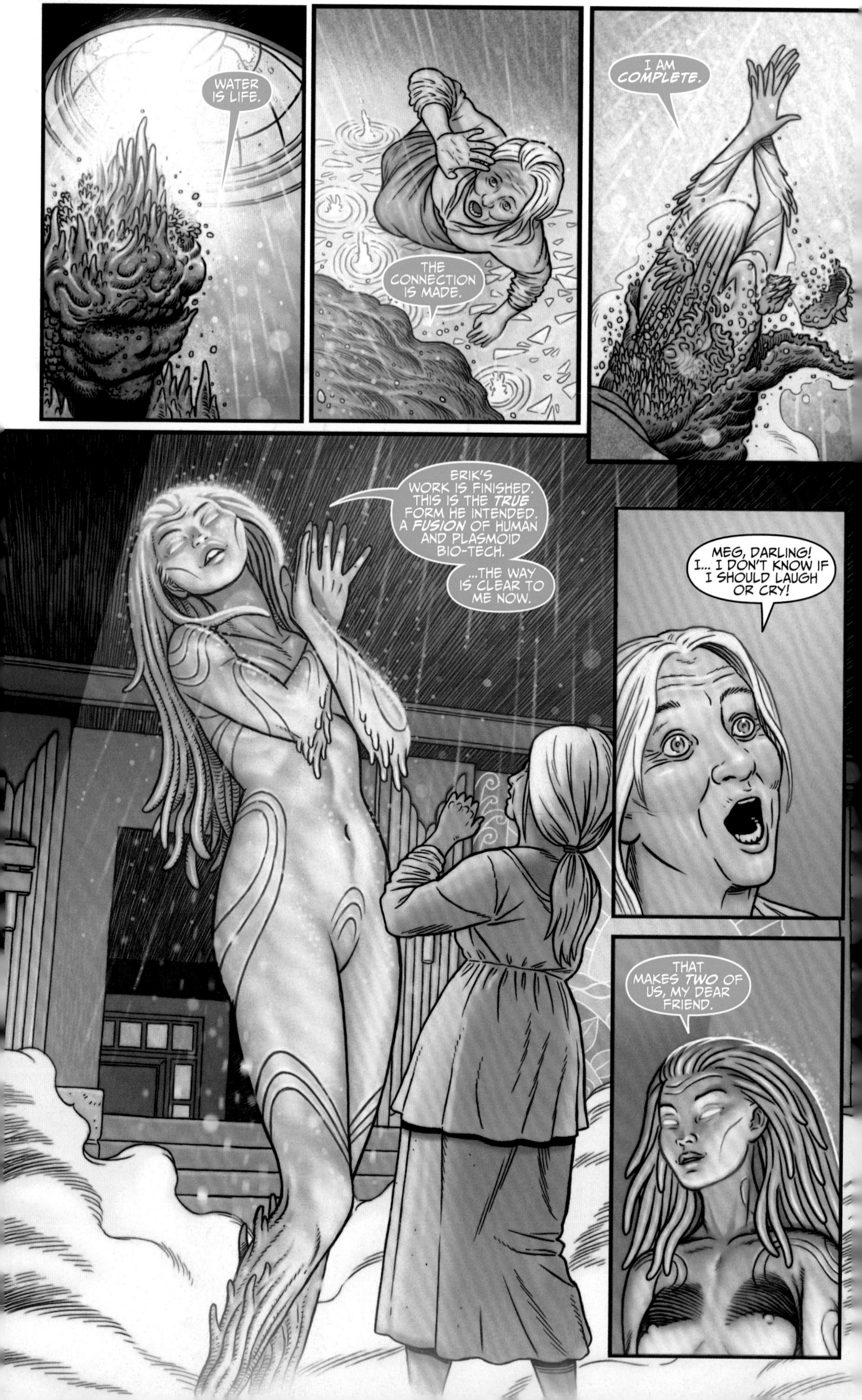
WATER IS LIFE.
THE CONNECTION IS MADE.
I AM COMPLETE.
ERIK'S WORK IS FINISHED. THIS IS THE TRUE FORM HE INTENDED. A FUSION OF HUMAN AND PLASMOID BIO-TECH.
...THE WAY IS CLEAR TO ME NOW.
MEG, DARLING! I... I DON'T KNOW IF I SHOULD LAUGH OR CRY!
THAT MAKES TWO OF US, MY DEAR FRIEND.

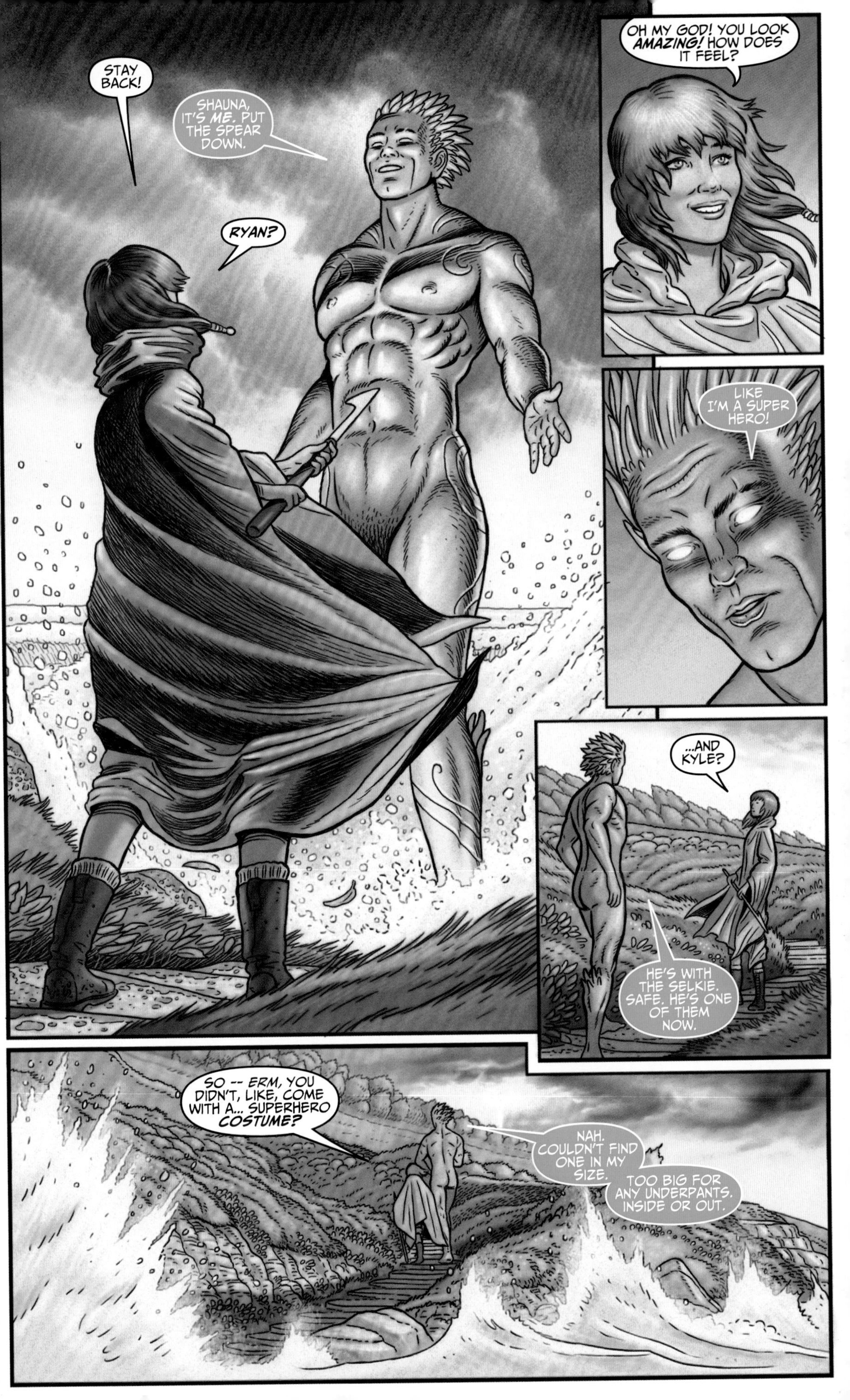
STAY BACK!
SHAUNA, IT'S ME. PUT THE SPEAR DOWN.
RYAN?
OH MY GOD! YOU LOOK AMAZING! HOW DOES IT FEEL?
LIKE I'M A SUPER HERO!
...AND KYLE?
HE'S WITH THE SELKIE. SAFE. HE'S ONE OF THEM NOW.
SO -- ERM, YOU DIDN'T, LIKE, COME WITH A... SUPERHERO COSTUME?
NAH. COULDN'T FIND ONE IN MY SIZE.
TOO BIG FOR ANY UNDERPANTS. INSIDE OR OUT.

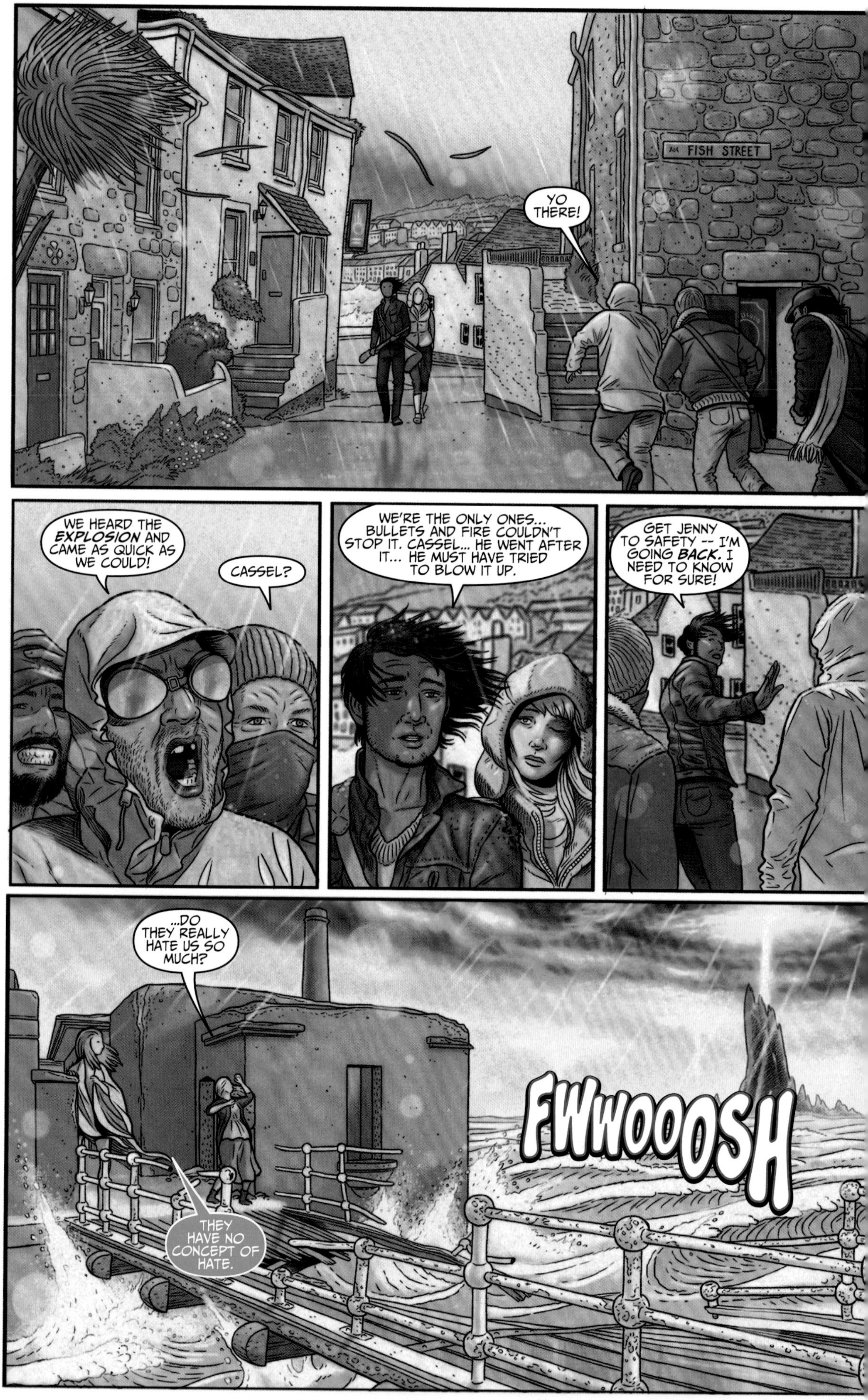
FISH STREET
YO THERE!
WE HEARD THE EXPLOSION AND CAME AS QUICK AS WE COULD!
CASSEL?
WE'RE THE ONLY ONES... BULLETS AND FIRE COULDN'T STOP IT. CASSEL... HE WENT AFTER IT... HE MUST HAVE TRIED TO BLOW IT UP.
GET JENNY TO SAFETY -- I'M GOING BACK. I NEED TO KNOW FOR SURE!
...DO THEY REALLY HATE US SO MUCH?
THEY HAVE NO CONCEPT OF HATE.
FWWOOOSH

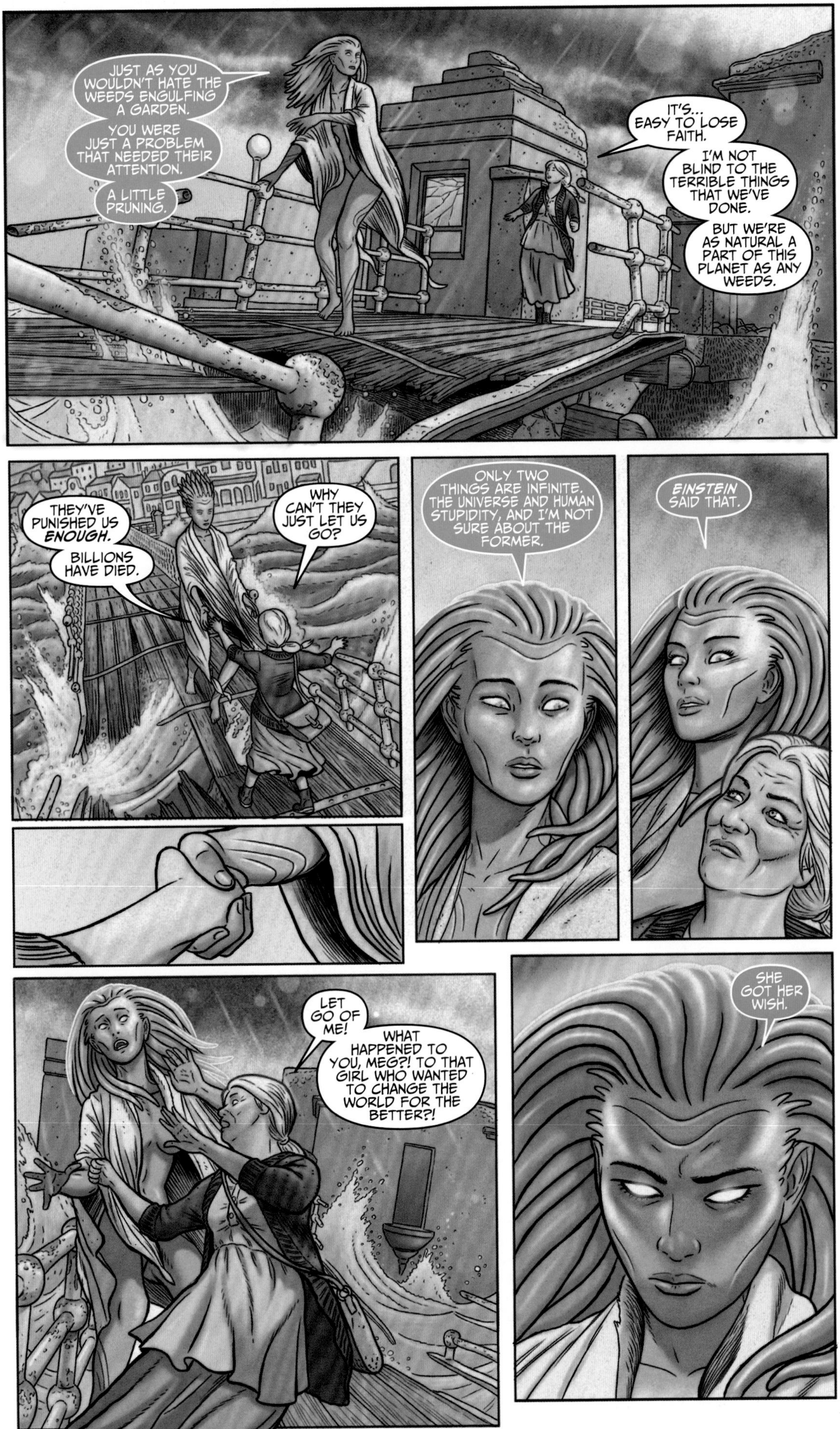
JUST AS YOU WOULDN'T HATE THE WEEDS ENGULFING A GARDEN.
YOU WERE JUST A PROBLEM THAT NEEDED THEIR ATTENTION.
A LITTLE PRUNING.
IT'S... EASY TO LOSE FAITH.
I'M NOT BLIND TO THE TERRIBLE THINGS THAT WE'VE DONE.
BUT WE'RE AS NATURAL A PART OF THIS PLANET AS ANY WEEDS.
THEY'VE PUNISHED US ENOUGH.
BILLIONS HAVE DIED.
WHY CAN'T THEY JUST LET US GO?
ONLY TWO THINGS ARE INFINITE. THE UNIVERSE AND HUMAN STUPIDITY, AND I'M NOT SURE ABOUT THE FORMER.
EINSTEIN SAID THAT.
LET GO OF ME!
WHAT HAPPENED TO YOU, MEG?! TO THAT GIRL WHO WANTED TO CHANGE THE WORLD FOR THE BETTER?!
SHE GOT HER WISH.

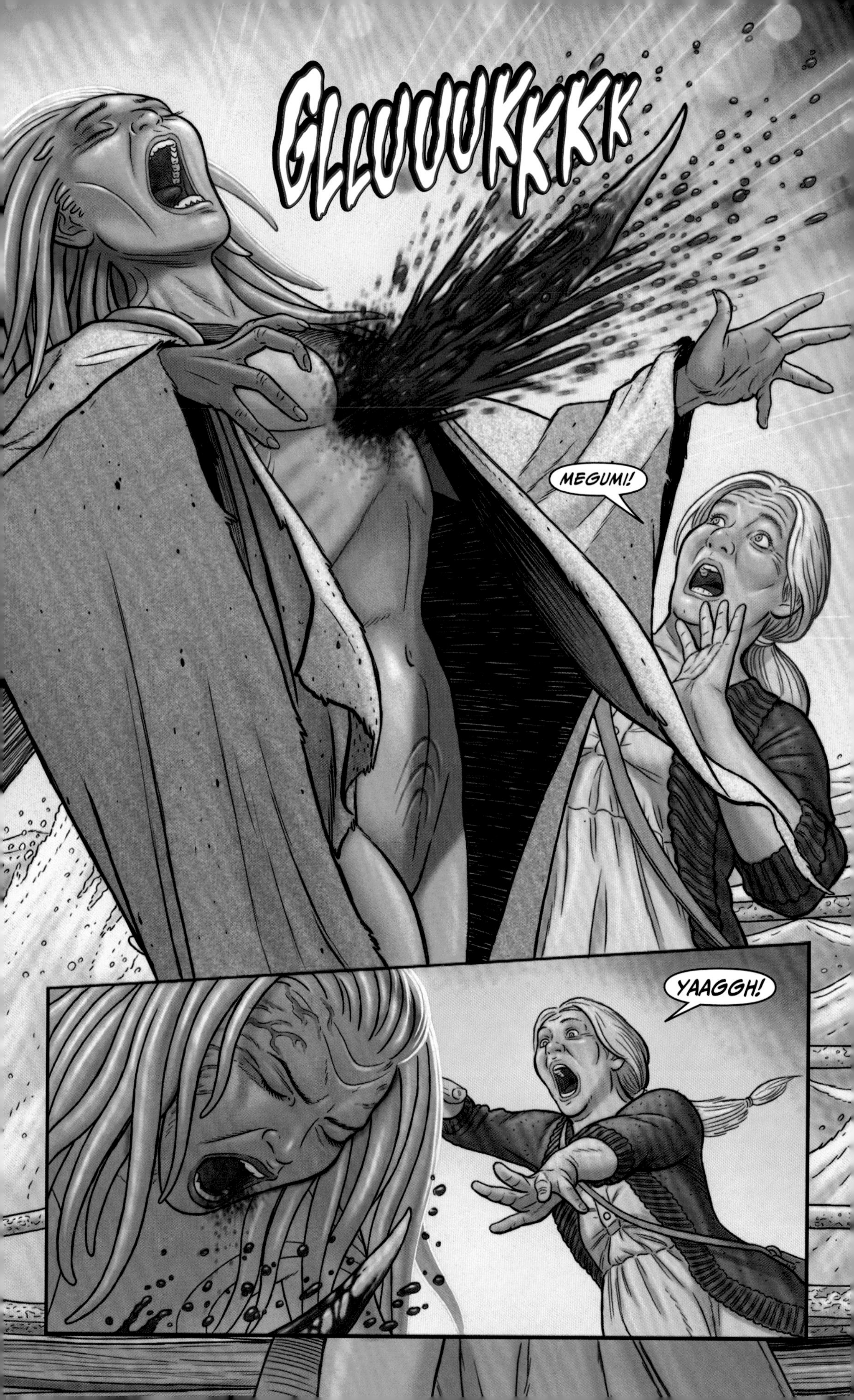
GLLUUUKKKK
MEGUMI!
YAAGGH!

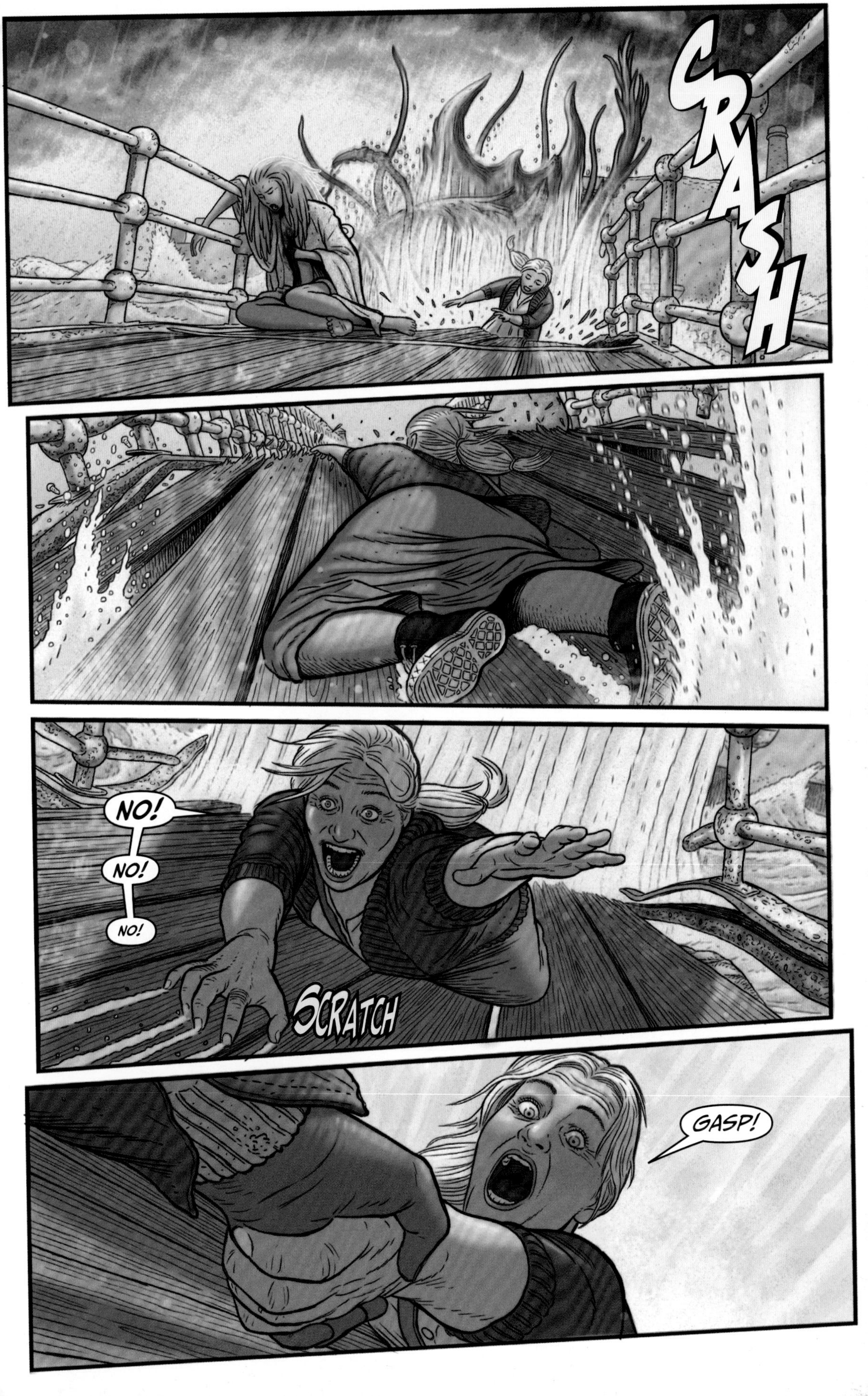
CRASH
NO!
NO!
NO!
SCRATCH
GASP!

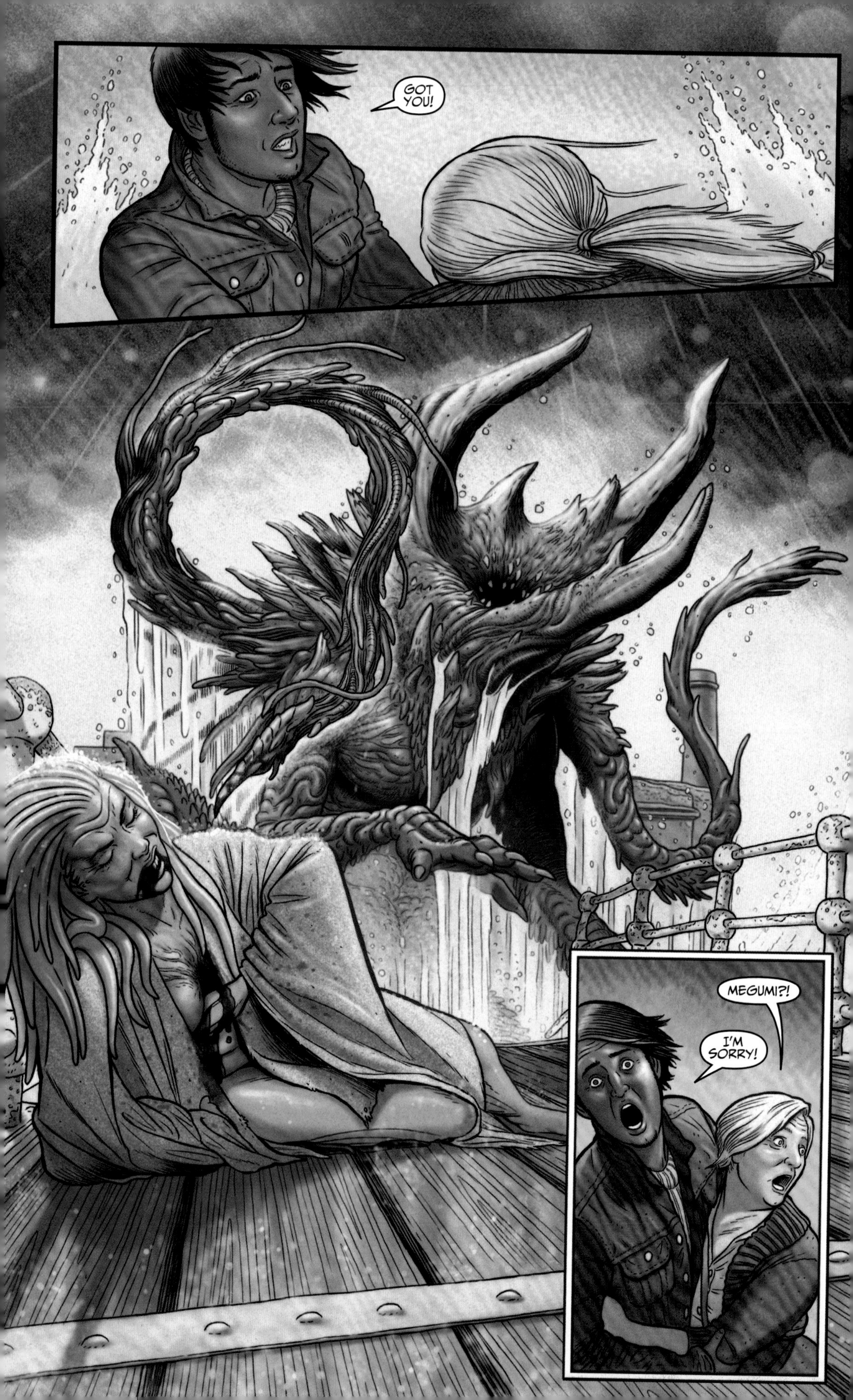
GOT YOU!
MEGUMI?!
I'M SORRY!

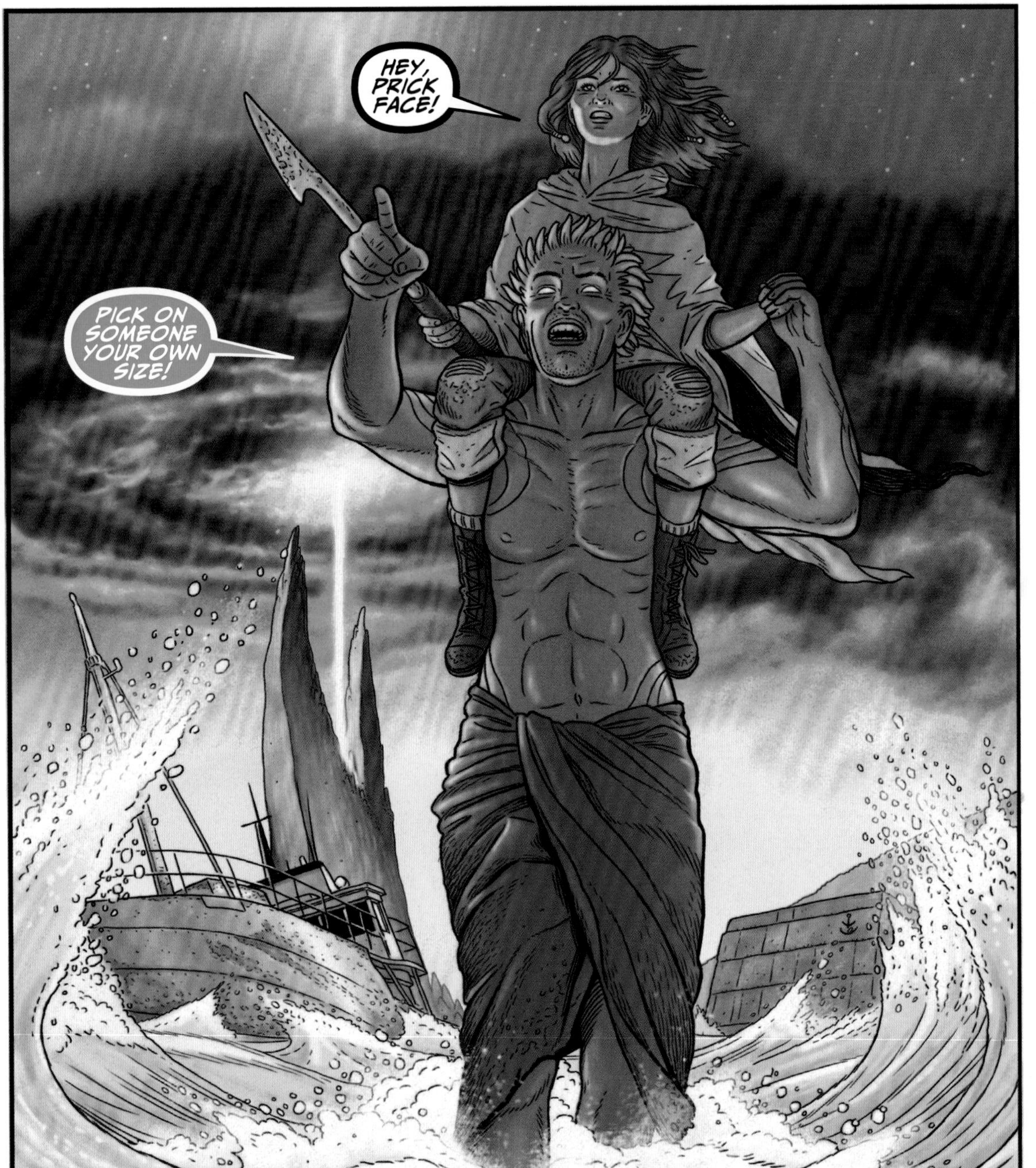
HEY, PRICK FACE!
PICK ON SOMEONE YOUR OWN SIZE!

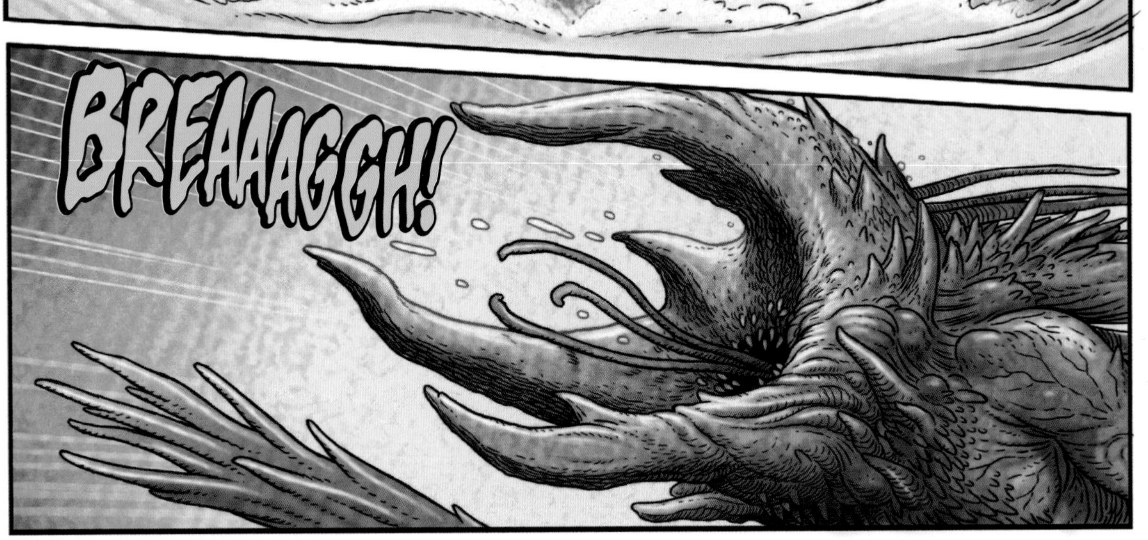
BREAAAGGH!

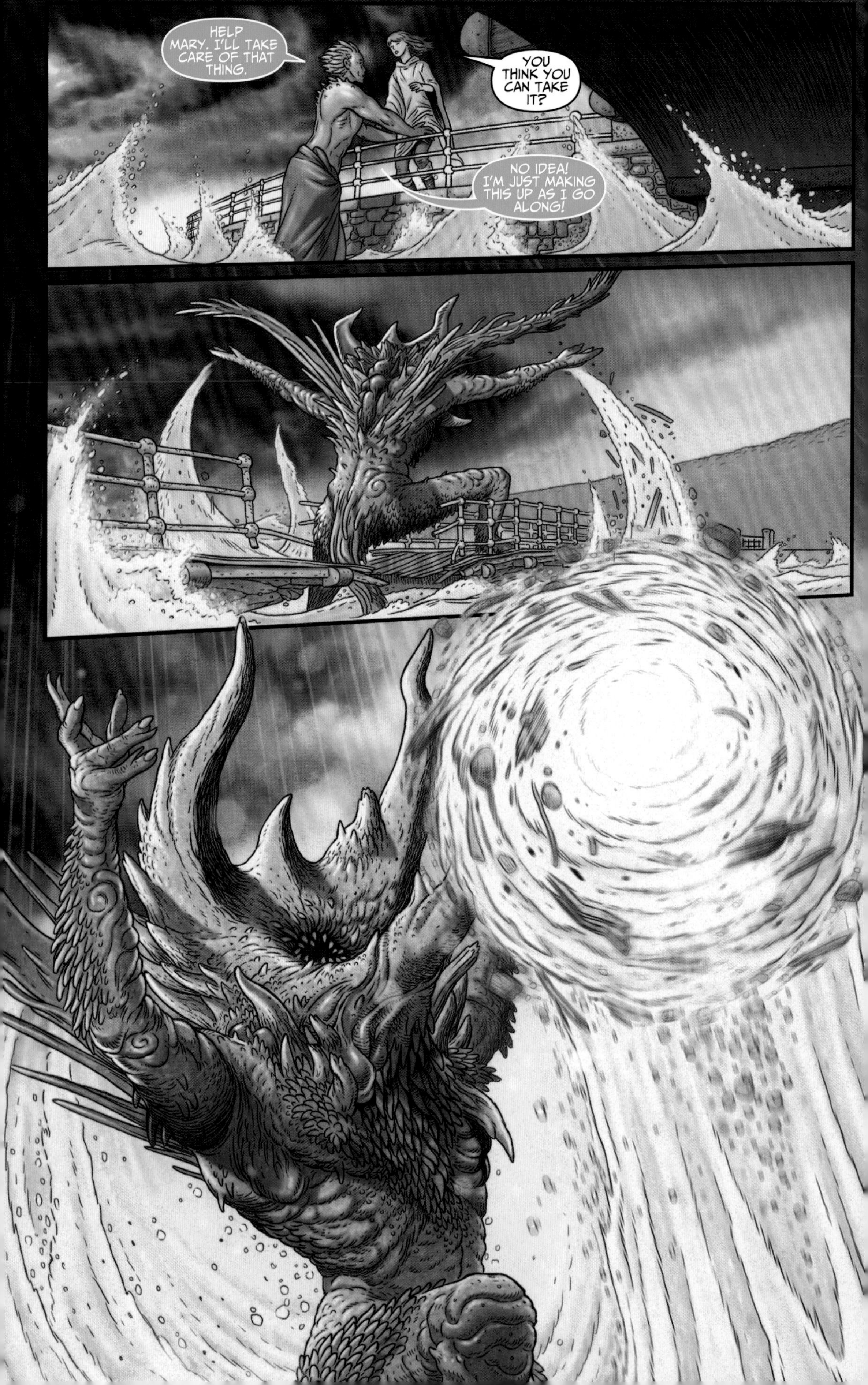
HELP MARY. I'LL TAKE CARE OF THAT THING.
YOU THINK YOU CAN TAKE IT?
NO IDEA! I'M JUST MAKING THIS UP AS I GO ALONG!

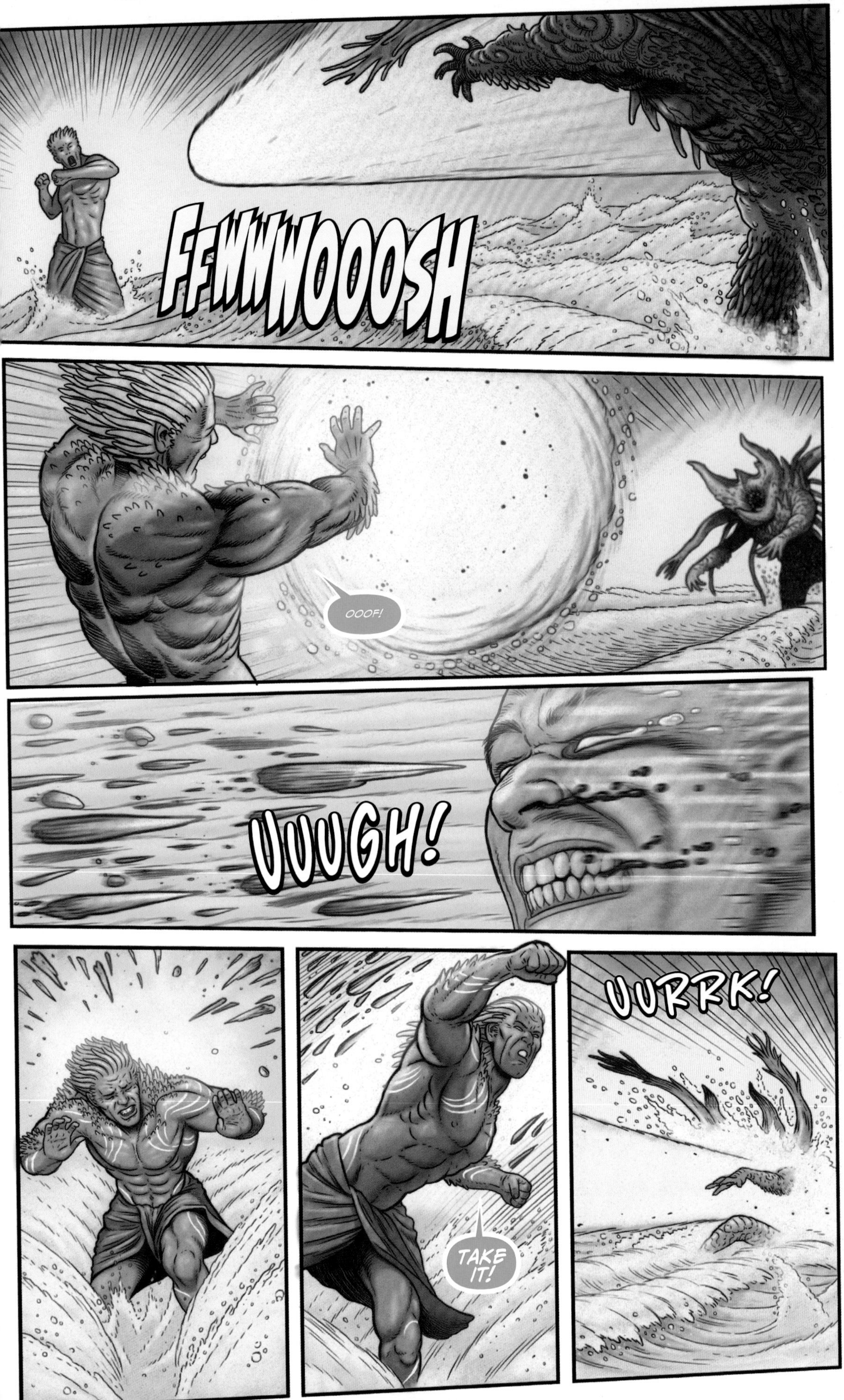
FFWWWOOOSH
OOOF!
UUUGH!
TAKE IT!
UURRK!

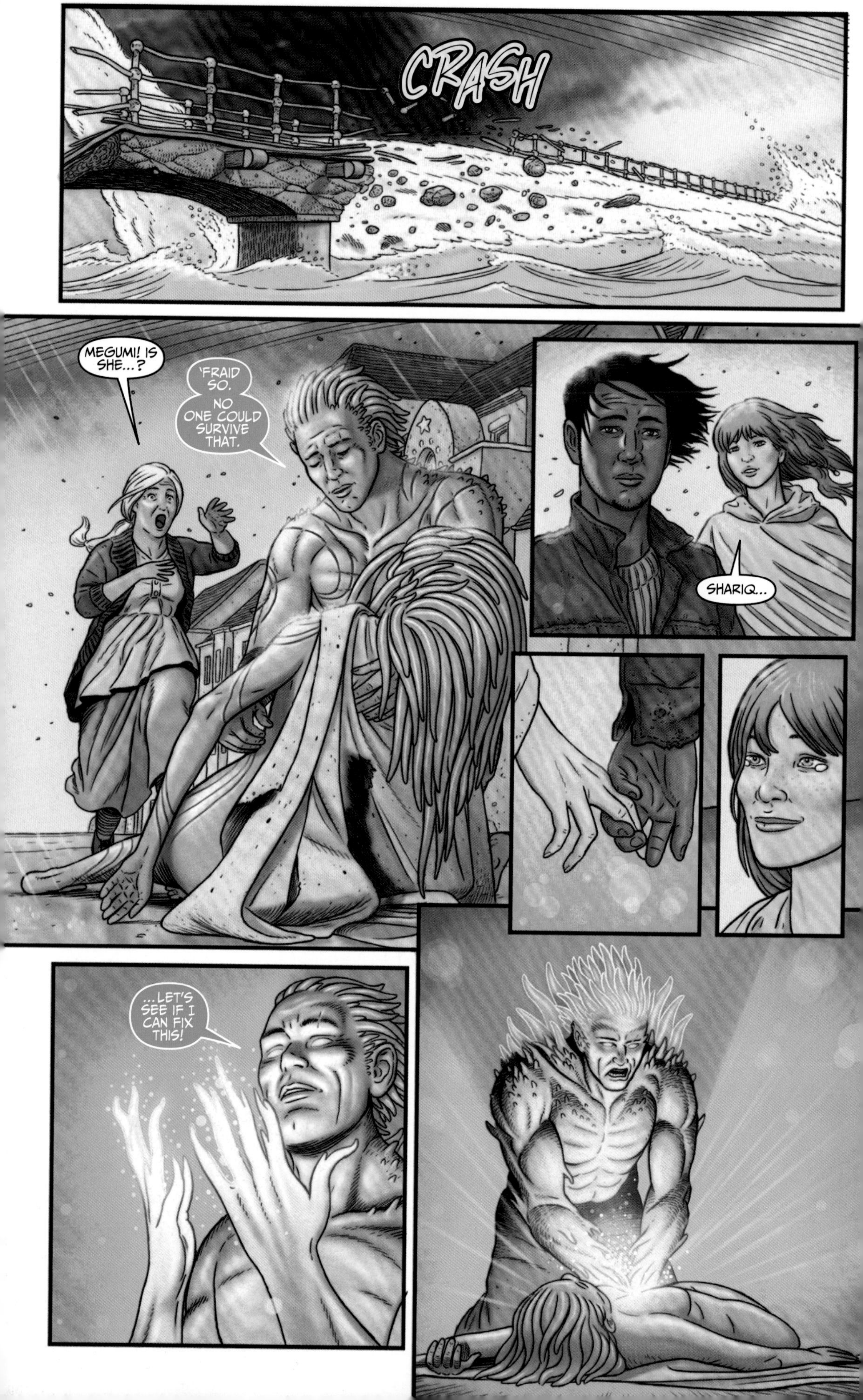
CRASH
MEGUMI! IS SHE...?
'FRAID SO. NO ONE COULD SURVIVE THAT.
SHARIQ...
...LET'S SEE IF I CAN FIX THIS!

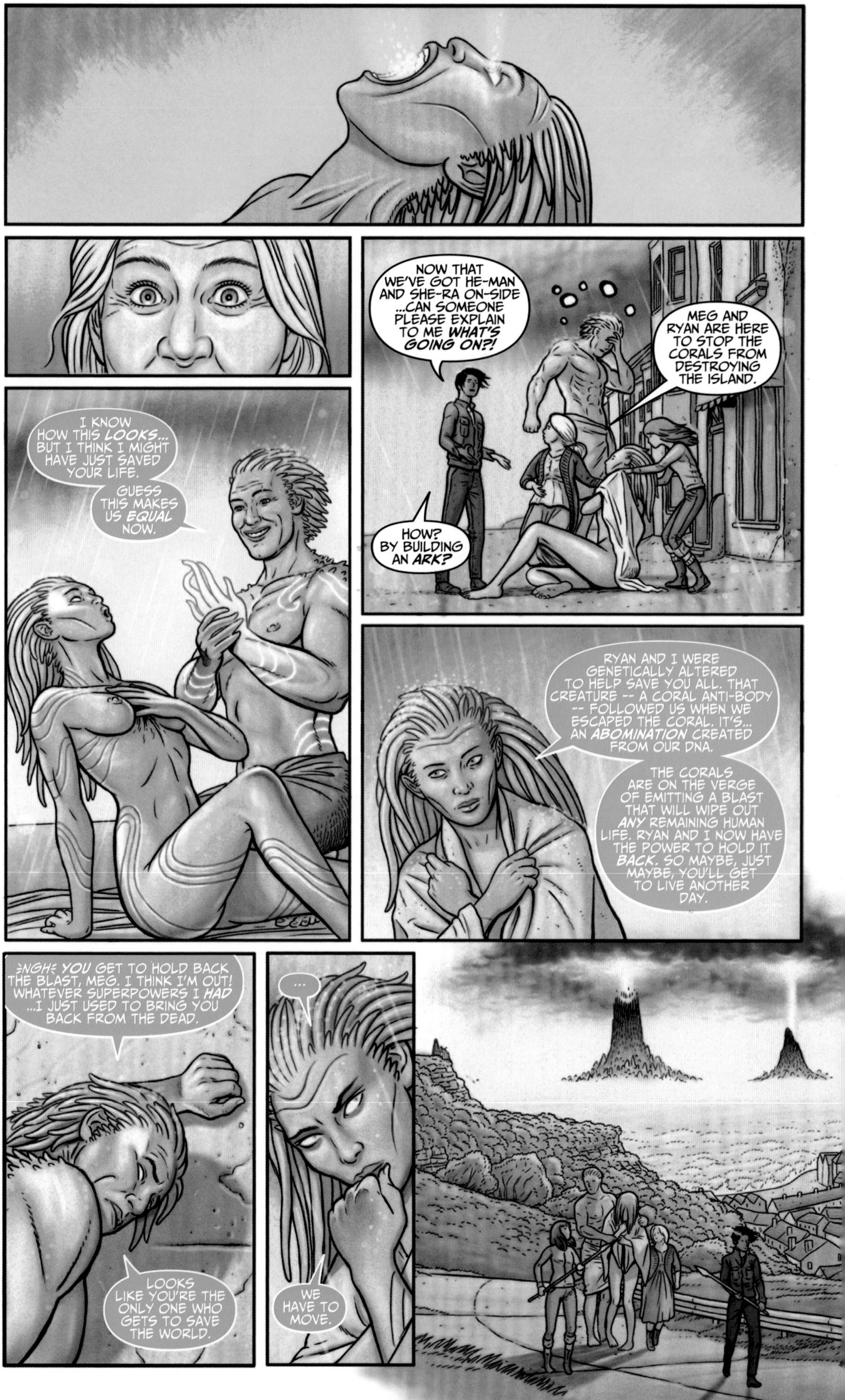
NOW THAT WE'VE GOT HE-MAN AND SHE-RA ON-SIDE ...CAN SOMEONE PLEASE EXPLAIN TO ME WHAT'S GOING ON?!
MEG AND RYAN ARE HERE TO STOP THE CORALS FROM DESTROYING THE ISLAND.
HOW? BY BUILDING AN ARK?
I KNOW HOW THIS LOOKS... BUT I THINK I MIGHT HAVE JUST SAVED YOUR LIFE.
GUESS THIS MAKES US EQUAL NOW.
RYAN AND I WERE GENETICALLY ALTERED TO HELP SAVE YOU ALL. THAT CREATURE -- A CORAL ANTI-BODY -- FOLLOWED US WHEN WE ESCAPED THE CORAL. IT'S... AN ABOMINATION CREATED FROM OUR DNA.
THE CORALS ARE ON THE VERGE OF EMITTING A BLAST THAT WILL WIPE OUT ANY REMAINING HUMAN LIFE. RYAN AND I NOW HAVE THE POWER TO HOLD IT BACK. SO MAYBE, JUST MAYBE, YOU'LL GET TO LIVE ANOTHER DAY.
<NGH> YOU GET TO HOLD BACK THE BLAST, MEG. I THINK I'M OUT! WHATEVER SUPERPOWERS I HAD ...I JUST USED TO BRING YOU BACK FROM THE DEAD.
LOOKS LIKE YOU'RE THE ONLY ONE WHO GETS TO SAVE THE WORLD.
...
WE HAVE TO MOVE.

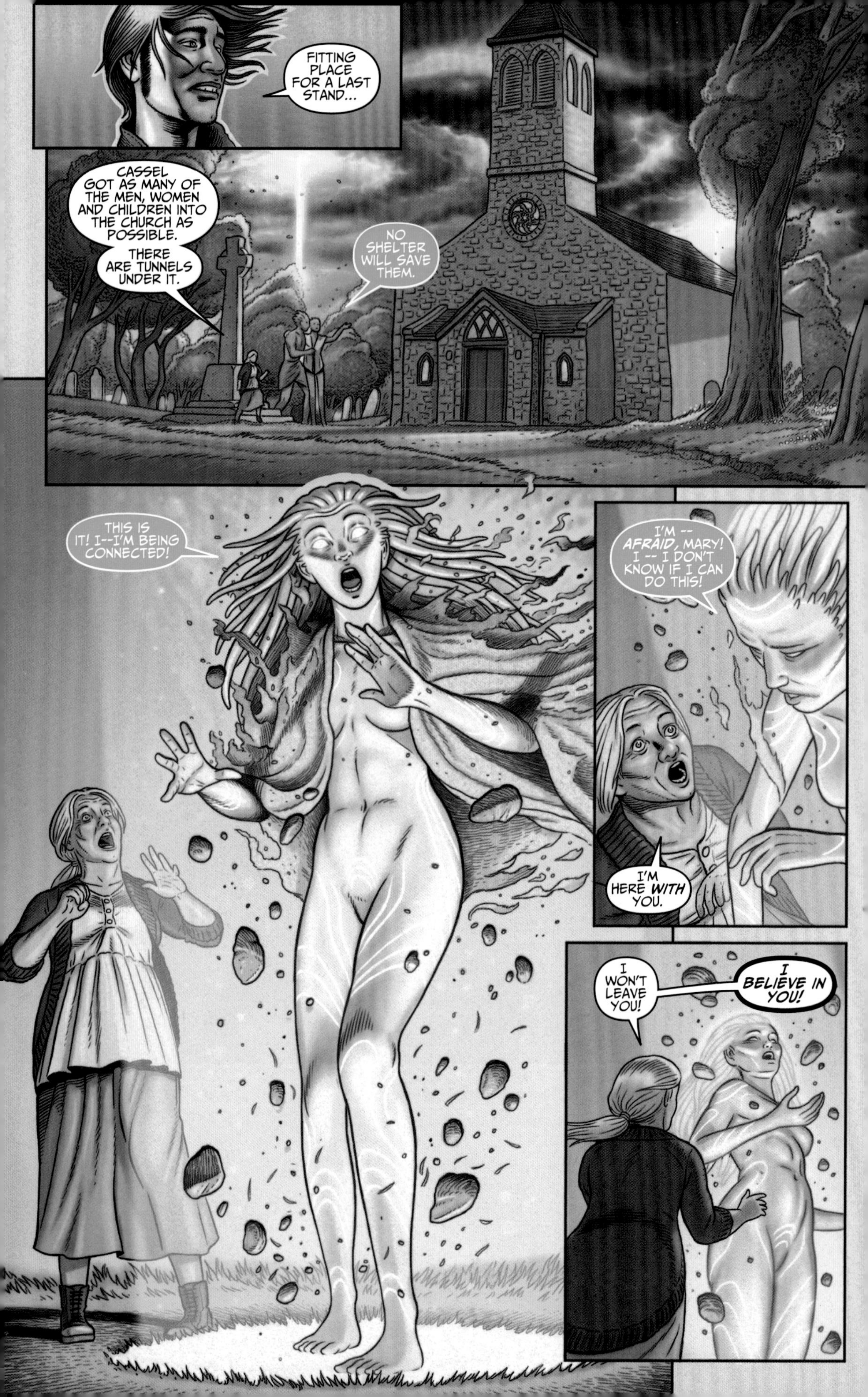
FITTING PLACE FOR A LAST STAND...
CASSEL GOT AS MANY OF THE MEN, WOMEN AND CHILDREN INTO THE CHURCH AS POSSIBLE.
THERE ARE TUNNELS UNDER IT.
NO SHELTER WILL SAVE THEM.
THIS IS IT! I--I'M BEING CONNECTED!
I'M -- AFRAID, MARY! I -- I DON'T KNOW IF I CAN DO THIS!
I'M HERE WITH YOU.
I WON'T LEAVE YOU!
I BELIEVE IN YOU!

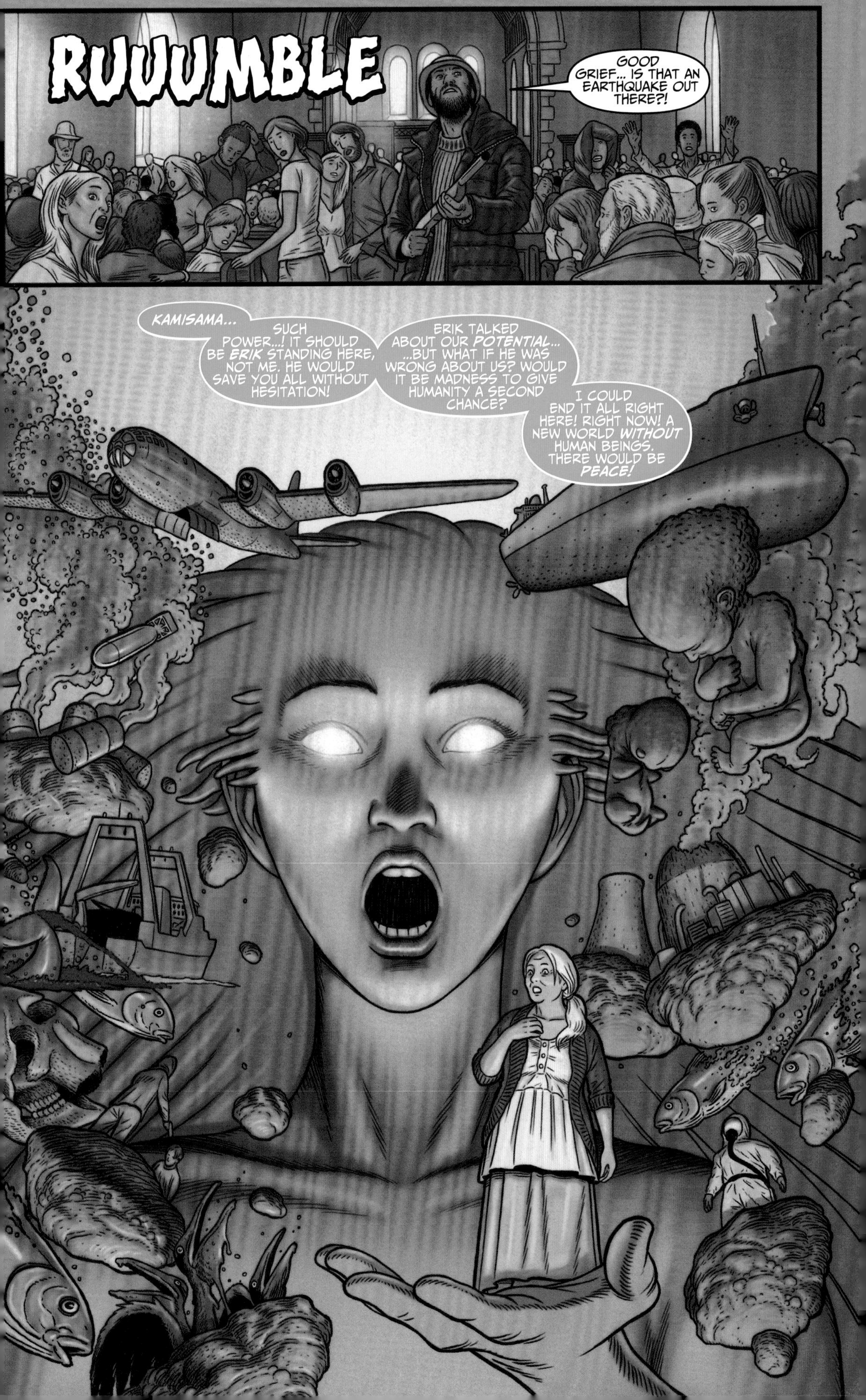
RUUUMBLE
GOOD GRIEF... IS THAT AN EARTHQUAKE OUT THERE?!
KAMISAMA...
SUCH POWER...! IT SHOULD BE ERIK STANDING HERE, NOT ME. HE WOULD SAVE YOU ALL WITHOUT HESITATION!
ERIK TALKED ABOUT OUR POTENTIAL... ...BUT WHAT IF HE WAS WRONG ABOUT US? WOULD IT BE MADNESS TO GIVE HUMANITY A SECOND CHANCE?
I COULD END IT ALL RIGHT HERE! RIGHT NOW! A NEW WORLD WITHOUT HUMAN BEINGS. THERE WOULD BE PEACE!

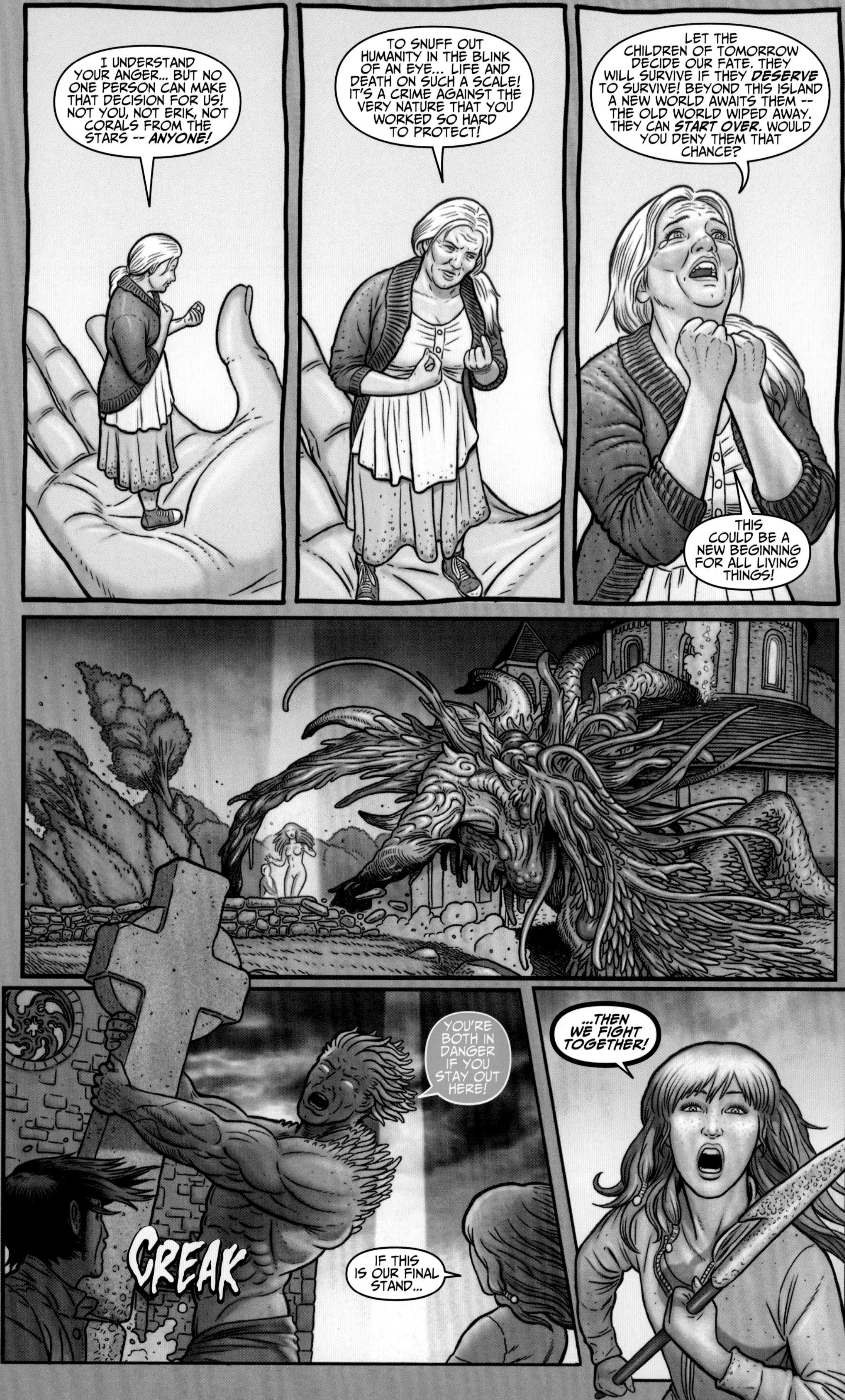
I UNDERSTAND YOUR ANGER... BUT NO ONE PERSON CAN MAKE THAT DECISION FOR US! NOT YOU, NOT ERIK, NOT CORALS FROM THE STARS -- ANYONE!
TO SNUFF OUT HUMANITY IN THE BLINK OF AN EYE... LIFE AND DEATH ON SUCH A SCALE! IT'S A CRIME AGAINST THE VERY NATURE THAT YOU WORKED SO HARD TO PROTECT!
LET THE CHILDREN OF TOMORROW DECIDE OUR FATE. THEY WILL SURVIVE IF THEY DESERVE TO SURVIVE! BEYOND THIS ISLAND A NEW WORLD AWAITS THEM -- THE OLD WORLD WIPED AWAY. THEY CAN START OVER. WOULD YOU DENY THEM THAT CHANCE?
THIS COULD BE A NEW BEGINNING FOR ALL LIVING THINGS!
YOU'RE BOTH IN DANGER IF YOU STAY OUT HERE!
CREAK
IF THIS IS OUR FINAL STAND...
...THEN WE FIGHT TOGETHER!

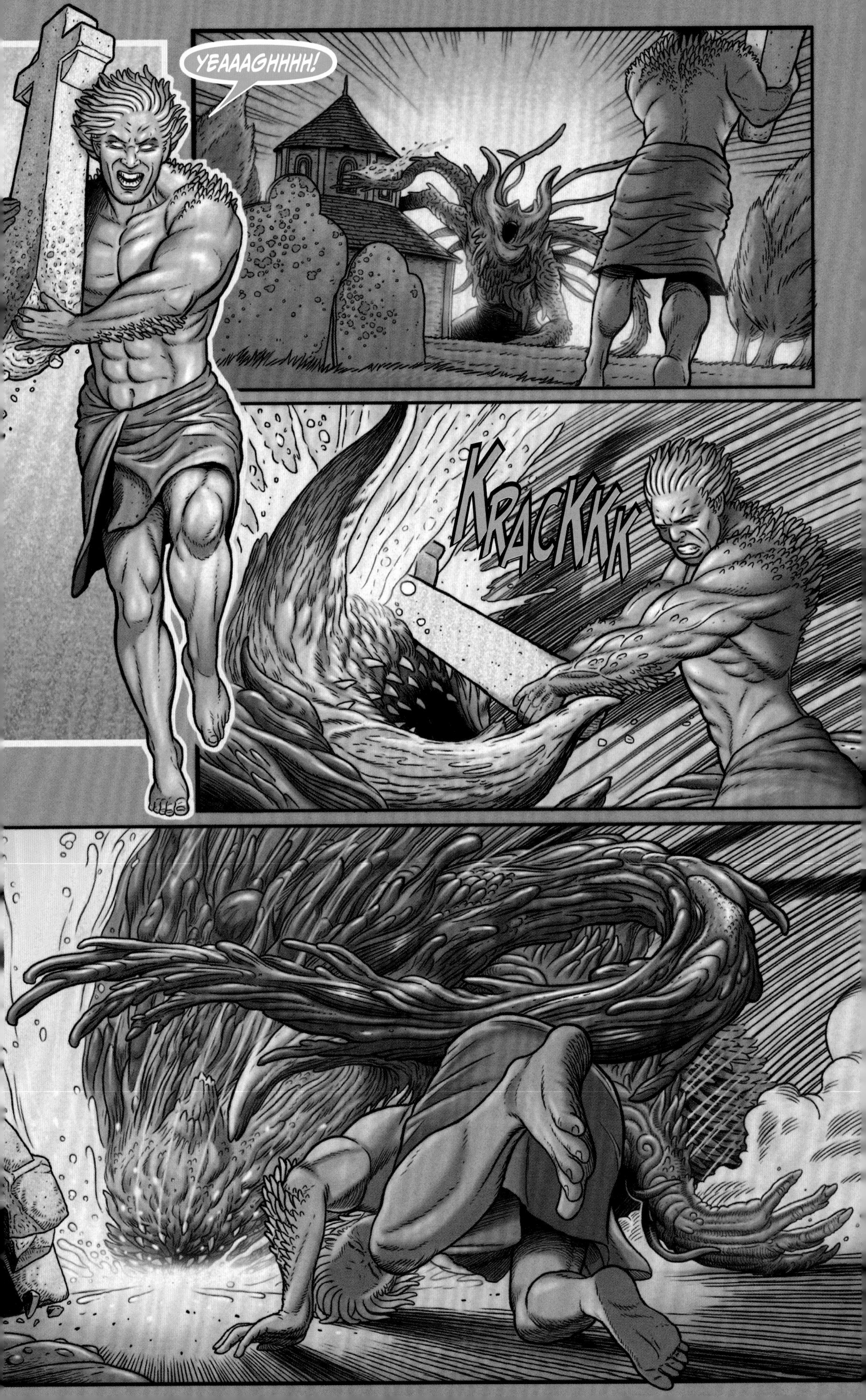
YEAAAGHHHH!
KRACKKK

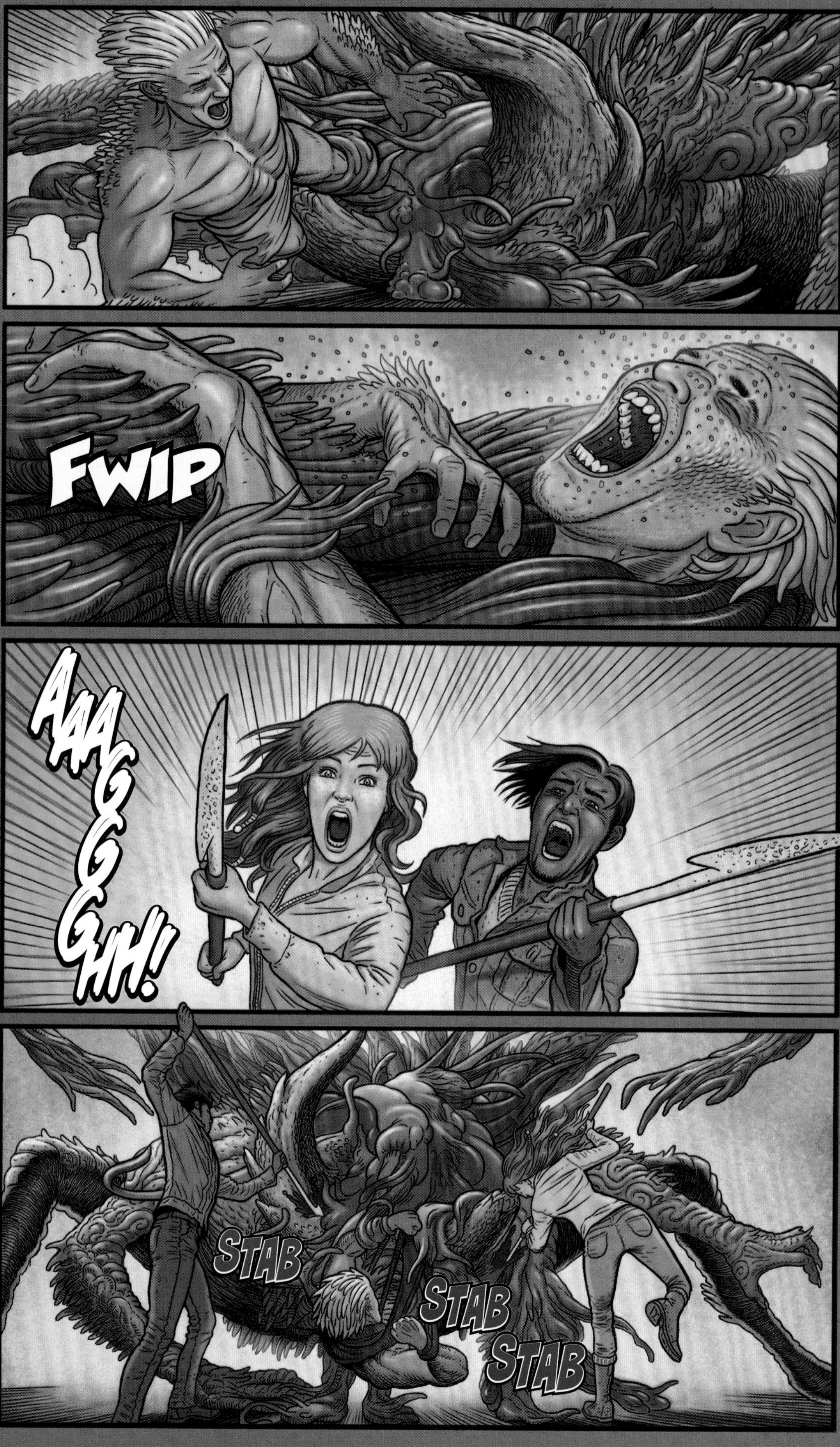
FWIP
AAAGGGGHH!
STAB
STAB
STAB

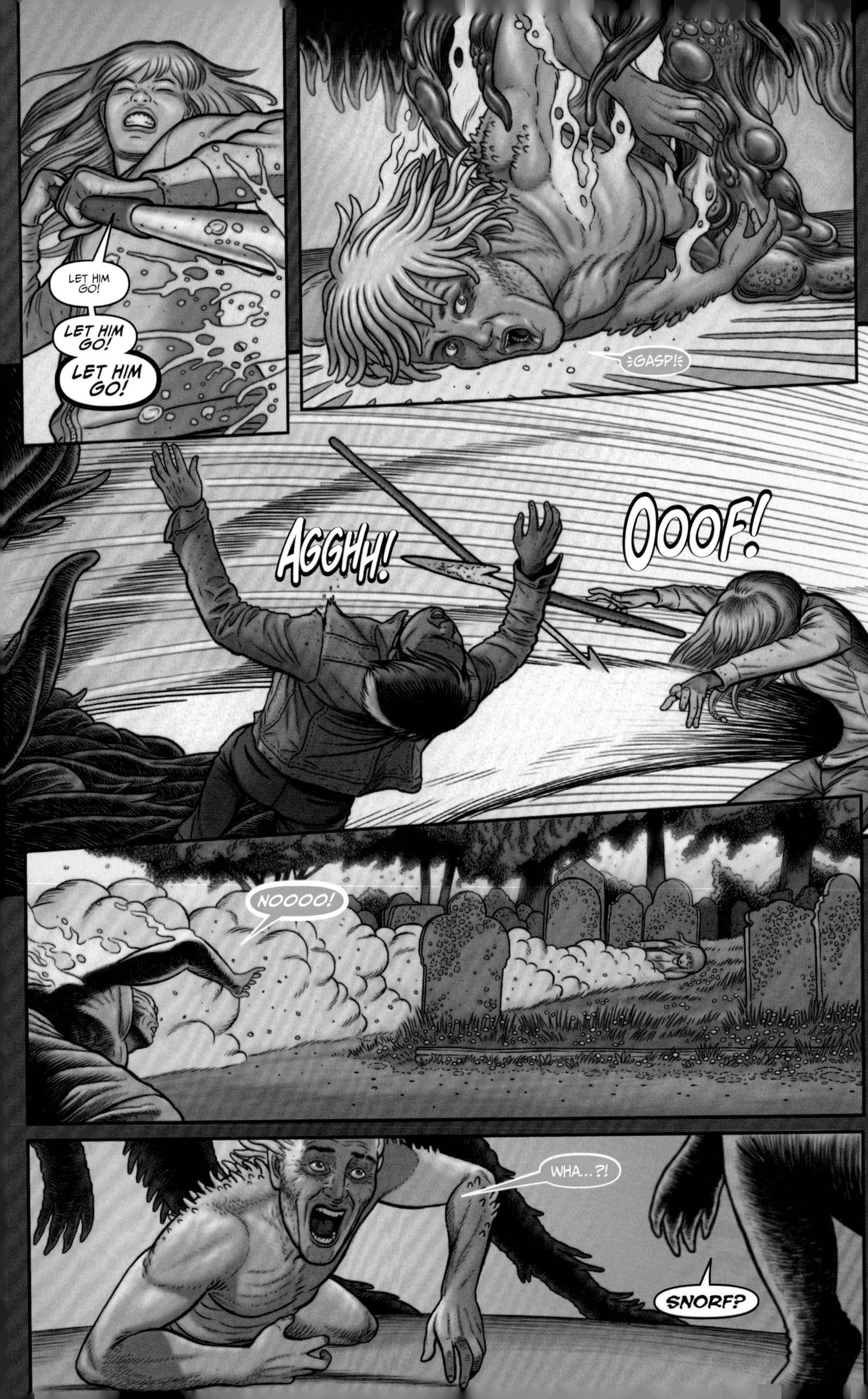
LET HIM GO!
LET HIM GO!
LET HIM GO!
GASP!
AGGHH!
OOOF!
NOOOO!
WHA...?!
SNORF?

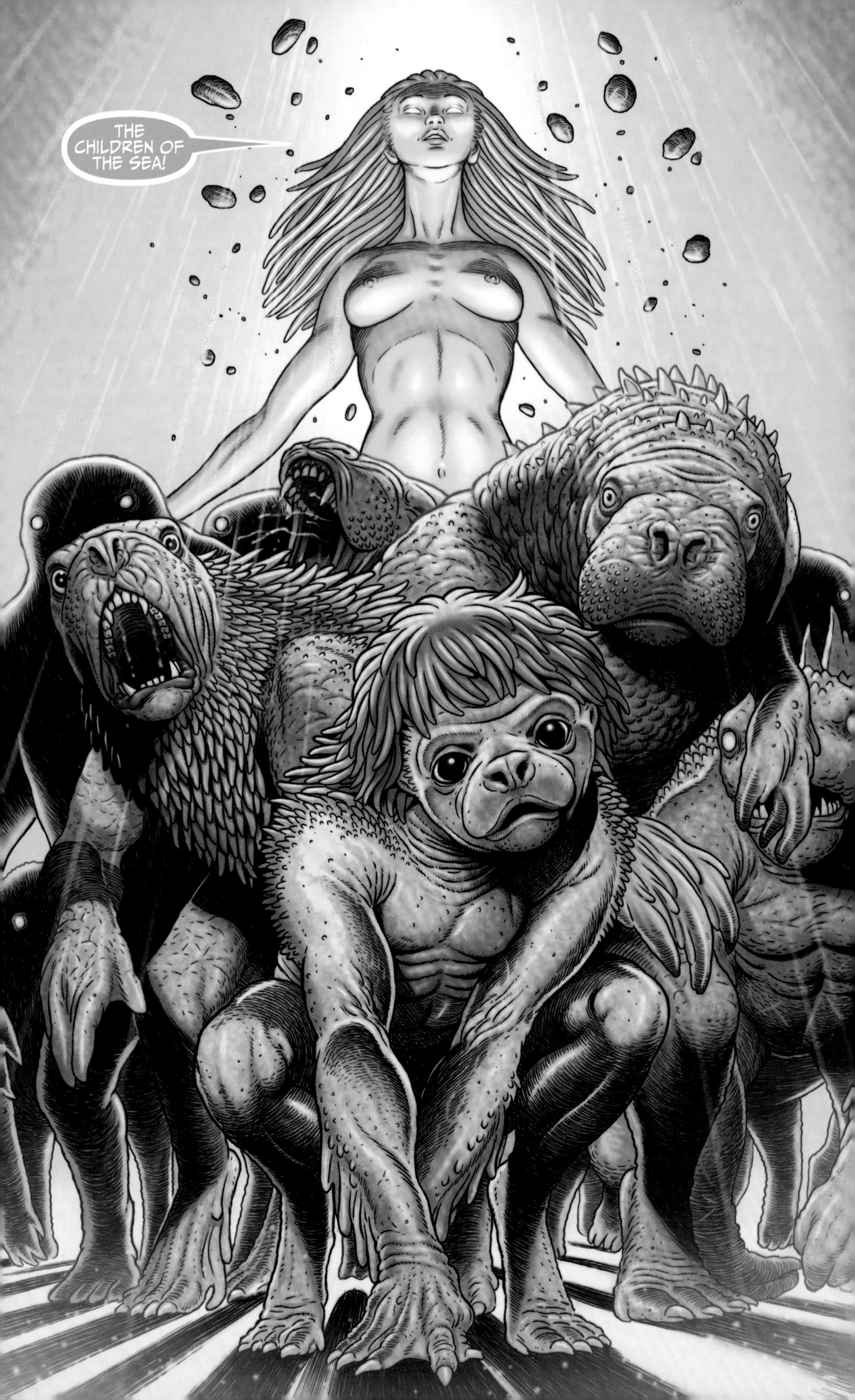
THE CHILDREN OF THE SEA!

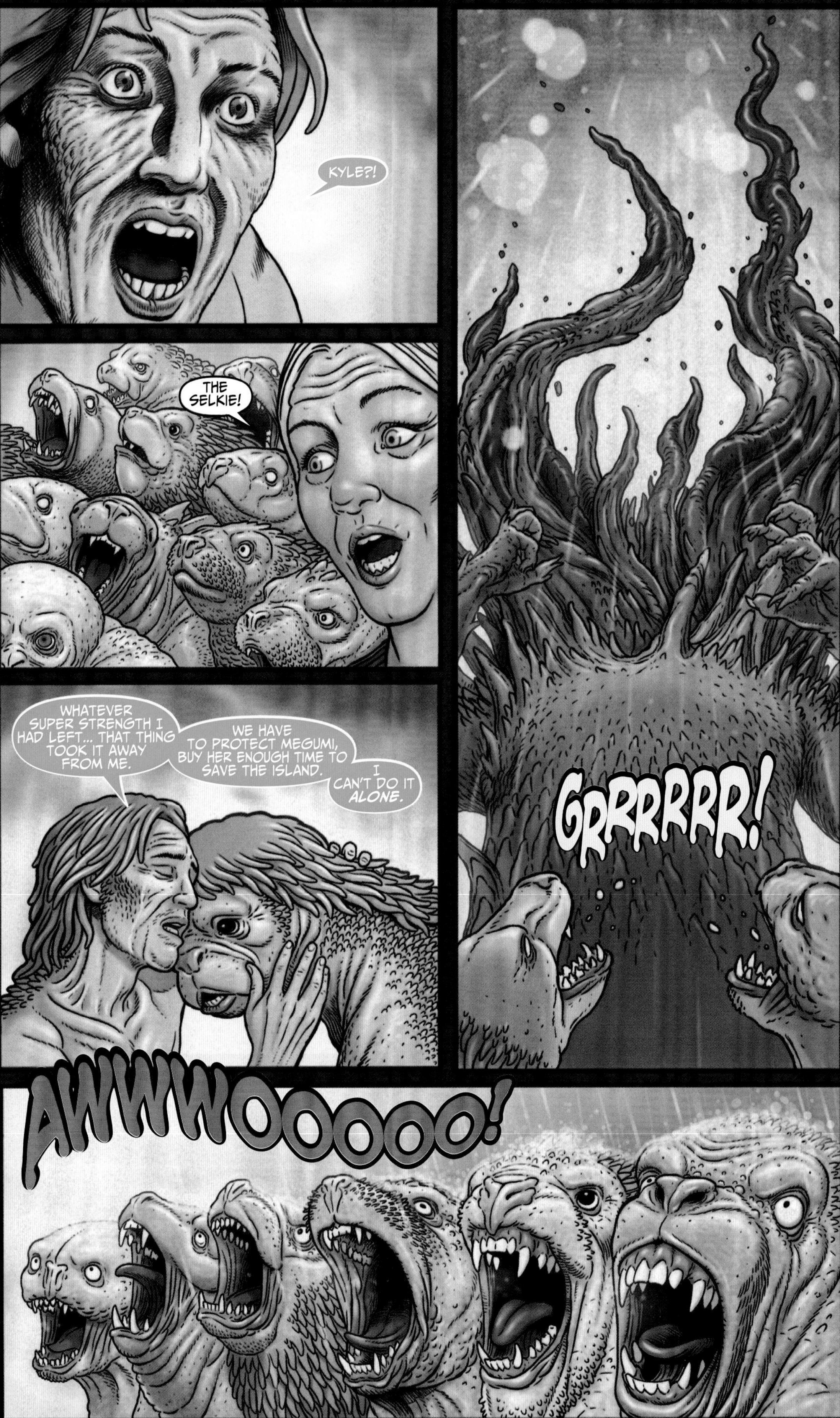
KYLE?!
THE SELKIE!
WHATEVER SUPER STRENGTH I HAD LEFT... THAT THING TOOK IT AWAY FROM ME.
WE HAVE TO PROTECT MEGUMI, BUY HER ENOUGH TIME TO SAVE THE ISLAND.
I CAN'T DO IT ALONE.
GRRRRRR!
AWWWOOOOOO!

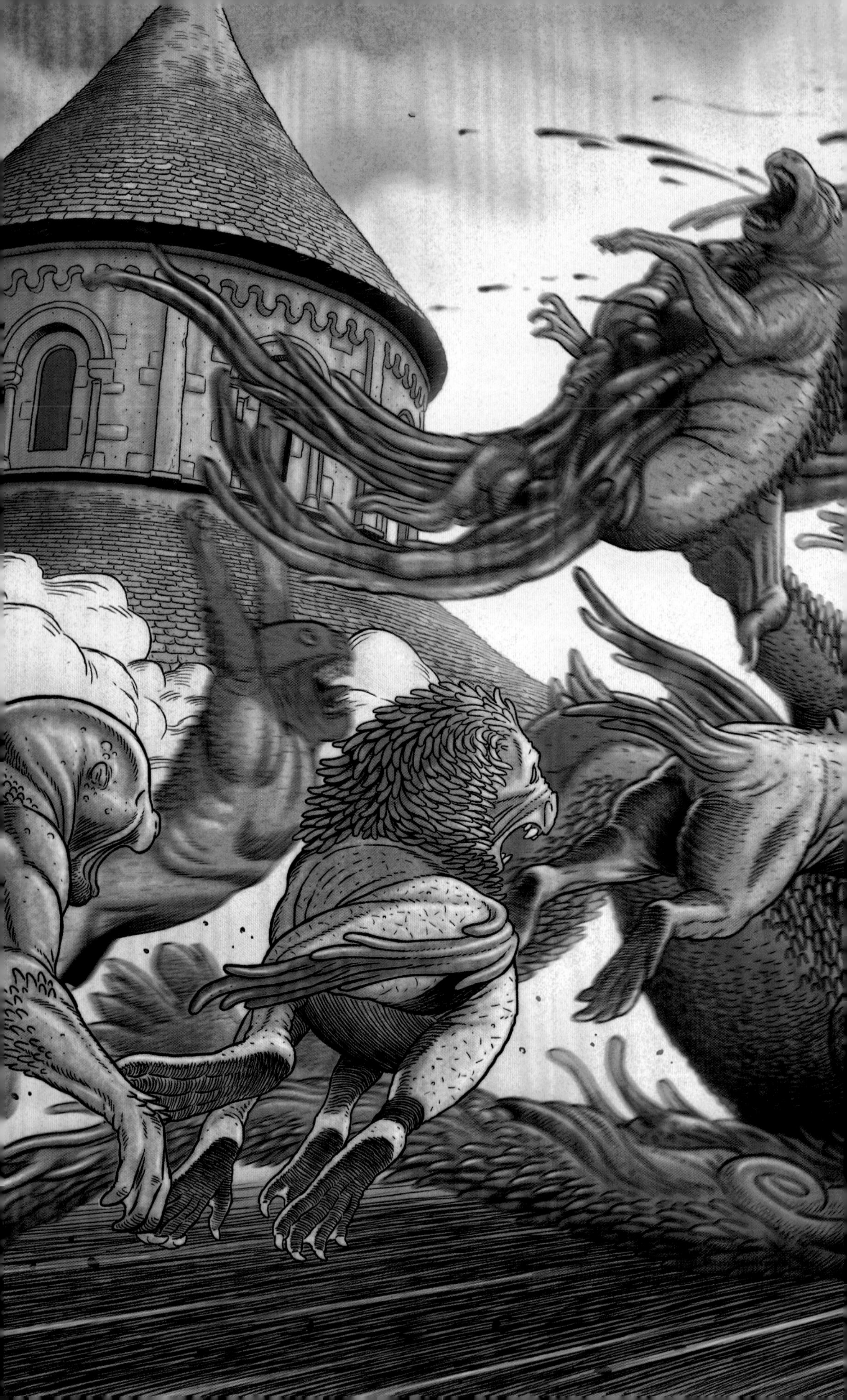

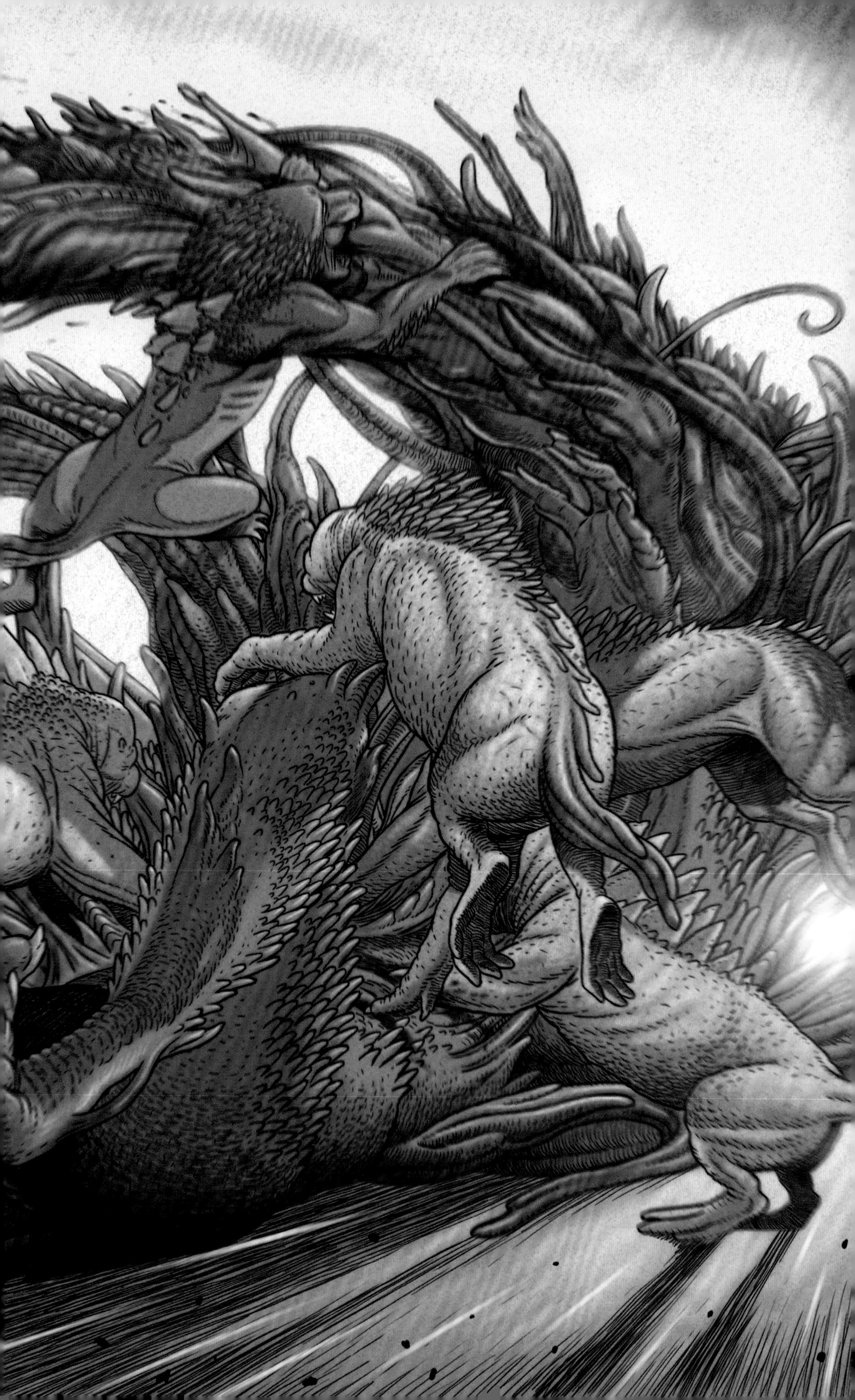

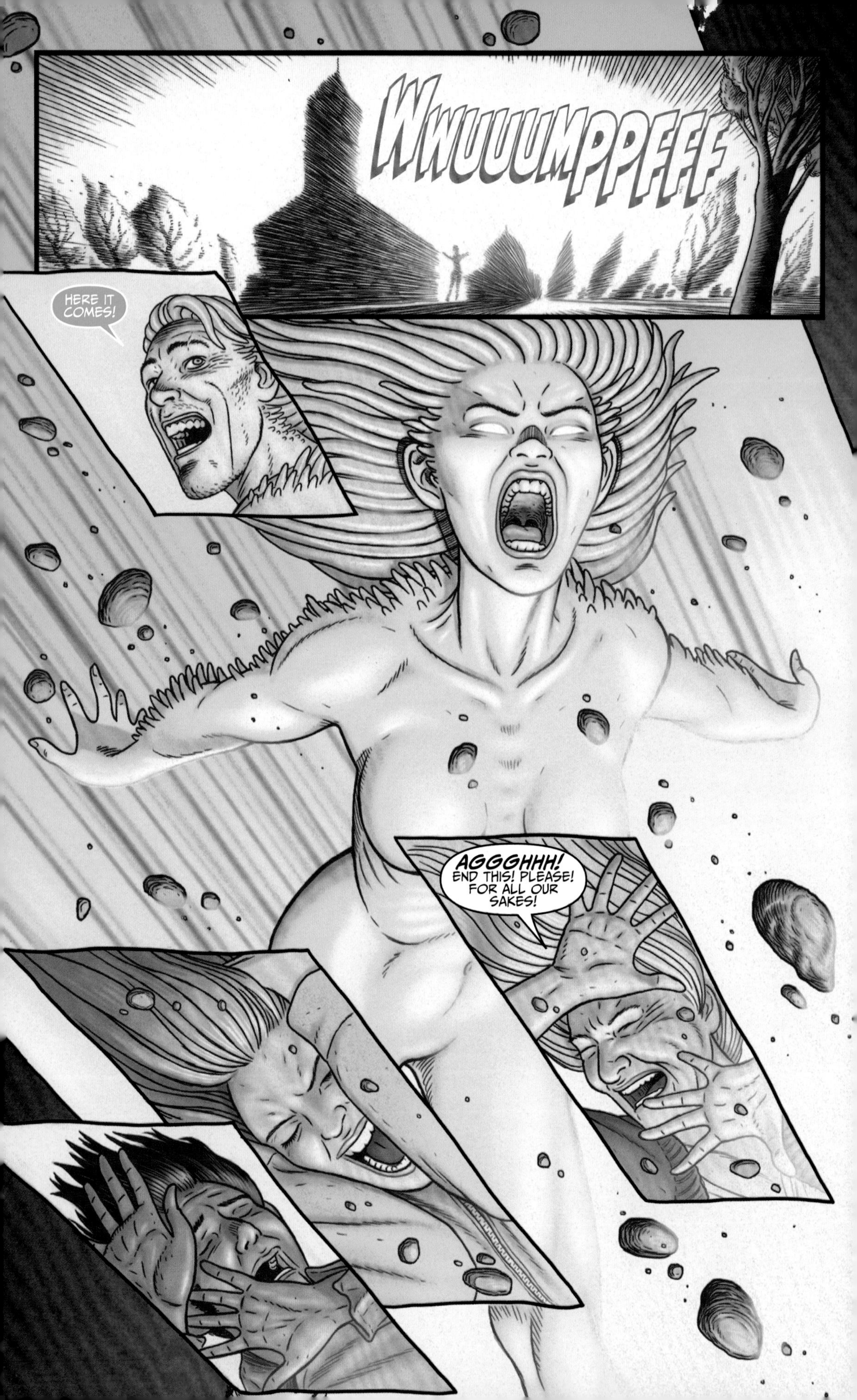
WWUUUMPPFFF
HERE IT COMES!
AGGGHHH! END THIS! PLEASE! FOR ALL OUR SAKES!

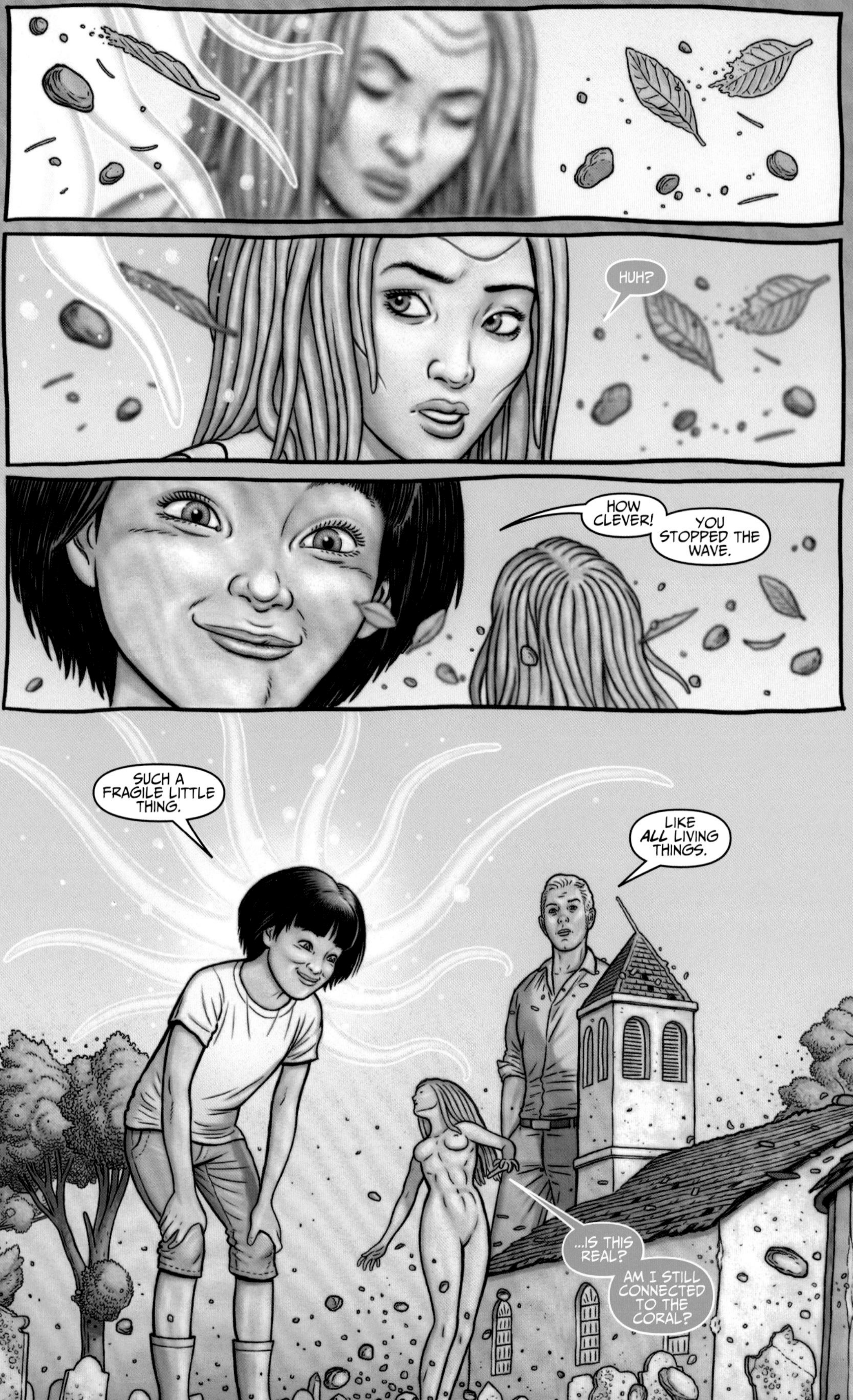
HUH?
HOW CLEVER!
YOU STOPPED THE WAVE.
SUCH A FRAGILE LITTLE THING.
LIKE ALL LIVING THINGS.
...IS THIS REAL?
AM I STILL CONNECTED TO THE CORAL?

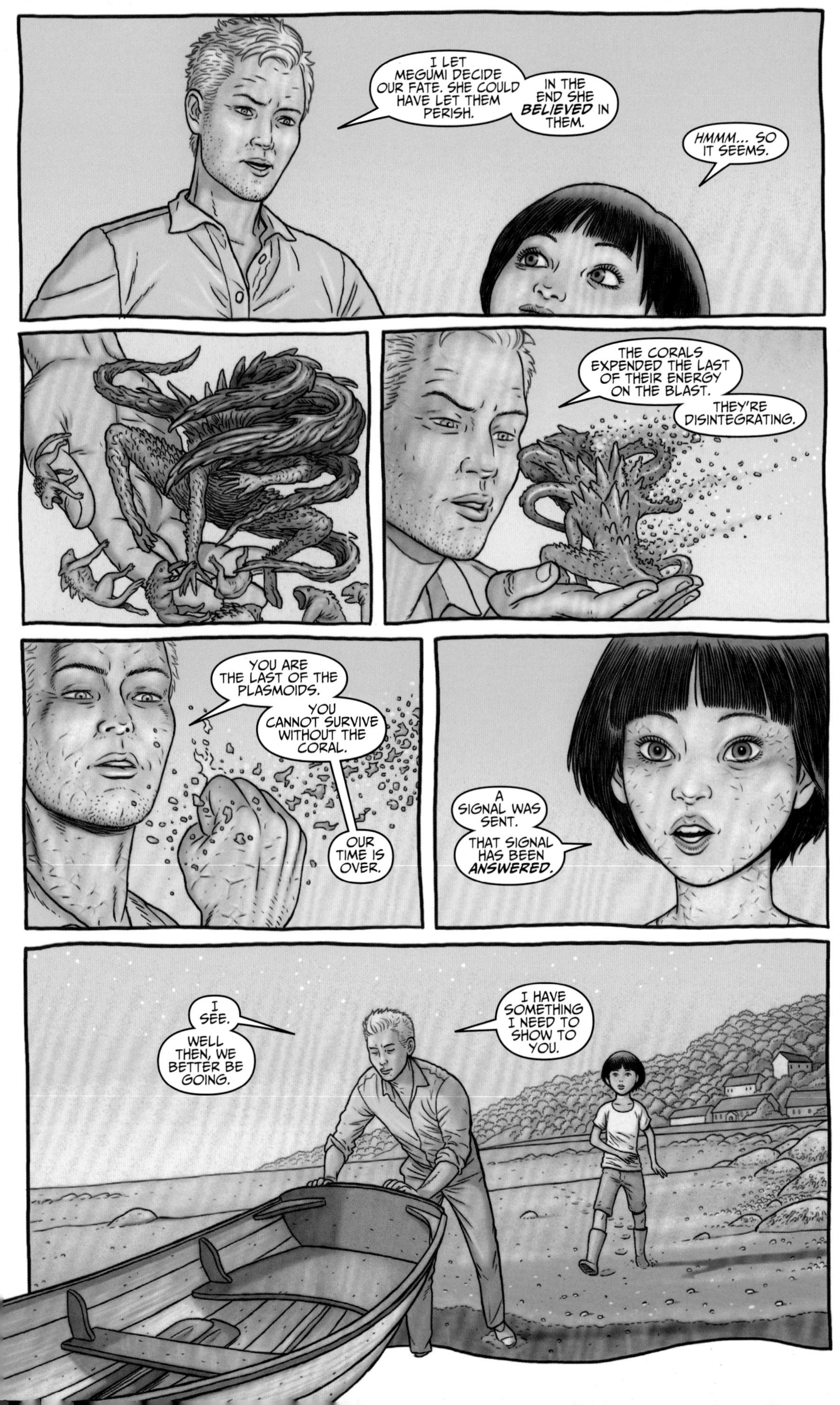
I LET MEGUMI DECIDE OUR FATE. SHE COULD HAVE LET THEM PERISH.
IN THE END SHE *BELIEVED* IN THEM.
HMMM... SO IT SEEMS.
THE CORALS EXPENDED THE LAST OF THEIR ENERGY ON THE BLAST.
THEY'RE DISINTEGRATING.
YOU ARE THE LAST OF THE PLASMOIDS.
YOU CANNOT SURVIVE WITHOUT THE CORAL.
OUR TIME IS OVER.
A SIGNAL WAS SENT.
THAT SIGNAL HAS BEEN *ANSWERED.*
I HAVE SOMETHING I NEED TO SHOW TO YOU.
I SEE.
WELL THEN, WE BETTER BE GOING.

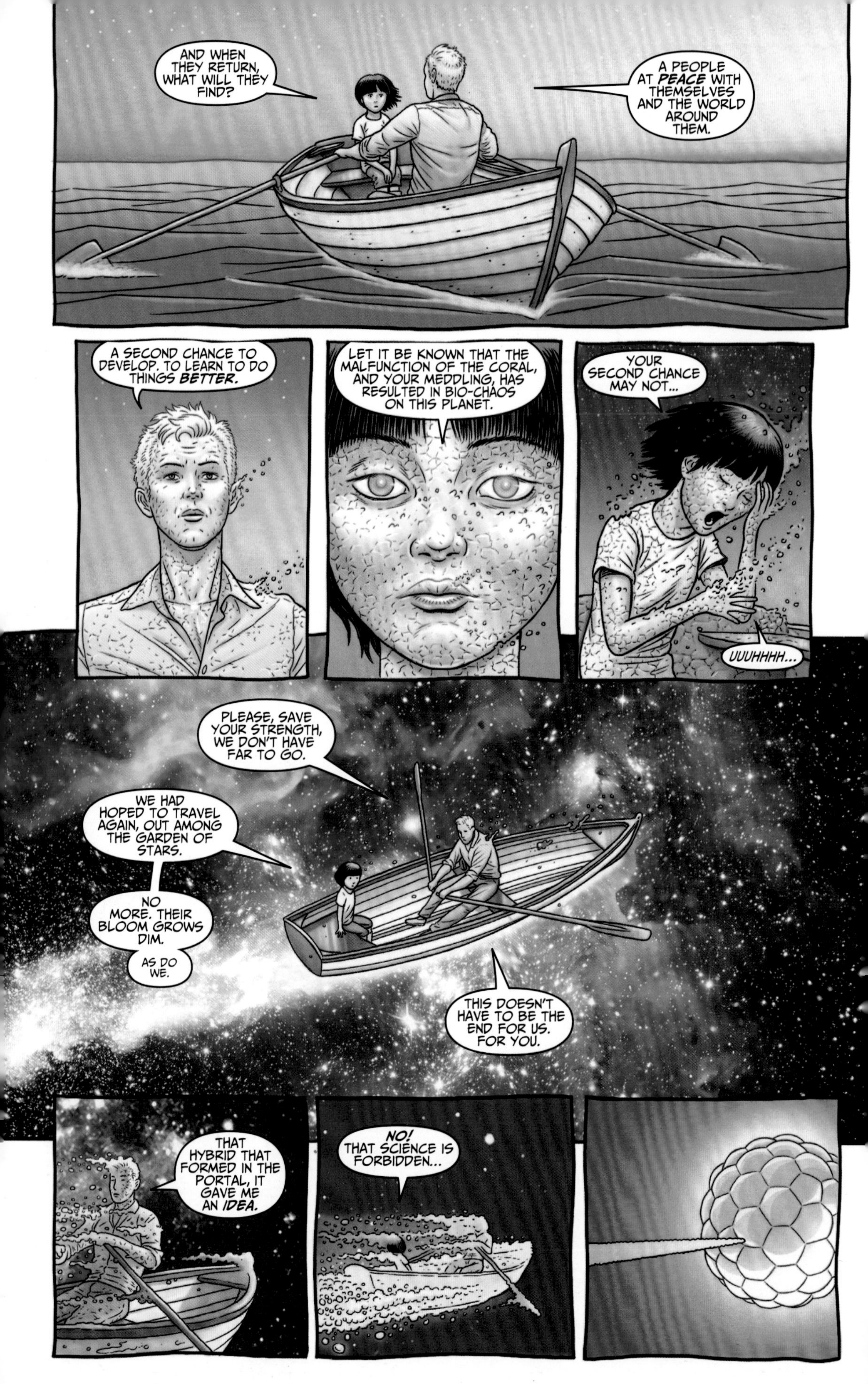
AND WHEN THEY RETURN, WHAT WILL THEY FIND?
A PEOPLE AT PEACE WITH THEMSELVES AND THE WORLD AROUND THEM.
A SECOND CHANCE TO DEVELOP. TO LEARN TO DO THINGS BETTER.
LET IT BE KNOWN THAT THE MALFUNCTION OF THE CORAL, AND YOUR MEDDLING, HAS RESULTED IN BIO-CHAOS ON THIS PLANET.
YOUR SECOND CHANCE MAY NOT...
UUUHHHH...
PLEASE, SAVE YOUR STRENGTH, WE DON'T HAVE FAR TO GO.
WE HAD HOPED TO TRAVEL AGAIN, OUT AMONG THE GARDEN OF STARS.
NO MORE. THEIR BLOOM GROWS DIM.
AS DO WE.
THIS DOESN'T HAVE TO BE THE END FOR US. FOR YOU.
THAT HYBRID THAT FORMED IN THE PORTAL, IT GAVE ME AN IDEA.
NO! THAT SCIENCE IS FORBIDDEN...

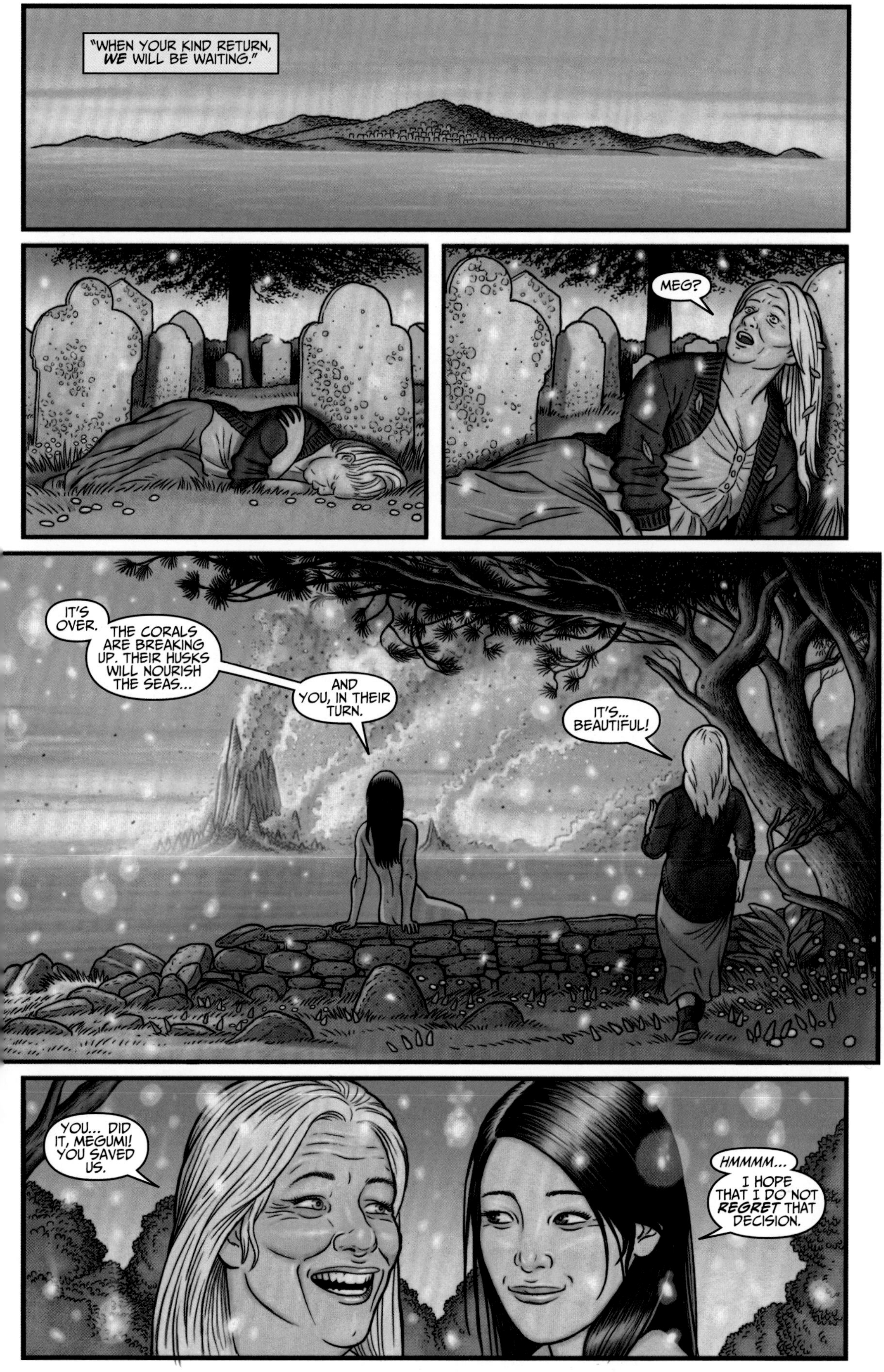
"WHEN YOUR KIND RETURN, WE WILL BE WAITING."
MEG?
IT'S OVER.
THE CORALS ARE BREAKING UP. THEIR HUSKS WILL NOURISH THE SEAS...
AND YOU, IN THEIR TURN.
IT'S... BEAUTIFUL!
YOU... DID IT, MEGUMI! YOU SAVED US.
HMMMM... I HOPE THAT I DO NOT REGRET THAT DECISION.

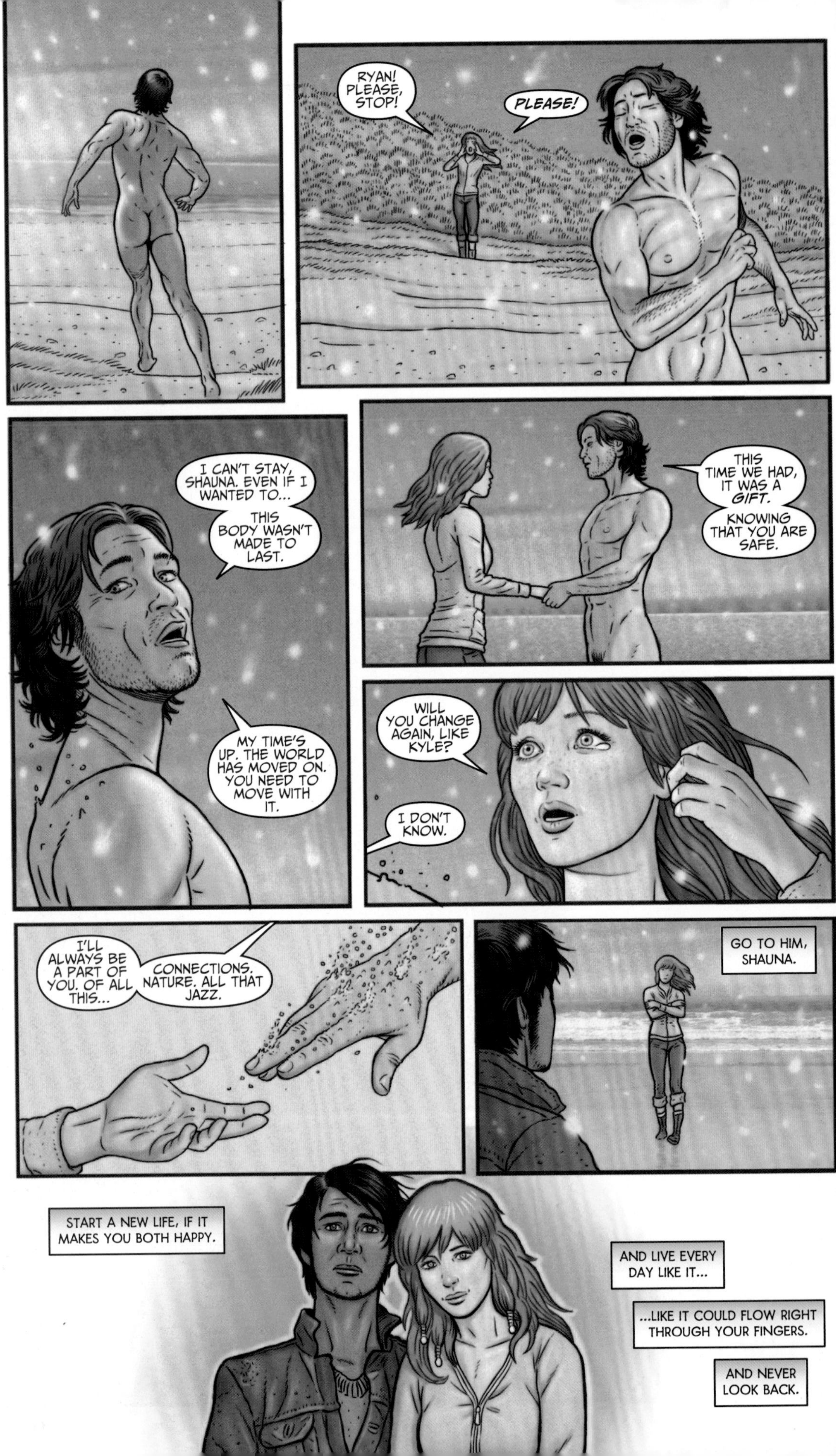
RYAN! PLEASE, STOP!
PLEASE!
I CAN'T STAY, SHAUNA. EVEN IF I WANTED TO...
THIS BODY WASN'T MADE TO LAST.
MY TIME'S UP. THE WORLD HAS MOVED ON. YOU NEED TO MOVE WITH IT.
THIS TIME WE HAD, IT WAS A GIFT.
KNOWING THAT YOU ARE SAFE.
WILL YOU CHANGE AGAIN, LIKE KYLE?
I DON'T KNOW.
I'LL ALWAYS BE A PART OF YOU. OF ALL THIS...
CONNECTIONS. NATURE. ALL THAT JAZZ.
GO TO HIM, SHAUNA.
START A NEW LIFE, IF IT MAKES YOU BOTH HAPPY.
AND LIVE EVERY DAY LIKE IT...
...LIKE IT COULD FLOW RIGHT THROUGH YOUR FINGERS.
AND NEVER LOOK BACK.

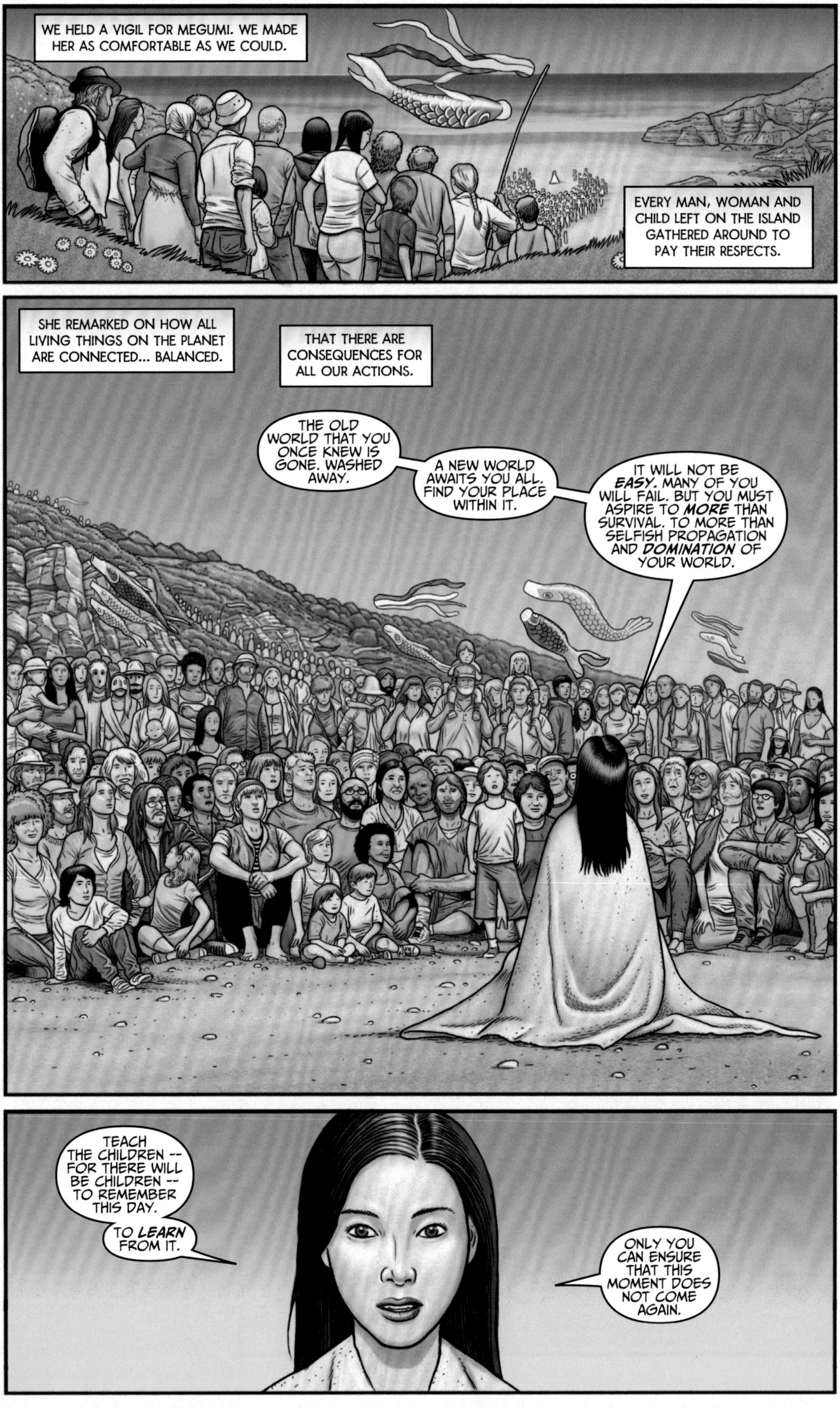
WE HELD A VIGIL FOR MEGUMI. WE MADE HER AS COMFORTABLE AS WE COULD.
EVERY MAN, WOMAN AND CHILD LEFT ON THE ISLAND GATHERED AROUND TO PAY THEIR RESPECTS.
SHE REMARKED ON HOW ALL LIVING THINGS ON THE PLANET ARE CONNECTED... BALANCED.
THAT THERE ARE CONSEQUENCES FOR ALL OUR ACTIONS.
THE OLD WORLD THAT YOU ONCE KNEW IS GONE. WASHED AWAY.
A NEW WORLD AWAITS YOU ALL. FIND YOUR PLACE WITHIN IT.
IT WILL NOT BE *EASY.* MANY OF YOU WILL FAIL. BUT YOU MUST ASPIRE TO ***MORE*** THAN SURVIVAL. TO MORE THAN SELFISH PROPAGATION AND ***DOMINATION*** OF YOUR WORLD.
TEACH THE CHILDREN -- FOR THERE WILL BE CHILDREN -- TO REMEMBER THIS DAY.
TO ***LEARN*** FROM IT.
ONLY YOU CAN ENSURE THAT THIS MOMENT DOES NOT COME AGAIN.

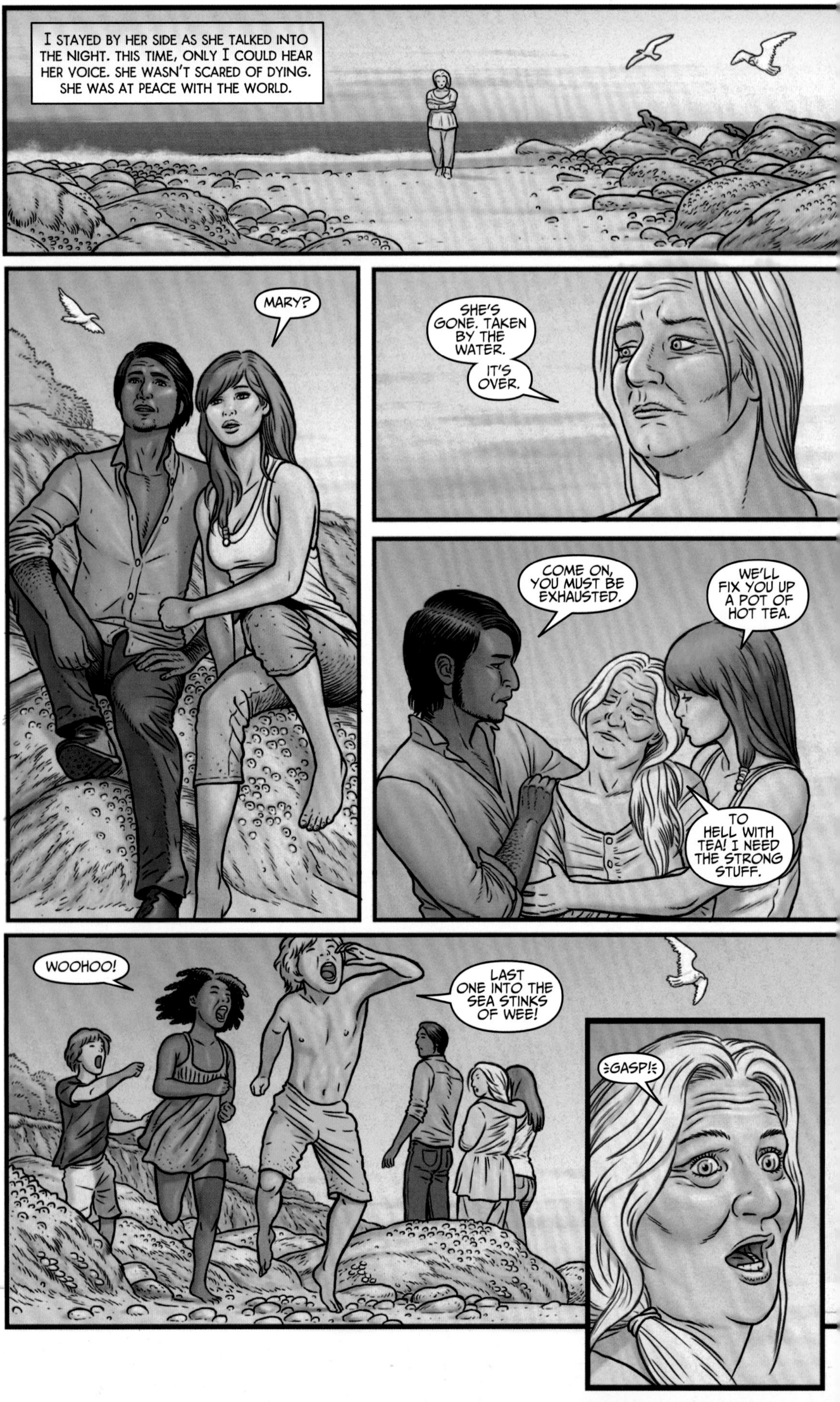
I STAYED BY HER SIDE AS SHE TALKED INTO THE NIGHT. THIS TIME, ONLY I COULD HEAR HER VOICE. SHE WASN'T SCARED OF DYING. SHE WAS AT PEACE WITH THE WORLD.
MARY?
SHE'S GONE. TAKEN BY THE WATER.
IT'S OVER.
COME ON, YOU MUST BE EXHAUSTED.
WE'LL FIX YOU UP A POT OF HOT TEA.
TO HELL WITH TEA! I NEED THE STRONG STUFF.
WOOHOO!
LAST ONE INTO THE SEA STINKS OF WEE!
GASP!

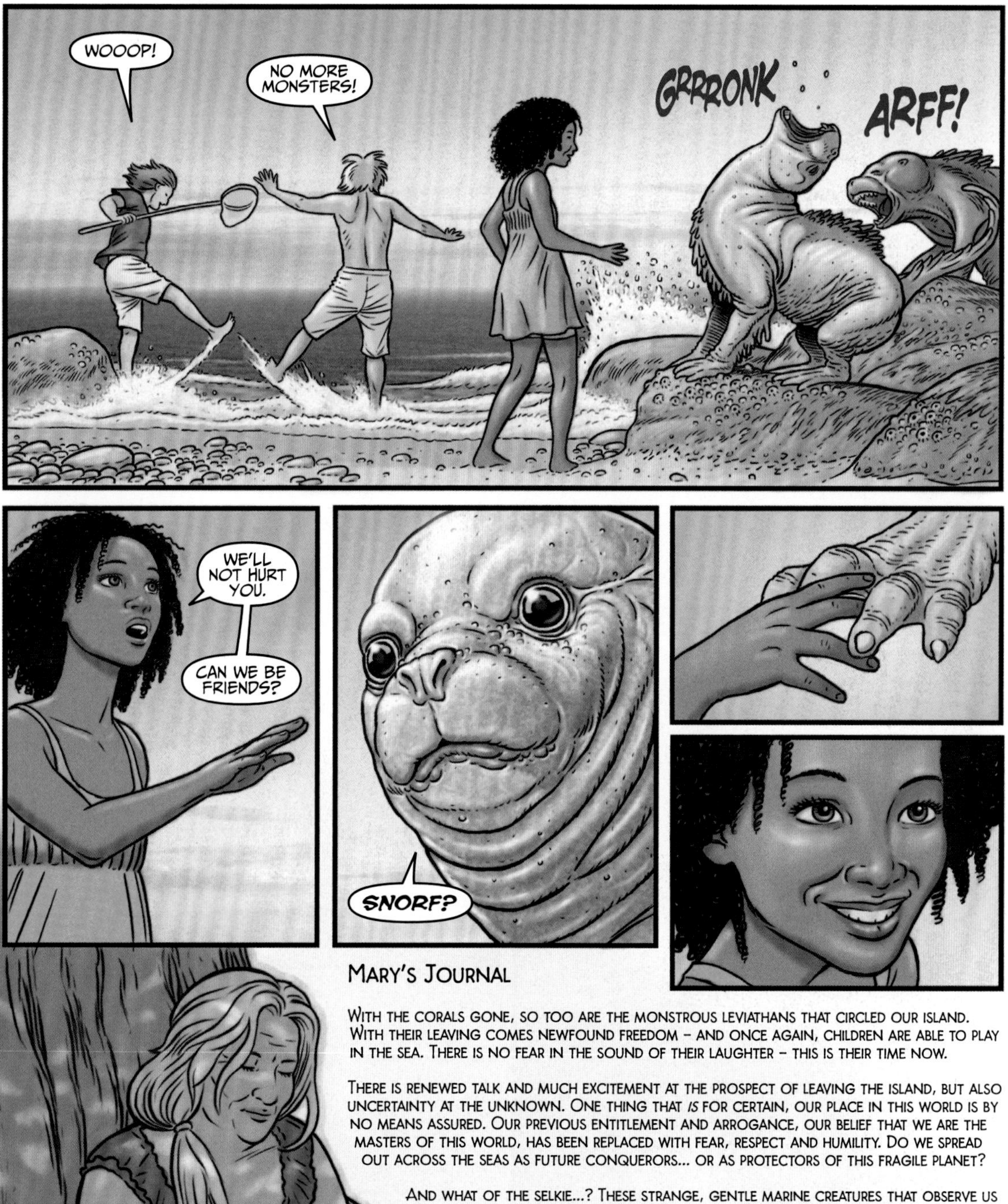
WOOOP!
NO MORE MONSTERS!
GRRRONK
ARFF!
WE'LL NOT HURT YOU.
CAN WE BE FRIENDS?
SNORF?

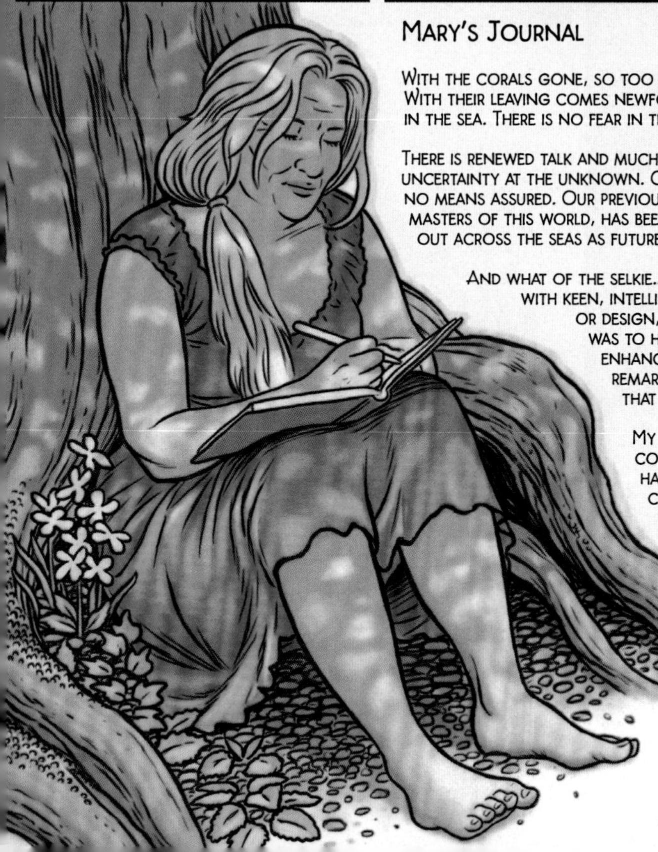

Mary's Journal

With the corals gone, so too are the monstrous leviathans that circled our island. With their leaving comes newfound freedom – and once again, children are able to play in the sea. There is no fear in the sound of their laughter – this is their time now.

There is renewed talk and much excitement at the prospect of leaving the island, but also uncertainty at the unknown. One thing that *is* for certain, our place in this world is by no means assured. Our previous entitlement and arrogance, our belief that we are the masters of this world, has been replaced with fear, respect and humility. Do we spread out across the seas as future conquerors... or as protectors of this fragile planet?

And what of the selkie...? These strange, gentle marine creatures that observe us with keen, intelligent eyes. At once familiar and yet so alien. By mistake, or design, the selkie have evolved from the biological soup that was to have been the end of our species. With their evolution enhanced by the science of the corals, the selkie have adapted remarkably well to their new environment. It's quite possible that they are the *true* heirs of this new world.

My thoughts turn to the cosmic beings that built the corals. Undoubtedly a remarkably advanced civilization, had we been able to communicate with them, what wisdom could they have bestowed? Wiped out by our hand, without our even being aware of their presence on this Earth. How many *other*, terrestrial species have been lost due to human activity – with no mark of their passing? Perhaps the extinctions that ultimately resulted from our unchecked and untimely destruction were always going to prefigure our inevitable demise. If not by the sea-sickness, then some other unforeseen catastrophe. Everything is connected.

When and if they return to this world, will they do so as vengeful gods? Or will they look upon us with forgiveness?

...That is a story for another day.

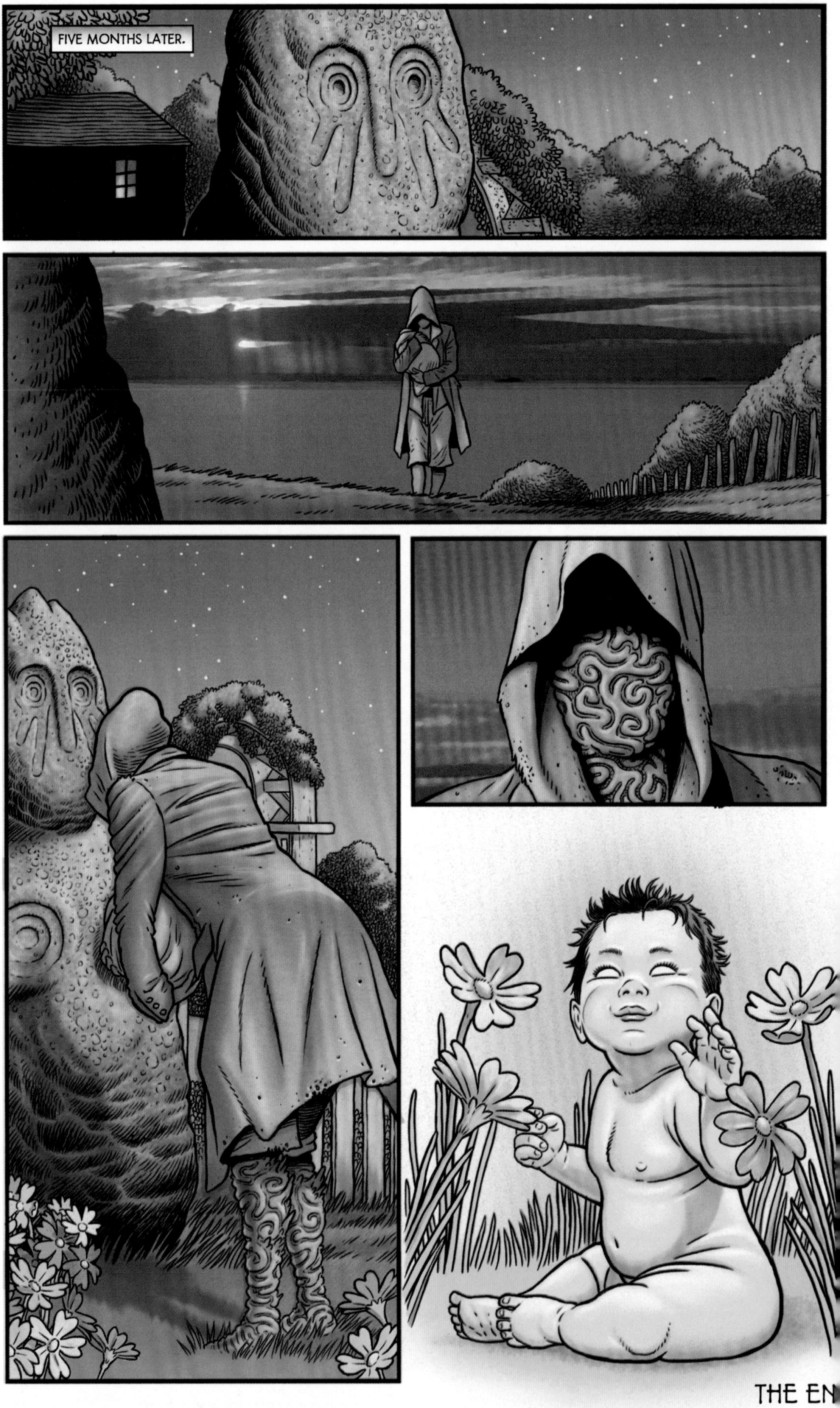
FIVE MONTHS LATER.
THE EN

THE MAKING OF
SURFACE TENSION

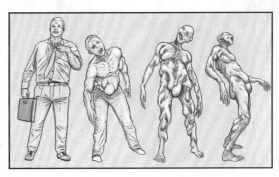

THE SEA-SICK

My intention with the Sea-Sick was to have the infected take on a wet appearance: their physical form is liquefying, like melting, running wax. During the process they lose their physical form but retain the same organic mass, until they are just an animated blob of flesh and bone. Once the Sea-Sick reach the sea, their organic matter dissolves into the water.

Early stages of the sickness involve a complete loss of pigment in skin and hair, the lymph-nodes swell, and flesh begins to bubble and lose definition.

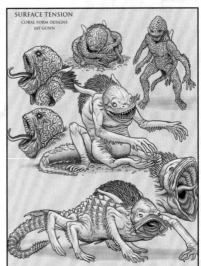

SURFACE TENSION
CORAL FORM DESIGNS
JAY GUNN

THE CORAL-FORM MONSTER

The creature that follows Megumi and Ryan from the sea posed a difficult design challenge. I could have easily gone in one of two directions: have the creature take the form of a tentacle-sprouting blob, or draw something very aquatic in form. I quickly concluded after my early concept drawings that aquatic monsters are very common in comics and it just seemed too obvious and tired as a design.

The 'coral-form' creature represents the physical wrath of nature, and so I made the decision to have the monster shift its form throughout the story; blurring the line between human, alien coral and animal. When the coral-form is attacking, it takes on a more human-like appearance: at times a horned, vengeful, demonic figure, rather like a wolf or a stag. At other times we see it going about on four legs, becoming more animal and benign in appearance and behavior. Only at the end of the story does the creature begin to lose its earthly forms and become more alien and abstract.

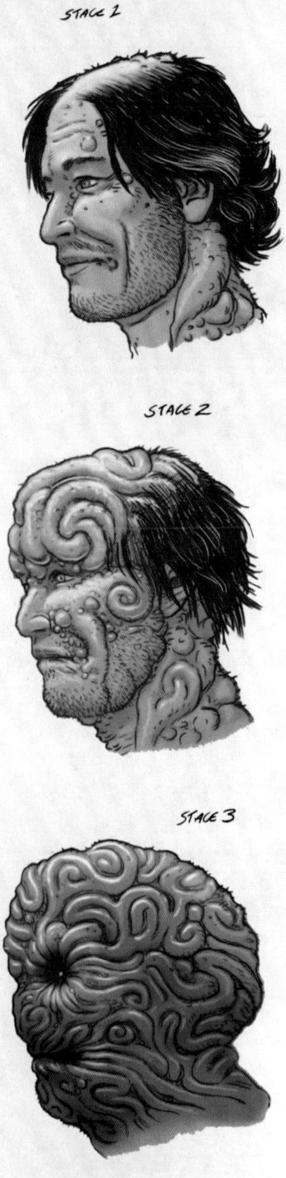
STAGE 1
STAGE 2
STAGE 3

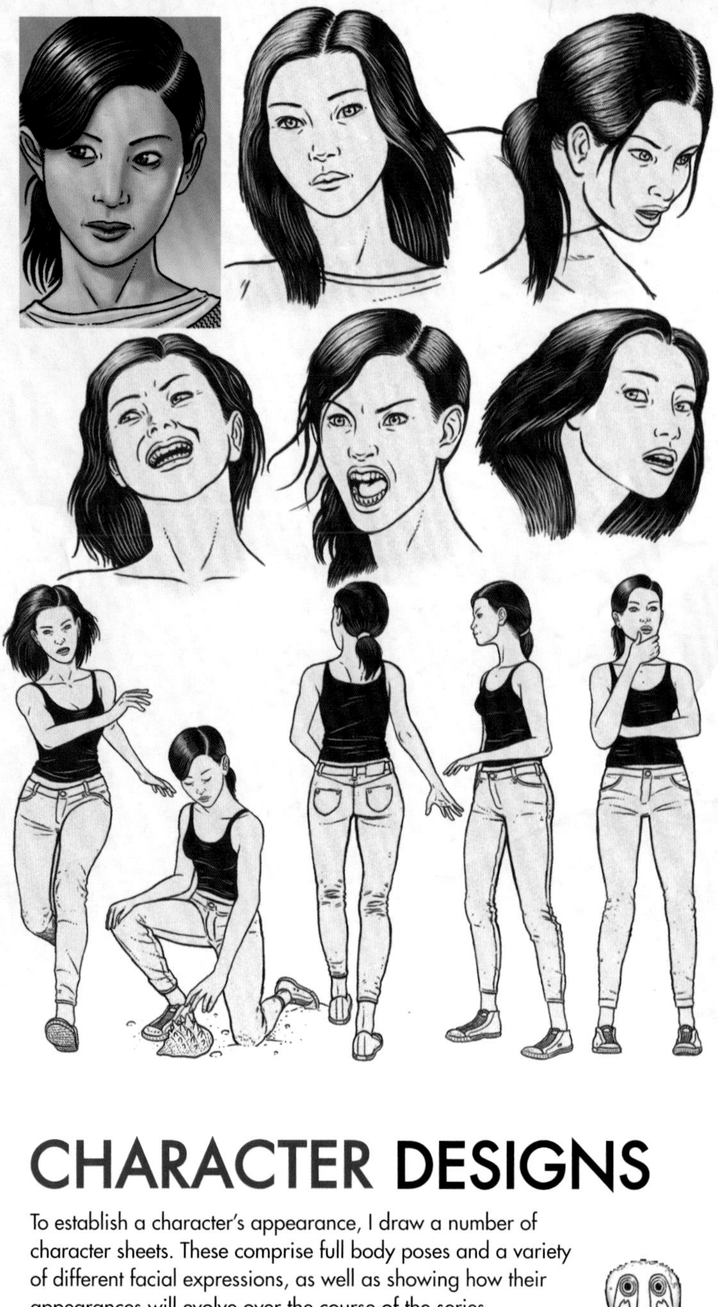

CHARACTER DESIGNS

To establish a character's appearance, I draw a number of character sheets. These comprise full body poses and a variety of different facial expressions, as well as showing how their appearances will evolve over the course of the series.

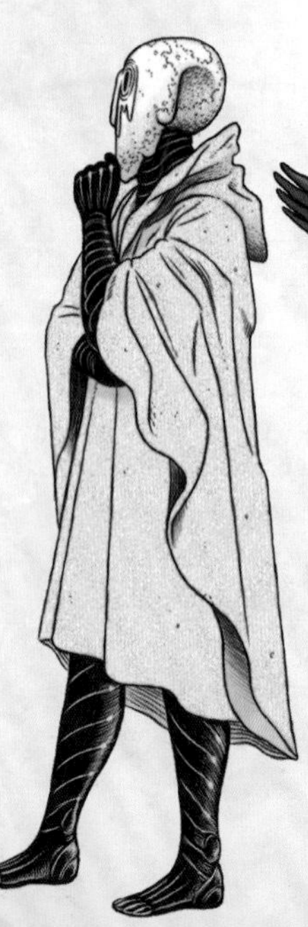

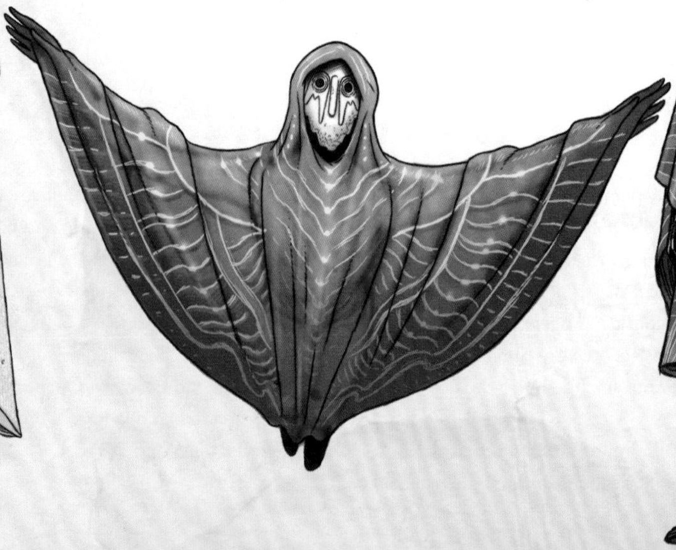

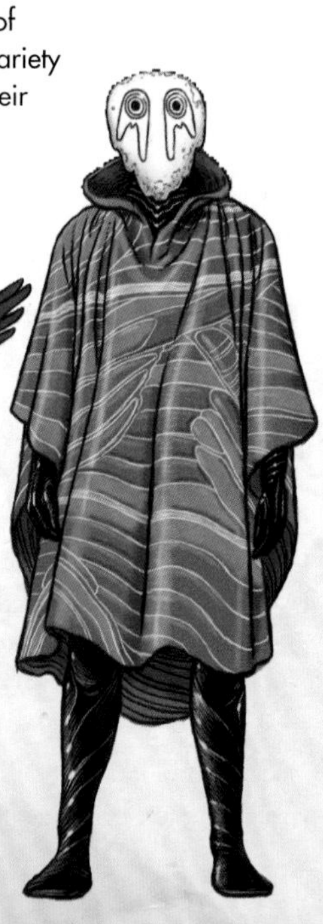

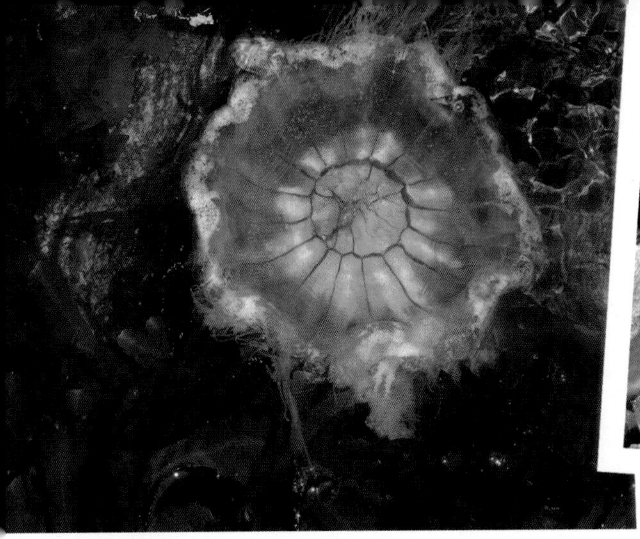

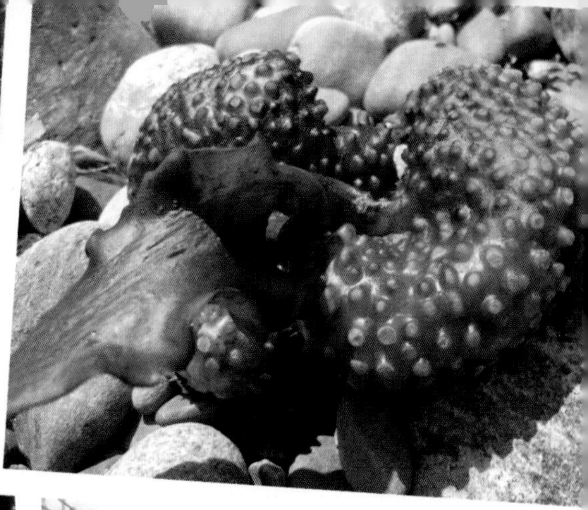

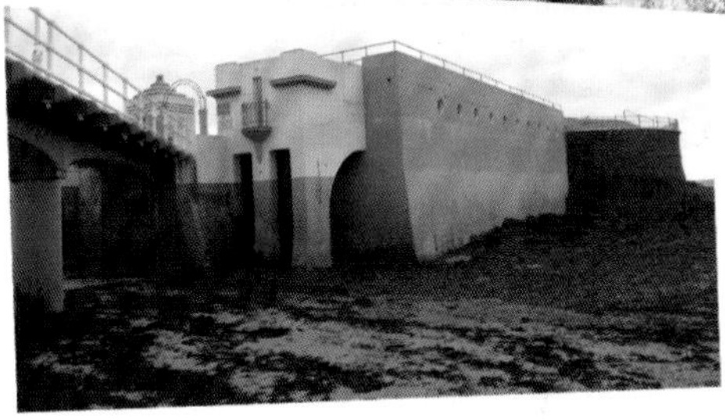

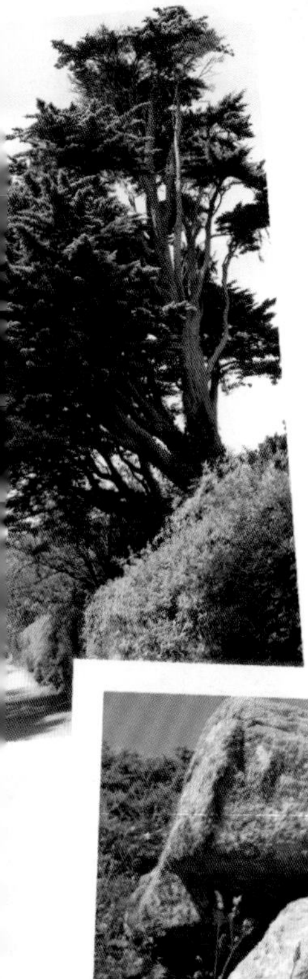

RESEARCH TRIPS

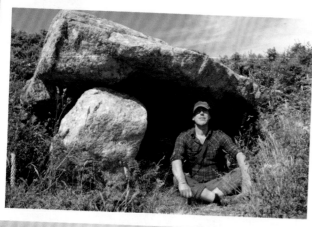

It was very important that Breith felt like a real location, so I traveled to a number of British coastal locations, in particular the British Channel Islands – Jersey, Guernsey and Sark. It was during these trips that I made a number of discoveries that I incorporated into the script – such as the German bunkers that were built during the Nazi occupation of the islands during World War II, and the Neolithic sites (featuring *dolmans* and *menhirs)* that can still be found on the islands.

My favorite discovery was a whimsical art deco Edwardian swim hall that is located on the coastline of Jersey. The outdoor swim hall becomes an island during high tide and is connected to the island by a pier. It was love at first sight and I just knew that I had to feature this wonderfully eccentric building in *Surface Tension*. I made a few adjustments to the location to transfer it to the page, but it is very similar to how it appears in real life.

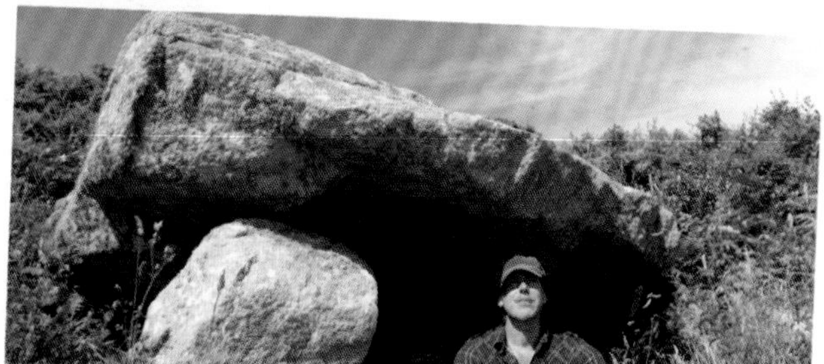

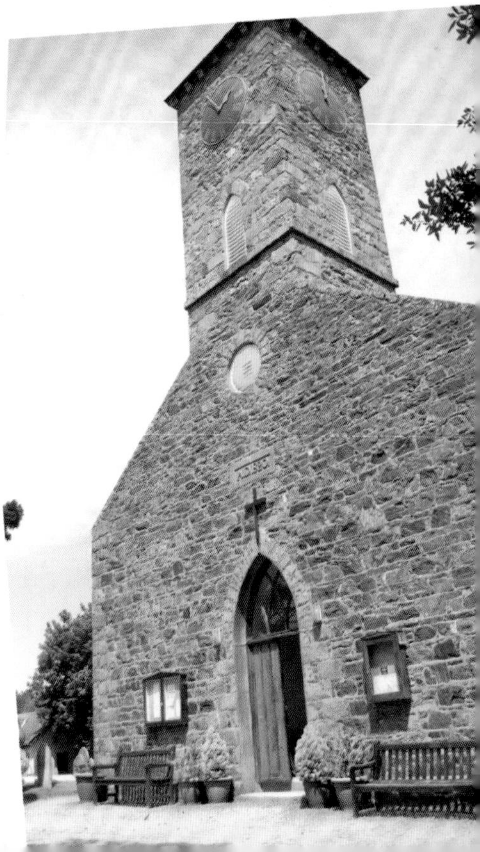

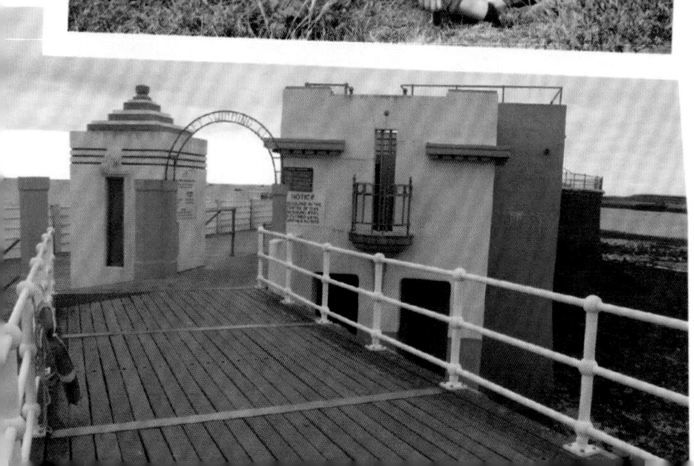

COVER ILLUSTRATION - STAGES

1 **Inspiration.** I was trying to figure out what to draw for #3: I'd doodled a number of ideas that I wasn't particularly enamored with, so I went out for an early morning walk. I often find that if I'm stuck for inspiration, it's best to get out of your environment and walk. During this particular walk I happened upon a horse and trap – perfect! I waved down the owners of the horse and politely asked if I could take a reference photo; the owners duly obliged.

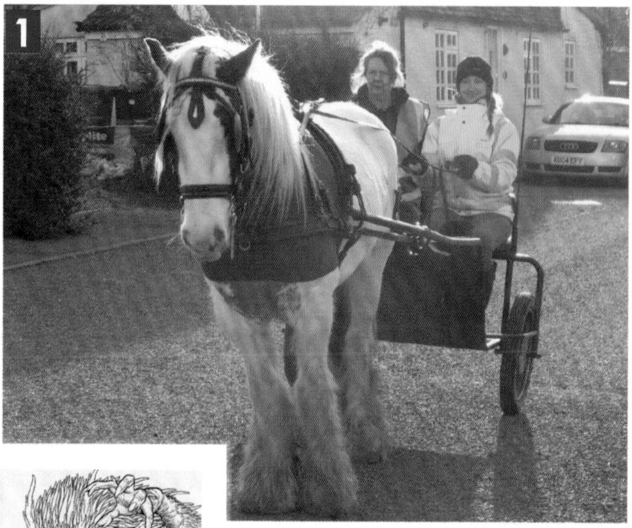
1

2 **Rough pencils.** After a thumbnail doodle I jump into drawing a small page of the final piece. This is the final composition with rough details.

3 **Final inks.** I then enlarge the pencils page from A4 to A3 and begin to ink over the pencils on a separate page or layer (I can never settle on a process – real ink or digital) and add more details. At this stage I may fix a number of elements from the pencils. In this case I altered the mouth and legs of the horse.

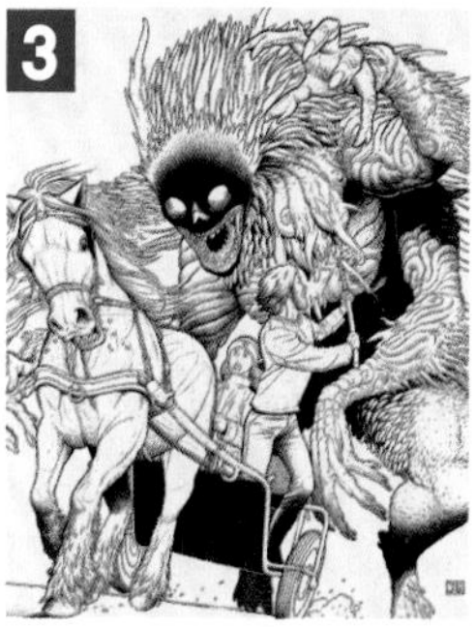
3

4 **Color.** All my coloring is done digitally. I try to make my colors vivid and striking, and so I'll try out a number of different background hues in order to make the foreground image pop. I don't use too many fancy digital tools, so I can keep my color work as painterly as possible.

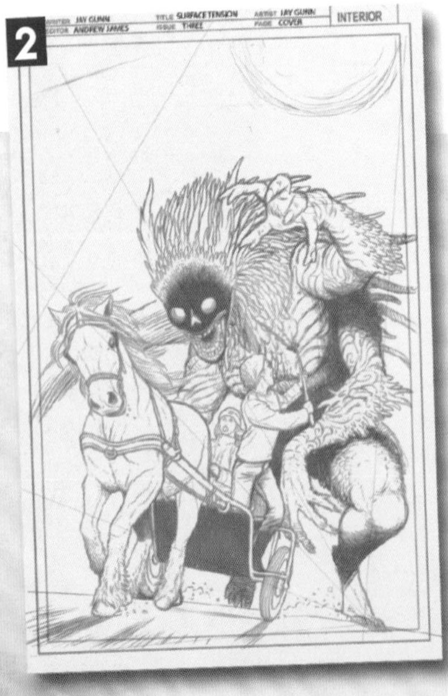
2
ANDREW JAMES
SURFACE TENSION
COVER
INTERIOR

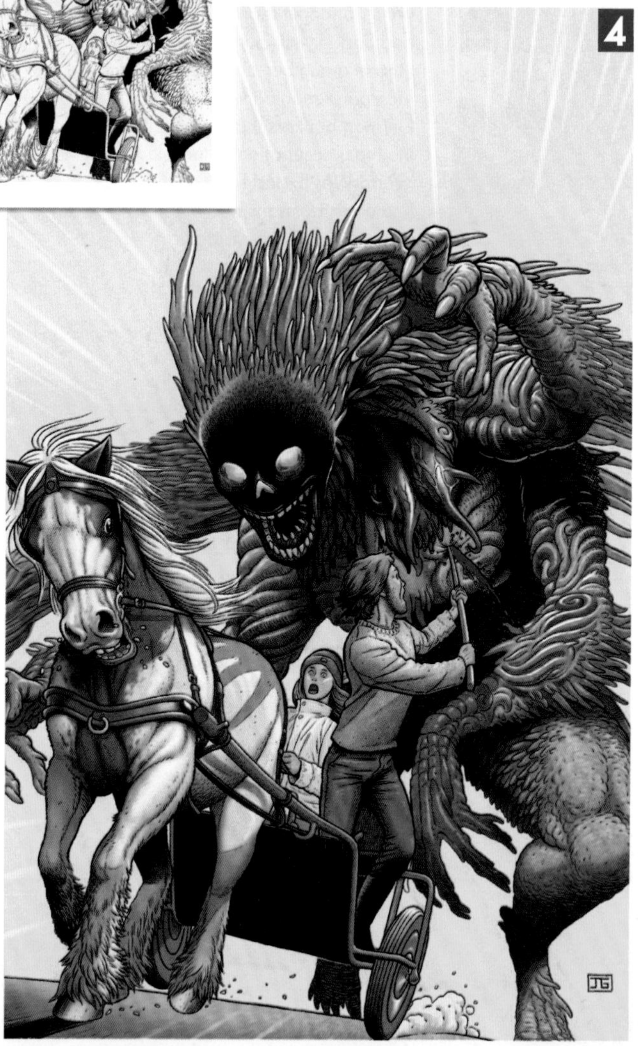
4
JG

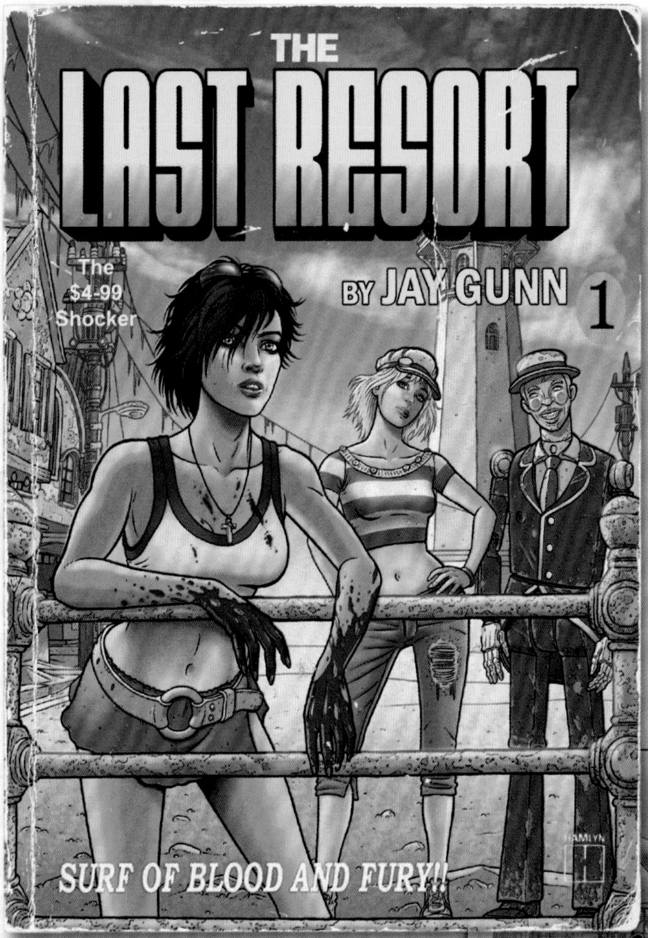
THE
LAST RESORT
The
$4-99
Shocker
BY JAY GUNN
1
SURF OF BLOOD AND FURY!!

DEMO COMIC PAGES

To hone my skills as a first-time comic creator, I created a 22 page 'pilot' episode, which became an early prototype draft of *Surface Tension*. I did this work on weekends and evenings, outside of my day job, and it helped me understand the incredible amount of work required to create a comic. It also helped me establish and hone a style and working method. I still like these early pages, but I can also see where there was room for lots of improvement. I was overcompensating for my lack of experience by adding way too much distracting detail, when I should have been focusing on improving my character anatomy and rendering.

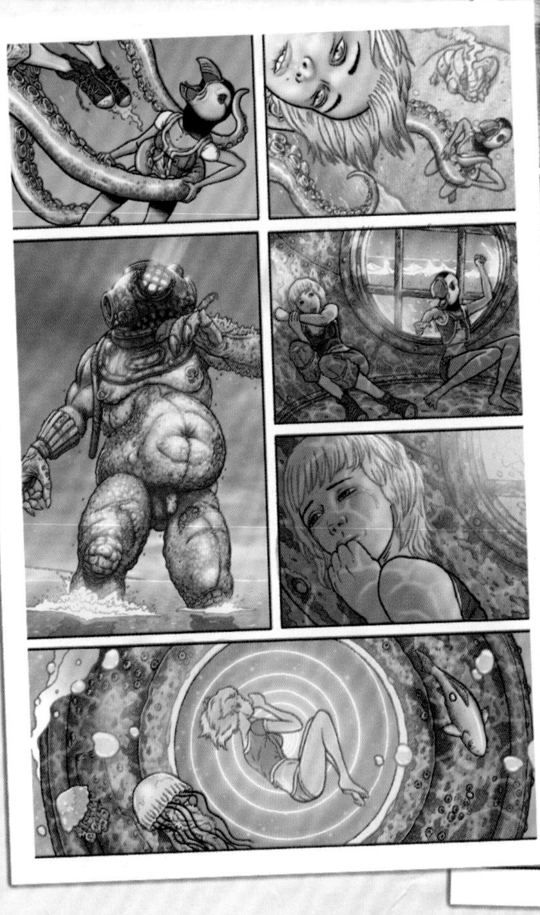

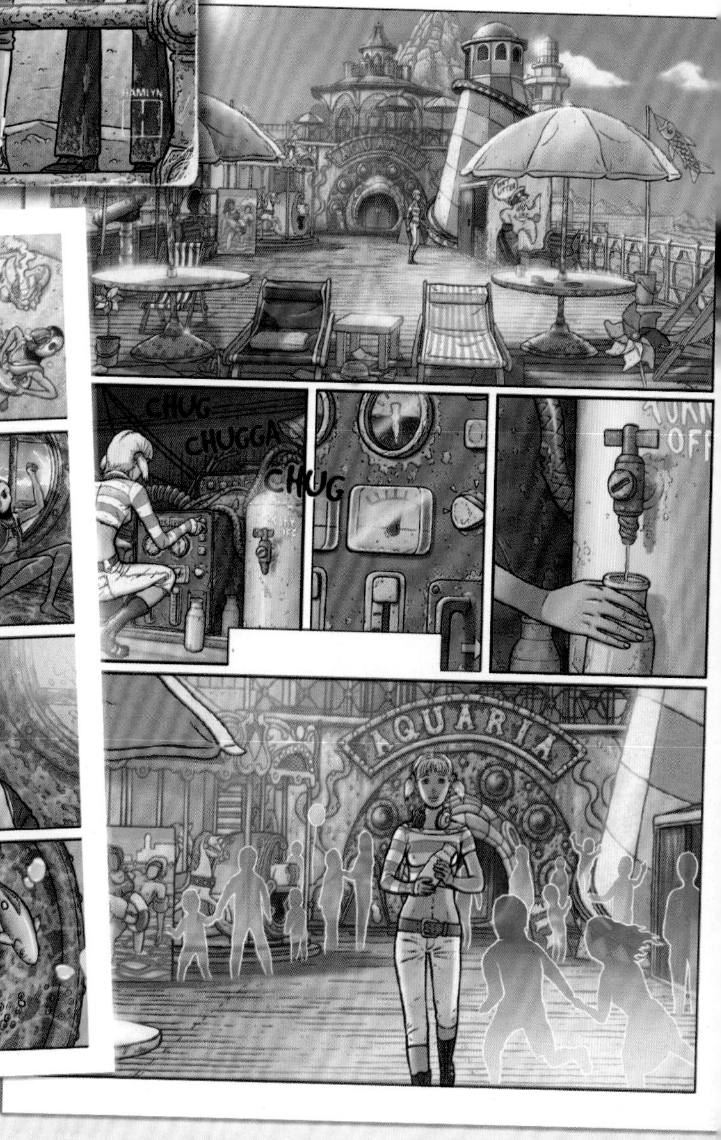
CHUG
CHUGGA
CHUG
AQUARIA

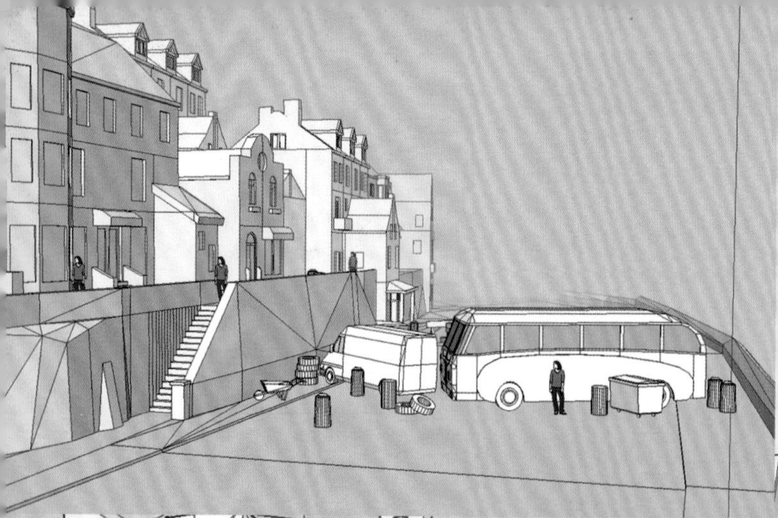

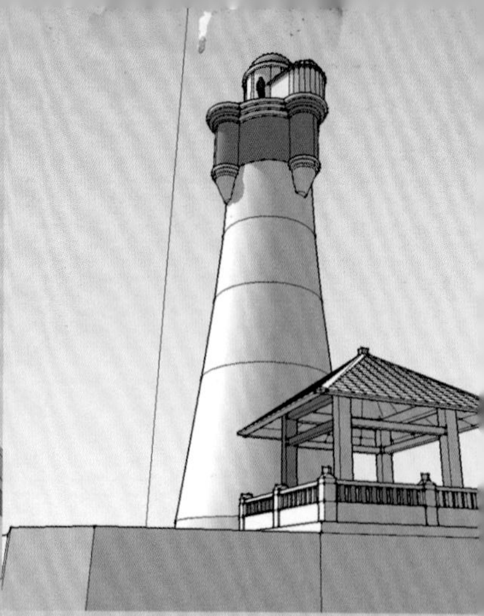

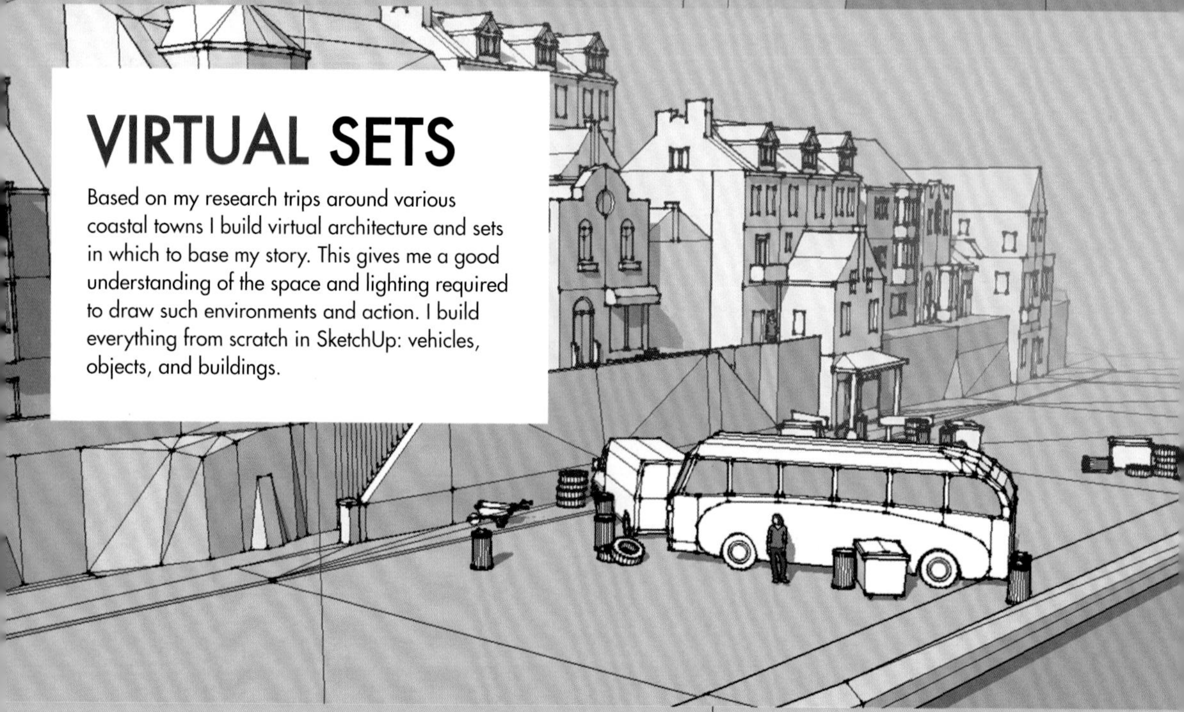

VIRTUAL SETS

Based on my research trips around various coastal towns I build virtual architecture and sets in which to base my story. This gives me a good understanding of the space and lighting required to draw such environments and action. I build everything from scratch in SketchUp: vehicles, objects, and buildings.

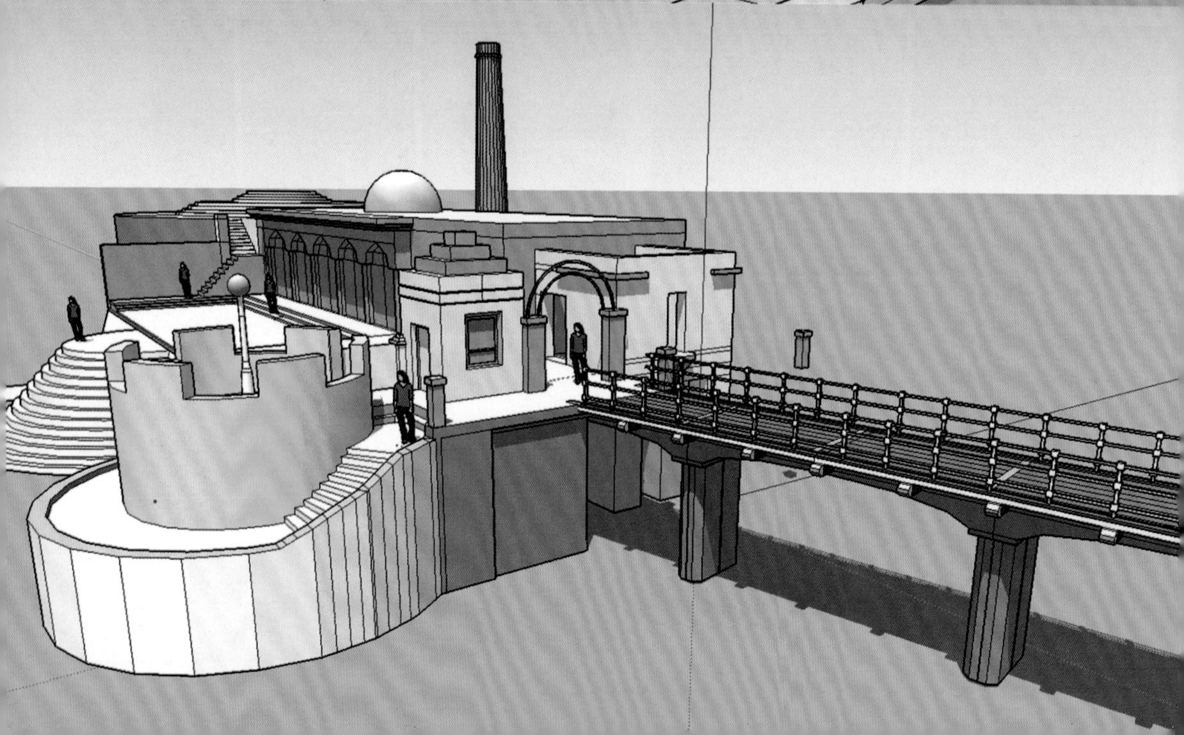

SURFACE TENSION

CREATOR JAY GUNN

Surface Tension is Jay's first foray into the world of comic books and we're delighted he was able to take time out of his busy schedule to talk to us about the project.

downthetubes: How did you come up with Surface Tension?

Jay Gunn: Throughout my life I've spent a lot of time by the coast. When I was a child my parents owned a caravan by the sea and we would stay there for much of the summer. During that time I would read lots of science fiction and horror novels that I had bought with my pocket money: John Wyndham, H.G. Wells, and the schlocky pulp of Guy N Smith. I would browse the seaside book stalls for second hand copies of the beautifully illustrated *Hammer's Halls of Horror* comic magazine. A lot of the stuff I read wasn't intended for children, but the lurid covers always captured my imagination – and anything that gets a child to read is a good thing, right? Even if one's reading would include stories about giant crabs eviscerating victims at dreary British coastal resorts!

Because of this I've always made a connection between the sea and sci-fi and horror. Some people have asked me if I was influenced by Lovecraft as he wrote several stories about aquatic horrors and I would have to say that I was not. Thematically, *Surface Tension* is much more sci-fi fantasy with a tinge of horror than it is the all-out cosmic dread of Lovecraft.

downthetubes: What were your inspirations for the story? There are echoes of the work of John Wyndham's SF novels in the tale, for example, but were there other influences? Quatermass, perhaps?
Jay: I think a lot of my inspiration for the story stems from one singular moment in my life. When I was very young, I lived in a very small village by a wide river that ran out

to sea. Downriver was a large chemical plant and my father worked in the steel mill that neighbored the plant. Thankfully, he wasn't at work on the day that the chemical plant – Flixborough – exploded!

At the time it was Britain's biggest postwar explosion. Lots of chemicals spewed into the air and into the river and I often wondered if the dead fish that would wash up in our backyard were a result of having been poisoned by the leak. I vividly remember the day, some months after the explosion, when my parents drove our family car through the devastated area. The twisted, mangled structure of the chemical plant, the empty houses of the nearby village, the pieces of peoples' lives scattered about the roadside... they left an indelible mark on my young mind.

I guess the disaster was responsible for my fascination for contemporary science fiction. I would go on to see films like Nigel Kneale's *Quatermass 2*, which was set in a chemical plant with shapeless alien beings occupying its metal domes. That film doubtlessly fired my imagination as to the possible cause of the explosion at the chemical plant!

In turn, this lead me to discover the works of John Wyndham: *Day of the Triffids* and *The Kraken Awakes*. Both books feature an ecological theme. I have very fond memories of watching Kneale's *The Quatermass Conclusion* TV series and finding it to be especially scary, as it was set in a then-contemporary time and place that I could relate to. I became fascinated with how Kneale would take British mythology and history and then fold them into contemporary science fiction concerns. I actually found Kneale's work to be a great source of inspiration for aspects of *Surface Tension*.

downthetubes: Has the project had a long gestation, and how did you come to partner with Titan Comics to publish it?
Jay: I did produce an early version of *Surface Tension* in the form of a demo comic back in 2006. It was about 30 pages long, but was quite different to the story that I have now. It still had the island setting and the event that had changed the world, but it was much more action-orientated, and was more of a romp than a science fiction story of any real depth. I took the comic to San Diego Comic Con and it was met with a very positive response. I was ready to quit my job and pursue a new career in comics but I was talked into staying at Sony (where I was working at the time as game designer) for a few more years, and so my love of comics remained a hobby.

It was at the London "Kapow" comic event that I approached Steve White of Titan. I discussed a couple

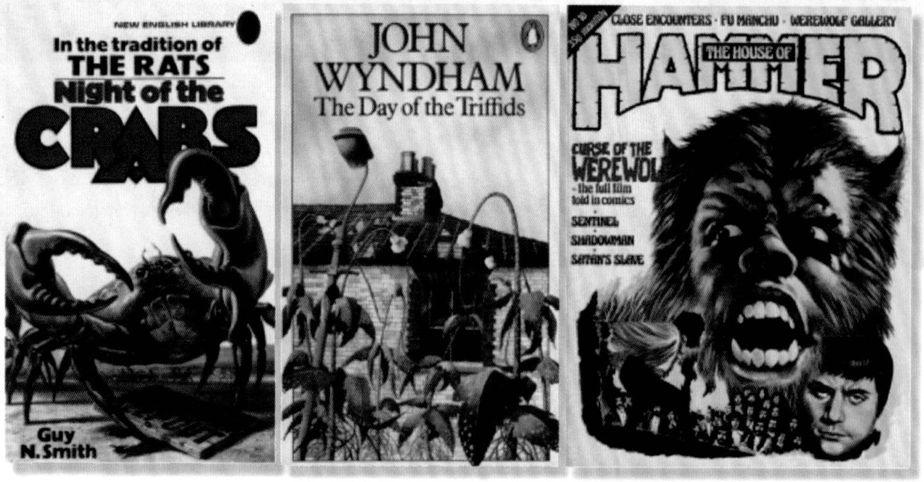
NEW ENGLISH LIBRARY
In the tradition of
THE RATS
Night of the
CRABS
Guy
N.Smith
JOHN
WYNDHAM
The Day of the Triffids
CLOSE ENCOUNTERS · FU MANCHU · WEREWOLF GALLERY
THE HOUSE OF
HAMMER
CURSE OF THE
WEREWOLF
- the full film
told in comics
SENTINEL
SHADOWMAN
SATAN'S SLAVE

Early seaside inspirations.

of ideas that I had, and the one that stuck was *Surface Tension*. I had intended to finish work on the comics sooner than I did – but this was partly due to being diagnosed with Stage 2 cancer when I was three months into writing and drawing the comic. I needed surgery on my neck to remove a rapidly growing tumor.

Understandably, this was a devastating blow for all concerned. I was just embarking on my dream job of writing and drawing a comic book and I decided that I didn't want the cancer to become a negative influence – so I used it as a source of inspiration and turned it into a positive creative energy. It helped me to develop the notion that the characters in the story are undergoing both a physical and mental transformation, which pretty much mirrored my own state at the time. The characters in the story need to save the sickened planet, but they are questioning their place in the world, whether the fight is worth it, if they win in the face of overwhelming odds?

Environmental disaster became my metaphor for cancer. This was the question I was asking myself when I was drawing the comic – should I continue the crazy dream or just give it up? Physical transformation, coupled with the notion of transcending beyond the limits of the physical, became a theme for me to hang the story around.

downthetubes: How much pre-production work did you put into the project – character design, locations, artefacts and 'world building'?

As I was writing the script, I traveled around the British Channel Islands to study island life and to gather reference. The ornate Edwardian art deco bath house you first see in Chapter One is actually based on a real swim hall that I discovered on Jersey. Sark in particular became a great reference point for the fictional island of Breith.

The organic texture of the setting is very important to me, and I wanted to capture the functional moments of island life before the action kicks into gear.

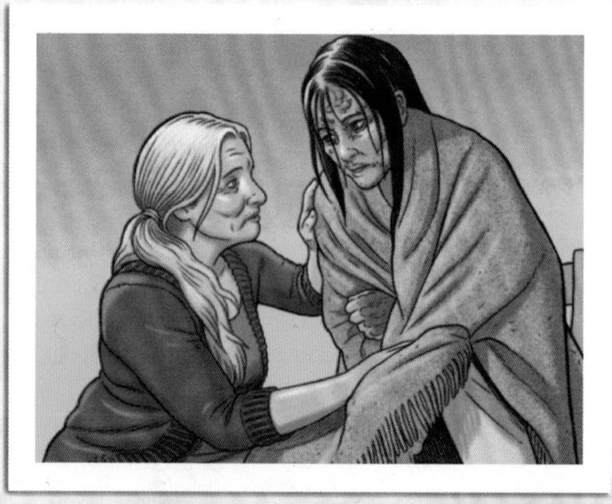

I'm a big fan of the quieter moments of Japanese cinema, those moments where we are simply observing characters going about their lives.

I'm a big fan of the quieter moments of Japanese cinema, those moments where we are simply observing characters going about their lives, I'm particularly thinking of the films by animator Hayao Miyazaki. With *Surface Tension* it was important to see characters framed by nature. The story is all about our relationship with the environment so I had to make the backgrounds seem as integral and as appealing as possible. You will notice that as the series progresses we see less and less of the natural environment, as if the survivors are being separated from the world of nature.

During my research I discovered that the Channel Islands have a Neolithic pagan past. On Sark, I had the pleasure of meeting a Cambridge archeologist who was living on the island and excavating ancient sites and he was kind enough to show me his work and answer my questions. On the islands I visited ancient Menhirs (standing stones) and dolmans (burial sites). I wove some of these neolithic elements into the fabric of the story. I also borrowed a few elements from Irish mythology such as the selkie – human/seal hybrid creatures.

downthetubes: Without giving anything away, is there scope for further tales in the same world once the initial run is published?

Jay: Oh, yes! I had to cut a number of interesting ideas from the original script, so there's a lot of mileage for further stories. For instance, we don't see what has happened to the rest of the world. Are there other survivors, and what challenges are they overcoming? What other creatures exist in this strange new world?

I do have a sequel story planned out, one that expands the concept beyond the island setting – and I'd love to do it – but in the end it comes down to financing. I think that it would make a wonderful story, but creator-owned work doesn't pay a page rate, and it's a long time to go without an income. Maybe I would write and have another artist illustrate it; that would save me some time.
However, I do have a number of smaller comic stories that I want to publish before I return to *Surface Tension*.

downthetubes: Do you work digitally or traditionally to create your pages?

Jay: A mixture of the two; I'm still undecided which is better or faster. Sometimes I'll feel like drawing out a page or a panel traditionally with pencil and ink on card and then some days I'll draw digitally. I do still like raw pencil work and so I worry that digital can take away that organic texture. Sometimes I wish I was looser in my line work, I'd like to get more impressionistic as I develop. I do all my colors digitally, but I do miss using colored pencils. I'd like to get back to them someday, perhaps for a short story that I'd like to draw.

In the end, traditional or digital, it's all drawn by hand and both are about ideas and storytelling.

downthetubes: How do you plan your day as a creator? (Do you plan your day?)

Jay: I try to keep consistent times, start at 9.00am and finish at 8.00pm. I also usually work at least half a day on the weekend. There's a tendency to keep working into the night, but you can easily burn yourself out and working too many late hours is the law of diminishing returns!

downthetubes: Jay, thanks very much for taking the time to talk with us.

SURFACE TENSION
SURFACE TENSION
1
2
3
4

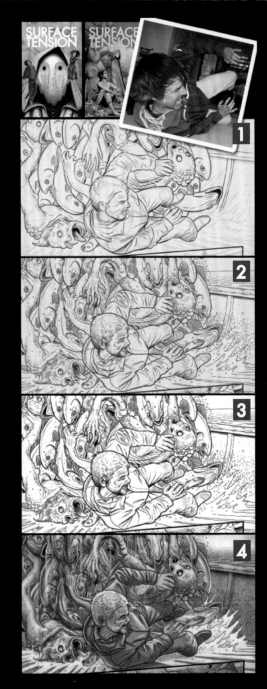

DRAWING STAGES:

1 – After doodling an incredibly rough thumbnail of a page, I'll decide if I need any reference photos for poses or clothing. In the case of this panel I took a photograph of myself rolling across the floor.

It is important never to trace or copy a photo as it will just look weird! Instead, I use it as the basis for a sketch, and then embellish it. I'll draw a very low resolution digital sketch of the composition and form.

2 – I then print out a larger version of the digital sketch and draw a detailed pencil of the final panel or page. Sometimes I will ink over the pencil, depending on how I feel.

3 – I scan the detailed pencil and clean up the image, making any digital improvements necessary.

4. I turn the image into different layers – foreground, middle ground and background. This way I can add depth and color to each layer independently. I gave the falling fish and melting bodies a blurred effect to give the impression of movement.

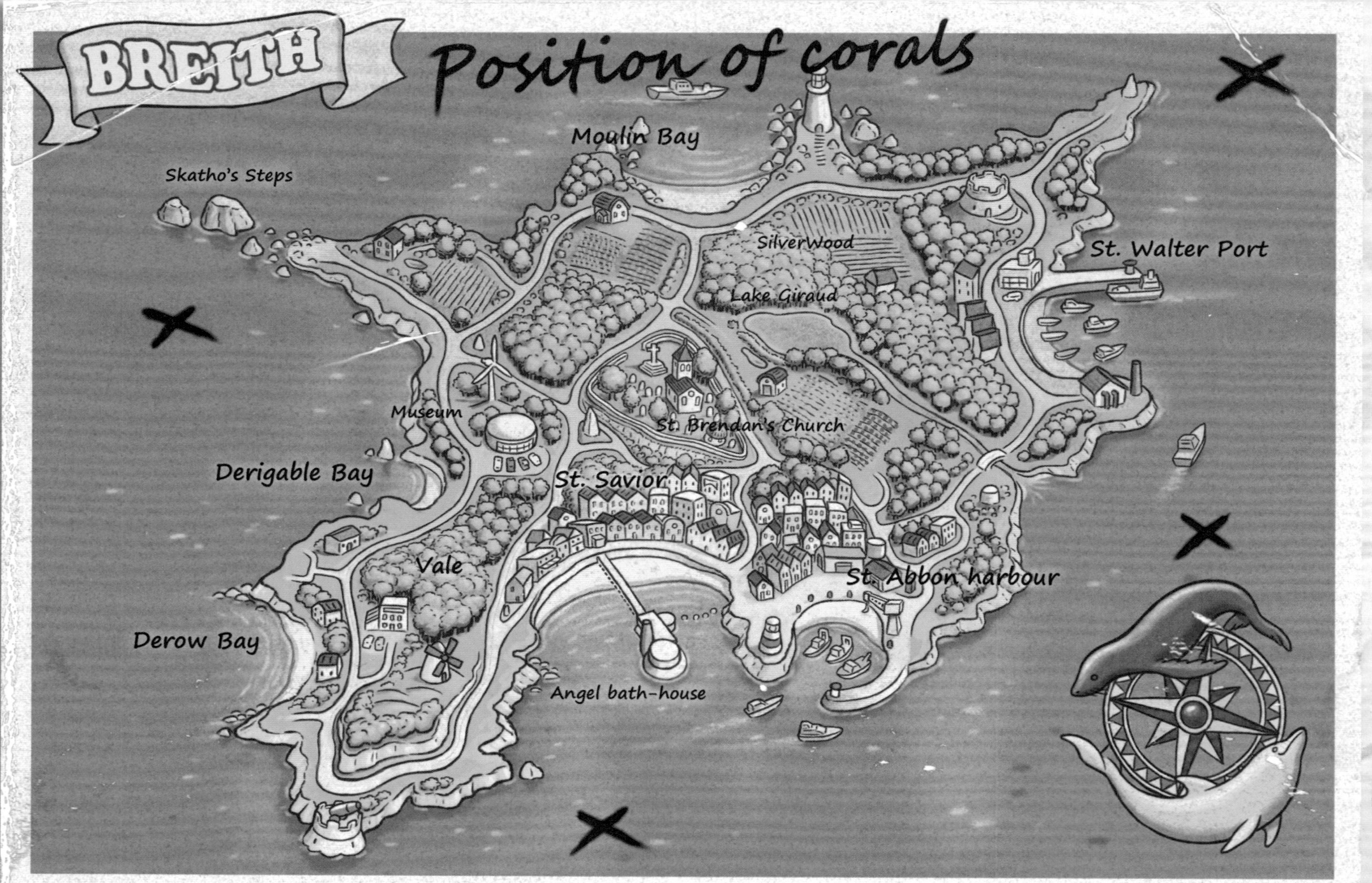
BREITH
Position of corals
Moulin Bay
Skatho's Steps
SilverWood
St. Walter Port
Lake Giraud
Museum
St. Brendan's Church
Derigable Bay
St. Savior
Vale
St. Abbon harbour
Derow Bay
Angel bath-house